The
Mac® OS X v. 10.2
Jaguar Book

Mark R. Bell

PARAGLYPH
PRESS

The Mac® OS X v. 10.2 Jaguar Book

Limits of Liability and Disclaimer of Warranty

The author and publisher of this book have used their best efforts in preparing the book and the programs contained in it. These efforts include the development, research, and testing of the theories and programs to determine their effectiveness. The author and publisher make no warranty of any kind, expressed or implied, with regard to these programs or the documentation contained in this book.

The author and publisher shall not be liable in the event of incidental or consequential damages in connection with, or arising out of, the furnishing, performance, or use of the programs, associated instructions, and/or claims of productivity gains.

Trademarks

Trademarked names appear throughout this book. Rather than list the names and entities that own the trademarks or insert a trademark symbol with each mention of the trademarked name, the publisher states that it is using the names for editorial purposes only and to the benefit of the trademark owner, with no intention of infringing upon that trademark.

Paraglyph Press, Inc.

2246 E. Myrtle Avenue

Phoenix, Arizona 85202

Phone: 602-749-8787

Paraglyph Press ISBN: 1-932111-73-5

Printed in the United States of America
10   9   8   7   6   5   4   3   2   1

President
Keith Weiskamp

Editor-at-Large
Jeff Duntemann

Vice President, Sales, Marketing, and Distribution
Steve Sayre

Vice President, International Sales and Marketing
Cynthia Caldwell

Editorial Director
Sharon Linsenbach

Production Manager
Kim Eoff

Cover Designer
Kris Sotelo

The Paraglyph Mission

This book you've purchased is a collaborative creation involving the work of many hands, from authors to editors to designers and to technical reviewers. At Paraglyph Press, we like to think that everything we create, develop, and publish is the result of one form creating another. And as this cycle continues on, we believe that your suggestions, ideas, feedback, and comments on how you've used our books is an important part of the process for us and our authors.

We've created Paraglyph Press with the sole mission of producing and publishing books that make a difference. The last thing we all need is yet another tech book on the same tired, old topic. So we ask our authors and all of the many creative hands who touch our publications to do a little extra, dig a little deeper, think a little harder, and create a better book. The founders of Paraglyph are dedicated to finding the best authors, developing the best books, and helping you find the solutions you need.

As you use this book, please take a moment to drop us a line at feedback@paraglyphpress.com and let us know how we are doing - and how we can keep producing and publishing the kinds of books that you can't live without.

Sincerely,

Keith Weiskamp & Jeff Duntemann
Paraglyph Press Founders

Paraglyph Press
2246 East Myrtle Ave.
Phoenix, AZ 85020

email:
feedback@paraglyphpress.com
Web: www.paraglyphpress.com
Phone: 602-749-8787
Fax: 602-861-1941

Look for these related books from Paraglyph Press:

Windows 2000 Security Little Black Book
By Ian McLean

Also Recently Published by Paraglyph Press:

Visual Basic .NET Programming with Peter Aitken
By Peter Aitken

Visual Basic .NET Black Book
By Steven Holzner

Mac OS X Version 10.1 Little Black Book
By Gene Steinberg

C++ Black Book
By Steven Holzner

C# Core Language Little Black Book
By Bill Wagner

To Virginia and Margaret Morgan, with whom one little room is, truly, an everywhere.

⁊♣

About the Author

Mark R. Bell is a best-selling author of over 22 computer books, articles, and software manuals, including *The Mac Web Server Book*, *The Mac OS 8 Book*, *Mac OS 8.5 Black Book*, *The Mac OS 8.6 Book*, *The Mac OS 9 Book*, *Mac OS 9.1 Black Book*, *Mac OS X Book*, and *Mac OS X Version 10.1 Black Book*. He is also a technical editor and contributing author, and has spoken at several conventions and workshops, including Mactivity/Web and Macworld Expo.

Mark holds a bachelor's degree from MTSU, and a master's degree from Duke University. He and his wife, Virginia D. Smith, live in Chapel Hill, North Carolina with their daughter, a small heard of Cocker Spaniels, and a network of Macs.

Acknowledgments

I'd like to acknowledge the many colleagues with whom I've worked over the past few months to complete this book. Paraglyph Press has many ward-working staff who have been essential to this project, including Keith Weiskamp and Steve Sayre, who got the ball rolling and stepped in on several occasions to move the project forward, and Sharon Linsenbach served as project manager. Also, Kim Eoff laid out the book, and Kris Sotelo, designed the cover. I'd also like to thank my wife Virginia Smith for her valuable and consistent contributions to this, and all of my books; my long-time colleague and coauthor Debrah D. Suggs, her technical reviewing skills; my friends at Apple Computer, including Grace Kvamme; and Rob Terrell, with whom I wrote my first Mac book many years ago, and on whom I place the blame for my success.

Contents at a Glance

Table of Contents

Introduction

I purchased my first Mac as a graduate student at Duke University in the 1980s after trying to use a PC, and failing miserably. A friend saved me from my PC-induced frustration by showing me how to use a program called MacWrite on a Macintosh SE. In those days, most Macs didn't have an internal hard drive. Instead, dual floppy drives where the order of the day—one floppy for the operating system and a second floppy for storing applications and documents. The computer used an operating system called System 6, which featured a graphical user interface and mouse instead of the blue background, white text and mouse-less blinking cursor of the PC. Within five minutes, I wasn't *learning* how to use the Macintosh, I was *using* the Macintosh, and I never looked back.

That was in the 1980s, and now Mac OS X Version 10.2 is here, and anyone who has used the Mac OS in the past will be instantly familiar with the basic Macintosh concepts of icons, Desktop, menu bar, printing, launching applications, creating documents, and managing files and folders. Recent users of Mac OS X and its stunningly beautiful graphical user interface called Aqua will be impressed with the 150 or so new, features enhancements and applications compared to the initial release of Mac OS X. iMovie, iPhoto, iTunes and QuickTime provide the tools necessary to explore the digital lifestyle; Mail, Address Book, iChat, Sherlock, and the built-in firewall will help you safely and intuitively navigate the Internet; and Darwin, Quartz Extreme, OpenGL, Java 2, AppleScript, and the Aqua interface provide the industrial-strength core operating system upon which all these wonderful applications rely.

Despite all the technical advances and wow-factors of Mac OS X, however, it still retains a tremendous level of backward-compatibility with earlier, "Classic" versions of the Mac OS. In fact, you can probably run the vast majority of you old applications within Mac OS X using the Classic compatibility environment and an installation of Mac OS 9.x.

This book covers it all—from the most basic concepts of using and customizing the user interface, using old and new applications, mobile computing, printing, multimedia and Internet applications, networking, using your Mac to share with others, troubleshooting and getting help, installing and updating the operating system, and even a thing or two about using the command-line interface.

Who Needs This Book?

This book is for anyone who is new to Mac OS X, such as a new iMac owner, or anyone who has used a previous version of the Mac OS and recently upgraded to a G3 or G4 and needs to master what's new in Mac OS X Version 10.2. Of course, some of you who are experienced users will already know much of what lies ahead in this book, such as managing aliases, switching among multiple applications, or customizing your Desktop. An equal number of you who are experienced users will be surprised to learn a thing or two about such tricks as customizing the Dock, typing commands in the Terminal application, and configuring the firewall. So, this book is for the earliest beginner, as well as the experienced user.

Hardware Requirements

Mac OS X will run on any Macintosh with a G3 or G4 processor, except the original G3 PowerBook. Specifically, Mac OS X also requires:

- 128MB of RAM

- 3GB of free disk space

- An built-in display, or an external display and an Apple-installed video card

The list of supported machines includes all Power Mac G4, Power Macintosh G3, iMac, iBook, and G3 or G4 PowerBooks except the very first G3 PowerBook.

And although Mac OS X uses a sophisticated and persistent form of virtual memory, experience tells me that you will be happier with the performance of your computer if it has at least 256MB of RAM instead of the minimal 128MB. To take advantage of Quartz Extreme, you must also have a NVIDIA GeForce2 MX, GeForce3, GeForce4 MX, GeForce4 Ti, or any AGP-based ATI RADEON video card with at least 16MB of video RAM. Mac OS X Version 10.2 will work even if you don't have one of these cards, but video performance will be up to twice as fast if you have one of these Quartz Extreme-supported video cards.

What's Inside

Here is a chapter-by-chapter rundown of what you will find in this book:

- *Chapter 1, Getting to Know Mac OS X*—Provides an overview of tasks performed by the Mac OS, looks at its various components, and explains how to use its basic features and how to configure the basic System Preferences.

- *Chapter 2, Working with the Finder and Desktop*—Explores the various drop-down menus in the Finder and how to use them; how to manipulate Finder windows; advanced Finder and Desktop features; and how to use the Trash and Get Info windows.

■ *Chapter 3, Customizing Mac OS X*—Explores how to customize the Mac OS using built-in features and third-party utilities, as well as how to create user accounts to make sharing your computer easier and safer than ever.

■ *Chapter 4, Configuring the Classic Environment*—Explores how to best configure Mac OS 9.x to run in the Classic environment under Mac OS X, or boot directly into Mac OS 9.x.

■ *Chapter 5, Organizing Your Data*—Looks at the various ways you can manage the Mac OS X file structure and the contents of your hard drives using aliases and comments, as well as how to search for information using the new Find command, and how to compress, decompress and encrypt data.

■ *Chapter 6, Mac OS X for PowerBooks and iBooks*—Explains issues that mobile users are likely to encounter, including power, performance, display, remote access, and security.

■ *Chapter 7, Working with Mac OS X Applications*—Addresses the various levels of compatibility between the three types of Mac OS X applications, how to launch applications, assign applications to certain types of documents, use stationery documents, layered windows, and attached sheets.

■ *Chapter 8, Working with Classic Applications*—Explains the differences between working with Classic versus Carbon and Cocoa applications, including memory management and using multiple applications.

■ *Chapter 9, Exploring Multimedia*—Shows off the impressive multimedia capabilities and utilities in Mac OS X, including QuickTime, QuickTime VR, Preview, speech capabilities, and the basics of iTunes, iMovie, and iPhoto.

■ *Chapter 10, Managing Fonts and Printers*—Describes the Quartz Extreme imaging model, various types of fonts that may be used in Mac OS X, how to use the Fonts panel and a few third-party utilities, and how to configure ColorSync to manage color matching more efficiently.

■ *Chapter 11, Scripting Mac OS X*—Explains the basics of AppleScript, how to use the Script Editor to record and save scripts, and how to use the Script Menu.

■ *Chapter 12, Using Java*—Shows how you can run Java applets on your Mac using Applet Launcher, Web browser, and Java Web Start, and how Java applets can take on the look and feel of various operating systems.

■ *Chapter 13, Troubleshooting Mac OS X*—Explains the various errors you might encounter, what to do about them, and the best tools for fixing problems.

■ *Chapter 14, Connecting to the Internet*—Explains the different types of Internet access and how to configure ports and protocols, switch among Internet locations, and connect to a dial-up ISP using the Internet Connect application.

- *Chapter 15, Accessing Network Services*—Explores how to use the Connect To Server command to access remote servers and volumes, how to access .Mac services, how to use FTP and SSH connections, how to share screen information using several third-party applications, and how to store Internet passwords in the Keychain.

- *Chapter 16, Sharing Internet Services*—Demonstrates how you can use the many built-in sharing features to share your files, folders, and documents over a local area network or the Internet, as well as how to configure ownership and access privileges for folders and activate the built-in firewall to increase the security of your Mac.

- *Chapter 17, Mastering Internet Applications and Utilities*—Provides an overview of the Internet configuration features, applications, and utilities installed by Mac OS X, as well as a handful of essential applications and utilities from third-party developers.

- *Appendix A, Getting Help*—Shows you the various ways you can get online help.

- *Appendix B, Shortcuts*—Lists the most commonly used keyboard shortcuts available in Mac OS X.

- *Appendix C, Learning Unix Shell Commands*—Introduces the basics of using the Terminal application to execute commands.

- *Appendix D, Mac OS 9.x and Mac OS X Feature Comparison*—Gives a brief overview of the differences in features between Mac OS 9.x and Mac OS X.

- *Appendix E, Installing and Updating Mac OS 9.x and Mac OS X*—Explains how to use the installation CDs to install, reinstall, add, and remove Mac OS 9.x and Mac OS X components, as well as how to use the Software Update feature to update the Mac OS over the Internet.

- *Appendix F, Additional Resources on the Web*—Lists several categories of Web sites for additional information about Apple and the Mac OS.

Contacting the Author

Finally, the publisher and I welcome your input on how to make this book even better. If you have any suggestions, rants, or raves, please send them my way. You can find my contact information, as well as errata and other information, on the official Web site for this book at **www.MacOSBook.com**.

Happy reading!

Part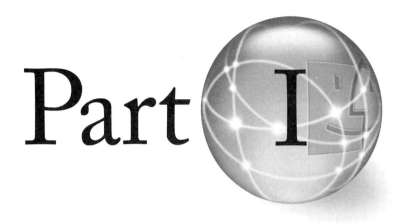

The Operating System

Getting to Know Mac OS X Version 10.2

Computer operating systems make it easy for you to perform complex tasks without having to navigate the intricate maze of computer code that controls everyday actions. An operating system enables you to accomplish these tasks by way of symbolic gestures such as clicking on an icon to open a document, dragging a file to the Trash to delete it, and clicking on a URL to access a Web site. By distilling complex, industrial-strength tasks down to a few elegant steps—a click of the mouse here, a keystroke there—Mac OS X gives you the power to execute unwieldy commands with the grace and style that have always been synonymous with the Macintosh operating system.

Don't be fooled by Mac OS X's deceptively simple appearance, however—underneath it all lies an enterprise-class operating system. OS X offers more flexibility than previous versions of the Mac OS, especially where ease of use and Internet access are concerned. But before you can make the most of its expanded capabilities, you need to understand how the OS works. This chapter defines the functions of Mac OS X and offers a quick tour of operating system basics, including some of the most commonly used commands and features.

This tour is designed for readers who are using the Mac OS for the first time, as well as Mac OS 9 and Mac OS X version 10.1 users who are upgrading to Mac OS X version 10.2. Because Mac OS X is a significant departure from previous versions of the Mac OS, I suggest reading this chapter before diving into the details of Mac OS X's features in subsequent chapters. If you're comfortable using Mac OS X, you can probably skim the sections entitled "What Tasks Does the Operating System Perform?" and "Using the Mac OS" before moving on to Chapter 2.

What Tasks Does the Operating System Perform?

What makes your computer chime when you turn it on? Why does the CD-ROM icon appear on the Desktop when you insert an audio CD? How can you access the Internet and check your email? How are fonts shared among all your applications? The answer to these questions is an easy one: the operating system makes it all happen for you.

The operating system (abbreviated OS, which computer geeks rhyme with *boss*) has three main functions: controlling the hardware built into your computer (and any peripherals you have connected to it), providing common elements and features to all your software applications, and helping you manage your hard drive(s), files, and directories. Let's briefly look at each of these areas:

■ *Hardware control*—In order for your Mac to work, its random access memory (RAM), disk drives, video monitor, keyboard, mouse, printer, digital versatile disc (DVD) drive ,and other peripherals must be collectively managed. Saving files to disk, drawing images on the screen, and printing are examples of hardware tasks managed by the OS.

■ *Common software elements*—Mac OS software applications have common elements such as menus, windows, and fonts. These elements are perpetuated when application programmers follow Apple's suggested human interface design principles.

■ *Disk and file management*—The Finder is an application that provides a graphical user interface (GUI) that employs icons and windows. These windows and icons represent the complex operations necessary to manage your disks and files. The Finder enables you to easily navigate disks and remote file servers; allows you to find, copy, move, rename, and delete files; and displays icon- and text-based information about disks and files. The Finder also allows you to launch applications and acts as the "home base" from which you start up or quit applications.

One remarkable feature of Mac OS X is its backward compatibility with earlier versions of the OS. This feature dates back to Apple's transition from the old Motorola 68000 series of microprocessors to the PowerPC processor. The Mac OS allowed PowerPC processors (such as the G3 and G4 processors), which are Reduced Instruction Set Computing (RISC) microprocessors, to run programs and software libraries written for the much older Complex Instruction Set Computing (CISC) microprocessors—albeit more slowly than software written specifically for the Power Macintosh.

Mac OS X is also compatible with applications written for earlier versions of the Mac OS. Under Mac OS X, programs can be executed in five distinct types of application environments:

■ *Classic*—For applications written for Mac OS 9.x and much earlier versions of the Mac OS, including System 6, System 7, and Mac OS 8. To run in Mac OS X, Classic applications require that a copy of Mac OS 9.1 or later be installed on your computer. Classic applications written for 68K or PowerPC processors will run in the Classic environment but cannot take advantage of the advanced features of Mac OS X. See Chapters 4 and 8 for detailed information about configuring the Classic environment and running Classic applications.

1

- *Carbon*—For applications written for Mac OS 8 and 9 .x that have been "tuned up" for Mac OS X and can take advantage of many of its advanced features (see the "Mac OS X Components" section for more information). Carbon applications may run in Mac OS X only, or Mac OS 9.x and Mac OS X.

- *Cocoa*—For applications that take full advantage of Mac OS X's advanced features and user interface.

- *Java 2*—For applications written for the Java programming language. This is not so much an application environment as an execution environment. Mac OS X includes a Java Virtual Machine that allows Java applets to be executed without modification.

- *Berkeley System Distribution (BSD) commands*—For executing command-line instructions from within the Terminal application to execute commands, navigate the file system, and view documents. Anyone with Unix experience will find a host of familiar commands to execute here.

By coordinating these application environments, Mac OS X allows you to continue accessing your old applications. Mac OS X's consistent user interface provides continuity from one application to the next and allows software developers to focus on creating unique and sophisticated programs while leaving the complexities of the modern OS to Apple.

Mac OS X Components

Unlike its predecessors, the core functions of Mac OS X are not easily extensible through the addition of third-party modifications such as Extensions and Control Panels. Although it's possible for software developers to implement additional features (such as mouse drivers and Dock enhancements) and even extend the functionality of the inner core (kernel) of the operating system, these types of enhancements typically require the owner of the computer (or someone else with administrative privileges) to enter their user name and password to authorize the modification of the Mac OS. Modifications are more strictly limited by the Mac OS's new application Programming Interfaces (APIs) when compared to Mac OS 9.x and earlier. At first, this may sound like a limitation to the flexible tradition of the Mac OS, but it's actually a good thing—third-party modifications to the Mac OS often caused it to be unstable or slow. Furthermore, many of the programming elements of the Mac OS that enabled extensibility also prevented it from implementing advanced features that Mac OS X is now fully capable of. These features include:

- *Preemptive multitasking*—The OS's ability to ensure that processing time is shared appropriately between the OS and running applications. Earlier versions of the Mac OS employed cooperative multitasking, which relies on applications to "play well" with one another and is a far less efficient method for dividing processor resources.

■ *Protected memory*—Dedicated RAM space that other applications cannot compromise. This eliminates the memory errors associated with previous versions of the Mac OS.

■ *Persistent virtual memory (VM)*—An advanced virtual memory system that is managed by the Mac OS and cannot be disabled. Earlier versions of the Mac OS have user-configurable virtual memory options that are accessible through the Memory Control Panel.

■ *Symmetric multiprocessing (SMP)*—The ability to use two or more processors in unison. Despite Apple's tinkering with multiprocessor support in previous versions, the OS has never been capable of using more than one processor.

These improvements are only the tip of the iceberg. To really begin to appreciate the radical differences between Mac OS X and its predecessors, let's take a look at how the components of the new OS work.

Core Operating System

The core, or foundation, of Apple's operating system is Darwin, *open source* software named after Charles Darwin, the English naturalist who popularized the modern theory of evolution. Open source means that (under the Apple Public Source License) Darwin belongs in the public domain. Developers are encouraged to improve upon Darwin in the hope that their input will eventually make the OS stronger and better-suited to the real-life environments in which Macs are used. Figure 1.1 illustrates Darwin and all the other layers of Mac OS X.

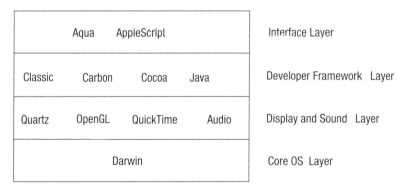

Figure 1.1
You can think of Mac OS X as a series of layers built on top of Darwin, an open source operating system.

Darwin provides low-level operating services, such as pre-emptive multitasking and symmetric multiprocessing, that allow Mac OS X to be as rock-solid as any operating system available today. Darwin features a high level of security and is based on established standards, including Transmission Control Protocol/Internet Protocol (TCP/IP) networking and Kerberos authentication. Darwin's firm foundation is actually a collection of technologies woven together, including:

- *Mach kernel*—The central portion of Darwin that connects the Mac OS to the computer's hardware.

- *Berkeley Software Distribution (BSD)*—Also an open source Unix operating system, this version of BSD supplies file system and networking services for Mac OS X.

- *I/O Kit*—A customized device driver support that allows for fast plug-and-play access to external hardware such as scanners, cameras, and storage drives.

- *Network Kernel Extensions (NKEs)*—Extensions to Darwin that allow you to add and configure third-party networking features to the OS.

- *Virtual File System (VFS)*—Darwin's VFS allows the Mac OS to access hard drives and file server volumes in several formats, including Hierarchical File System (HFS), Hierarchical File System Plus (HFS+), Unix File System (UFS), Universal Disk Format (UDF) for DVD discs, and International Standards Organization (ISO) 9660 for CD-ROMs. VFS allows for file names of up to 255 characters (up from 32 in Mac OS 9.1) in length ,as well as access to hard drives via the Apple File Sharing Protocol (AFP), Server Message block (SMB), and Network File Service (NFS) protocol.

As operating systems go, Darwin is about as sophisticated as they come—it pulls off the feat of tying legacy services (from Mac OS 9.x and earlier) into the new OS without burdening users with its underlying complexity. All we see is a wonderfully crisp, colorful, and intuitive graphical interface.

Display and Sound

The display and sound layer that sits on top of Darwin is composed of several new and familiar technologies. These components control all of Mac OS X's visual and audible effects, including icons, windows, 2D and 3D graphics, multimedia, sound, and printing. In fact, some of Mac OS X's most obvious improvements can be seen in the larger icons, drop shadows, and sharply drawn windows of the Aqua theme interface. For example, Figure 1.2 shows the contents of the same hard drive viewed in Mac OS X (top) and Mac OS 9.2.2 (bottom).

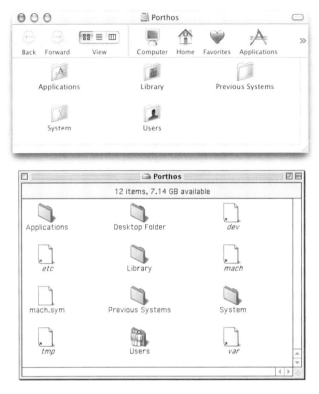

Figure 1.2
The 2D and 3D graphics capabilities of Mac OS X are more impressive than ever, thanks to Quartz Extreme.

Like the foundation layer of the OS, the display and sound layer (known as the graphics layer in previous versions of Mac OS X) consists of several technologies that work together behind the scenes to present a unified front:

■ *Quartz Extreme*—Handles screen drawing, cursor manipulation, anti aliasing of fonts and graphics, and 2D graphics acceleration. Because the default screen and document format are based on the Portable Document Format (PDF) standard, all documents can be manipulated and saved in PDF format with crisp colors and special effects such as vector graphics and drop shadows. Carbon-based applications can still take advantage of QuickDraw, the graphics standard for Mac OS 9.x. Computers with one of the following video cards with at least 16MB of VRAM (video random access memory) will be capable of roughly twice the video perfor-mance compared to earlier versions of Mac OS X: NVIDIA GeForce2 MX, GeForce3, GeForce4 MX, or GeForce4 Ti, or AGP-based ATI RADEON GPU.

- *OpenGL*—Allows OS X to run games and a variety of applications (including modeling, animation, video, and scientific) that render 3D objects. OpenGL, produced by Silicon Graphics, is the industry standard for 3D graphics rendering.

- *QuickTime*—Powers the MPEG-4 movie, and MP3 audio capabilities of Mac OS X ,enabling users to view movies, sounds, and images in dozens of formats. QuickTime has long been the multimedia standard for the Mac OS; the standard edition of QuickTime 6 is installed as part of Mac OS X version 10.2. You can upgrade to the Professional Edition for around $30.

- *Audio*—Provides professional-level audio, including multichannel recording and playback, 24-bit resolution, integrated Musical Instrument Digital Interface (MIDI) support, and multiple sound-in and sound-out options.

Developer Frameworks

The developer framework, or application layer, of Mac OS X consists of the application execution environments mentioned earlier in this chapter. These environments make it possible for applications that were developed for previous versions of the OS to run simultaneously under Mac OS X. The main application frameworks include:

- *Classic*—For Mac OS 9.x (and earlier) applications. The Classic environment allows these applications to run in conjunction with Mac OS X.

- *Carbon*—For Mac OS 8 and 9 applications that have been modified to take advantage of many, but not all of, Mac OS X's advanced features and Aqua interface. Carbon and Mac OS 9.x (i.e., Classic) applications share approximately 70 percent of the same programming code. The remaining code base is stripped out of Carbon applications and replaced with APIs that enable the new features. Some carbon applications run only under Mac OS X, while others can run under both Mac OS 9.x and Mac OS X. Also, it is possible to write an application from the ground up as a Carbon application that will only run under Mac OS X, but I believe most programmers would use Cocoa APIs instead to be able to take advantage for all of Mac OS X's advanced features.

- *Cocoa*—For applications written specifically for Mac OS X and all its advanced features. In other words, Cocoa applications contain little or no *legacy code* from earlier versions of the Mac OS.

- *Java 2*—For applications written in Java 2 Standard Edition (J2SE), a cross-platform programming language from Sun Microsystems. Mac OS X was the first major desktop OS to include certified J2SE support.

■ BSD—For applications used by the Unix environment, advanced users, and pro-grammers.

Interface

The topmost layer of Mac OS X is the interface layer, which consists of Aqua and AppleScript. Aqua is only the third major interface change in the history of the Macintosh, following the original (System 6 and earlier) and Platinum (Mac OS 8 and 9) interfaces. Compared to previous OS interfaces, Aqua is characterized by some dramatic changes, including:

■ Multicolor interface elements

■ Pulsating buttons

■ Greater depth of color

■ Larger icons

■ Translucence

■ Drop shadows

■ Animated windows

■ "Sheet" dialog windows

■ Column views

■ The Dock

■ Finder window toolbars

■ Searchable Finder windows

For example, Figure 1.3 shows many of the new features, including the column list, Dock, larger icons, and multicolor interface elements.

Aqua's design principle provides a fluid, deep interface that mimics Apple's award-winning computer hardware, including the Titanium PowerBook, Cube, and the flat-panel iMac. Because some graphic designers may find the colors of the new interface distracting, Apple also includes Graphite, an Appearance theme that uses gray buttons in place of the red, yellow, green, and blue buttons featured in Aqua. Most users, however, will be happy to discover that Aqua provides more interactivity and more opportunities for customization—and does so more intuitively —than previous interfaces. We'll explore the basic features of Aqua in the next section, and learn in detail how to customize the user interface in Chapter 3.

Figure 1.3
The new Aqua interface is a radical departure from earlier versions of the Mac OS.

AppleScript is not so much a distinguishing element of the user interface as it is an integrated part of Mac OS X that allows developers and ordinary users the ability to interact with, and modify, the user experience. AppleScript is an object-oriented programming language that is integrated into the Mac OS and many popular applications and utilities. Whether simple or highly complex, all AppleScripts are accessible from the Finder (and often from within an application)and are intended to control the computer or one or more applications. We'll discuss AppleScripts in detail in Chapter 11.

Using Mac OS X

Mac OS X is loaded from the hard drive when the computer is turned on, and remains in use until the computer is physically turned off. Any additions, deletions, or modifications you make to the OS, such as changes to the Finder Preferences or System Preferences, are saved back to the hard drive; when you choose Restart or Shut Down from the Apple menu and the Mac OS is loaded again, your changes are in place and ready for use. To further help you understand the role of the Mac OS, let's take a look at a few of the essential tasks it controls:

- *Startup*—Almost immediately after the power is turned on, Mac OS X takes control of the start-up process, verifies that your hardware is functioning properly, and loads the Desktop and Finder, or login window (if automatic login has been disabled).

- *File management*—When you manipulate windows and icons in the Finder and on the Desktop, your actions are translated from the on-screen graphical display into actual code changes to the files on disk. As you know, files aren't stored on disk as cute little icons—they're actually strings of ones and zeroes. The OS transforms them into meaningful text, beautiful graphics, stirring sounds, and moving images.

- *Application launching*—When you run a software program, Mac OS X accesses the computer to ensure that the correct portions of the file are read from disk, that the available memory is properly managed, and that data files (and sometimes temporary work files) are created and maintained on disk.

- *Font usage*—Whenever a font—whether it's bitmapped, Type 1, TrueType, or OpenType—is used, Mac OS X supplies information about that font, including the way it should look in any particular size and style. This ensures proper on-screen display and printing of the font.

- *Windows and dialog boxes*— Mac OS X provides the basic format for all windows and dialog boxes. For the Open and Save As dialog boxes, the Mac OS now enables programmers to incorporate a drop-down sheet attached to the document in question. This window replaces the old modal dialog boxes that often stopped everything on your computer until the document was saved or closed.

- *Printing*—An application must pass its data through one of the OS's printer drivers in order to convert it into a format that the printer can understand. After this has been taken care of, the OS communicates the file to the printer and, in some cases, receives feedback from the printer during output.

- *Screen display*—The OS is responsible for producing the display that appears on your computer's screen. Applications communicate the display information to the OS using Quartz Extreme, which converts this information and draws it on the screen.

- *Networking and peripheral connectivity*—Nearly every aspect of communication between the Mac and its peripherals is controlled by the OS. This includes data transfer from the disk to the Internet or other networked services, such as printers or file servers; the timing of network communications while other software is running onscreen; two-way communications with sophisticated printers, modems, and storage drives.

As you can see, almost every task you perform on your Macintosh—from the smallest mouse click to the largest data transfer—relies on the OS. Fortunately it isn't necessary to understand the technical intricacies of how the OS performs these tasks in order to use your Macintosh. An appreciation for the range and depth of the OS's functions is useful, nonetheless.

Basic Mac OS X Operations

Let's turn from technical descriptions of the Mac OS to the easiest and most fundamental aspects of using the OS. This section looks at the things you need to know in order to use Mac OS X efficiently, and defines terms you'll encounter throughout the book. This information is intended primarily for readers who are using Mac OS X as part of their first Macintosh experience.

The Graphical User Interface

The first and most fundamental requirement for using the Mac OS is understanding its graphical user interface. Instead of communicating your commands in words, you select pictures—or icons—that represent Macintosh hardware and software functions and features. The mouse cursor also plays an important role in communicating with the Macintosh. (Yes, you'll use the keyboard too, but I'll assume you've already mastered that device!)

Let's look at each of the elements of the graphical user interface.

Icons

Icons are graphics (pictures) of various sizes that appear on the Macintosh screen. They represent items such as disks and folders and, in fact, they actually look like a hard drive or folder, as you saw in Figure 1.3. Different icons are used to symbolize the various types of files stored on your disks. Figure 1.4 shows examples of an application icon (top left) and a document icon (top right) for the application Preview (a PDF and image viewing program).

Most applications and their associated documents use application-specific icons as a means of providing additional information about the type of document. For example, Adobe Acrobat Reader document icons look similar to the Adobe Acrobat Reader application icons, just as Preview document icons look similar to the Preview application icon. Most document icons are in the shape of a dog-eared page. A custom document icon also contains a small version of the application's icon. If an application or document doesn't have a custom icon, Mac OS X assigns a generic icon instead, depending on the document's general type. For example, generic text documents are assigned the TextEdit application's icon, because TextEdit is capable of opening text documents.

Preview   Picture 1.pdf

Acrobat Reader 5.0   Document 1.pdf

Figure 1.4
An example of application icons (left) and document icons (right) used by two applications.

Windows

When a file, folder, or disk is opened, its contents are displayed in a Finder window. The most common type of window, which looks like the one shown in Figure 1.2, usually includes a title bar at the top and scrollbars on the right and bottom edges. Because many windows are customizable under Mac OS X, they may not look exactly like the one shown here. You can move a window around (by dragging its title bar), close a window (by clicking the close button), increase the size of the window (by clicking the zoom button), change the size of a window (by dragging the resize tab), or minimize the window (by double clicking on the title bar or clicking on the minimize button). Minimized windows are automatically placed in the Dock. Mac OS X features other types of windows as well, including application-specific windows that have fewer (or more) elements than the window shown in Figure 1.5.

You won't see as many dialog boxes as in previous versions of the OS—Apple recommends that programmers replace them with drop-down windows called *sheets* . These small, specialized windows usually present a set of options that allow you to *Save* or *Save As*. And unlike the old modal dialog boxes, you can switch to another application or the Finder while the window is open without the Mac OS coming to a screeching halt. Figure 1.6 illustrates the way in which one of the new windows is "attached" to its document.

Close Minimize Zoom   Titlebar   Show / Hide Toolbar

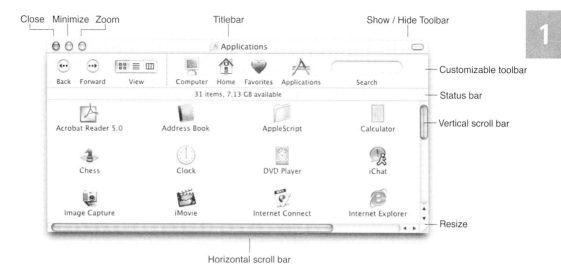

Customizable toolbar

Status bar

Vertical scroll bar

Resize

Horizontal scroll bar

Figure 1.5
A sample Finder window.

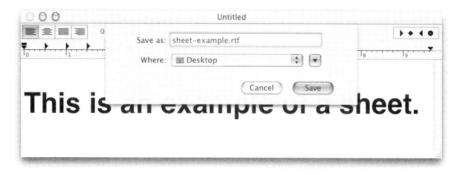

Figure 1.6
In Mac OS X, the drop-down sheet replaces the old Save As dialog box.

An alert window, another new type of window, simply provides information—usually feedback concerning a command or action you're engaged in or a message from one of your hardware devices. Along with this information, an alert window usually has an OK button and nothing else. An example of an alert window is displayed in Figure 1.7.

Finally, a floating palette is yet another type of window used in some software applications. Palettes "float" on top of active document windows and the Desktop and cannot be obscured by them. Unlike an ordinary window, which disappears after you've selected options or closed it, a palette may remain open for the duration of a work

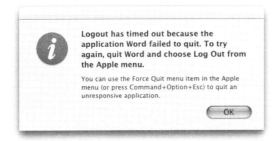

Figure 1.7
A standard alert window in Mac OS X.

session (although it may also become invisible when the application is minimized). A
floating palette displays a collection of icons that represent the tools that are available
to you, in much the same way that an artist's palette displays her paints. Sometimes a
palette presents a text list of commands or options for you to choose from. Figure 1.8
shows several types of palette windows.

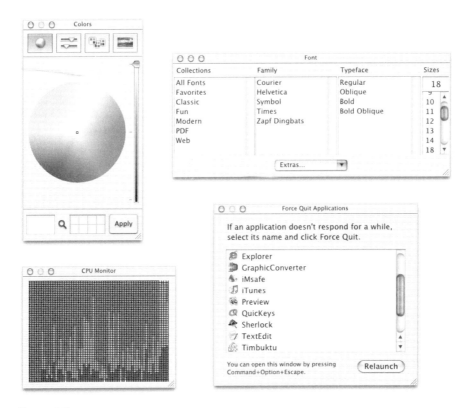

Figure 1.8
A sampling of floating palettes.

Menus

In Mac OS X and most applications written for the Mac OS, commands are presented in a persistent menu bar at the top of the screen. In some other operating systems, including all versions of Microsoft Windows and many versions of Linux, the menu bar is attached to each application window and does not appear at the top of the Desktop. Compared to the Mac OS, this approach is inefficient because it dictates that if you have 10 windows open, you also have 10 menu bars. A single menu bar is always present in Mac OS X, and commands are usually grouped logically and have names befitting their functions. The menu bar is one of the most distinctive elements of the Mac OS. The familiar fonts Chicago and Charcoal, specifically designed for the purpose of attractive screen display on the original Macintosh menu bar, have been replaced in Mac OS X by Lucida Grande.

TIP: In Mac OS X, menus drop down and stay open until you make a menu selection or click somewhere else on the screen. In fact, they're sometimes referred to as "sticky" menus. Drop-down menus relieve you from holding down the mouse button while navigating the menu.

When you click on the name of any menu, the menu drops down and stays down until you make a selection or click somewhere else on the screen (this feature was introduced in Mac OS 8, but was available only when using third-party utilities). As you drag the mouse along the menu each command is highlighted as the mouse cursor passes over it. If you release the mouse while a particular command is highlighted, that command will be executed; the selected command flashes once to confirm that it has been executed successfully. (Using the mouse will be covered more fully later in this chapter.) In Mac OS X, activated menus, which are translucent, do not time out as they did in earlier versions of the OS.

The Mac OS employs four basic types of menu commands. Some commands execute as soon as they're selected. Others act as a toggle to turn a feature on and off. Command names that end with ellipses (...) bring up a dialog box of related options. A fourth type of menu command offers you a hierarchical submenu of commands. To select an item from one of these normal, toggling, or elliptical menus, click the item once. Figure 1.9 shows an example of a hierarchical, translucent menu with the Automatic option toggled in the On position.

Pointing Devices

Each of the graphical elements we've discussed so far is conventionally manipulated using a pointing device such as a mouse or trackpad. Operating a pointing device is simple enough: You move the mouse and the cursor moves onscreen accordingly. The mouse is a relative pointing device, whereas some devices, such as graphics tablets, are

Figure 1.9
Mac OS X adds several new features to drop-down menus, including translucence, and menus remain open until dismissed.

absolute pointing devices, meaning that each point on their surface maps to a specific point on your screen. In Mac OS X, the cursor provides information about where you are and what you are doing with the mouse. The type of cursor that appears at any given time depends on many variables, including the item you're pointing to, the software you're using, the commands you've chosen, and the keys you've pressed.

Arrow cursors appear whenever you're pointing to the menu bar, regardless of the application in use. When you're working in the Finder, the mouse cursor appears as a left-pointing arrow. Macintosh applications also use the arrow cursor to select and manipulate objects. Custom cursors are employed by applications to indicate the specific tool being used, or the type of operation being performed by an application. For example, a cursor in the shape of a pencil could represent the ability to draw freehand in a graphics application. Similarly, a cursor in the shape of a magnifying glass might be used to indicate that you can zoom in or out on a document in a painting program.

With the cursor, you can perform five common actions that enable you to manipulate icons, invoke commands, and control application tools. These actions are:

1

- *Pointing*—Positioning the cursor over a particular icon, object, or window element. When the cursor takes the form of an arrow, the arrow's tip marks the exact spot you're pointing to. Other cursor styles have their own "hot spots," or specific points of action.

- *Clicking*—Quickly pressing and releasing the mouse button. In most cases, the click executes as soon as the button is fully released—not while it's being pressed. Mouse clicks select objects, including icons, buttons, and dialog box options.

- *Double—clicking*—Pressing and releasing the mouse button twice in rapid succession. Most beginners don't double-click fast enough to prevent the Mac OS from interpreting two single clicks instead of one double—click. Double clicking controls many Macintosh actions, such as opening icons to display their windows. The sensitivity with which the OS responds to double—clicking can be changed in the Mouse System Preferences pane.

- *Pressing*—Holding down the mouse button while a command or action is completed.

- *Dragging*—Moving the mouse—and therefore the cursor—while holding down (pressing) the mouse button. This action usually moves an item or employs the active cursor tool (such as when you're drawing a line with a pencil tool).

You can also use the keyboard to perform many of the mouse's functions, including activating menus and making menu selections, choosing items in the Dock, and manipulating Finder and application windows. A discussion of the Full Keyboard Access feature is described in Chapter 2, "*Working with the Finder and Desktop*."

Files and Folders

Now that you understand icons and windows and are comfortable working with your mouse, you're ready to put all that knowledge and skill to work. Manipulating files on the Desktop is one of the most important tasks you'll undertake, so let's start here.

Files come in many different types, including applications, documents, OS files, utilities, fonts, and dictionaries. The best way to keep all these files organized is to put them into folders. The File menu's New Folder command enables you to create folders to hold any type of file. You can also create folders within other folders to establish a hierarchical arrangement of files and folders. The importance of this will be explained in Chapter 5, "*Organizing Your Data*."

In Mac OS X ,you can see a list of your files and folders through the new column view, which replaces Mac OS 9.x's button view. An example of the column view is shown in Figure 1.10. Although this way of viewing your files and folders takes some getting used to, the column view really streamlines the process of browsing through multiple layers of folders.

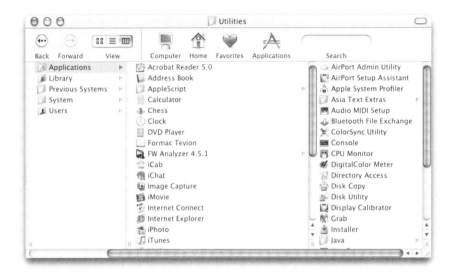

Figure 1.10
A hierarchical view of a collection of related files and folders as seen in the new column view.

To reposition files or folders (that is, to add them to a folder or copy them to another disk or hard drive), point to the icon of the file or folder you want to manipulate, click and hold the mouse button, drag the file onto the destination icon, and then release the mouse button. If you drag files to a different folder on the same disk, the files are moved (rather than copied) and will appear in the new location only. If you drag files to a different disk, or to a folder on a different disk, they're copied rather than moved, and therefore exist in both the new and old locations. To select multiple items for repositioning, hold the Command key while selecting the additional items (Mac OS X uses the Command key instead of the Shift key, as was the case in Mac OS 9.x and earlier). Finally, if you hold the selected files over the destination folder or volume and wait a few seconds, the destination folder will "spring" open and you can drop the files into this folder or hover the cursor over another folder and repeat the process. This is known as the "spring-loaded folders" option that was present in Mac OS 9.x, but not the versions of Mac OS X prior to Version 10.2.

Popular Macintosh Activities

To accomplish common tasks such as accessing files and folders, customizing the user interface, and locating information, you'll find yourself turning again and again to the same handful of utilities. Mac OS X has come up with new ways to perform these tasks, which are routine for experienced Mac users. Let's take a quick look at some of these innovations.

1

Using the Dock
The Dock is one of the most interesting additions to the Mac OS—even though some people may think of it as a replacement for the old Application menu rather than an entirely new feature. The Dock, shown in Figure 1.11, displays the running applications just as the old Application menu did, but it also stores shortcuts to minimized windows as well as frequently used files, folders, disks, and URLs.

Many of the Dock's features, including the order, size, and visibility of its contents, can be customized. For detailed instructions on how to customize the Dock, as well as information on third-party Dock alternatives such as DragThing, see Chapter 3, "*Customizing Mac OS X.*"

Browsing the Apple Menu
The Apple menu, one of the most familiar elements of the Mac OS interface, has undergone some serious changes under Mac OS X. The new Apple menu is not customizable without the aid of third-party utilities, and familiar utilities such as the Calculator, Scrapbook, and Stickies are missing. However, the Apple menu does contain many of the essential commands previously found in the Special menu, including Sleep, Restart, and Shut Down. It also features a few commands that are unique to Mac OS X, such as System Preferences, Dock, Location, Force Quit, and Log Out. Figure 1.12 shows an example of the Apple menu, including the Recent Items submenu.

Configuring System Preferences
One of the guiding principles of Mac OS X is the consolidation of like features into a central location for easier access. Mac OS 9.x did this to some degree, for example, by placing all the Control Panels into a folder called—you guessed it—Control Panels. However, each Control Panel was an individual item that had to be opened separately

Figure 1.11
The Dock replaces the functionality of the Application menu and is far more customizable.

Figure 1.12
Although the new Apple menu preserves some aspects of the old menu, such as the hierarchical Recent Items submenu, its design is different in Mac OS X.

and had its own interface design. Mac OS X changes this with System Preferences, a single utility for system-wide configuration. System Preferences is accessible from the Apple menu or the Dock (in its default configuration). The following sections, or *panes*, of the System Preferences control several familiar elements of the Mac OS user experience:

■ General System Preferences —Allows you to configure the overall appearance of the Mac OS. You can choose the Blue (Aqua) or Graphite (grayscale) Appearance options, as well as the color of highlighted items in the Finder. This is also your opportunity to configure the placement and behavior of the scrollbars of Finder and application windows, the number of recent applications and documents included in the Apple menu, and font smoothing options, as illustrated in Figure 1.13. Options found in the old General Controls Panel such as Desktop show/hide, cursor blinking, improper shutdown warnings, and default document locations are no longer applicable under Mac OS X.

■ Date & Time System Preferences —Used to set the date and time, time zone, and network time server information. In this pane, you can set the Mac OS's internal clock, which determines the date and time that appear in your menu bar as well as the creation and modification times of files. Many applications, including the Clock application itself, refer to the Date & Time System Preferences pane. Figure 1.14 shows the Date & Time System Preferences pane with the translucent, digital

Figure 1.13
The new General System Preferences pane.

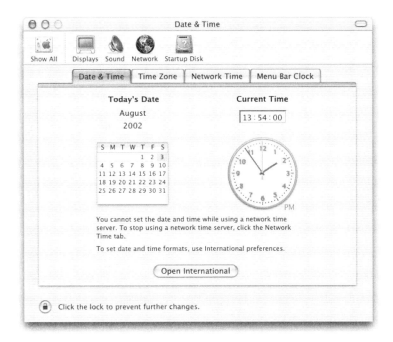

Figure 1.14
The Date & Time System Preferences pane controls most of the same tasks as its predecessor, the Date &
Time Control Panel.

version of the Clock application hovering over the right side of the pane. You normally set the date and time parameters once; then an internal battery runs the clock under its own power. If your Mac isn't keeping time accurately, your battery may be low.

■ Displays System Preferences —Determines your monitor's display of colors, refresh rate, and resolution (if you have a multiresolution monitor). You can also set the relative position of each monitor if you have more than one monitor connected to your Macintosh. ColorSync preferences are now accessible through the ColorSync System Preferences pane instead of the Displays System Preferences pane.

■ Sound System Preferences —Establishes the volume of your system and alert sounds, as well as speaker balance preferences. These sound functions were previously controlled through the Monitors & Sound (and later just Sound) Control Panel in Mac OS 9.x.

■ Mouse System Preferences —Allows you to adjust the speed of your on-screen cursor relative to the speed with which you move the mouse. You can also determine the delay interval between clicks. The double-click speed setting determines if two clicks will be interpreted as two separate clicks instead of one double—click. A PowerBook-and iBook-specific Mouse pane lets you make similar adjustments to the Track pad.

■ International System Preferences —Replaces the old Text and Numbers Control Panels. This pane supports language, text, and number formats. The Languages section offers three options: Language (such as English or Nederlands), Script (the method of writing characters, such as left to right for Roman languages or right to left for Hebrew or Arabic), and Behaviors (which specifies character sets, such as English versus German case sorting). In the Date, Time, and Numbers sections of the International System Preferences pane, you can specify how information that falls under these categories is displayed in the Finder and in applications. You can also choose to display the Input menu to the left of the Help menu in the Finder by selecting additional keyboard layouts in the Input Menu section, as shown in Figure 1.15. Previously known as the Keyboard section, this is a helpful feature for users who frequently switch between keyboard layouts.

■ Login Items and the Accounts System Preferences —Enable you to determine the items that will be launched at startup and the default user (if any) for your computer. Whereas earlier versions of the Mac OS supported multiple users as an option, Mac OS X is based on the concept of multiple users from the ground up—therefore the login options are especially important for security purposes. Figure 1.16 shows the Accounts pane that permits a user to log in automatically at startup without having to enter a username or password. The multi—user configuration options found in the Login Items, My Account, and Accounts panes are discussed in Chapter 3, "*Customizing Mac OS X.*"

Figure 1.15
The International System Preferences pane consolidates all of the configuration options for language localization, keyboard, and input methods.

Launching Classic Applications

Launching Classic applications is another task that you're likely to encounter on a regular basis. We'll cover Classic in great detail in Chapter 4, "*Configuring the Classic Environment*," and Chapter 8, "*Working with Classic Applications*." For now, all you need to know is that once you've told Mac OS X the location of a valid installation of Mac OS 9.x on your computer, your Classic applications can be launched by double clicking on the application's icon or alias. The Classic environment will load, and your Classic application will launch pretty much as usual. Or, if you prefer, you can have the Classic environment load automatically when you log your computer into Mac OS X, including any Classic applications in the Mac OS 9.x System Folder's Startup Items folder. In other words, Mac OS X will start up Classic automatically, and then Classic will start up your favorite Classic applications. How's that for a smooth transition between operating systems?

Figure 1.16
The new Accounts System Preferences pane replaces some of the functions of the Users System Preferences pane in earlier versions of Mac OS X.

Connecting to Printers and Servers

Under Mac OS X, the Chooser is no longer used to connect to printers and file servers. The Chooser has been replaced by the Print Center utility for accessing printers that are connected via Universal Serial Bus (USB) or over an AppleTalk or TCP/IP network (including the Internet). Mac OS X installs print drivers for a wide array of laser and ink jet printers; check your printer manufacturer's Web site for the latest information about Mac OS X compatibility. The Chooser and Network Browser have been replaced by the Connect To Server command (Command+K from within the Finder), to access every major type of file server available today. We'll discuss printing in detail in Chapter 9, "*Managing Fonts and Printers.*" Connecting to file servers is covered in Part III, "*Networking.*"

Mounting Removable Media

Removable media such as CD-ROM, DVD-ROM, DVD-RAM, Zip, Jaz, and even floppy disks are mounted and accessed in Mac OS X just as they were in the past—but with one important exception. In the Finder Preferences menu (Finder|Preferences), you can choose to hide disks, including removable media, on the Desktop. You may still access and eject removable media from within a Finder window, however.

Searching and Sherlock

If you're anything like me and have more than 50,000 files on your computer, you'll need to learn how to use the new Find command , which enables you to search local and networked volumes from within the Finder. With the Find command, you can construct fairly complex searches using much of the criteria found in previous versions of Sherlock, an example of which is shown in Figure 1.17. Sherlock 3, new to Mac OS X version 10.2, is an Internet-only search utility designed for finding a broad range of information, including Web sites, pictures, stock quotes, ZIP code-specific local movie listings, and much more. See Chapter 5, "*Organizing Your Data*" for information on the new Find command, and Chapter 17, "*Mastering Internet Applications and Utilities*" for the scoop on the new Sherlock application.

Transferring Data

The Clipboard is the Mac OS's built-in method for transferring text, sounds, graphical elements, and even movies from one application to another. You can use the Clipboard to move items within a document or from one document to another—even if the documents were created by different software applications. The metaphor of the Clipboard is continued in the commands used to manipulate it—Cut, Copy, and Paste—each of which can be found in the Edit menu of Mac OS X.

Figure 1.17
The Find command is reintroduced in Mac OS X version 10.2, and replaces the local and networked volumes searching features found in Sherlock 2.

Because you never observe the information being transferred, it's easy to make mistakes with Clipboard operations. Even when you're careful and check the contents of the Clipboard using the Show Clipboard command, Clipboard transfers are at least a two-step operation; checking the Clipboard for content adds a third step.

Drag-and-drop is a more direct method for moving information in Mac OS X, even among application environments (such as Classic, Carbon, and Cocoa). With drag-and-drop, you click and drag information to other locations on your Desktop, hard drive, or in other applications. You'll be glad to know that the Dock is fully drag-and-drop compliant as well.

Using drag-and-drop, you can even move data to the Desktop in the form of clipping objects—text as text clippings, graphics as picture clippings, sound as sound clippings, video as video clippings, and Internet addresses and URLs as any of eight different types of Internet clippings. Many types of applications are capable of creating clippings—just drag-and-drop them to the Desktop or to any open Finder window. Applications written for Mac OS 8 or higher most likely include drag-and-drop support. You can also use this method to start processes such as opening files (by dragging-and-dropping a file onto an application icon). We'll pay particular attention to drag-and-drop as we proceed through the book.

Cut and Paste: Using the Clipboard

You rarely access the Clipboard directly; instead, you manipulate the contents of the Clipboard using the Cut, Copy, and Paste commands. In fact, you'll use these commands so frequently that it's a good idea to remember their keystroke equivalents:

- Command+X (Cut)

- Command+C (Copy)

- Command+V (Paste)

These commands provide you with the following capabilities:

- *Cut*—Removes the selected objects from their current location and places them on the Clipboard, overwriting the previous Clipboard contents. (The Clipboard can contain only the result of the most recent Cut or Copy command.)

- *Copy*—Places the selected objects on the Clipboard, but leaves them in their current location as well. The copied objects replace the previous contents of the Clipboard.

- *Paste*—Places a copy of the objects now on the Clipboard into the current document at the cursor location. Using the Paste command does not remove items from the Clipboard; you can paste the same item repeatedly.

1

Although the Clipboard has many uses, the most common is moving an element such as a paragraph or graphical item from one place to another within the same document. To do so, select the element (such as a paragraph of text) using the mouse or keyboard, choose the Cut command, position the cursor at the new location, and choose the Paste command.

The Clipboard is also used to copy or move elements—even elements created by different applications—between different documents. For example, to move a chart from a file you created with your spreadsheet into a word processor document, follow this procedure:

1. Open the spreadsheet and select the chart. Use the Copy command, rather than Cut, to ensure that the chart remains in the spreadsheet even after it has been moved to the word processor.

2. Open the word processor, or switch to it if it's already open. Open the document that will receive the copied chart. You can quit the spreadsheet if you like, but it's not required.

3. Position the cursor at the point in the word processor document where you want the chart placed. Choose the Paste command.

Chances are that if you can select some information, you can copy it to the Clipboard and move it around. In addition to simple ASCII text, the Clipboard supports stylized text and various graphics formats. The Clipboard even supports sound and QuickTime video clippings. Because the Clipboard can hold only one item at a time and is not saved out to a file, it is overwritten whenever it is modified.

 TIP: If you want to remove selected items without involving the Clipboard, use the Clear command or the Delete key.

It's easy to forget the contents of your Clipboard. Some applications have a menu item called Show Clipboard; its location varies. In the Finder, this command is found in the Edit menu. Microsoft Word X has its own special Clipboard menu, the Office Clipboard, which holds multiple clippings and can float above your Word documents. Other programs place the Show Clipboard command in a View menu. In the Finder, the Edit|Show Clipboard command opens a window that shows you the Clipboard's contents and tells you what kind of data it contains. Figure 1.18 shows an example of the contents of the Clipboard (a frame from a QuickTime movie).

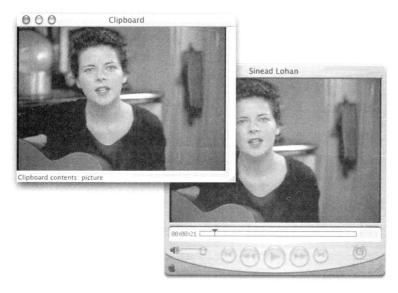

Figure 1.18
Use the Show Clipboard command in the Finder to reveal the contents of the Clipboard.

Macintosh Drag and Drop

Drag-and-drop is a technique for sharing data among documents, applications, and volumes. Various aspects of drag-and-drop behavior were introduced many years ago in System 7, where it was possible to open a file by dragging the file's icon onto an application—assuming the application was capable of opening and translating that type of file. Drag-and-drop is a terrific method for data exchange because it is intuitive. If you've used drag-and-drop in other applications (such as Microsoft Word), then you're familiar with the basics: simply select the data, drag it to a new location, and drop it. Figure 1.19 shows an example of moving a paragraph of text within a document using drag and drop.

Mac OS X also allows you to drag and drop selections to the Desktop or any other local or networked folder to which a user has write privileges. The resulting objects are called *clippings* and are given a default file name, such as "text clipping," to indicate the data type. You can later edit the file name using standard Macintosh editing techniques: click once on the file name, wait a moment for the file name field to become highlighted, type a new name, and press the Return key to put the new name into effect. If you're working in an application that was written to take advantage of the auto-naming feature for clippings (often found in applications written for Mac OS 9 or higher), the clipping may be automatically named using the first 18 to 40 or so

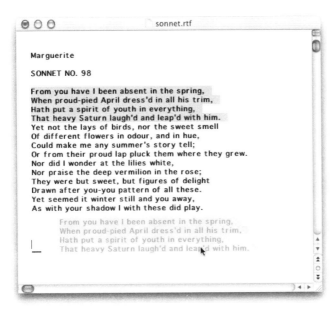

Figure 1.19
An example of drag and drop in Microsoft Word.

characters of the clipping contents. This feature only works for text clippings. Figure 1.20 contains clippings from four different applications, some of which incorporate the auto-naming feature.

To use a clipping, simply double-click on it to view its contents or open the clipping in the appropriate application, such as your Web browser for a URL clipping. Clippings are a convenient way to transfer logos or headers to documents or to other items you may have stored for future reference.

Stickies

Mac OS X has a handy little application called Stickies, located in the Applications folder. With Stickies, you can create windows of text that float on your Desktop, as shown in Figure 1.21. They resemble the paper notes found in most offices and homes that are stuck to desks, lamps, doors, and refrigerators. You can scroll the text of Stickies using the arrow keys and collapse the windows to a single bar.

The Stickies accessory supports Cut, Copy, and Paste and can import and export text. It even supports formatted text images. You can vary the colors of notes and make them any rectangular size down to a single line. When you're done with a note, you can close it and save it to a file, or simply delete it.

MacNN | The Macintosh
News .url

To use a clipping, simply
dr.textClipping

Mac OS X also allows you
to .textClipping

Picture
clipping.pictClipping

Figure 1.20
Several examples of Desktop clippings that take advantage of auto-naming.

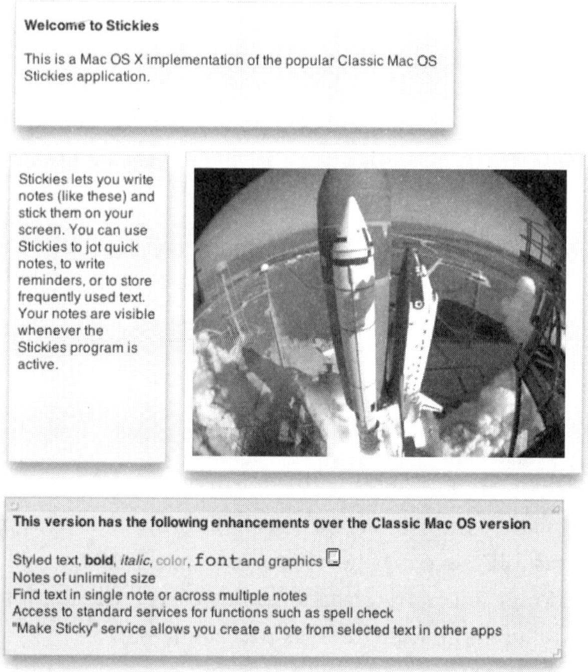

Figure 1.21
The Stickies application, rewritten for Mac OS X.

Wrapping Up

The OS is the core of what we think of as the Macintosh, and the core of Mac OS X, Darwin, is the foundation upon which many layers are built. The Mac OS makes it possible for you to interact with the computer, enables the computer to communicate with your applications, and allows you to connect to the Internet and access peripheral hardware such as printers, scanners, and storage devices.

Some of the basic features of Mac OS X that all users should understand include:

- Icons, windows, and dialog boxes instead of endless lines of computer code and obscure syntax

- Mouse controls and menus instead of just keystrokes

- The various types of windows and palettes

- Configurable System Preferences

- The purpose of the Clipboard

- The many uses of drag-and-drop

In Chapter 2, "*Working with the Finder and Desktop*," we'll explore the Finder and the Desktop, two important aspects of the OS that provide the interface and tools you use to manage your disks and files on the Mac OS.

Working with the Finder and Desktop

Just like your word processor, spreadsheet, or Web browser, the Finder is an application—even though most people don't think of it that way. Whereas each of those other applications is dedicated to creating and manipulating one specific type of data, the Finder focuses on helping you manage your disks and files.

The new Finder in Mac OS X version 10.2 provides you with features that make navigating your disks and drives easier than ever. These include the distinctive Macintosh Desktop, where icons represent files, folders, disks, and servers; the Dock; the indispensable Finder menus; the Column view; a new Find command; and the return of the "spring-loaded folder" feature. Best of all, the Finder is now multithreaded, which provides users with more speed when working in the Finder and the ability to execute multiple searches while continuing to work with other Finder windows. Of course, you can still use the Finder to launch applications, open documents, and view and modify the contents of your disks in many different ways.

Compared to earlier versions of the Mac OS, the Finder in Mac OS X gives you more information about your disks and files, more consistency in commands and features, and additional customizing capabilities. However, if you were comfortable working in earlier versions of the OS, including Mac OS 8 through OS 9.x, you'll have few problems taking advantage of the Finder's expanded capabilities in Mac OS X.

This chapter starts by examining the Finder's menu commands and then looks at Finder windows. Advanced features, such as customizing the Finder toolbar, Column views, the Dock, and icon proxies are covered, along with other well-known Finder features, including Mac Help, the Trash, the enhanced Get Info command, and the new Find command.

This chapter is not the only place in this book where you'll read about new Finder and Desktop capabilities. Several of the new Finder features were introduced in Chapter 1, "Getting to Know Mac OS X," and will be elaborated upon where the context is more appropriate. For example, customizing the Dock, windows, and the Desktop are covered in Chapter 3, "Customizing Mac OS X," and aliasing and advanced searching with the new Find command are discussed in Chapter 5, "Organizing Your Data."

Finder Menus and Commands

The Mac OS X Finder and Desktop represent both radical change and sophisticated refinement of the most basic of Mac OS elements. Despite the changes, all users can grasp the fundamentals of the latest version of the Mac OS by learning how to navigate the file system, operate menus, and open, close, and minimize windows. For starters, take a look at Figure 2.1, which shows the Finder menus and commands as they appear when Mac OS X is first installed.

Although Mac OS X has enhanced a few of the Finder menus, many (if not most) of the Finder commands should be familiar to anyone who has used previous versions of the Mac OS. The following sections offer an overview of the menus offered in the Mac OS X Finder.

Figure 2.1
The many Finder menus in Mac OS X.

Apple Menu

The Apple menu is a compilation of Apple and Special menu items from previous versions of the Mac OS, plus a few new commands:

- *About This Mac*—Opens a window that displays information about your computer, such as available memory and a description of your Mac's processor(s). This menu choice was previously called About This Macintosh or About This Computer., In Mac OS X version 10.2, the new More Info buttons opens the Apple System Profiler, where you can find even more information about your computer.

- *Get Mac OS X Software*—Launches a Web browser, and then opens a page on the Apple Web site that contains categories of downloadable software.

- *System Preferences*—Opens the System Preferences application, where you can customize many aspects of Mac OS X.

- *Dock*—Offers choices to help you configure the Dock, including options for magnifying, hiding, and positioning.

- *Location*—Reveals any configured network profiles, called locations, as well as a shortcut to open the Network Preferences System Preferences pane, where you can add, delete, and modify network locations (discussed in Chapter 14, "Connecting to the Internet").

- *Recent Items*—Shows a list of recently used applications and/or documents, as configured in the General System Preferences pane.

- *Force Quit*—Brings up a command that allows you to force an application to quit. See Chapter 13, "Troubleshooting Mac OS X", for information on how and when to use the Force Quit command.

- *Sleep*—Places your computer in energy-saving mode, according to your Energy Saver System Preferences settings. Press any key or jiggle the mouse to wake your computer from sleep.

- *Restart*—Commands your Mac to close any open documents, quit all open applications, and then restart the computer. If you have any unsaved documents or active applications, you'll be prompted to attend to them.

- *Shut Down*—Commands your computer to log out the current user, close any open documents, quit all open applications, and then turn itself off. If you have any unsaved documents or applications performing ongoing tasks, you'll be asked to attend to the documents and applications (just like with the Restart command).

- *Log Out*—Commands your computer to log out the current user, close any open documents, quit all open applications, and then present the login screen. If you have any unsaved documents or active applications, you'll be asked to attend to them (just like with the Restart and Shut Down commands). If no documents need saving and you do not confirm the logout command, it will proceed after waiting two minutes.

Application Menu Items

The Application menu, located next to the Apple menu, contains commands associated with the foremost application (i.e., the one that's operating in the foreground of your screen). The Application menu goes by the name of the foremost application; for example, if BBEdit is the foremost application, you'll see BBEdit in bold lettering next to the Apple menu, and users will refer to it as the *BBEdit* menu. Depending on the application, the options in this menu will vary. For example, the following list describes the Application menu options you'll see when working in the Finder:

■ *About Finder*—Displays a small window with information about the version of the Finder, such as "Finder Mac OS X (v10.2)."

■ *Preferences*—Opens the Finder Preferences window, which is shown in Figure 2.2. The Preferences command allows you to configure the way the Desktop opens windows and displays background images and icons. See Chapter 3, "Customizing Mac OS X," for details on how to configure the look and feel of your computer's Desktop.

■ *Empty Trash*—Empties the Trash. In previous versions of the Mac OS, this command was located in the Special menu. If the Trash is already empty, this menu option will be inactive.

■ *Services* —Activates a selected service for the item(s) selected in the foremost application, such as Finder services (Open, Reveal, or Get Info for an item in the Finder) or speech services (speak a paragraph of highlighted text in a speech-savvy word processor).

■ *Hide Finder*—Moves the Finder into the background and hides all open Finder windows. However, the windows are still accessible in the Windows menu or the Dock; an example of the latter is shown in Figure 2.3. You can un—hide the Finder by selecting any of the hidden windows from the Dock, or by selecting Show All from the Application menu of the current application (discussed next).

■ *Show All*—Reveals all hidden applications and returns hidden Finder windows that were previously minimized to the right side of the Dock.

Figure 2.2
The new Finder Preferences.

Figure 2.3
Hidden Finder windows are accessible from the Dock.

File Menu

The File menu is almost a universal constant in the Mac OS cosmos. Virtually all applications have a File menu, and the contents are predictable: New, Save, Save As, Page Setup, and Print. In Mac OS X, the only surprises are the addition of Finder windows and the relocation of the Quit option from the File menu to the Application menu. The Finder offers the following File menu options:

■ *New Finder Window*—Opens a window in the Finder for browsing the contents of your computer, local area network (LAN), servers, and removable media such as CD-ROMs. This feature, which is not found in versions of the Mac OS prior to Mac OS X, is described in detail later in this chapter.

- *New Folder*—Creates a new folder in the active Finder window or on the Desktop, but not in the root level of the computer (where your computer's hard drives and Network folder are listed).

- *Open*—Opens the selected item(s) —including files, folders, aliases, or volumes—in a Finder window or on the Desktop, just as in previous versions of the Mac OS.

- *Open With*—Opens the item(s) with a user-selected application. Mac OS X will provide a list of applications that are appropriate for the selected items, or you can browse local and remote volumes for a specific application.

- *Close Window*—Closes the foremost window on your screen.

- *Get Info*—Reveals detailed information about a selected item in the Finder, such as a file, folder, volume, or server. This command has been completely rewritten in Mac OS X version 10.2 and is explained in detail later in this chapter.

- *Duplicate*—Makes a copy of whatever is selected in the Finder, including multiple selected items, just as in earlier versions of the Mac OS.

- *Make Alias*—Creates an alias of the item that is selected in a Finder window or on the Desktop. The concept of aliases is discussed in Chapter 5, "Organizing Your Data."

- *Show Original*—Enables you to select an alias and then reveal its original in the Finder. The Show Original menu option is identical to the Reveal Original option of System 7.x and the Show Original command in Mac OS 9.x.

- *Add to Favorites*—Makes an alias of the item selected in the Finder or on the Desktop and places it in a user's Favorites folder.

- *Move to Trash*—Allows you to throw selected items into the Trash without dragging them to the Trash icon in the Dock. To use this command, select one or more items in the Finder or on the Desktop; then choose the Move to Trash command or use the keyboard equivalent (Command+Delete).

- *Eject*—Ejects the item selected in the Finder or on the Desktop if it is a removable media, such as a CD-ROM or disk image, or unmounts nonremovable media, such as a server. The Eject command has the same effect as dragging the item to the Trash icon in the Dock—both cause the Trash icon to turn into the new Eject icon.

- *Burn Disc*—Writes the data that has been copied to a writable or rewritable CD-ROM.

■ *Find*—Launches the new Find command to help you find files on your computer or network volumes. The Find command can search for files by name, size, creation date, label, and so on. See Chapter 5, "Organizing Your Data," for more information about Find.

Edit Menu

In Mac OS X, the Edit menu is pretty much the same as it is in Mac OS 9.x—with a few exceptions. The Clear command is no longer present, and the Preferences command has been relocated to the Finder's Application menu (discussed earlier). The enhanced Undo command allows you to undo Finder commands, such as moving an item back to the Desktop after moving it to the Trash. On the whole, the commands in the Edit menu are very straightforward:

■ *Undo/Can't Undo*—Allows you to reverse an action, such as changing the name of a file or folder, moving items to the Trash, or relocating a file you've downloaded from the Web to another location on your computer. Not all commands can be undone, however. In those instances, you'll see Can't Undo in the View menu instead of Undo Rename or Undo Move of "Really Important Stuff", as illustrated in Figure 2.4.

■ *Cut*—Removes (cuts) the text or image selected in the Finder. Like all the commands in the View menu, the purpose of the Cut command depends on the active application. When you're working in an imaging editing program such as GraphicConverter, for example, the Cut command cuts the selected image data; when you're working in a word processor, on the other hand, the Cut command removes a selected block of text and places it in the Clipboard.

■ *Copy*—Makes a duplicate of the selected data and stores it in the Clipboard.

■ *Paste*—Takes the data that is stored in the Clipboard and copies it to the cursor insertion point.

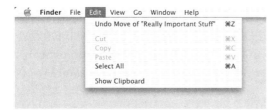

Figure 2.4
The enhanced Undo command can undo Finder actions such as renaming or moving files.

- *Select All*—Selects all the items on the Desktop or in a Finder window. And like the Cut, Copy, and Paste commands, the Select All command is found in many types of applications such as word processors, HTML editors, and imaging programs.

- *Show Clipboard*—Displays the contents of the Clipboard in a special type of window in the Finder. Many applications include this command, which opens the Clipboard contents in a window belonging to the active application rather than in the Finder.

View Menu

The commands in the View menu affect how you view the contents of the Desktop and Finder windows. Mac OS X replaces the button view with the Column view and allows you to configure both your global and window-by-window viewing preferences; however, the View menu's purpose in Mac OS X is the same as in Mac OS 8.5 through 9.x. The following options are available in the Mac OS X View menu:

- *As Columns*—Configures a Finder window to the new Column view. Column, Icon, and List views are discussed in great detail later in this chapter.

- *As Icons*—Changes a Finder window to the familiar Icon view.

- *As List*—Organizes the contents of a Finder window in the form of a list.

- *Clean Up Selection*—Unclutters the contents of a view-by-icon window so that icons and file names do not overlap and obscure each other. This command only pertains to the Desktop and to Finder windows in the icon view.

- *Arrange By Name, Date Modified, Date Created, Size or Kind*—Alphabetizes the contents of the Desktop and Finder windows in Icon views. In previous versions of the Mac OS, the Arrange By Name command could arrange lists by date modified, date created, and so on (as well as by name); however, this is not possible in Mac OS X. Refer to the View as List section later in this chapter for List view sorting options.

- *Hide/Show Toolbar*—Shows or hides the toolbar, a major new feature in the Mac OS X Finder. The toolbar is a customizable navigation tool that is extraordinarily useful for maneuvering the contents of computers with large numbers of files, folders, and attached servers.

- *Customize Toolbar*—Allows you to modify the commands and icons in the toolbar, or restore the default set of commands. Chapter 3, "Customizing Mac OS X," contains presents detailed information on how to customize the toolbar.

- *Hide/Show Status Bar*—Toggles the display of the status bar off and on. In all previous versions of the Mac OS, the status bar could not be hidden. In Mac OS X, it displays the number of items in a Finder window and the amount of free space on the disk to which the window belongs. Figure 2.5 shows a Finder window with the status bar shown (top) and hidden (bottom).

- *Show View Options*—Allows you to customize global Icon and List view options, including icon size, the arrangement of items in the Finder window, default display of columns, and the use of relative versus exact dates. The Show View Options command also lets you override the global view and select viewing options on a window-by-window basis. In Mac OS X, this command doesn't work for the Desktop, although it did under Mac OS 9.x. The Desktop view options are now configured through the Preferences menu in the Finder. All the options for the Show View Options command are discussed in the next section of this chapter.

Go Menu

The Go menu, another new addition to the Mac OS X Finder, has been revised since its introduction in Mac OS X version 10.0. It now contains shortcuts to commonly used folders and services. Some Mac purists may find this feature a little odd for an operating system that has always used icons and mouse clicks rather than lengthy commands to accomplish tasks. You'll find the following options under the Go menu:

- *Back*—Navigates to the previously selected folder or volume (this option is available only a Finder window that was not opened as a new window).

- *Forward*——Takes you to the next folder (but only if that folder has already been selected from within the same Finder window, and only if the current Finder window was not opened as a new window).

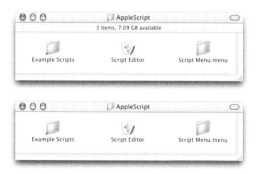

Figure 2.5
The status bar can be toggled on (top) and off (bottom) in Mac OS X.

- *Computer*—Opens a Finder window (if no windows are already open) that displays the root level of the computer, including your hard drives, removable media, network folder, and connected servers. If a Finder window is already open, the view of the top-most window will be replaced with the Computer view.

- *Home*—Takes you to the Home location of the user who is currently logged in to the computer.

- *iDisk*—Logs into your iDisk account (if you have an .Mac account configured in the Network section of the System Preferences) and mounts the iDisk.

- *Applications*—Opens the Applications folder.

- *Favorites*—Opens the Favorites folder in the Finder.

- *Favorites*—Displays the contents of the Favorites folder as shown in Figure 2.6.

- *Recent Folders*—Lists the folders recently opened in the Finder.

- *Go to Folder*—Allows you to open a folder in a new Finder window by typing its path, but only if no Finder windows are already open. If a Finder window is open, the folder will open in the top-most window. The term *path* refers to the location of a file or folder as expressed with words and punctuation, similar to the way you might type a URL of a document on a Web server using forward slashes to separate folder names. For example, you would type "Porthos/Applications/Utilities/" to go to the Utilities folder on a drive named Porthos. Figure 2.7 shows how to use a variation of this command to open the *home folder* for a user named mbell. Every user account in Mac OS X has a home folder where user-specific documents and applications can be stored. To go to your home folder, just type a tilde (~) followed by your login name.

Figure 2.6
The Favorites folder gives you easy access to items you have bookmarked with the Add to Favorites command.

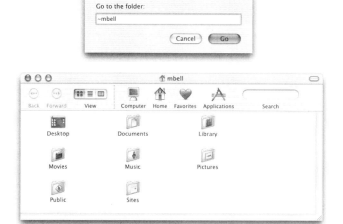

Figure 2.7
The Go To Folder command allows you to open a folder in the Finder by typing in the folder's path, by typing a tilde (~) to go to your home folder, or the tilde and a user's short name to open that user's home folder.

- *Connect to Server*—Replaces the Chooser and Network Browser of previous versions of the OS as a means of connecting to file servers. This command is covered in detail in Chapter 15, "Accessing Internet Services."

Window Menu

The Window menu provides easy access to Finder windows, including minimized (Docked), active, and inactive windows. This menu is similar to the Window menu that was added to Mac OS 9.1, but with a few added features:

- *Zoom Window*—Zooms, or enlarges, a Finder window.

- *Minimize Window*—Minimizes the active Finder window and places it in the Dock. When minimized, the window's name will be prefixed with a diamond in the Window menu; the active Finder window will be prefixed with a checkmark. Because only one window can be active in the Finder at any time, only one menu item will have a checkmark. However, multiple Finder windows may be minimized. For examples of these indicators, refer back to Figure 2.1, which shows the Window menu with one active window (Porthos), one minimized window (Archer), and one inactive window (Enterprise).

■ *Bring All to Front*—Brings all Finder windows to the front of the screen so they are grouped together. Mac OS X uses a layered windowing system that allows you to stagger windows belonging to different applications in an alternating fashion. In earlier versions of the Mac OS, an application's windows were always grouped together on screen—your Web browser's windows were on top of all your word processor's windows, which were in turn on top of all your QuickTime windows. In Mac OS X, the Bring All to Front command allows you to show one window from each application in successive layers.

Help Menu

Mac OS X version 10.2 sports a revised interface that should be very familiar to anyone who has ever surfed the Web or used any broad range of Mac OS X-native applications. You may be disappointed to learn that the venerable Apple Guide and Balloon Help are no longer supported by the Mac OS; however, some applications provide tool tips, Balloon Help-like displays of information that appear when the cursor hovers over a context-sensitive area of the Finder or application. When in the Finder, the Help menu displays only one option, Mac Help. Figure 2.8 shows the result of choosing this option.

The Help menu is available at all times in most applications, not just in the Finder. The quality and quantity of help content is determined by how the developers of your software chose to implement a Help menu. The options under the Help menu are specific to the application that is active; for example, if you're using QuickTime you'll

Figure 2.8
The new Help menu in the Finder.

see an option called QuickTime Help, rather than Mac Help. Individual applications may provide additional Help menu options as well.

Input Menu

Many users refer to the Input menu as the keyboard layout menu., It is visible only if you have more than one input device selected in the Input Menu section of the International System Preferences. For example, Figure 2.1 shows three items in the Input menu: the Australian keyboard layout, the TypeIt4Me keyboard shortcut input utility, and the U.S. keyboard layout. Selecting the Customize Menu option at the bottom of this menu opens up the Input Menu section of the International System Preferences.

Utility Menu

The Utility menu is the section of the menu bar that contains information and shortcuts to several items, including the clock, sound level, display settings, iChat, and various third-party utilities such as QuicKeys and Timbuktu. Several applications and Mac OS X features provide quick access to settings and information using the Utility menu; check for an option to show or hide this setting in a particular System Preferences pane, such as the Displays and Sound panes.

Finder and Desktop Basics

Menu commands are only a small segment of the Finder's overall function as a disk and file management tool. Most of the time, you move, copy, delete, arrange, and open files by using the mouse to directly manipulate icons on the Desktop and in Finder windows, instead of using a menu command.

In Mac OS X, your ability to see and manipulate files and folders in windows is dramatically improved compared to all earlier versions of the Mac OS. The basic features of Finder windows include the following:

■ Windows are created each time a volume or folder is opened.

■ Each window has a title bar; close, minimize, and maximize buttons, and an optional toolbar.

■ Windows can be freely positioned by dragging their title bars.

■ Windows can be resized by dragging on the resize tab.

■ The window display is controlled via the View menu.

■ The icon size and type of information displayed in Finder windows can be customized.

- Keyboard commands enable you to navigate windows and select files without using the mouse.

- Smart zooming opens windows only enough to display their content, or to the maximum available display area.

- The contents of any folder or subfolder can be displayed hierarchically in any window.

- Hierarchical levels of folders allow files in different folders to be manipulated simultaneously.

- Icon proxies (in the title bar) allow you to move, copy, or alias Finder windows.

- List view columns may be resized and reordered.

When compared to earlier versions of the Mac OS, the improvements to the Finder in Mac OS X give you more control over windows, a more consistent user interface, and a wider range of display options, including:

- The Dock replaces the functionality of the Application and Apple menus.

- Finder windows can display the files and folders for an entire computer (use the Go|Computer menu command and then select the new Column view).

- The toolbar provides customizable shortcuts that allow you to navigate to the contents of the Finder.

- You can now browse the contents of your computer by way of Finder windows, thereby circumventing the need for hard drive icons on the Desktop.

For a better perspective about the how the Finder has evolved, consider that in the early days of the Mac OS the presentation of text and icons in Finder windows was preset and could not be modified. Text was always shown in 9-point Geneva, and icons appeared only in preset sizes in each icon view. In System 7, the Views Control Panel provided a variety of options that enabled you to control the information and the way it was displayed in Finder windows. In Mac OS 8, the options relating to viewing the contents of a folder or hard drive became even more flexible and customizable, as well as more a part of the core OS rather than a branch of it. Mac OS 8.6 went even further to allow users to customize more Finder elements, including spring-loaded folders and Finder labels (the latter is not present in Mac OS X). Several elements of the Mac OS X Finder are configurable in the Finder|Preferences menu, as shown earlier in Figure 2.2. Mac OS X separates the preferences for configuring the behavior of the Finder and Desktop into four locations:

- Finder|Preferences menu

- View|Show View Options menu

- Apple|Dock|Dock Preferences menu

- Desktop System Preferences

The trend in Mac OS X is to centralize the configuration options that were previously scattered in various locations, making them easier to find. Because they have strong ties to Finder configuration options in earlier versions of the Mac OS, let's take a look at the first two configuration options; the Dock and Desktop will be discussed in the next section of this chapter.

The following sections will help you understand the basic configuration options for the Finder, and how to use the different views in Finder windows to get the most out of Mac OS X.

Finder Preferences

The Finder Preferences window options affect the behavior and appearance of items on the Desktop and in Finder windows. In the first release of Mac OS X, the Desktop picture was also managed through the Finder Preferences but that has been moved to the Desktop System Preferences. The following options are found when you select the Finder|Preferences menu:

- *Show these Items on the Desktop*—Check the items you want to show on the Desktop: hard drives, removable media (including CD-ROMs, DVDs, and disk images), and connected servers (such as file servers and Macs running Personal File Sharing).

- *New Finder Window Shows*—Choose whether you want new Finder windows to open to your home folder or to the root level of your computer, revealing all in your home folder or at the root level of your computer, revealing all hard drives, removable media and connected servers.

- *Always Open Folders in a New Window*—When checked, any folder in a list or icon view that is double-clicked will open in a new Finder window; if unchecked, the new location will be opened in the same Finder window.

- *Open New Windows in Column View*—Causes Finder windows created using Command+N or File|New Finder Window to open in a Column view, which many people find to be the best way to navigate the file system.

■ *Spring-Loaded Folders and Windows*—When checked and configured using the sliding scale, allows you to drag an item onto a closed Finder window and have that window "spring open" so that you can drop the item into the selected Finder window. With spring-loaded folders, you can easily and quickly navigate through a series of hierarchical folders to deposit a selected document, folder, application, or any other drag-and-droppable item in the Finder. To immediately open the target folder, drag the selected item(s) over the folder or volume and press the space bar; to cancel navigation through a series of folders without actually moving the selected item, press the Escape key before releasing the mouse.

■ *Show Warning before Emptying the Trash*—When selected, a standard warning will appear when you choose the Empty Trash command.

■ *Always Show File Extensions*—When checked, filenames with extensions such as .html and .pdf will reveal their extensions. This is a global setting; if unchecked, it can be set on a per-file basis using the Get Info command, which is explained later in this chapter. Also, when this option is not selected, a warning like the one shown in Figure 2.9 will appear when you change the extension of a file. To avoid these warning, make sure the Always Show File Extensions option is selected.

■ *Languages for Searching File Contents*—Click the Select button to choose which languages you want the Mac OS to index for full-text searches of your files. To speed up the search process and cut down on the disk space required for the indices, only select the languages you intend to search.

■ *Folders in a New Window*—When checked, any folder in a list or icon view that is double-clicked will open in a new Finder window, which mimics the behavior of Mac OS 9.x and earlier. If this option is unchecked, the new location will be opened in the same Finder window.

■ *OpenNew Windows in Column View*—Causes Finder windows created using Command+Nor File|New Finder Window to open in a column view, which may people find to be the best way to navigate the file system.

■ *Spring-loaded Folders and Windows*—When checked and configured using the sliding scale (short-to-long), allows you to drag and item onto a closed Finder window and have that window "spring open" and let you drop the item into the selected Finder window. With spring-loaded folders, you can easily and quickly navigate through a series of hierarchical folders to deposit a selected document, folder, application, or anything else that you are able to drag and drop in the Finder. To immediately open the target folder, press the space bar; to cancel navigation through a series of folders without actually moving the selected item, press the Escape key before releasing the mouse.

- *Show Warning Before Emptying the Trash*—When selected, a standard warning will appear when you choose the Empty Trash command.

- *Always Show File Extensions*—When checked, filenames with extensions such as .html and .pdf, for example, will reveal their extensions. This is a global setting that if unchecked, can be set on a per-file basis using the Get Info command, which is explained later in this chapter. Also, when this option is not selected, a warning like the one shown in Figure 2.9 will appear when you change the extension of a file. To avoid these warning, make sure the Always Show File Extensions option is selected.

- *Languages for Searching File Contents*—Click the Select button to choose which languages you want the Mac OS to index for full-text searches of your files. To speed up the search process, and cut down on the disk space required for the indices, only select the languages you intend to search.

Window View Options

When viewed as icons, lists, or columns, any Finder window can be customized to meet the needs of the task at hand. For example, a folder containing a large number of HTML documents might best be viewed using a list or column view, whereas a folder of images may be viewed best in the List or Column formats, and a folder of images may best be viewed as large icons arranged by name. Mac OS X allows you to set global preferences for all three views, but you can always override the global setting and further customize the view options for a particular folder. Most people will want to mix the three views to meet their needs.

Column Views

The main strength of the Column view is not simply in viewing the contents of a folder or hard drive, but also in navigating the file system of your computer or a server for quick access to an item. I like to be able to highly customize certain windows, but view others in a way that promotes speedy navigation. For example, I like to keep the root level of my hard drive very lean, using only those folders created by Mac OS X

Figure 2.9
Check the Always Show File Extensions option in the Finder Preferences to avoid this warning.

(Applications, Library, System, and Users) and the default folders found in every user's home folder (including Desktop, Documents, Library, Movies, Music, Pictures, Public, and Sites). The new Column view is perfect for navigating a computer organized in this way. However, when I'm working on a project like a Web site, I need to view the contents of a folder using a customized Icon or List view in order to work with my files. To navigate using a Column view from within the Finder, follow these steps:

1. Open a new Finder window by selecting Command+N or File|New Finder Window.

2. Choose View|As Columns, or select the Columns icon in the toolbar.

3. Select an item in the window's far-left column to display the contents of that folder in the column to the right.

Column views may have one or more columns; if you enlarge the window using the grow button in the lower-right corner of the Finder window, the number of columns will increase proportionately—as far as the size of your Desktop will allow. For example, Figure 2.10 shows two versions of a Column view.

Of course, you can navigate to a depth that exceeds the number of columns your Desktop is capable of displaying. The columns will drift to the left of the window as you navigate deeper into a folder hierarchy. The reverse is true as well—the columns will drift to the right as you go backward in the hierarchy—but you must drag the scroll tab to the left to navigate backward. The width of one or more of the columns in a column view can be changed as follows:

1. To evenly change the width of all columns, drag the resize tab of any of the visible columns to the right to increase, or to the left to decrease the width. The cursor in Figure 2.11 points to the column resize tab.

2. To individually change the width of a specific column, Option+drag the resize tab located at the right of the column to the right to increase the width or to the left to decrease the width.

With Mac OS X version 10.2, you can globally customize three aspects of the Column view by opening any window and selecting from the following items:

■ *Test Size*—Choose a text size between 10 and 16 points.

■ *Show Icons*—Show or hide icons for each item in a column.

■ *Show Preview Column*—Show or hide the display of the selected item's Finder attributes in the right-most column.

Figure 2.10
You can resize a column window to increase or decrease the number of columns shown.

For example, Figure 2.12 shows the new Column view configuration options as applied to the Applications folder. Note how reducing the text size, icons, and preview column allows for more Finder items to be listed in the column view.

Once you get the hang of it, Column views are kind of nifty because they provide a fast method of navigating a complex file hierarchy.

Icon Views

The Icon view is probably the most flexible of the three Finder window views, because you can arrange the contents of a window both creatively (using icon placement, background colors, and pictures) and logically (by sorting the contents using the Keep Arranged By option). For example, Figure 2.13 shows a portion of the Utilities folder viewed in a highly customized Icon view.

Figure 2.11
Use the column resize tab to resize all the columns, or a specific column.

Figure 2.12
The new Column view options.

To configure a window in Icon view, select any Finder window. Choose View as Icons and Show View Options (or press Command+J), as illustrated in Figure 2.13, and then choose from the following configuration options:

■ *This Window Only*—Applies the view options to the selected window only.

■ *All Windows*—Applies the view options to all Finder windows viewed as icons.

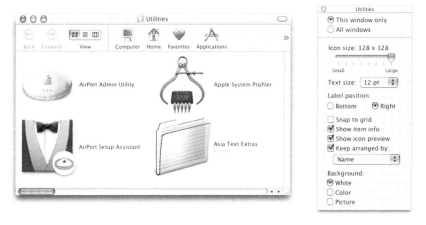

Figure 2.13
The Icon view for a Finder window is, for many users, the most flexible of the three view options.

2

■ *Icon Size*—Changes the size of icons on a sliding scale between 16x16 pixels and 128x128 pixels.

■ *Text Size*—Determines the text size (between 10 and 16 points) used in Icon views.

■ *Label Position*—Displays the text that accompanies the icons either at the bottom or to the right of the icons (in Figure 2.13, the Label Position is set to the right).

■ *Snap to Grid*—Forces any repositioned icons on the window to automatically snap to the nearest point on an invisible grid. This is the same invisible grid used by the View|Clean Up command in Finder windows. The concept of always keeping files grid-aligned in this way may sound appealing, but it can be disconcerting when the Finder grabs and relocates files while you're trying to position them precisely. In most cases, it's probably better to leave this option off and use the Clean Up command as needed to correct any icon alignment problems in Finder windows.

TIP: You cannot determine the amount of space between items displayed in Icon view, or when the Always Snap to Grid option is selected in the Finder Preferences. Versions of the Mac OS prior to OS X version 10.1 allow you to choose between tight and wide grid spacing, but Mac OS X defaults to somewhere in between.

■ *Show Item Info*—Displays the number of items inside folders viewed as icons (see the Asia Text Extras folder in Figure 2.13 for an example).

■ *Keep Arranged By*—Forces the arrangement of icons in the Finder window according to one of the following:

■ *By Name*—Sorts files and folders alphabetically (A through Z), from top to bottom.

■ *By Date Modified*—Sorts files by the date on which they were last modified, with the most recently updated files at the top of the list. This view is useful when you're looking for files that are much older (or much newer) than most of the other files in a particular folder.

■ *By Date Created*—Sorts files by the date they were created, with the most recently created files at the top of the list. When you copy a file or folder from another source, it retains its original creation date.

■ *By Size*—Sorts files in descending size order. Otherwise, files are grouped alphabetically at the end of the list. Commonly, the By Size command is used to find files known to be either very large or very small, or to locate large files that could be deleted to free up space.

■ *By Kind*—Sorts files alphabetically by a short description based on the *file type*, a designation assigned by the creator of the application. Files associated with a particular application often include the name of that application as the kind. Viewing files by kind is useful if you know the kind of file you're looking for and if the window containing that file has many different types of files in it.

■ *Background*—Selects the color or picture for the Icon view window. A selected color will fill the entire window with color, no matter how you resize the window. A background image, on the other hand, will display its natural size and will not "tile" itself to cover the Finder window if it is enlarged beyond the original size of the window. If you stretch the window beyond the size of the background picture, the outlying portions of the Finder window will appear white.

List Views

The List view is a popular way of viewing Finder windows because it enables you to easily sort a window's contents. Finding items displayed in a List view is intuitive because most people are accustomed to scanning top to bottom to find items alphabetically. Figure 2.14 shows a customized List view window in which the contents are sorted by name.

To configure the appearance of folders viewed as lists, choose from the following options:

■ *This Window Only*—Applies the view options to the selected window only.

■ *All Windows*—Applies the view options to all Finder windows displayed in a List view.

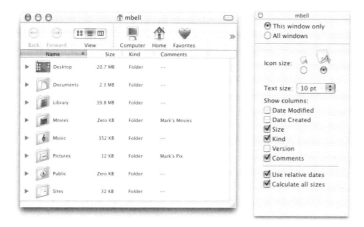

Figure 2.14
A customized List view.

- *Icon Size*—Determines the size of icons used in List views.

- *Text Size*—Changes the text size (between 10 and 16 points) used in List views.

- *Show Columns by: Date Modified, Date Created, Size, and Kind*—These options work just as they do when viewing the contents of a window as icons. See the preceding section for a description.

- *Show Columns by: Version*—Useful only for application files, this command sorts according to the software developer's assigned version number. Ancillary application files (such as dictionaries and references) and data files that you've created usually do not have this type of version number.

- *Show Columns by: Comments*—This command sorts files alphabetically by the text contained in their Get Info window comment fields. Displaying comment text in Finder windows is a handy file management feature; however, it's useful only if the first characters of the comment are significant or if you just want to separate all files that have comments from those that don't. Files that have no comments are placed at the top of any windows sorted using the View menu's Show Columns by Comment command. The Movies and Pictures folders in Figure 2.14 have custom comments.

- *Use Relative Dates*—Documents created or modified recently will be listed as Today (*time*) and Yesterday (*time*), and all others will be listed as *Date* (*time*). This is helpful when you have a long list of documents and want to find the ones you've worked on recently.

- *Calculate All Sizes*—Checking this option will cause the total number of items in a window's subfolders to be calculated and displayed in the List view. Mac OS X version 10.2's Finder is multithreaded, and can calculate the sizes of enclosed folders much faster than previous versions of the Mac Os.

Viewing Hierarchical Lists

List views may not be the most aesthetically appealing way to look at your files and folders, but most people have so much data on their hard drives that viewing them as lists is the most practical way to find things. List views are also pragmatic because they can be manipulated more easily than Icon or Column views. Furthermore, they're more versatile because they can be expanded hierarchically or collapsed back into a single list with great ease. With this feature, you can display the contents of any folder without having to open a new folder window. In older versions of the Mac OS, the only way to view and manipulate folder contents was to open the folder, thereby creating a new window.

In System 7 and all subsequent versions of the Mac OS, the contents of any folder can be displayed by clicking on the small triangle (referred to as a disclosure triangle or button) that appears to the left of the folder icon. A hierarchical view allows you to view several levels of nested folders (folders inside of folders) at one time simply by clicking on the triangle next to the appropriate folder. Folder aliases, which are discussed in Chapter 5, "Organizing Your Data," do not have a triangle and cannot be displayed hierarchically.

If you drag hierarchically displayed folders from one List view window to another, however, they will appear as closed, unexpanded folders. You may drag files or folders from a list window to other volumes (copying the files), to other open Finder windows (moving the files), to the Desktop, or to the Trash (deleting the files), just as you would with items selected in icon and column windows. Eliminating clutter is the primary benefit of the hierarchical view—there's no need to open a new Finder window for every folder you want to view, as some people are known to do. In addition, hierarchical views allow you to simultaneously select and manipulate files and folders from different hierarchical levels; this was not possible in some earlier versions of the Mac OS, because each time you clicked the mouse in a new window, the selection in the previous window was released.

Figure 2.15 illustrates this capability by showing the selection of three different folders, each on a different hierarchical level. The folders in this selection can now be

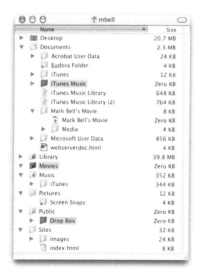

Figure 2.15
In a hierarchical display, you can select folders and/or files in different folders at the same time using the Command+click method.

copied, moved, deleted, or manipulated as easily as a single file. To select files and folders at multiple levels of the hierarchy at the same time, hold down the Command key while clicking on the file names or icons.

To collapse a folder's hierarchical display, click the triangle next to the folder icon; the enclosed files and folder listing will disappear. When you close a window viewed as a list, the OS will not remember the hierarchical display settings (unlike Mac OS 9.1).

Of course, you can still open a completely new window for any folder, if you prefer. Simply double-click on the folder icon rather than on the triangle, or select the folder icon and then choose the Open command from the File menu.

Resizing List Columns

Mac OS X enables you to resize the width of a column in a List view. Although the Mac OS no longer limits the length of file names to 32 characters, a practical limit on the width of a column remains a good idea. The lack of space on your display is just one of many possible reasons to shrink a column's width. Figure 2.16 shows an example of a List view before (top) and after (bottom) the column widths have been manipulated, as well as the three types of cursors that indicate the direction of the column expansion or contraction (right).

To manipulate a column's width, follow these steps:

1. Open a window to a List view.

2. Position the cursor between two column headings, such as Name and Date Modified, until the cursor changes when the mouse is depressed. The cursor will change from the normal pointer cursor into one of three types of cursors (shown in Figure 2.16), which indicate whether a column may be expanded, expanded or contracted, or contracted. The direction of the cursor will indicate the direction(s) you can adjust the column width.

The OS limits the maximum and minimum sizes for columns. Watch for the cursor to change as a visual clue as to how far you are allowed to resize a column.

Reordering List Columns

In Mac OS X, you can reorder any visible column except the Name column, which cannot be reordered or removed from view in the Show View Options configuration window for a List view. This capability is useful for anyone who wants to sort a list without having to scroll horizontally to bring a particular column into view. Now you can just drag that column closer to the Name column on the left side of the window, as illustrated in Figure 2.17.

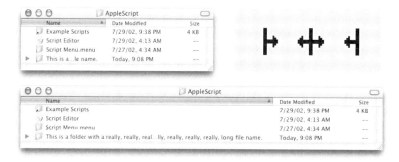

Figure 2.16
Resize columns to better view the contents of List views.

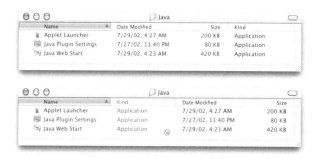

Figure 2.17
You can reorder all but the Name column in a List view by dragging the column to the left or right.

To manipulate a column's position in a list window, follow these steps:

1. Open a window to a List view.

2. Place the cursor in the center of a column heading, such as Size; drag it horizontally to a column occupied by another heading; then release it.

Advanced Finder and Desktop Features

Now that I've covered the basics of how windows work and how they can be configured to enhance your access to applications, documents, folders, and volumes, let's look at a few advanced features for working with the Finder and Desktop.

The Dock

It's easy to get lost when you have a number of windows open on your screen—particularly a problem on PowerBooks or Macs with very small displays. Most applications, including the Finder, have a Window menu to help you out of such a predicament. The Dock incorporates two clutter-management features that are not found in Mac OS X: collapsible windows (also called window shade) and pop-up windows. Whereas both features help to temporarily hide windows, the Dock can do even more to manage Finder and application windows. But don't worry if you really, really miss these two features. Chapter 3, "Customizing Mac OS X," shows you how to download and install utilities that restore these features.

In addition to the collapsing and pop-up windows, the Dock replaces other features found in previous versions of the Mac OS. It incorporates elements of the Apple menu, the Application menu, the Application Switcher, and the Control Strip. And if you think it can do even more—you're right. In the next chapter, we'll cover third-party utilities that significantly enhance the Dock and even replace the features of the Dock with something altogether different.

By default, the Dock is configured to appear at the bottom center of your Desktop and to display a standard set of items. As you can see in Figure 2.18, the default version of the Dock includes the following items (shown from left to right):

- Finder

- Mail

- iChat

- Address Book

- Internet Explorer

- iTunes

- iPhoto

- iMovie

- Sherlock

Figure 2.18
The default Dock icons for Mac OS X.

- QuickTime Player
- System Preferences
- Divider line
- Mac OS X home page link (URL)
- Trash

In addition to displaying the default applications, documents, and URLs, the Dock serves as a menu switching utility. A small black triangle appears below the icon for any application that is running in the Mac OS; as the application is being launched, the triangle will blink or the icon will bounce up and down on the Dock. Most Dock icons offer contextual information about associated windows or processes, revealed by Control+clicking on the icon. For example, Figure 2.3 shows several Finder windows that are accessible via the Finder icon in the Dock; Figure 2.18 shows an iChat message in its Dock icon. .

You can also use the Dock to store frequently accessed folders, a folder filled with shortcuts to groups of applications and utilities, or even hard drives. When activated with a Control+click, the folder reveals its contents in a hierarchical fashion, growing wherever it finds room. For example, Figure 2.19 shows my Favorites folder accessed through the Dock, revealing several levels of subfolders.

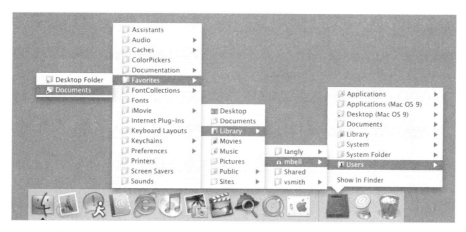

Figure 2.19
Docked folders can be expanded hierarchically for easy access to documents, folders, applications, and volumes.

When adding and deleting items in the Dock, the only rules to remember are these:

- Applications may only go to the left of the divider line.

- Documents may only go to the right of the divider line.

- The Finder and Trash icons cannot be removed.

- Everything but the Finder, divider line, and Trash can be repositioned by dragging them to the left or right, as long as you stick to the first two rules.

The Dock has only a few options to configure. You can access them via the Apple menu, the System Preferences, or by Control+clicking on the divider line, the results of which are shown in Figure 2.20. The configuration options in the Dock pane of the System Preferences include:

- *Dock Size*—Changes the size of the Dock via a sliding scale. Clicking on the divider line and dragging the Dock resizer up or down will also accomplish this task (visible when Control+clicking on the divider bar).

- *Magnification*—Increases the size of the icon when the cursor passes or hovers over it.

- *Position on Screen*—Places the dock against the left, bottom, or right side of the screen.

- *Minimize Using*—Chooses between the Genie or Scale visual effects when mini-mizing or restoring Finder or application windows.

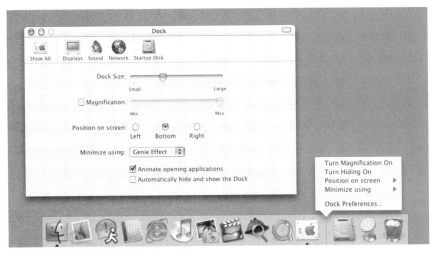

Figure 2.20
Control+click on the divider bar in the Dock to reveal several dock configuration options.

■ *Animate Opening Applications*—Causes an application icon to bounce up and down when launching.

■ *Automatically Hide and Show the Dock*—When selected, this option hides the Dock until the mouse cursor meets the bottom of the Desktop, triggering the Dock to pop up. After a Dock item is selected or the focus of the mouse changes, the Dock goes back into hiding. When in the Finder, press Command+Option+D to toggle between showing and hiding the Dock.

Navigating from the Keyboard

Even though the Mac OS relies primarily on its graphical interface and the mouse, keyboard control is, at times, a necessity. A variety of keyboard shortcuts can be used to select files, move between file windows, and manipulate icons. For a complete list of keyboard shortcuts, see Appendix B, "Shortcuts." The following keyboard commands are available in all List-viewed Finder windows and on the Desktop:

■ *Jump to File Name*—Type the first few letters in a file name to select that file. For example, if you want to select a file named Budget, type B and the first file name starting with a B is selected. When the u is typed after the B, the selection will be the first file name starting with Bu, and so on. Don't pause between letters, or the Mac OS will interpret each additional letter as the first letter of a new search. If you don't know an exact file name, type an A to cause the display to scroll to the top of the list, an L to scroll to the middle, or a Z to scroll to the end.

■ *Select Next Alphabetical File Name*—Press the Tab key to select the next item when in an Icon view.

■ *Select Previous Alphabetical File Name*—Press Shift+Tab to select the previous item when in an Icon view. This is useful when you press the Tab key one time too many and need to go back one step in reverse alphabetical order.

■ *Select Next File*—Use the down and up arrow keys to select the next file or folder icon in the corresponding direction.

■ *Open Selected Folder*—Press Command+down arrow to open the selected file or folder. If the selected file or folder is already open, pressing this key combination brings its window to the front. Command+O will also open the selection.

■ *Open Selected File or Folder and Close Current Window*—Press Command+Option+down arrow. If the selected file or folder is already open, this key combination brings its window to the front and closes the current folder or volume window. Command+Option+O performs the same function.

■ *Open Parent Folder Window*—Press Command+up arrow. If the selected file or folder is already open, this key combination brings its window to the front.

■ *Open Parent Folder Window, Close Current Window*—Pressing Command+Option+up arrow closes the current window and opens the parent window.

■ *Edit File Name*—Press Return to enter into editing mode for a window or Desktop item that isn't locked. Files can also be prepared for editing with the mouse by clicking the cursor on the text of the file name twice, with a one-second delay between clicks. You can tell that the name has been selected for editing when its display is highlighted and a box is drawn around the file name. Once the file name is open for editing, the backspace key deletes characters and the right and left arrow keys position the cursor. Pressing Return again saves the file name changes. Items that are locked or whose names are reserved by the Mac OS, such as *Desktop*, cannot be edited.

■ *Make Desktop Active*—Pressing Command+Shift+up arrow makes the current window inactive and the Finder Desktop active.

■ *Throw Item into the Trash*—Pressing Command+Delete will move the selected item to the Trash; Shift+Command+Delete will activate the Empty Trash command.

The following keyboard commands are available only when working in Finder windows viewed as lists (By Name, Size, Kind, Version, Label, or Comment):

■ *Expand Hierarchical Folder*—Command+right arrow displays the folder contents hierarchically.

■ *Expand All Folders*—Command+A selects all the items in a folder, then Command+right arrow.

■ *Expand All Hierarchical Subfolders*—Command+Option+right arrow displays the contents of the current folder and all of its enclosed folders hierarchically.

■ *Collapse Hierarchical Display*—Command+left arrow collapses the hierarchical display of the current folder.

■ *Collapse All Folders*—Command+A selects all the items in a folder, then Command+left arrow.

■ *Collapse All Hierarchical Subfolders*—Command+Option+left arrow collapses the hierarchical display of the current folder and all enclosed folders.

Dragging Files between Inactive Windows

Mac OS X allows you to select and move a file from one window to another—even from one inactive window to another. In some earlier versions of the OS, as soon as an icon was selected in an inactive window, the window containing that icon became the active (and, consequently, the foremost) window. This created a problem when that window overlapped and obscured other folder icons. In the Mac OS X Finder, any visible icon in any window can be selected and dragged to a new location without the source file window becoming active.

 TIP: To move a Finder window without making it active, hold down the Command key while dragging the window's title bar.

To copy an item from an inactive Finder window:

1. Point the mouse over the item to be moved.

2. While holding the Command key, drag the item to its new location.

As long as the mouse button is not released, only a single mouse movement is required to move the file.

This method cannot be used to move more than one file at a time. To move multiple files from one inactive window to another, the window containing the files must be made active.

When you drag items over and into a window, the inside of the window that will contain the item becomes outlined for a brief moment, a feature that first appeared in System 7.1 as a means of telling the user where the item would land if dropped. In Mac OS X, if you drag an item onto an inactive window and pause, the inactive window will then become active.

Working with Multiple Files

Selecting one item in a Finder window or on the Desktop is easy enough, but you'll often want to select more than one item at a time to duplicate, alias, or move to the Trash. To perform any operation on one or more items in a window or on the Desktop, first select the file or group of files. Most aspects of selecting files in Mac OS X are the same as in previous versions of the Mac OS:

■ *Immediate Marquee Selection*—The marquee, or selection rectangle, (created by clicking the mouse button and dragging with the button pressed while in an Icon or List view) selects files as soon as any part of the file name or icon is inside the selection rectangle.

- *Command Select*—Use the Command key while drawing a marquee to select non-contiguous sections of any Finder window.

- *File Dragging*—It's still possible to drag files by clicking on their names and moving them while the mouse is depressed.

- *Finder Scrolling*—When dragging with a marquee, the Finder window scrolls automatically as soon as the cursor hits one of its edges.

Title Bar Pop-up Menu

Column and List window views make it easy to navigate a folder hierarchy—and with the title bar pop-up menu, you can move up the folder hierarchy of any window, column, icon, or list. You'll find a pop-up menu in the title bar of any window when you hold down the Command key and click on the folder's name in the title bar. For example, Figure 2.21 shows a pop-up menu for the folder named Utilities, which is many layers deep inside the hard drive named Porthos.

Selecting a folder or volume name from this pop-up menu opens a new Finder window that displays the folder or volume contents. If a window for the selected folder or volume is already open, that window is brought forward and made active. This feature is a real time-saver when hunting down folders in the Finder.

Icon Proxies

A great advanced Finder feature in Mac OS X is the icon proxy. Each window has a small icon positioned to the left of the window's name. This icon serves as a proxy for the folder itself in the Finder. You can move, copy, alias, or delete a folder by manipulating its icon proxy as follows:

Figure 2.21
Click and hold the icon proxy in the title bar of a Finder window to reveal its path in the file system.

1. Click once and hold on the icon proxy for a brief moment.

2. Drag the icon proxy to the Desktop, Trash, or anywhere else.

3. Option+drag the icon proxy to copy the item, or Command+Option+drag the icon proxy to make an alias of the item. Figure 2.22 demonstrates aliasing a folder to the Desktop.

Figure 2.22
Use an item's icon proxy to move, copy, or alias an item in the Finder.

When I'm working with a group of folders and have to rearrange them frequently as my project progresses, icon proxies are especially useful. Manipulating the icon proxy saves several steps each time a change is made.

Resizing Windows

Although windows don't always open up to the size you need, you can use any of several methods to resize them. To resize an open window, you can drag the size tab (also referred to as the size button, although it isn't a button in the way that most people think of buttons) in the lower-right corner of a window, or click on the maximize button in the window's title bar, as illustrated in Figure 2.23. The maximize button expands the window just enough to display the complete file list or all file and folder icons, or as much as possible if the window will exceed the monitor's display area. Clicking on the maximize button while holding the Option key no longer opens the window to the full size of the screen.

Option Key Options

The Option key performs many functions beyond just assisting with title bar navigation. Holding down the Option key closes windows in a variety of situations. In other words, the Option key gives you more options when working in the Finder, including:

■ *Folders*—While opening a folder by double-clicking on its icon in the Finder, the current folder will close as the new one is opened.

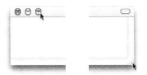

Figure 2.23
Resize your windows using the zoom button (left) and the size tab (right).

- *Multiple Windows*—While clicking the close button, all open windows will close; also, while clicking the minimize button, all open windows will minimize.

- *Applications*—While launching an application, the window in which the application icon appears will close.

Trash and Empty Trash

The Trash has undergone at least two significant changes in Mac OS X. First, the Trash icon no longer appears on the Desktop—instead, the Trash has been integrated into the Dock. For me, this makes it harder to discern whether it is empty or contains unwanted files ready for deleting. The key, of course, is to configure the size of the Dock so that it's large enough for you to see the Trash icon more clearly. For example, Figure 2.24 shows two views of the Trash icon when it is empty (left) and when it contains one or more items (right).

Note that instead of revealing the names of the items in the Trash when you Control+click on the Trash icon, it instead offers the command Empty Trash. When the Trash is empty, you can still see the Empty Trash command, but it is an inactive command (and therefore grayed out). Believe it or not, the Trash was emptied automatically in really old versions of the Mac OS. In Mac OS X, of course, you have to tell the Mac OS to empty the Trash using the Finder|Empty Trash command. Here's the second difference in the new Trash feature: it doesn't provide any feedback relating to the number of files in the Trash or the total amount of disk space the files occupy. It still

Figure 2.24
Views of the Trash icon in the Dock.

Figure 2.25
Compared to earlier versions of the Mac OS, the Empty Trash command in Mac OS X provides less information about the contents of the Trash.

presents a confirmation message, as shown in Figure 2.25. Compared to the empty Trash command in Mac OS 9.x, however, this version leaves a little to be desired.

The Empty Trash command is accessed from the Application menu when in the Finder; by pressing Shift+Command+Delete; or by Control+clicking on the Trash icon and selecting Empty Trash from the contextual menu. I prefer to know how many files are being deleted and how big they are, because I once accidentally deleted an entire collection of project files totaling 30MB. What I thought I was throwing away was 30KB of duplicate files, and had I enabled the old "warn me before empty-ing the Trash" option, I would have been saved from my own blunder. In Mac OS X, you know less about what you are deleting than in Mac OS 9.x. Fortunately, you can see what's in the Trash by double-clicking on the Trash icon in the Dock, which opens a Finder window displaying the contents of the Trash.

> **WARNING!** Mac OS X no longer counts the number of files being deleted or calculates how much space they consume. You'll have to manually open the Trash and see for yourself.

Although using the Trash is straightforward, you should be aware of several less obvious aspects of this process:

■ *Avoid Trash Warnings*—If you hold down the Option key while choosing Empty Trash, the confirmation dialog box will not appear and the Trash will be emptied immediately. Alternatively, press Command+Option+Shift+Delete to empty the Trash without warning.

■ *Retrieving Trashed Items*—At any time before the Empty Trash command is chosen, items inside the Trash may be recovered and saved from deletion. This is done by double-clicking on the Trash icon and dragging the file icons you want to recover out of the Trash window and back onto the Desktop or to any Finder window.

- *Freeing Disk Space*—Only when the Trash has been emptied is disk space released. In previous systems, dragging items to the Trash was sufficient to free disk space— although not always immediately.

- *Trash for Removable Media*—Although the Trash icon will appear empty, items from removable media (such as Zip or Jaz cartridges) that have been placed in the Trash will not be deleted when the cartridge is ejected. You must empty the Trash to delete them.

TIP: Don't be in too much of a hurry to empty the Trash. Do it every so often when you need to recover disk space, but be sure to give yourself a chance to retrieve mistakenly trashed items first. Once the Trash is emptied, deleted files can often be recovered with the help of a third-party undelete utility such as Symantec's SystemWorks or MicroMat's Tech Tool Pro, among others.

Locating Files in the Finder

In Mac OS X, the ability to search local files and folders has been extracted from the Sherlock application and put back into the Finder, where it was several OS generations ago. And since the Finder is multithreaded, searching for files has never been faster—or easier. There are two ways to search local or networked volumes from within the Finder; by using the toolbar's Search feature or by pressing Command+F while in the Finder to open the Find window. Let's look at the first way here; the Find command is discussed in detail in Chapter 5, "Organizing Your Data."

The default toolbar in Mac OS X version 10.2 includes a new command called Search. To search one or more volumes or folders, select them in the Finder window using the Command+click method described earlier in this chapter, and enter a term in the Search window. In Figure 2.26, for example, I have selected one volume named Porthos to search for the term "web" and pressed the Return key.

The Finder will search for the term only in the file names of the selected volume or folder, and then display the results in the upper half of the window. Clicking on an item in the upper half of the window will display the path to the item in the lower half of the window. As in all other types of Finder windows, you may select Command+J and configure the size of the icons (small or large) and text (10 through 16 points) of the search results, as well as what columns to display (Date Modified, Date Created, Size, Kind, Version, and Comments).

Figure 2.26
The new Search feature from within a Finder window.

Displaying Information about Finder Objects

As in previous versions of the Mac OS, you can select any file, folder, or drive icon and get more information about it by choosing File|Get Info or by selecting the Get Info contextual pop-up menu (known as the Show Info command in previous versions of Mac OS X). The Info window displays basic information and related options for all Finder objects, such as documents, folders, disks, and mounted server volumes. The Info window for the graphic editing program GraphicConverter, as shown on the left in Figure 2.27, is very different from the Info window in previous Finder versions of

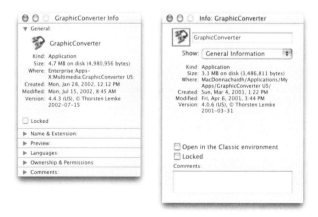

Figure 2.27
The Get Info window for GraphicConverter in Mac OS X version 10.2 (left) and Mac OS x version 10.0 (right).

Mac OS X (on the right). The new Info window contains several levels of information, depending on the type of Finder object:

- General

- Name & Extension

- Content Index

- Open with

- Preview

- Languages

- Ownership & Permissions

- Comments

The Memory section of the Get Info window is no longer required for editing for non-Classic applications. The advanced virtual memory feature of Mac OS X does not allow users to manually configure memory requirements for applications. However, it is possible to change the memory settings for Classic applications from within Mac OS X using the Get Info command, which is discussed in Chapter 8, "Working with Classic Applications."

The Info window is now available in at least six different flavors—one each for documents, folders, applications, volumes, the Desktop, and aliases. Options may differ among these types of Finder objects, but the General, Name & Extensions, Preview, Ownership & Permissions, and Comments sections appear in all Finder objects. The following sections describe the information you are most likely to find in the various sections of an Info window.

General

The General section of the Get Info window shows the basic information for Finder objects, including:

- *Kind*—A brief description of the selected file. For data files, this usually includes the name of the application that created the file.

- *Size*—The amount of disk space the item and its contents (if it's a folder) consume on a volume.

- *Where*—The location of the selected file, including all folders enclosing it and the volume it's stored on.

- *Created*—The date and time the file was created. The date is reset when a file is copied from one volume to another, or if a new copy is created by holding down the Option key while moving the file into a new folder.

- *Modified*—The date and time the contents of the file were last changed.

- *Version*—The software application's version number. No information on data files, folders, or volumes is provided.

- *Stationery Pad*—Available for data files only, this turns the selected document into a template (a master document on which new documents are based). With this option, a copy of the file is created each time the selected document is opened; any changes or customizations are made to this copy, leaving the original Stationery Pad document available as a master at all times. (A complete discussion of Stationery is provided in Chapter 7, "Working with Mac OS X Applications.")

- *Locked*—Makes it more difficult to change or delete the selected file. The Locked option appears for data files, applications, and aliases. Locking ensures that un-wanted changes are not accidentally made to data files. In most applications, locked data files can be opened but changes cannot be saved unless you use Save As to create a new file. Locked files are protected from accidental deletion because they must be unlocked before they can be moved to the Trash or have their names modified. If you try to delete a locked file, a warning dialog box will appear telling you, vaguely, that you do not have sufficient privileges to delete the item (instead of telling you the item is locked).

- *Original*—The location of the original file when the selected object is an alias.

- *Select New Original*—The location of a new parent object when the selected object is an alias.

- *Format*—The type of file format used by the selected volume, such as Mac OS Extended.

- *Capacity*—The storage capacity of a selected volume.

- *Available*—The amount of storage space available on a selected volume.

- *Used*—The amount of storage space consumed on a selected volume.

Name & Extension

The Name & Extension section of the new Info window replaces the name field in previous versions of the Get Info window It allows you to rename the selected item. Some versions of the Info window also allow you to select whether you want to show

Figure 2.28
Two versions of the Name & Extension section of the Info window.

or hide the file extension. For example, Figure 2.28 shows two versions of the Name & Extension sections, one for iMovie (left) and one for an HTML document (right).

Content Index

The Content Index section of the Info window is used only by folders and volumes Their content may be indexed for full-text searches using the Find command, which is explained in detail in Chapter 5, "Organizing Your Data." Whereas indexing was possible in many previous versions of the Mac OS, it was configured via the Sherlock application rather than the Info command. In Mac OS X version 10.2, the Content Index section has the following options:

- *Status*—Indicates whether a folder or volume has been Indexed or Not Indexed.

- *Date*—Gives the date and time of the last indexing

- *Index Now*—Updates the index immediately.

- *Delete*—Removes the index for the selected item.

Open With

The Open With section of the Info window allows you to choose what application to use to open a document with a particular extension. For example, Adobe Acrobat Reader documents ending in .pdf may be opened using Preview, as well as Adobe Acrobat Reader. The options in the Open With section are:

- *Open With*—Allows you to select an application from the drop-down menu, or select Other from the bottom of the menu and locate the appropriate application.

- *Change All*—Applies your selection to all documents with the extension in question.

Languages

Mac OS X supports localization of applications, meaning that multiple-language support may be incorporated by the application's author (see Figure 2.28 for an example). The Languages section allows you to make the following selections:

- *Check Language*—Selects the language to enable within the selected application.

- *Uncheck Language*—Temporarily disables a language for the selected application.

- *Add*—Provides additional language support for an application.

- *Remove*—Removes a language for the selected application.

Preview

The Preview section displays a 128x128 pixel version of the icon seen in the Finder, the largest size an icon may be viewed in Mac OS X version 10.2.

Ownership & Permissions

Mac OS X incorporates Unix-style file permissions that are easily changed from within a Finder selection's Get Info window. File permissions are discussed in detail in Chapter 16, "Sharing Internet Service," especially in the context of providing access and services on your computer to other users. Ownership and permissions of files are essential to the multiple-user support built into the OS, which is also the basis of all security in Mac OS X. The following summary will help familiarize you with Mac OS X's file ownership and permissions, examples of which are shown in Figure 2.29:

- *Owner*—Permits the highest level of permission (ownership) for the selected item.

- *Access*—Selects the owner's level of permission: Read & Write, Read Only, Write Only, or No Access.

- *Group*—Names a group of users who will have a secondary level of permission for the selected item.

- *Access*—Specifies the group's level of permission: Read & Write, Read Only, Write Only, or No Access.

- *Others*—Selects the level of permission for everyone else for the selected item (also Read & Write, Read Only, or No Access).

Figure 2.29
Configuring ownership and permissions in the new Info window.

- *Apply to Enclosed Items*—Copies the ownership and permissions to all folders within the selected folder.

Comments

The Comments field is a text field into which you can enter up to several hundred characters to describe the contents if the file or folder, or use as a means of categorizing. I use the Comments field to enter numbers or letters that I can use to create a customized list and then sort in a List view, an example of which you can see back in Figure 2.14.

Wrapping Up

The Finder is the most visible part of the Mac OS, As you've seen in this chapter, it gives you powerful and intuitive tools to manage the disks and files you're using with your computer, including:

- The new Finder menus

- Basic Finder operations

- Advanced Finder features such as the Dock and Column views

- The many ways you can see and manipulate data in Finder windows

- The Trash and Empty Trash commands

- The new Get Info window

Next, in Chapter 3, "Customizing Mac OS X," we'll look at the various elements in Mac OS X that you can use to give your computer a more personal look and feel. In addition, we'll cover a few inexpensive third-party utilities that can add a lot of cool features to the Mac OS, as well as restore a few that are missing in Mac OS X!

Customizing Mac OS X

Without a doubt, the fierce loyalty among Mac users is due in large part to the Mac OS's capacity for customization. Mac OS X is just as customizable as earlier versions of the Mac OS—and it has several new features that make it even more flexible. With so many ways to personalize your Mac, you'll never feel locked into using the same computer day after day.

In this chapter, we'll look at Mac OS X's redesigned System Preferences, its many customizable user interface elements, several freeware and shareware utilities for customizing your Mac, and everything you need to know to start sharing your computer with multiple users.

Mac OS Customization Features

Mac OS X employs numerous features and System Preferences to allow you to customize the way your Mac looks and functions. You'll probably do a lot of experimenting with the options that affect the way your computer looks before discovering which options work best for you. If you're like most people, your needs change over time; you should be able to change the way your computer displays icons, the Desktop, the Dock, and Finder windows to suit your needs. Why not treat yourself to a different interface every day?

Using the New System Preferences

The Mac OS X System Preferences has been modified several times since the initial release of version 10.0, with each tweak adding or recategorizing the various panes of customizable elements. The number of individual panes has increased to 25, and they're grouped into several categories. You can view the contents of the System Preferences alphabetically, similar to a Finder window in Icon view and arranged by name. Figure 3.1 shows both views of the revised System Preferences.

Figure 3.1
The new System Preferences in Mac OS X version 10.2 may be viewed by category (top) or alphabetically (bottom).

The following sections describe the System Preferences by category. Some of the categories have been, or will be, described in more detail elsewhere in this book.

Personal

The System Preferences pane in the Personal section allow various elements of the Mac OS interface to be customized by any user, even if the user has not been granted administrative privileges or had the "Open All System Preferences" deselected in the Accounts sections (more on that in a minute). The following list describes the main features of each System Preferences pane in the Personal category:

■ *Desktop*—Select the Desktop picture and determine how often the picture is automatically changed.

■ *Dock*—Configure the appearance and behavior of the Dock.

■ *General*—Select appearance, highlight color, scroll arrows, recent applications and documents, and font smoothing options.

■ *International*—Select a primary language and script behavior, and the ways in which the date, time, numbers, and Input menu are presented on screen.

■ *Login Items*—Selects item(s) to be automatically opened or launched at login.

■ *My Account*—Configure the user's password, login icon, and Address Book card.

■ *Screen Effects*—Select and configure a screen saver.

Hardware

The appearance and behavior of the various hardware components of your computer, including the central processing unit (CPU), monitor, keyboard, mouse, and removable media devices, are configured in the Hardware section of the System Preferences. A user with limited System Preferences access may only configure the last three items in this category. The System Preferences panes in the Hardware category allow you to:

■ *CDs & DVDs*—Control what the computer should do when a CD or DVD disc is inserted.

■ *ColorSync*—Select a color matching profile and color matching method to determine how colors should be rendered on screen.

■ *Displays*—Calibrate a monitor and choose a display resolution, color depth, and refresh rate to create a custom Color Sync profile.

■ *Energy Saver*—Customize energy consumption for the CPU and monitor, as well as for certain behaviors of your computer.

■ *Keyboard*—Configure keyboard repeat rate.

■ *Mouse*—Select the mouse tracking and double-click speed of the mouse or trackpad, as well as access to keystrokes to replace certain mouse functions.

■ *Sound*—Choose an alert sound, as well as sound input and output options.

Internet & Network

System Preferences related to the Internet, network adapters and protocols, QuickTime, file and Web sharing, firewall security, and the sharing of Internet access through your Mac are all located in the Internet & Network section. QuickTime configuration settings are included here because QuickTime is a multimedia format that is "streamed" over the Internet, as well as a multimedia file format. The Internet & Network System Preferences panes allow you to configure:

- *Internet*—Your .Mac account settings, iDisk storage space and access privileges, email account preferences, and Web browser home page.

- *Network*—Network interface hardware settings for such devices as modem and Ethernet cards, as well as collections of settings called Locations.

- *QuickTime*—All aspects of QuickTime preferences, including the type of network over which your computer will receive QuickTime audio and video.

- *Sharing*—Internet services to share over a network, such as Mac and Windows file sharing, Web, File Transfer Protocol (FTP), and printers, as well as the built-in firewall and the new Internet sharing feature, which allows your computer to provide Internet access to other computers.

System

In the System section of the System Preferences, users with administrative access may configure preferences that affect certain aspects of the OS, as well as speech recognition. All users have access to the final item in this category. The System panes of the System Preferences permit you to:

- *Accounts*—Create and manage multiple user accounts on your Mac.

- *Classic*—Configure the Classic environment for running Mac OS 9.x and pre-Mac OS X applications on your computer.

- *Date & Time*—Select the date, time, time tone, network time server, and menu bar clock options.

- *Software Update*—Configure manual or schedule automatic updates of the OS.

- *Speech*—Enable or disable speech recognition and configure related options.

- *Startup Disk*—Select a volume containing a valid OS from which to boot the computer.

- *Universal Access*—Configure user interface features that enhance visual and audible accessibility of the Mac OS.

The "Other" Category

Mac OS X allows developers of third-party utilities to add an item to the System Preferences for easy access to a utility. These items are placed in /**Macintosh HD/ Library/PreferencePanes/** and appear in the System Preferences window in a category called Other. The location of user-installed System Preferences panes is slightly different than in previous versions of Mac OS X, in which users could install System Preferences panes inside their own home folder hierarchy. In Mac OS X version 10.2, a user with administrative access may restrict non-administrative users' ability to access all of the System Preferences—including user-installed System Preferences panes.

Numerous utilities offer access to their features via the Other section of the System Preferences. Several of my favorites, such as Default Folder X and WindowShade X, are discussed later in this chapter. Figure 3.2 shows the System Preferences, including the Other category, and a column view of the location of these items in the Finder.

Figure 3.2
Third-party utilities may install an item in the Other section of the System Preferences for easy access to its features.

Customizing the System Preferences Toolbar

Like the Finder toolbar, the System Preferences toolbar can be easily customized to provide one-click access to a particular System Preferences pane (such as the Desktop pane). By default, the System Preferences toolbar contains icons for the Displays, Sound, Network, and Startup Disk panes, as you saw in Figure 3.1. However, you can ditch these items and add your own choices, or even hide the System Preferences toolbar altogether by choosing View|Hide Toolbar while in the System Preferences. To restore the toolbar, just choose View|Show Toolbar. Follow these steps to customize the items in the System Preferences toolbar:

1. Open the System Preferences from the Apple menu, Dock, or Applications folder.

2. Display the toolbar (if it isn't already visible) by choosing View|Show Toolbar.

3. Remove an item by dragging it to the Desktop. You'll see a "poof" animation that tells you the item has been removed, but don't worry—you've deleted the item from the toolbar, not the System Preferences itself.

4. Rearrange an item by moving it to the left or right within the toolbar.

5. Add an item by dragging it from the list of icons onto the System Preferences toolbar.

6. Quit the System Preferences.

A customized System Preferences toolbar like the one shown in Figure 3.3 makes customizing the look and feel of the computer faster and easier.

To restore the System Preferences toolbar to its original settings, follow these steps:

1. Quit the System Preferences, if it is currently running.

2. Locate/**Macintosh HD/Users/username/Library/Preferences/ com.apple.systempreferences.plist** and move it to the Trash.

3. Choose Logout from the Apple menu, and then log back in. A preference file with the new default settings will be recreated automatically, revealing the Displays, Sound, Network, and Startup Disk icons.

Changing the Desktop

Changing the Desktop is probably the most popular way to customize the look and feel of your Mac. In the old days, you could only modify the Desktop Pattern feature. The minute that Desktop pictures and custom icons were enabled, the race was on to see who could create the wackiest Desktop.

In the initial release of Mac OS X, configuring the Desktop began with in the Finder Preferences window Since the advent of Mac OS X version 10.1, however, the

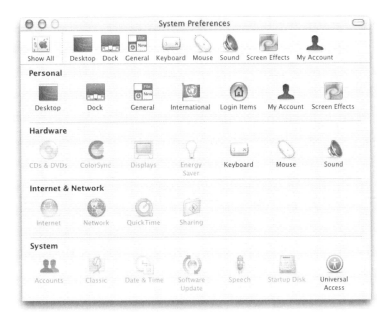

Figure 3.3
A customized System Preferences toolbar.

starting point for customizing your Desktop has been the Desktop pane of the System Preferences. If none of the default Desktop pictures suit you, you can add your own picture or pattern as long as it's in one of the many supported file formats, such as:

■ Adobe Acrobat Portable Document Format (PDF)

■ Joint Photographic Experts Group (JPEG)

■ Portable Network Graphics Image (PNG)

■ Tagged Image File Format (TIFF)

To change the Desktop pattern, follow these steps:

1. Open the System Preferences and select the Desktop pane, or Control+click on the Desktop and select Change Desktop Background.

2. Click the Collection menu and select a preinstalled image from categories such as Apple Background Images, Nature, Abstract, or Solid Colors. Alternatively, you may choose an image from another folder by selecting Pictures Folder, Desktop Pictures, or by selecting Choose Folder and locating a folder containing a valid image format.

3. To automatically rotate through the images in the selected folder, choose the Change Picture option and select the frequency to change the picture, the options for which are shown in Figure 3.4.

4. Select the Random Order checkbox to rotate the images in the selected folder in random order.

5. A single image may also be chosen as the Desktop picture by dragging an image onto the Current Desktop Picture preview well.

Mac OS old-timers will recall the days when it was possible to customize a Desktop *pattern*, but not a *picture*. In the days of System 7, small 32x32 pixel patterns were *tiled* across the screen to cover the Desktop and present the illusion of one large pattern. On the Web, background images may be similarly tiled to cover the background of a Web page—thereby using a small file and saving bandwidth. In Mac OS X, follow these steps to select a small image to tile:

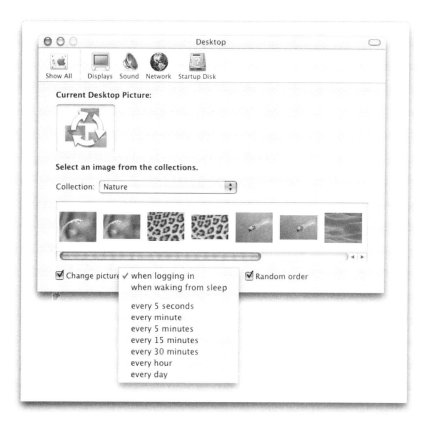

Figure 3.4
Mac OS X allows you to automatically rotate the Desktop picture.

1. Open the System Preferences and select the Desktop pane, or Control+click on the Desktop and select Change Desktop Background.

2. Select a small image using the Collection menu or by dragging an image onto the Current Desktop Picture preview well.

3. If Mac OS X determines the image is small enough, a new menu will appear to the right of the preview well, as shown in Figure 3.5.

4. From the pop-up menu, select how you would like to position the image: Fill Screen, Stretch to Fill Screen, Center, or Tile.

5. If you choose to center the image, a color picker icon will appear and let you choose a background color for the space not covered by the centered image.

Customizing the Dock

The Dock, discussed in detail in the previous chapter, is perhaps the most noticeable addition to the Mac OS. It is highly configurable and replaces the functionality of features found in previous versions of the Mac OS, including the collapsing windows, pop-up windows, Apple menu, Application menu, Application Switcher, and Control Strip. And, as we'll see in the next section, several of the Dock's capabilities become even more usable when enhanced by third-party utilities. The default Dock configura-

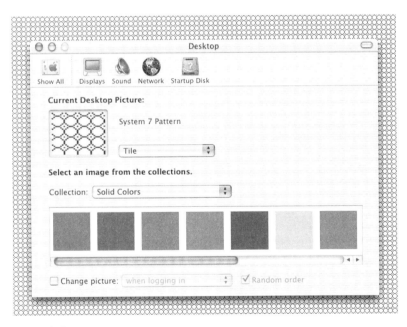

Figure 3.5
Selecting a small image file as a Desktop picture will present additional options, including the old-fashioned tile option.

tion contains shortcuts to several useful items—but why not start from scratch and make the Dock work the way *you* want it to work?

To start customizing the Dock, try this approach: Get rid of all the shortcuts except the Finder and the Trash, which cannot be removed, by dragging each item to the Desktop until you see the trademark "poof" animation. When you've successfully completed this task, the icons that remain in the Dock are for the Finder, the Trash, and any running applications (which you cannot remove). Next, place folders you access the most, as well as one or more custom folders containing categories of shortcuts to your favorite applications, projects, or resources in the Dock. Remember, there is no "best" way to configure the Dock or any other aspect of the user interface. The ideal configurations enhance your productivity and entertain you, too. I like to use the Dock as a one-stop source for shortcuts to my favorite applications and documents, which I group according to function. For example, because I do a great deal of Web development and network management, my Dock (shown in Figure 3.6) contains

Figure 3.6
A customized version of the Dock.

folders that I created to house shortcuts to the appropriate applications and documents, as well as my primary hard drive and home folder.

To remove your customizations and return to the default Dock, follow these steps:

1. Quit all open applications.

2. Locate/Macintosh HD/Users/*username*/Library/Preferences/com.apple.dock.plist and move it to the Trash.

3. Choose Logout from the Apple menu and then log back in. The default Dock size and icons view will be restored.

Finally, to hide the Dock from view, press Command+Option+D; to restore the Dock, press this keyboard shortcut again. Alternatively, place the mouse at the bottom center of the screen and the Dock will pop into view. Drag the mouse away from the Dock and it will again be hidden.

Selecting an Appearance

You can also change the appearance of the Mac OS by selecting one of two appearances in the General Controls pane of the System Preferences, as illustrated earlier in Figure 1.13. Mac OS X provides only two appearances—Blue and Graphite. They are essentially the same, except that the Graphite appearance uses gray buttons in place of the blue, red, yellow, and green buttons of the Blue appearance. Graphic designers proposed the Graphite option as Mac OS X was being developed because the jewel-tones of the Blue appearance were thought to be too distracting. In the General Controls pane, you can configure the following options:

■ *Appearance*—Allows you to choose an appearance that controls the look and feel of buttons, menus, and certain window elements, such as scroll bars. Other means of enhancing the appearance are discussed in the next section of this chapter.

■ *Highlight Color*—Enables you to determine the color used to select items in the Finder, as well as to select blocks of text for drag, drop, cut, copy, and paste commands. You may choose from one of seven pre-defined colors, or choose Other to open the color picker and select practically any color.

■ *Place Scroll Arrows*—Provides scroll arrows at the top and bottom of windows, or together at the bottom of the window.

■ *Click in the Scroll Bar to*—When working with long documents or windows, allows you to choose whether you want to skip to just the next page, or to the location just clicked in the scroll bar area.

■ *Recent Number of Items*—Choose from between zero and 50 of the most recently used applications and documents.

■ *Font Smoothing*—Choose from one of several styles, or techniques, for smoothing screen fonts.

■ *Turn off Text Smoothing for Font Sizes ___and Smaller*—Disables the smoothing of screen fonts for fonts smaller than 8, 9, 10, or 12 points in size.

Customizing Date & Time Display

Mac OS X contains a clock powered by a small battery on the logic board (for times when your Mac is unplugged or if the power is lost). It's important to configure the computer's date, time, and time zone settings so that email messages and documents can be tracked according to the date and time they were created or last modified. A file with an incorrect date and time stamp may very well elude you in a search for items created on a particular date. Mac OS X can display the time (and the date, when the time is single-clicked with the mouse) in the menu bar as well as in a small application appropriately named Clock, which is located in the Applications folder. The settings in the Date & Time System Preferences pane control all of your Mac's time and date features. You can review and configure your date and time settings by following these steps:

1. Open the Date & Time System Preferences pane.

2. Enter the current date and time in the Date & Time tab.

3. Select the appropriate information in the Time Zone tab; Mac OS X automatically configures Daylight Saving Time.

4. In the Network Time section, determine whether you want to use a network time server to automatically set the time on your computer. Refer to **http://time.apple.com** for the URL of a time server.

5. Under the Menu Bar Clock tab, you can choose to display the time and date in the menu bar and set several clock display options.

The Clock application, a small clock that has both analog and digital interfaces, can be displayed in the Dock or as a floating window with varying degrees of transparency. You may reposition the clock by dragging it to the desired location on the Desktop.

Setting Displays and Sound System Preferences

You can go beyond customizing how your Mac looks by tailoring the way it displays information on your monitor and plays sounds. This flexibility is yet another example of the capacity for individualization that makes the Mac OS so popular. In Mac OS X, the

Displays System Preferences pane replaces the old Monitors Control Panel, and the Sound System Preferences pane replaces the Sound Control Panel. Depending on what type of computer and monitor you have, your options may look slightly different from the examples that follow.

Customizing Displays

To customize the style in which your Mac displays information received from the operating system, go to the Displays System Preferences pane. The color depth, or the number of colors your monitor can display, will depend on the amount of video RAM (also called VRAM) and the type of display. Most video cards installed in new computers are capable of displaying millions of colors; however, if you don't have enough VRAM, you may only be able to display thousands of colors. A good rule of thumb is to set your monitor to display millions of colors if it is capable of doing so. If you have a PowerBook or iBook, which I'll talk about more in Chapter 7, additional customization features may apply to the Displays System Preferences.

The optimal Displays setting is highly personal. Because the monitor is the primary avenue through which you interact with the computer, I suggest you thoroughly explore the following settings to determine what works best for you:

- *Resolutions*—The various resolutions available to your computer, measured in pixels, horizontal and vertical. For example, 1024 horizontal pixels by 768 vertical pixels is commonly noted as *1024x768*, and is considered to be the minimal resolution acceptable for ease of viewing.

- *Colors*—The number of colors displayed at a particular resolution, typically millions, thousands, or 256. The Mac OS X interface is designed for display using millions colors to bring out the detail of the user interface and photographic qualities of Desktop pictures and screen savers.

- *Refresh Rate*—The frequency with which images are displayed on your monitor, measured in Hertz (Hz). Refresh rates of 75Hz and higher are easiest on the eyes; rates lower than 75Hz appear to flicker and can cause eye strain and even nausea.

- *Show Modes Recommended by Display*—When checked, only those resolutions thought to be safe will be displayed. If unchecked, all possible resolution and refresh rates will be displayed, some of which are not thoroughly supported by your computer's combination of video card and display.

- *Show Displays in Menu Bar*—Shows a drop-down menu for changing display settings in the upper-right of the menu bar.

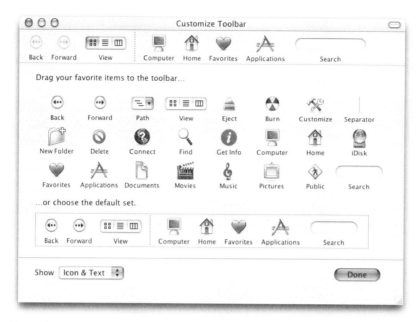

Figure 3.7
The Displays System Preferences and menu bar shortcut.

Figure 3.7 shows the Displays pane and the menu bar shortcut, which provides quick access to change your display resolution and color depth.

The Color section of the Displays System Preferences pane may be new to many users (we'll cover it in more detail in Chapter 10, "Managing Fonts and Printers"). The Color section enables you to select a ColorSync display calibration profile or launch the Display Calibrator Assistant, examples of which are shown in Figure 3.8. The

Figure 3.8
The Color configuration portion of the Displays System Preferences and the Display Calibrator Assistant.

calibration profile affects the display of colors on your screen, as well as how they are transmitted to color printers. In short, the Displays System Preferences pane is the "one-stop shop" for configuration options that determine how your computer manages color, and ColorSync assists in these color management capabilities.

What's a Good Monitor?

A good CRT (cathode ray tube) monitor has a 17-inch or larger screen and is capable of displaying at multiple resolutions with a good refresh rate and acceptable dot pitch. An LCD (liquid crystal display) monitor should have a 15-inch or larger screen, but usually doesn't have as fine a dot-pitch as a CRT monitor. But what does all this mean and why should you care?

- The size of a monitor is measured diagonally from the top-left of the viewable area to the lower-right, not including the monitor's plastic casing. Early Apple monitors were as small as 8 inches on the diagonal, but the emerging standard these days is 19 inches. A 17-inch monitor is the current standard.

- Resolution refers to the width and height of your display, measured in pixels. For example, 1024x768 pixels is a standard resolution for contemporary monitors, whereas first-generation monitors usually displayed at a fixed resolution of 640x480. A good monitor will display multiple resolutions of 1600x1200 and higher.

- The refresh rate refers to the frequency at which the image displayed on your screen is refreshed, or redrawn, per second, measured in Hertz (abbreviated Hz). The human eye usually can't detect refresh rates higher than 75Hz or so, but if the rate is any lower the image will appear to flicker.

- Dot pitch refers to the size of the tiny elements in a monitor that pass light to the eye, measured in millimeters. Several different technologies, such as shadow mask and invar mask, are used to create these elements. Just remember that smaller is better when it comes to dot pitch. Look for a monitor with a dot pitch of .26mm or smaller. The typical range will be from .30mm (unacceptable) to .22mm (excellent).

Customizing Sound

Of all the customizable elements of your Mac's interface, the Sound System Preferences is probably the most familiar—or at least a close second to everybody's favorite, the changeable Desktop picture. Longtime Mac users remember when this feature made us say to our friends, "Hey, listen to this. My Mac thinks it's a duck!" Now, of course, you can purchase sample sounds or download them from the Web, so instead of just quacking at you, your computer might have Bart Simpson talk back to you or Captain Archer beam you aboard.

With Mac OS X, you can choose from many new, high-quality alert sounds—or select the venerable Sosumi, for old time's sake. Although the Sound System Preferences pane allows you to customize the way your Mac plays alert sounds, you cannot record new alert sounds from within the Sound pane, as you could in pre-Mac OS X versions of the operating system. As illustrated in Figure 3.9, you can choose among many sound-related options.

The Sound Effects tab lists options effecting how the Mac OS should behave when issuing alert sounds, including:

■ *Choose an Alert Sound*—Select a sound for the computer to use to alert you to various conditions or warnings.

■ *Alert Volume*—Raises or lowers the volume level for alert sounds only.

■ *Play User Interface Sound Effects*—Uses audible feedback on certain Finder actions, such as removing an icon from the Dock.

■ Play Feedback When Volume Keys are Pressed—Enables a subtle sound effect when the Volume Up or Volume Down keys are pressed (not available on all keyboards).

■ *Output Volume*—Raises or lowers the volume level for applications and portions of the Mac OS that produce sound.

■ *Mute*—Mutes all sound output when checked.

■ *Show Volume in Menu Bar*—Adds a volume adjustment shortcut to the menu bar.

The Output and Input tabs list options for any available sound output and input devices, such as the built-in audio controller (output) and microphone (input). These options include:

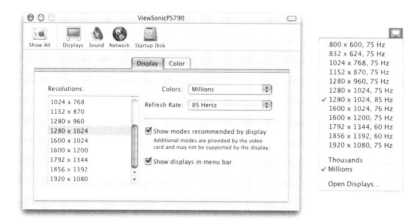

Figure 3.9
The Sound System Preferences (top) and the result of pressing the volume key (bottom).

■ *Choose a Device for Sound Output/Input*—Select a sound output or input device to configure.

■ *Settings for Selected Device*—Determine various settings for a sound output device, such as Balance, which adjusts the balance between right and left speakers, if you've attached speakers to your Mac. An example of a sound input device setting would be the sound input volume level for an internal or external microphone.

As with displays, you should customize your sound settings as necessary—and don't be afraid to tinker with and explore your computer's options. It's a Mac, after all! To record your own alert sounds, you'll need a sound recording and manipulation application, such as those listed here, and a PlainTalk microphone or other source for sound input, such as a CD-ROM or DVD:

■ *Audacity (Dominic Mazzoni, et al.)*—**audacity.sourceforge.net**

■ *Sound Studio (Felt Tip Software)*—**www.felttip.com/products/soundstudio/**

Be sure to limit the size of your "homemade" alert sound files; large sound files take so long to replay that the system slows down every time an alert is triggered.

 TIP: Mac OS X system sounds are stored in **/Macintosh HD/System/Library/Sounds/** in AIFC format (also known as Audio Interchange File Format, Audio IFF, or AIFF format), which also supports compression.

Customizing Energy Saver Preferences

Although you may not think of the Energy Saver System Preferences pane as a customization feature, it has a useful purpose, especially for PowerBook and iBook users. (See Chapter 6, "Mac OS X for PowerBook and iBook Users," for a detailed explanation of Energy Saver features from the perspective of mobile computers.) As shown in Figure 3.10, the Energy Saver System Preferences pane allows you to tell the Mac OS when the computer should revert to a power-saving mode. With Mac OS X, however, you no longer have the options of telling the computer to shut itself off after a specified period of inactivity or start itself up at a certain time and on certain days, as was possible (and popular) in earlier versions of the Mac OS.

Under Mac OS X, the options in the Sleep tab of the Energy Saver System Preferences pane are:

■ *Put the Computer to Sleep When it is Inactive for*—Determines how much time should pass before the computer goes into sleep mode.

■ *Use Separate Time to Put the Display to Sleep*— Establishes how long the OS should wait before putting just the display into sleep mode (independently of the entire computer).

Figure 3.10
Use the Energy Saver System Preferences to configure your Mac to go into sleep mode.

■ *Put the Hard Disk to Sleep When Possible*—Allows the hard drive to go into sleep mode when possible. In Mac OS X, the hard drive is used for virtual memory and is therefore engaged on an almost constant basis, making its sleep options different from those found in Mac OS 9.x and earlier.

The Options tab contains a few more configuration options, including:

■ *Wake When the Modem Detects a Ring*—Brings the computer out of sleep mode if the modem receives a call from various networking utilities or fax software.

■ *Wake for Network Administrator Access*—Brings the computer out of sleep mode if the Ethernet port receives communication from an administrative application.

■ *Restart Automatically after a Power Failure*—Turns the computer on as soon as power has been restored after a power outage.

Configuring Screen Effects

Many users find Screen Effects, a feature introduced in Mac OS X Version 1.0 called Screen Savers, very entertaining. The example screen—effects modules included with the OS really show off the powerful image rendering capabilities of Mac OS X's Quartz Extreme display engine. These modules gently walk you through still images of beaches (Beach), outer space (Cosmos), and forests (Forest) as if you were actually in the scenes displayed on your monitor. Other screen saver examples include a basic black screen with an Apple logo (Computer Name), a collection of familiar Desktop pictures (Abstract), a module that you can customize by identifying a folder of images to be used as part of the screen saver slide show of images (Pictures Folder), and a new .Mac screen effect that allows users to store images on their iDisk account and use them from any computer running Mac OS X version 10.2 connected to the Internet. Visit www.apple.com/downloads/macosx/apple/macslidespublisher.html and download the utility called Mac Slides Publisher to optimize, rename, and upload images to your .Mac account for use with the .Mac screen effect.

To activate a screen saver using Screen Effects:

1. Open the System Preferences.

2. Switch to the Screen Effects pane, as shown in Figure 3.11.

3. Select a module in the Screen Effects tab.

4. Press the Configure button to change any additional settings for modules that require additional configuration. Each module may have different configuration options.

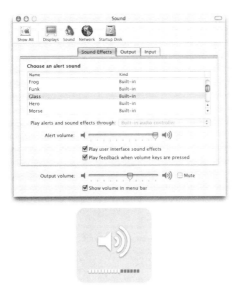

Figure 3.11
The Screen Effects pane includes several built-in screen saver modules, and many third-party modules have been created as well

5. Switch to the Activation tab to decide how long the keyboard and mouse should be inactive before the module is activated (five to 60 minutes, or never) and whether a password is required to dismiss the screen saver.

6. In the Hot Corners tab, select which corners of the display will activate the screen saver whenever the mouse cursor lingers over that area; use a minus sign to identify corners of the screen that should not activate the screen saver if the mouse were to be in that corner.

 TIP: Download

Chapter 6, "Mac OS X for PowerBooks and iBooks," goes into a little more depth about the screen saver as it relates to battery consumption and using the screen saver password requirement as a security measure. For more Screen Saver modules, visit the following Web sites and check out what they have to offer:

■ *VersionTracker*—**www.versiontracker.com/macos/screensavers**

■ *SaverLab (Dozing Cat Software)*—**www.dozingcat.com**

■ *MacOSXScreenSaver (Epicware)*—**www.epicware.com/macosxsavers.html**

■ *SETI@home (Search for Extraterrestrial Intelligence)*—**http://setiathome.berkeley.edu**

Customizing Finder Window Toolbars

Customizing the toolbar for Finder windows makes navigating the contents of your hard drive just as easy as using the customized Dock to navigate among applications. For each Finder window, you can show or hide the toolbar; you can also customize the toolbar in two ways. First, you can include one or more of the shortcuts installed by Mac OS X in your customized toolbar by following these steps. In this example, I'm customizing the toolbar for the Applications folder:

1. Switch to the Finder by clicking on the Finder icon in the Dock.

2. Open a Finder window by pressing Command+N.

3. Choose View|Customize Toolbar. This opens the window shown in Figure 3.12.

4. Drag and drop one or more shortcuts to the toolbar area.

5. Click the Done button to return to the Finder window, which will contain the new toolbar.

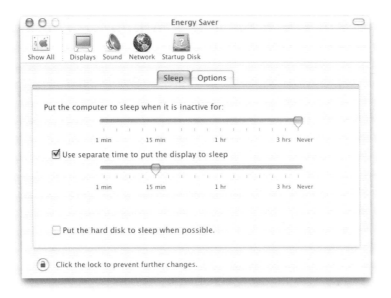

Figure 3.12
The default set of toolbar shortcuts provided by Mac OS X.

The default set of toolbar shortcuts includes many handy features, including:

■ *Back*—Moves back one step in the Finder.

■ *Forward*— Moves forward one step in the Finder.

■ *View*—Provides buttons to change the view of the current window to Icon, List, or Column view.

■ *Separator*—Places a vertical separator in the toolbar to help you group shortcuts.

■ *Computer*—Goes to the root level of your computer's file system.

■ *Home*—Opens your Home folder.

■ *Favorites*—Opens your Favorites folder.

■ *Applications*—Accesses the main Applications folder

■ *Search*—Presents a text entry field to search the contents of the current folder by name.

To customize the toolbar, you can choose from a default set of approximately 24 icons. However, you can always revert to the default toolbar by dragging the Default Set to the toolbar area, thereby deleting all your custom selections.

TIP: You can customize the toolbar in the System Preferences by dragging your favorite System Preferences shortcuts to the toolbar area. To delete a shortcut from the toolbar, drag the icon to the Desktop.

The second method of customizing the toolbar is to populate it with default shortcuts combined with shortcuts to applications, documents, files, and even the Trash. For example, I frequently use several of the default shortcuts, but I also like to be able to navigate to specific folders, including my favorite word processing applications, Web development tools, and the Utilities folder, with just one mouse click. In Figure 3.13, I removed several of the Default Set shortcuts, added the Path shortcut, and then added a divider to the right of the default shortcuts. On the other side of the divider, I put in shortcuts to my three favorite folders and another divider; I placed the Search shortcut to the far right, and also changed the toolbar to a Text view (instead of Icon & Text) to reduce the size of the toolbar. When I'm working on a particular project that requires a new shortcut, it's just as easy to add it to the toolbar as the Dock.

You can also add aliases to resources such as removable media and remote server volumes to the toolbar. When the resource is available, the toolbar icon for this shortcut will look and behave normally. If you log out from a server or eject a CD, for example, the shortcut icon will appear as a question mark until it again becomes available.

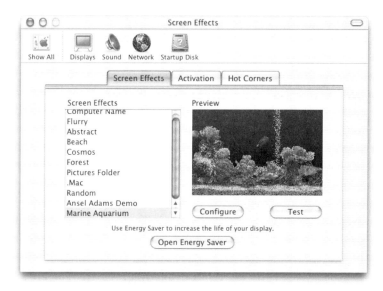

Figure 3.13
A customized—and personalized—toolbar.

Using Third-Party Customization Utilities

When compared to earlier versions of the OS, Mac OS X is highly customizable—despite the loss of several familiar features, such as the Control Strip, Launcher, and the appearance themes and sounds found in the old Appearance Control Panel. Software developers have wasted no time in coming up with new applications and utilities for Mac OS X to compensate for these changes and add even more customization features. They've also been busy adapting tried and true applications such as DragThing and Drop Drawers to work with the new operating system. Because many third-party solutions designed for earlier versions of the Mac OS rely on Control Panels and Extensions to provide functionality, they are not easily ported to Mac OS X. At the same time, however, entirely new utilities are being written to fill the gaps or to enable "hidden" features that Apple overlooked, such as the ability to reposition the Dock on the top of the screen. The following utilities (just a few of my favorites) allow me to customize Mac OS X so that I'm far more productive than before.

DragThing
www.dragthing.com

DragThing, created by James Thomson, is the consummate docking utility. Incredibly flexible and very easy to use, DragThing allows you to create several types of docks that you can customize in shape, size, color, location, and functionality. Docks can be minimized or maximized, single- or multilayered, vertical or horizontal—to name only a few of the configuration options. Use the customized docks to store shortcuts to applications, documents, folders, disks, and servers. DragThing also offers the Process Dock, a special type of dock whose purpose is to display foreground, background, and even hidden processes. You can customize the Process Dock to behave much like the "real" Dock or like the old Application Switcher's tear-off menu.

DragThing enables you to create as many docks as you like. For example, Figure 3.14 shows four docks that I'm using for very different purposes in Mac OS X:

■ The Process Dock (upper right) is a floating dock configured to display all non-hidden processes in the order in which they were launched; it also displays the Trash. This dock is very similar to the Application Switcher found in previous versions of the OS.

■ A Dock called Utilities (lower right) is a two-layered dock that houses shortcuts to frequently used utilities; one layer is for Mac OS X utilities and the other is for Classic utilities.

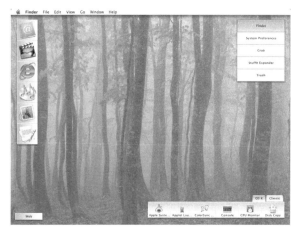

Figure 3.14
A sampling of docks created by DragThing.

■ A minimized dock called Web (lower left) provides quick access to my Web-related utilities, folders, and servers; when clicked, it expands to reveal its contents, and then automatically minimizes itself when not in use.

■ A single-layered dock (upper left) contains icons representing shortcuts to my favorite applications; the icons are arranged alphabetically by name.

DragThing has a set of application-wide preferences that are configured through the main Preferences configuration interface, shown in Figure 3.15, as well as individual preferences for each Dock. The general preferences control many aspects of DragThing's behavior, including Process Dock options; startup options; appearance configuration options, including fonts, color, and sound selections; hot keys to affect application switching and DragThing shortcuts; tool tips; contextual menu support; and dragging behavior. Two of my favorite features provided by DragThing are the keyboard shortcuts for each item in a Dock and the ability to group an application's many windows together when the application is brought to the front as the active application. Mac OS X's layered window feature allows Finder windows to be interleaved between windows belonging to any other application, which can lead to confusion when you want to see all the Finder windows or all of Internet Explorer's windows grouped together. DragThing solves this problem for you with the Bring All Windows to the Front When Switching option, also shown in Figure 3.15.

The flexibility that DragThing lends to the Mac OS X Desktop experience is so expansive that I could easily spend the rest of this chapter just describing its many features and benefits. Try customizing DragThing to help you organize and navigate Mac OS X.

Figure 3.15
DragThing's application-wide preferences.

Default Folder X

www.stclairsoft.com

Default Folder X gets its name from its ability to assign a default folder for opening and saving documents, in much the same way that a Web browser allows users to assign a folder as the default download location. In addition to this basic function, Default Folder X enables you to associate applications with folders, and provides numerous Finder-related shortcuts. Default Folder X allows you to:

■ Create multiple sets of default folders, such as Web development or graphic design sets.

■ Associate particular applications and their default folders with each set.

■ Associate keyboard shortcuts with the favorite folders of a specific set.

■ Easily open a Finder window from within an Open dialog box by clicking on one of four shortcut tabs or on an open Finder window.

My favorite Default Folder X shortcut makes it possible to select any Finder window that is visible from within an Open or Save dialog window, as illustrated in Figure 3.16. To enable this feature, open the Default Folder X pane in the System Preferences, select the Settings button, and check the Switch to Folders by Clicking on

Figure 3.16
Use Default Folder X to enhance Open and Save dialog windows and provide numerous Finder-related shortcuts.

Finder Windows option. Two additional options relating to this feature—Show Boundaries of Selected Finder Windows and Show Name of Selected Window—make the selection process even more user friendly. The example in Figure 3.16 shows all three of these options enabled. The Sites folder has been identified by hovering the mouse over the Sites folder; clicking once on the folder causes it to be selected in the BBEdit Open window.

WindowShade X

www.unsanity.com

WindowShade X brings the beloved windowshade feature back to Finder and applications windows, and leverages Mac OS X's Quartz Extreme display features to provide enhancements that are well worth the tiny registration fee. You can now collapse windows by double-clicking on the window's title bar, or you can configure the window so that it's minimized to the Dock, hidden, or made transparent. For example, Figure 3.17 shows the main features in the WindowShade X System Preferences pane as configured for a specific application (Internet Explorer). In the background of this example, there is a window that has been collapsed using the traditional windowshade feature (top) and a window that has been made transparent (lower right).

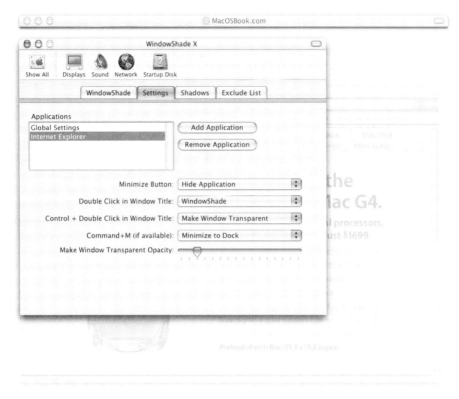

Figure 3.17
Use WindowShade X to collapse and customize windows.

For the Finder and all applications, WindowShade X settings can be global, or they can be configured to be application specific. Furthermore, WindowShade X version 2.0 enables you to customize the use of drop shadows throughout the Aqua interface, as well as exclude certain applications from all of WindowShade X's enhancements.

QuicKeys X

www.cesoft.com

QuicKeys X is a venerable application that allows you to customize keyboard and mouse shortcuts ranging from the simple to the very complex. Once QuicKeys X has been launched (or loaded at login), the availability of your shortcuts can be triggered by:

■ The passage of a specified amount of time after QuicKeys X has been loaded

■ A certain date or time

■ Pressing a keyboard combination

■ Repeating the shortcut after a specified delay

■ From the QuicKeys System Menu in the menu bar

Shortcuts can be single- or multistep. Multistep shortcuts may include pauses between steps that allow you to manipulate windows, menus, applications, Finder windows, keystrokes, mouse clicks, Internet resources, and much more. For example, Figure 3.18 shows a shortcut called Manage Files that uses a keyboard shortcut to copy the contents of one folder to another. The QuicKeys Editor, in the background, is the central location for managing your collection of shortcuts.

If you have any type of repetitive motion injury, such as Repetitive Strain Injury (RSI), Carpel Tunnel Syndrome (CTS), or computer-induced tendonitis, QuicKeys X is a sound investment for around $100.

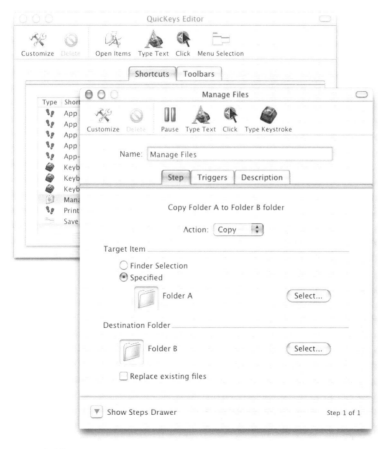

Figure 3.18
Use QuicKeys X to create simple or complex shortcuts in Mac OS X.

Show Desktop

www.everydaysoftware.net/

Screen clutter is an obstacle for which many solutions have been provided. Some users open so many application windows that locating an item in the Finder or simply focusing attention on one window becomes an exercise in frustration. For example, I use the Desktop as both my general workspace and the download location for my Web browser. Because my Desktop is usually littered with several dozen files and folders (see Chapter 5, "Organizing Your Data," which contains many tips on managing the contents of your hard drive), I often need to hide all open applications in order to reveal the Desktop.

Mac OS X is unable to switch to the Finder and then hide all other applications in one easy mouse click or keystroke. Fortunately, Everyday Software's Show Desktop picks up the slack for Mac OS X. When launched, Show Desktop has a few simple configuration options as well as a Dock or menu bar icon that, when clicked, switches to the Finder and hides all other applications. You can even configure Show Desktop to create a new Finder window, in the event that no Finder window is open and your goal is to navigate the file system using a Finder window.

TinkerTool

www.bresink.de/osx/TinkerTool.html

TinkerTool provides about a dozen customization capabilities that significantly enhance the usability of the Finder, Dock, and default fonts used by Mac OS X. TinkerTool is also freeware, which adds to the appeal of the following categories of enhancements:

- *Finder*—Enhances the animation of Dock icons; allows hidden and system files to be visible in the Finder; adds a Quit menu to the Finder; and enables you to change the number of label lines in the Finder when viewing windows as icons.

- *General*—Adds a transparency feature for hidden applications in the Dock; adds additional Dock position, placement, and minimization effects; offers additional scroll arrow options.

- *Fonts*—Allows you to change the system, fixed, and application fonts, as well as reset them to their defaults.

- *Font Smoothing*—Allows you to configure font smoothing for QuickDraw-based applications.

- *Reset*—Resets all TinkerTool attributes to their defaults.

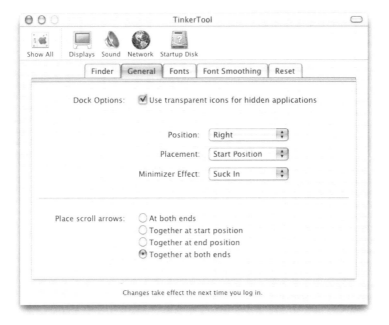

Figure 3.19
Use TinkerTool to customize several Mac OS appearance features, including the Dock.

Some of TinkerTool's enhancements are subtle, but they are definitely worth exploring. For example, Figure 3.19 shows my preferences for enhancing the Dock in four ways that are not supported by Mac OS X.

X-Assist

http://members.ozemail.com.au/~pli/x-assist/

Peter Li created X-Assist to restore several user interface features found in Mac OS 9.x that are missing in Mac OS X. The features reenabled by X-Assist include:

- A Mac OS 9.x-style Application menu

- A Shortcuts submenu

- A Recent Applications submenu

- A user-defined hierarchical submenu

- A plug-in architecture for developers to add additional features

In addition, X-Assist allows you to add multiple subfolders to a special folder in your Favorites folder. For example, I have added four folders named Audio, Graphics,

Internet, and Utilities to a folder called X-Assist Items, which is located in my Favorites folder. X-Assist knows to look in this folder and display its contents hierarchically when the Shortcuts submenu is activated from the Application menu, as illustrated in Figure 3.20.

Mac OS X uses a staggered or layered windowing approach so that an application's windows need not be entirely visible or grouped together on the Desktop. X-Assist provides a shortcut, found in the Preferences submenu, that brings all the windows belonging to a particular application (instead of just the selected window) to the front when any one of the windows is clicked.

Other Utilities

New utilities that allow you to customize Mac OS X to suit your needs are being written almost daily. Many of the utilities mentioned in this chapter focus on restoring or enhancing user interface features that—for whatever reason—were not carried over from previous versions of the Mac OS. Two great Web sites that can help you keep track of all the new and revised applications for Mac OS X are:

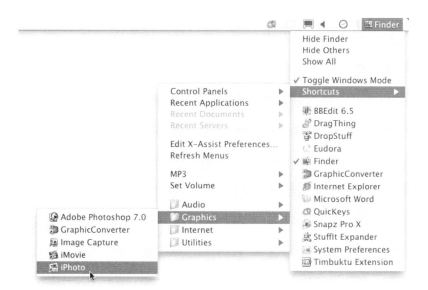

Figure 3.20
X-Assist has no limit to the number of items that can be displayed in its hierarchical menu.

- *Apple Downloads*—www.apple.com/downloads/macosx

- *VersionTracker*— www.VersionTracker.com/macosx/index.shtml

- *Mac OS X Apps*—**www.macosxapps.com**

Each of these sites is a fantastic resource for categorizing and tracking software. They also provide services such as bulletin boards, searchable archives, and news relevant to Apple and the Mac OS.

Working with Multiple Users

Mac OS X is a true multiuser operating system. After all, the core operating system was built to support this capability. In previous versions of the OS, the Multiple Users feature provided limited options for securely sharing one computer with multiple users. As the "owner" or administrator of your Macintosh, you can now create multiple user accounts and assign various levels of privileges to enable other users to customize the Mac OS. Although only one person at a time can use the physical components of your Macintosh—monitor, mouse, and keyboard—services such as file and Web sharing are accessible to other users while you are logged in. You can use the Accounts section of the System Preferences, shown in Figure 3.21, to create, edit, and delete user accounts.

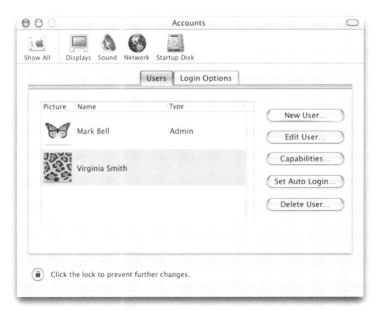

Figure 3.21
Manage user accounts with the Accounts System Preferences pane.

Creating User Accounts

The first time you used your computer, you were asked to create an initial user account with a username and password, among other things. The initial user account is given administrative privileges, and the owner of that account may create additional user accounts on the same computer via the New User dialog box, as shown in Figure 3.22.

To create a new, non-administrative user account on your computer, take the following steps:

1. Open the System Preferences from the Dock or Apple menu.

2. Switch to the Accounts pane and click the New User button.

3. Enter the appropriate information in the Name (e.g., *Jane Doe*), Short Name (e.g., *jdoe*), New Password, Verify, and Password Hint fields, and then select a login picture. The user's short name (i.e., username) should be four to eight lowercase characters (no spaces); the password must be at least four characters in length.

4. Click the Save button.

Non-administrative users have full access to their home folder and can use many of the System Preferences panes in the Personal section (described earlier in this chapter). However, they do not have access to most of the panes that affect network configuration, file and Web sharing, and firewall settings. These, and many other changes, require an administrative password.

Figure 3.22
Adding a new user account with the New User command.

Mac OS X version 10.2 reintroduces the Simple Finder feature that further allows Mac OS X administrators to restrict the use of the Finder, System Preferences, and even specific applications. To restrict the capabilities of non-administrative users, follow these steps:

1. Create a new user account or select a non-administrative user account in the Users tab of the System Preferences Accounts pane.

2. Select the user and click the Capabilities button; the window shown in Figure 3.23 will appear. The Capabilities button will be disabled for users with administrative access.

3. Select the features and applications to which the user may have access. Restricted items will yield an error message stating that insufficient access privileges restrict the user from accessing the resource or application.

4. Click the Simple Finder feature to force the account to use a nearly-featureless version of the Finder. For example, Figure 3.24 shows a user logged into an account with the Simple Finder feature enabled and access restricted to the six specific applications shown in the previous figure. Full access to the Finder is easily restored by choosing Run Full Finder from the Finder menu, and then entering an administrative username and password.

Figure 3.23
Use the Capabilities feature to restrict access to non-administrative users.

Figure 3.24
A user logged into an account with the Simple Finder capability enabled.

Users should not be granted administrative access to a computer unless you intend to allow that person to have unlimited rights. In Mac OS X, there is no in-between—users are either administrators or plain old users. Whenever a non-administrative user logs in and attempts to perform an administrative task such as installing software, the username and password of an administrative user will be requested. Administrative users can modify any of the System Preferences, including the option to have the computer automatically log in as that user when started or restarted, which is a useful shortcut if you're the primary user of the computer and if the computer is in a secure location. (Because of the security risk, you wouldn't want to enable this feature if your computer is located in a public area.) For example, if a user with administrative access entered her username and password and checked the Automatically Log In checkbox, no other user would be able to use the computer unless the administrative user is manually logged out via the Apple menu.

 TIP: You will be logged into Mac OS X automatically until you choose Logout from the Apple menu or create a second account on your computer.

To create a new administrative user account, or assign administrator privileges to an existing user, follow these steps:

1. Launch the System Preferences.

2. Choose the Accounts pane.

3. To select an existing account, double-click a user from the list in the Users tab, or select the user and click the Edit User button.

4. To create a new account, click the New User button and enter the information (described earlier in this section) required to create the account.

5. Select the checkbox entitled Allow User to Administer This Computer.

6. Choose OK and quit the System Preferences.

 TIP: It has been suggested that only one administrative account be created for each computer to better control the security of the computer.

Setting a Root Password

In addition to the first account created on your computer, which is granted administrative access by default, a root, or superuser, account is also created. No password is assigned to this account, however, and the root account is therefore inactive. You may never need to use the root password, but the possibility exists that someone may hack your computer and set the root password without your knowledge. With root access, it is possible to install stealth software and completely compromise the integrity of your computer. Therefore, it's essential that you set the root password from the outset to eliminate this avenue of vulnerability.

To set the root password for a computer running Mac OS X, follow these steps:

1. Locate the first of two Mac OS X installation CDs.

2. Insert the CD.

3. Choose Restart from the Apple menu while holding down the C key.

4. While the computer restarts, continue holding the C key until the computer begins booting from the CD instead of the hard drive. You'll know you're booting from CD when you hear the CD drive activate and the boot process takes longer than normal, because booting from CD is much slower than when booting from a hard drive.

5. Once the Installer has loaded, but before you have made any choices regarding the Installer application, choose Reset Password from the File menu.

6. Choose the hard drive associated with your installation of Mac OS X.

7. Select System Administrator (root) from the list of user accounts.

8. Enter and then reenter the root password.

9. Click the Save button and wait for a confirmation window telling you that the password was successfully reset.

10. Change any additional passwords for the computer, or quit the Reset Password application to return to the Installer application.

11. Choose Quit Installer from the Installer menu, then select the Restart button.

12. After the computer has restarted from the hard drive, log in as you normally would using your administrative account.

Changing Passwords

If multiple users will be using your computer on a regular basis, someone will inevitably forget their username or password. If you—the owner of the computer—forget your password, you'll need to use the Mac OS X installation CD and follow the directions in the preceding section to reset your password.

Follow these steps to change your own password—if you know the current password:

1. Launch the System Preferences.

2. Choose the My Account pane.

3. Click the Change button in the My Password section.

4. Enter the current password and the new password, and then verify the new password. Optionally, provide a hint to the new password in the Password Hint field.

5. Choose OK and then quit the System Preferences.

Once your password has been reset, you will again have full control over the user accounts and configuration capabilities, including software installation.

Follow these steps to change an unknown user password:

1. Launch the System Preferences.

2. Choose the Accounts pane.

3. Double-click a user from the list in the Users tab, or select the user and click the Edit User button.

4. Complete the New Password and Verify fields.

5. Choose OK and quit the System Preferences.

 TIP: See Chapter 16, "Sharing Internet Services," for additional information about user accounts and access privileges when providing File and Web Sharing services.

Customizing Auto Login

You may want to disable the auto login feature so that no one can gain access to your computer without entering the correct username and password. On the other hand, if security isn't a concern, you may want to automatically log in to your computer without being prompted for your username and password. Either way, you can customize the login process in Mac OS X by following these steps:

1. Launch the System Preferences.

2. Choose the Accounts pane.

3. Click the Set Auto Login button.

4. Enter the username and password of the account you want to login automatically.

5. Mac OS X will remember the last user designated for auto login; you may toggle this option on and off by selecting the checkbox entitled Log in Automatically as *username* in the lower half of the Users tab in the Accounts System Preferences.

6. Click the OK button and quit the System Preferences.

You can also customize several attribute of the login screen whenever a user is prompted for a username and password at login by following these steps:

1. Launch the System Preferences.

2. Choose the Accounts pane.

3. Select the Login Options tab, as illustrated in Figure 3.25.

4. Indicate whether you want to Display Login Window as Name and Password or as List of Users.

5. Choose Hide the Restart and Shut Down Buttons in order to hinder the ability of users to hack or hijack your computer by booting from an external source such as a CD or FireWire drive.

6. Click on Show Password Hint after 3 Attempts to Enter a Password to display a user's password hint (this is optional for each user account).

7. Quit the System Preferences.

Configuring User Login Items

Because Mac OS X is a true multiuser operating system, each user's preferences—including what applications, documents, or folders should be opened at login—are stored separately from other users' settings. In the old days of Mac OS 9.x, there was only one Startup Items folder, and whoever turned on the computer was greeted with the items in this folder once the startup process was complete.

To determine what items are loaded at login, follow these steps:

1. Login and Launch the System Preferences.

2. Select the Login Items pane, as shown in the example in Figure 3.26.

3. To select an item to add to the list of items to be opened automatically at startup, click the Add button; alternatively, drag and drop an item from the Finder onto the list of login items.

Figure 3.25
The Login Options tab of the Accounts System Preferences pane.

Figure 3.26
To customize the login process and save time, each user may enter items in the Login Items System Preferences pane.

4. Drag any of the items up or down to reorder their position in the list.

5. Click the Hide button beside an item if you want it to be hidden in the Finder at startup.

6. Select an item and click the Remove button to delete it from the list of login items.

7. Quit the System Preferences.

Deleting User Accounts

Deleting user accounts is at least as easy as creating them. In fact, it's even easier in Mac OS X version 10.2 than in previous releases of Mac OS X, in which file permissions often caused difficulties when tring to remove the home folders of the deleted user accounts. This is no longer the case, however. To delete a user account, follow these steps:

1. Log in and launch the System Preferences.

2. Select the Accounts pane.

3. Select the user's account and click the Delete User button.

4. When prompted, confirm that the account is to be deleted.

5. Quit the System Preferences.

The user's home folder is archived as a disk image in /**Macintosh HD/Users/Deleted Users/** and is accessible to anyone with administrative access.

Wrapping Up

Using the Mac OS for the first time is kind of like driving someone else's car—when you get behind the wheel, the first thing you do is adjust the mirrors and seat so that you're comfortable. Its many and varied opportunities for customizing the user interface have always been among the Mac OS's greatest attractions. Apple builds many of these opportunities right into the interface through:

- New System Preferences

- Desktop pictures and Appearance options

- Dock configuration options

- Finder window toolbars

- Time, date, display, and sound options

- Energy Saver features

- Screen effects

- Third-party utilities such as DragThing, Default Folder X, WindowShade X, QuicKeys X, Show Desktop, TinkerTool, X-Assist, and Web resources for locating additional utilities to customize Mac OS X

- The ability to create, manage, and customize user accounts

In the next chapter, we'll examine Mac OS X's ability to run older Classic applications. You'll learn how to configure Classic and Mac OS 9.x to best suit your needs when running the Classic environment or booting directly into Mac OS 9.x.

Configuring the Classic Environment

The Classic environment allows Mac OS X to run versions of the OS as far back as Mac OS 9.1 through Mac OS 9.x , as well as just about any "legacy" applications written for versions of the OS as far back as Mac OS 8. Mac OS X version 10.2 has added several configuration options that make running Classic even more flexible than before, not to mention much, much faster. Launch time for Classic is only a fraction of what it was in Mac OS X version 10.1.5. For example, on one of my computers the launch time has improved from at least one minute to only seven seconds.

To keep our terminology straight, however, I'll use *Classic* to refer to both Mac OS 9.1 through Mac OS 9.2.2, as well as to pre-Carbon or pre-Cocoa applications (Classic apps). I'll also refer to Mac OS 9.1 and later as Mac OS 9.x. When discussing components or features of Mac OS 9.x that are not available while running Classic within Mac OS X, I'll distinguish between the Classic environment and booting the computer directly into Mac OS 9.x, because there are a few tasks, and many applications, that behave differently or not at all unless you boot the computer directly into Mac OS 9.x. When Mac OS X was released in March 2001, fewer than 500 Carbon or Cocoa applications—compared to over 10,000 Classic applications—were available, and the number has grown to several thousand. However, it's probably safe to assume that Classic support won't be disappearing from Mac OS X altogether (at least not anytime soon), although Apple will stop making computers that boot into Mac OS 9.x beginning in January 2003. After that time, all new computers from Apple will only boot into Mac OS X.

In this chapter, I'll cover how to configure Mac OS 9.x, as well as how to configure Mac OS X to run the Classic environment to best suit your needs. Because Mac OS 9.x is actually a self-contained operating system into which you can boot your computer, I'll also cover the basics of working with Mac OS 9.x, paying special attention to the role of the Mac OS 9.x System Folder. The next chapter covers what you need to know to run your favorite Classic applications, including Classic application memory management and a few tips on troubleshooting Classic.

Configuring Mac OS 9.x

To run Classic on your computer, you must have Mac OS 9.1 or later installed on your computer. If you don't have Mac OS 9.1 installed or just need to update an earlier version of the Mac OS to the latest version (Mac OS 9.2.2), refer to Appendix E, *Installing and Updating Mac OS 9.x and Mac OS X*, for detailed instructions. For now, I'll assume you have Mac OS 9.1 or later installed and are ready to go.

Hard Drive Options

Mac OS X doesn't load Classic by default. If you launch a Classic application when Classic isn't running, OS X will look for a valid installation of Mac OS 9.x on your computer, load it, and then launch the Classic application. Mac OS X first searches for Mac OS 9.x on the same hard drive on which OS X resides. Then, if Mac OS 9.x cannot be found there, OS X searches for it on other hard drives or bootable media such as a CD-ROM connected to your computer.

If Mac OS 9.x cannot be located, the Classic environment cannot load and the application will not launch. If you intend to use Classic applications on a regular basis, or if you have multiple Mac OS 9.x System Folders on your computer, you should tell Mac OS X on which drive Mac OS 9.x is located. The following section contains instructions for doing this.

There are several options for where to locate Mac OS 9.x on your local hard drives, and all are equally acceptable. Since most computer share only one hard drive, the default option is to install Mac OS 9.x on the same drive as Mac OS X. Since Mac OS 9.x and Mac OS X use different folder names for their operating system files, don't worry about mixing and matching system files between the two.

A second option is to partition a single drive and install Mac OS 9.x and Mac OS X onto separate partitions. However, this requires that you move all your files onto a secondary drive, partition the primary drive into two or more partitions, then move all your Mac OS 9.x files onto one partition and reinstall Mac OS X on the other partition. Mac OS 9.x is easily moved from one drive to another, but Mac OS X is not easily moved around; it requires a reinstallation instead.

A third option is to install a second hard drive and use it in the same way as the second option above, with Mac OS 9.x on one drive and Mac OS X on the other. Hard drives are cheap these days, so it's not a bad option if you have several GB of Mac OS 9.x system and application files that you'd like to keep apart from Mac OS X. Of course, Mac OS X supports a drive file format called Unix File System (UFS) that is not compatible with Mac OS 9.x, so if you want to use this format you'll need two drives in order to have access to Classic on the same computer.

I have several Macs, and I prefer to have Mac OS X on one drive and Mac OS 9.x on another. Having two drives makes it a little easier to repair disk errors because you can boot from one drive and repair the other.

Booting into Mac OS 9.x

Occasionally, you may find that you really need to boot directly into Mac OS 9.x rather than use your Mac OS 9.x applications from within the Classic environment of Mac OS X. For example, I have several legacy applications that may not ever be converted into native Mac OS X applications and do not like running in Classic mode, so booting into Mac OS 9.x is the only option. Also, you'll need to boot into Mac OS 9.x occasionally to perform system software and firmware updates. Fortunately, Apple has made booting directly into Mac OS 9.x an easy operation to perform.

You can force most modern Macs to boot into Mac OS 9.x by holding down the Option key when starting or restarting the computer and selecting the drive containing Mac OS 9.x from the list of drives found by the built-in drive selection utility. If your computer doesn't respond to this procedure (typically because of old firmware), you'll have to select the drive by following these steps:

1. Choose System Preferences from the Apple menu.

2. Select Startup Disk from the list of icons or from the View menu.

3. Choose a drive containing Mac OS 9.x, as illustrated in Figure 4.1.

Figure 4.1
Use the Startup Disk pane of the System Preferences to select a startup drive containing Mac OS 9.x.

The folder icons in the Startup Disk pane indicate the general version of the operating system; the folder label indicates the version and the name of the volume containing the operating system. As you can see in Figure 4.1, hovering the mouse over the icon for a Mac OS 9.x folder for a moment reveals the name of the folder containing the actual operating system.

Booting into Mac OS X

Booting back into Mac OS X is very similar to booting into Mac OS 9.x. In earlier versions of the Mac OS, the Startup Disk utility could only identify one System Folder per drive; an additional utility such as System Picker was required to identify which version of the OS should be used to boot. Starting with Mac OS 9.x, however, the Mac OS can identify multiple System Folders and allows you to choose which is to be "blessed" (i.e., authorized) for booting. To boot back into Mac OS X:

1. Choose Control Panels from the Apple menu.

2. Choose Startup Disk from the list of Control Panels.

3. Choose a drive containing Mac OS X, two examples of which (Archer and Enterprise) are shown in Figure 4.2.

The Startup Disk utility displays a hierarchical view of disks and System Folders. Therefore, if you have multiple System Folders on one disk, you'll need to expand the view to see all of them.

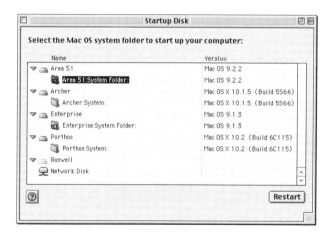

Figure 4.2
Choosing a startup disk containing Mac OS X.

Configuring Classic System Preferences

The Classic environment has a few configuration options that enable you to customize Mac OS 9.x on your computer. For example, configuring Classic to start up automatically can save time for users who want to access their Classic applications on a regular basis. Fortunately, Mac OS X makes it easy for you to sort out your Classic configuration options by putting them all in one place—the Classic pane of the System Preferences. To access the Classic configuration options:

1. Choose System Preferences from the Apple menu.

2. Select the Classic pane from the list of icons or from the View menu. If you have not already selected a valid System Folder containing Mac OS 9.x, you will be prompted to make a selection.

Within Mac OS X version 10.2, the new Classic pane has three tabs that contain a few additional configuration options. The following list describes the options found in the Start/Stop tab, which is shown in Figure 4.3:

■ *Classic Is*—Tells you if Classic is running, starting, stopping, or not running. If it's running or starting up, the path of the System Folder is also displayed (/Enterprise/ System Folder, in this example).

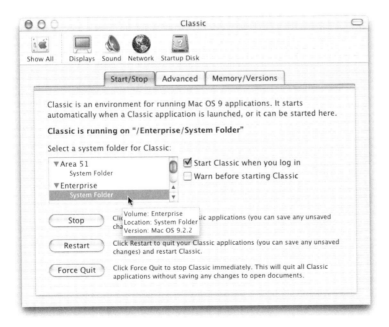

Figure 4.3
The Classic System Preferences pane in Mac OS X.

- *Select a Startup Volume for Classic*—Allows you to identify a specific drive from which Mac OS 9.x should be launched, similar in concept to how the Startup Disk System Preferences and Control Panels work in Mac OS X and Mac OS 9.x. Only drives with a valid Mac OS 9.x System Folder will appear as selectable options in this area. Drives lacking a valid System Folder will be grayed out, indicating their ineligibility.

- *Start up Classic on Login to This Computer*—Enables Classic to start automatically for some users, but not for others. Administrators with access to the Classics System Preferences pane can configure this setting; non-administrative users can only launch a Classic application, not select any configuration options such as loading on startup.

- *Warn before Starting Classic*—Issues a warning that Classic is starting up, and continues the startup process after 30 seconds if the Don't Start button is selected. Click the Start Classic button in the warning dialog to immediately continue the startup process.

- *Start/Stop*—Starts or stops (quits) the Classic environment. If you have any open documents, you'll be given an opportunity to save your work before Classic is stopped.

- *Restart*—Stops and then restarts Classic, allowing you to save any open documents.

- *Force Quit*—Stops Classic without saving open documents. Mac OS X gives you a warning dialog before carrying out the command to force quit, however. Figure 4.4 shows the Advanced section while Classic is running; when Classic is not running, the Restart Classic button will read Start Classic instead. The following commands, which are found under the Advanced section of the Classic System Preferences pane, give you a little more control over the Classic startup process

- *Startup Options*—When starting or restarting Classic using the Start/Restart Classic button, the following options are possible:

- *Turn off Extensions*—Turns off Extensions and Control Panels when Mac OS 9.x starts up.

- *Open Extension Manager*—Forces the Extension Manager to open at startup.

- *Use Key Combination*—Programs a key combination that will be pressed virtually (initiated by the OS) when Classic starts up. You can program a combination of up to five keys, which is useful for certain applications that look for such a key combination at startup.

- *Use Preferences from Home Folder*—Creates a set of folders containing various preferences for running Classic; these folders are stored in each user's home folder , thereby preserving various Classic attributes for each Mac OS X user. The section

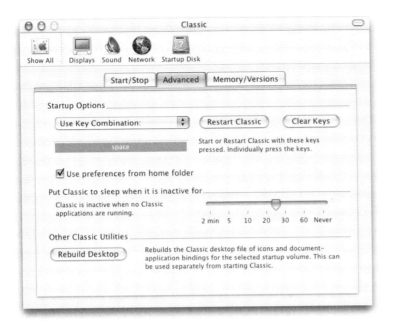

Figure 4.4
The Advanced pane of the Classic System Preferences.

below entitled *Configuring Classic for Multiple Users* explains in detail how this feature works, and why you would want to choose it.

* *Put Classic to Sleep When It Is Inactive for*—Tells Classic when to go to sleep if no Classic applications are running. All computer processes require system resources, and this option lets you redirect processing power for other purposes when Classic is not being used. You can configure Classic to sleep after as little as two or as many as 60 minutes of inactivity, or to never sleep at all. If you do allow Classic to sleep, it will take several seconds for it to "wake up" from sleep when you're ready to use a Classic application.

* *Rebuild Desktop*—Rebuilds the Desktop database of the Mac OS 9.x startup disk. The Desktop database keeps track of information about the files on your Classic startup disk, including the icon and application associated with each file (such as word processing applications and their associated documents). You can rebuild the Desktop using this option at any time, but only on the volume identified in the Start/Stop tab of the Classic System Preferences pane.

The Memory/Versions tab of the Classic System Preferences pane (new to Mac OS X) provides technical information about the applications and OS-related processes running as part of the Classic environment. Although this tab doesn't contain any real configuration options, the information provided may be useful at some point in time. This type of information is discussed in great detail in the following chapter.

Most users will not use the System Preferences to start and stop Classic, so let's take a quick look at the many ways you can actually start and stop the Classic environment.

Starting and Stopping Classic

If you have Classic applications and a valid version of Mac OS 9.x installed on your computer, you should be aware of the various methods of starting and stopping the Classic environment. Don't be surprised if you're a little perplexed about Classic versus native applications—because Apple has essentially incorporated an operating system within an operating system in order ensure backward compatibility with older applications, some confusion is to be expected. To top it off, some applications (the so-called dual applications discussed in the following chapter) work in both Mac OS 9.x and Mac OS X, whereas other applications work only under one operating system or the other. To use your Classic applications, consider the various ways you can first start the Classic environment:

- Choose Start Classic When You Log in from the Start/Stop tab of the Classic System Preferences pane

- Select the Start button in the Start/Stop tab of the Classic System Preferences pane

- Select the Restart button in the Start/Stop tab of the Classic System Preferences pane

- Select the Restart Classic button in the Advanced tab of the Classic System Preferences pane

- Launch a Classic application from the Finder

- Open a document belonging to a Classic application

- Add a Classic application or document to your Login Items pane in the System Preferences

- Launch */Macintosh HD/System/Library/CoreServices/Classic Startup.app*

Once the Classic startup process has begun, you can modify it by using the configuration options mentioned above . You can also use specific keystrokes to initiate various Mac OS 9.x-related startup features. These keystrokes include:

- *Command*+Option—Rebuilds the Desktop

- *Shift*—Turns off Extensions

- *Space bar*—Opens the Extensions Manager

For example, Figure 4.5 shows how programming the space bar (See Figure 4.4) to be depressed at startup using the Startup Options feature causes the Extensions Manager to open at the beginning of the Classic startup process. Once the Classic starts and opens the Extension Manager, you can make additional configuration changes to the Classic environment at startup by enabling or disabling selected items in the System Folder.

If you use Classic applications on a regular basis and have plenty of computing resources (i.e., a dual-processor G4 with at least 256MB of RAM), consider starting Classic at login and leaving it running. With this setup, loading a Classic application will only take a few seconds.

 TIP: You can optimize Mac OS 9.x by modifying the contents of the System Folder so Classic loads faster and causes fewer system-level conflicts with Mac OS X. Later in this chapter, the section entitled "*Optimizing Classic* "will explore the various techniques for tweaking Mac OS 9.x.

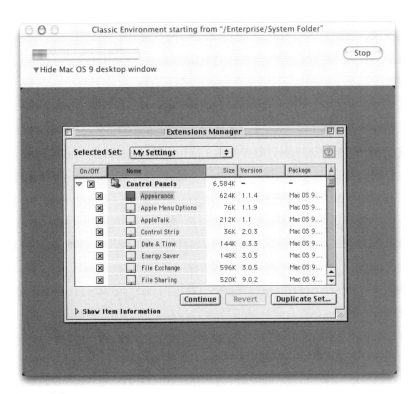

Figure 4.5
Use the Advanced tab of the Classic System Preferences pane to customize the Classic startup process, such as using the space bar to invoke the Extensions Manager when Classic starts up.

It's a snap to stop the Classic environment —and by stopping Classic, I mean quitting the Classic environment and unloading Mac OS 9.x. To stop Classic, choose from these methods:

■ Choose Log Out from the Apple menu

■ Choose Shut Down from the Apple menu

■ Select the Stop button in the Start/Stop tab of the Classic System Preferences pane

In a worst-case scenario, you may be unable to stop the Classic environment using the System Preferences. In such a case, it is possible to "kill" the Mac OS X system process called *TruBlueEnvironme* that supports the Classic environment using the Process Viewer utility, which is discussed in Chapter 13, "Troubleshooting Mac OS X." Using the force-quit command (Command+Option+Escape) will allow you to force quit any applications, but not the Classic environment itself.

Configuring Classic for Multiple Users

Mac OS X version 10.2 enables you to configure Classic for multiple users by storing each user's Classic preferences in their home folder. This is a wise addition to the OS because it allows you to maintain the integrity of the contents of the System Folder (discussed later in this chapter) while allowing each user to customize the Classic environment.

To configure Classic for multiple users, follow these steps:

1. Open the System Preferences from the Apple menu and choose the Classic System Preferences pane.

2. Switch to the Advanced tab.

3. Check the Use Preferences from Home Folder option.

The next time a user starts or restarts Classic, a dialog sheet like the one shown in Figure 4.6 will drop from the Classic startup window. The dialog sheets offers you two options relating to the files to be placed in your home folder at */Macintosh HD/Users/ username/Library/Classic/*:

■ Leave Empty—Leaves the newly created folders empty and allows you, using Mac OS 9.x, to create documents in these folders as needed.

■ Copy Folders—Copies the necessary folders from the System Folder into each user's home folder.

The folders that are copied to each user's home folder are as follows:

Figure 4.6
Users can now store their Classic preferences in their home folders instead of sharing one set of preferences in the System Folder.

- Apple Menu Items

- Favorites

- Internet Search Sites

- Launcher Items

- Preferences

- Startup Items

These folders are composed of the same items that perform the same functions as their counterparts in the Mac OS 9.x System Folder, but future changes to these folders are stored in your home folder and will not be copied to the System Folder. The contents of the Mac OS 9.x System Folder is explained in the next section.

Working with Mac OS 9.x

Because Mac OS X requires a fully functional version of Mac OS 9.x in order to run Classic applications, you're essentially responsible for maintaining two operating systems. If you install Mac OS X on a hard drive or partition other than the one where OS 9.x resides, maintaining the OS will be a more manageable task because system files, applications, and utilities are less likely to intermingle and cause problems with their Mac OS X counterparts. This section covers what you need to know to keep Mac OS 9.x happy and functioning well, whereas Chapter 5, "*Organizing Your Data,*" discusses the organization of Mac OS X's files and folders.

Exploring the Mac OS 9.x System Folder

In each Macintosh OS prior to Mac OS X ,the System Folder has been home to the operating system and many other important files. So it's no surprise that the System Folder requires special treatment from the operating system, other software applications, and you, the Mac OS user.

Because of the fundamental role that software in the System Folder plays in the operation of previous versions of the Mac OS, your freedom to change the organization of the System Folder is limited. However, the Mac OS hasn't always been organized the way it is in Mac OS 9.x—an important concept to keep in mind as you consider the role of Mac OS 9.x and the Classic application environment. Moreover, the System Folder of Mac OS X version 10.2 is subtly different in comparison to previous versions of Mac OS X.

In Mac OS 9.x, the System Folder includes a number of predefined subfolders, each designed to hold a specific type of file. This organizational system, which is created when Mac OS 9.x is installed, greatly reduces the potential for clutter. The actual number of items in the System Folder depends on the components chosen for installation and the type of Mac. (Appendix E, "*Installing and Updating Mac OS 9.x and Mac OS X,* "provides more detailed information regarding the options available for installation with Mac OS 9.x, as well as Mac OS X.) Depending on which components you install in addition to the OS, your Mac OS 9.x System Folder will include many items, such as:

- Appearance
- Apple Menu Items
- Application Support
- Clipboard

- ColorSync Profiles

- Contextual Menu Items

- Control Panels

- Control Strip Modules

- Extensions

- Favorites

- Finder

- Fonts

- Help

- Internet Plug-Ins

- Internet Search Sites

- Language & Region Support

- Launcher Items

- Login

- Mac OS ROM

- MacTCP DNR

- MS Preference Panels

- Panels

- Preferences

- PrintMonitor Documents

- Scrapbook File

- Scripting Additions

- Scripts

- Servers

- Shutdown Items

- Startup Items

- System

■ System Resources

■ Text Encodings

Once you launch the Extension sManager Control Panel to turn off or on Extensions—either from within Mac OS 9.x or using the Open Extensions Manager option from within the Classic System Preferences pane—you'll see the following subfolders in the System Folder as well:

■ Control Panels (Disabled)

■ Extensions (Disabled)

■ Shutdown Items (Disabled)

■ Startup Items (Disabled)

■ System Extensions (Disabled)

These folders are created "on the fly" (computer-speak for automatically) by the Extensions Manager program to store the parts of the OS that you've disabled. This is an example of one of the ways in which the System Folder in Mac OS 9.x is more complex than in previous versions of the Mac OS, where files could often be stored willy-nilly. Fortunately, as we'll see, Apple has built in an "invisible hand" to help ensure that System Folder files are always located correctly. The operating system files in Mac OS X are not managed in this way, and you'll rarely need to access the contents of the System and Library folders.

When you start Classic for the first time, Mac OS X adds a few more items to the System Folder to facilitate interoperability between the two operating systems. They include the following items:

■ Classic

■ Classic Support

■ Classic Support UI

■ ProxyApp

If any of these items is moved, renamed, or deleted from the System Folder, Mac OS X will detect the change and ask permission to reinstall the missing component. And finally, Mac OS X version 10.2 no longer requires the following System Folder components (in fact, they may no longer be visible after the Classic environment has been started for the first time):

■ Clipboard

■ PrintMonitor Documents

Because the System Folder and its subfolders are essential to the operation of your computer, it's important to understand what type of files should be placed in each subfolder. The following section describes the subfolders and provides some basic tips for organizing and using them.

Appearance

The Appearance folder serves as a storage area for many of the elements you use to customize the aesthetics of your computer. Desktop pictures, sound sets, and themes reside here in individual folders. In fact, the Mac OS automatically directs to the Appearance folder all images, sound sets, and theme files dropped onto the System Folder. This feature helps keep files where they belong within the System Folder (which is good for the overall stability of the OS) and reduces the number of steps needed to store files correctly. A typical alert dialog box will read something like, "Preparing to copy to System Folder. One or more items needs to be stored in special places inside the destination. Put the items where they belong?" All you have to do is choose the Stop or Continue button.

The Apple Menu Folder

The ability to access files, folders, applications, and documents through the Apple menu is one of the best features of the Classic Mac OS. Although Mac OS X also has an Apple menu, the Dock handles its traditional functions. Classic's Apple menu, independent of Mac OS X, and is fully functional in the Classic environment or if you're booting directly into Mac OS 9.x.

When Mac OS 9.x is installed, most of the following items are automatically placed in the Apple Menu Items folder:

■ Apple DVD Player

■ Apple System Profiler

■ Calculator

■ Chooser

■ Control Panels

■ Favorites

■ Key Caps

■ Network Browser

■ Remote Access Status

■ Scrapbook

■ Sherlock 2

■ Speakable Items

■ Stickies

Some of these items, such as the Apple System Profiler and Sherlock 2, are applications, whereas others are desk accessories, folders, or aliases to other files and folders.

 TIP: An alias is like a shortcut to an original file or folder. You can always tell an alias from the original when viewing it in a Mac OS 9.x Finder window because its name is italicized and often contains the word *alias* at the end.

Long-time Macintosh users will note the loss of the venerable Alarm Clock desk accessory from the Apple menu. The Alarm Clock was the preferred method for changing the system date and time in several whole-number versions of system software. The Alarm Clock was replaced by the Date & Time Control Panel in Mac OS 8, and is easily accessible in OS 9.1 through the Control Panels submenu of the Apple menu.

 TIP: Some users like to rearrange the Apple menu items to make them easier to work with. To modify the contents of the Apple menu, add files or aliases to (or remove them from) the Apple Menu Items folder. The Apple menu is updated immediately and alphabetically displays the first 50 items contained in the top level of the Apple Menu Items folder. The only item you can't remove is the About This Computer option, which is always the first choice in the Apple menu when the Finder is the active application.

To make frequently used folders and applications more easily accessible, add their aliases to the Apple Menu Items folder. For example, you can add the aliases of applications, documents, folders, and volumes. Choosing an item from the Apple menu is equivalent to double-clicking on the item's icon.

To avoid moving the file, folder, or volume icon from its original location, most of the files added to the Apple Menu Items folder should be aliases rather than original files. In the Apple Menu Items folder, the alias file name is displayed in italics, even though it appears in standard font in the Apple menu.

TIP: Because the Apple menu displays files alphabetically, you can reorder the menu items by modifying their names with numerical or alphabetical prefixes.

Application Support

The Application Support folder is created by the Mac OS for the benefit of applications (such as Adobe Acrobat, Aladdin StuffIt Deluxe, and Norton AntiVirus) that are designed to store important files and folders for their own use. By default, this folder is empty, and it cannot be renamed.

Clipboard

Under Mac OS 9.x, the Clipboard is a file that holds information (text, pictures, sounds, and so on) that has been cut or copied using the Cut (Command+X) or Copy (Command+C) commands found under the Edit menu of most applications. The Clipboard can hold only one piece of information at a time, although several utilities that allow users to have multiple clipboards now exist for Mac OS 9.x as well as Mac OS X. In Mac OS X version 10.2, however, the Classic Clipboard may not be accessible.

ColorSync Profiles

ColorSync is a system created by Apple to assist in the conversion and management of color values among computers displays, printers, scanners, and other imaging devices. Because monitors and printers use different methods of interpreting color values, ColorSync was created as a standard method of describing color that would ensure consistency across the board. For computers, ColorSync creates documents called *profiles*, which define colors using red, green, and blue (RGB); for printers, it creates profiles using cyan, magenta, yellow, and black (CMYK). It then attaches these profiles to a document. The ColorSync folder in the System Folder stores profiles for most models of Apple monitors, as well as custom profiles you create with ColorSync (also supported in Mac OS X).

Contextual Menu Items

Contextual menus are accessible in the Finder when booting directly into Mac OS 9.x and in most Mac OS 8-savvy applications by clicking the mouse while holding down the Control key. The Contextual Menu Items folder contains several contextual menu plug-ins that are automatically installed by the Mac OS, as well as any others installed by third-party applications. Several applications for Mac OS X, including the Finder and Super Get Info, also support contextual menus.

The Control Panels Folder

The Control Panels, a familiar concept to most Mac users, have undergone a dramatic transformation under Mac OS X. They are now consolidated into a single application called the *System Preferences*. Under Mac OS 9.x, however, Control Panels still work as they have for many years: as individual applications that are launched, have menu options, and are exited by quitting.

The individual files for each Control Panel are stored in the Control Panels folder, which resides inside the System Folder—mainly because Control Panels often contain special resources (like Extensions) that must be run during startup. If the Extensions portion of the Control Panel isn't loaded when Classic is activated, the Control Panel may not function properly. For example, the Location Manager and Control Strip both rely on corresponding Extensions to function.

The contents of your Control Panels folder depend on what Mac OS components you've installed. Figure 4.7 shows a typical Control Panels folder. However, bear in mind that different models of computers contain different Control Panels, which is most obvious when you compare the contents of the Control Panels folders of desktop Macs and PowerBooks. Most Macs with Mac OS 9.x have the following Control Panels in common:

- Appearance
- Apple Menu Options
- AppleTalk
- ColorSync
- Configuration Manager
- Control Strip
- Date & Time
- DialAssist
- Energy Saver
- Extensions Manager
- File Exchange
- File Sharing
- General Controls

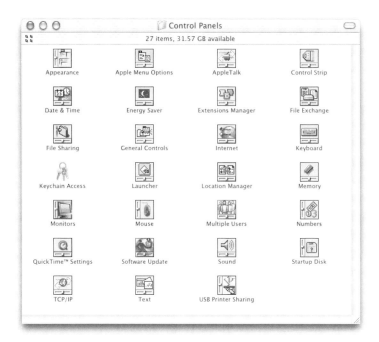

Figure 4.7
The contents of a typical Control Panels folder in Mac OS 9.x. .

- Internet
- Keyboard
- Keychain Access
- Launcher
- Location Manager
- Memory
- Modem
- Monitors
- Mouse
- Multiple Users
- Numbers
- QuickTime Settings
- Remote Access
- Software Update

- Sound

- Speech

- Startup Disk

- TCP/IP

- Text

- USB Printer Sharing

- Web Sharing

If you want to keep a copy of any Control Panel in another location, create an alias and move the alias to your preferred location. You could, for example, store aliases of frequently used Control Panels in the Apple Menu Items folder or in a folder containing other utility applications.

You should be aware, however, that not all Control Panels function in Classic mode. A few of them do not work at all, whereas others are partially disabled because the function they perform is handled by Mac OS X instead. For example, the Control Strip and Location Manager are not available at all. The General Controls Control Panel, on the other hand, is only partially functional, as illustrated in Figure 4.8.

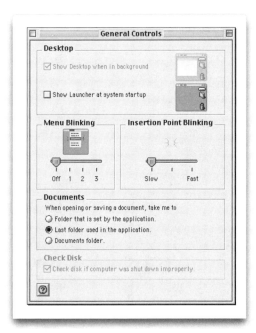

Figure 4.8
Several Control Panels are disabled while in Classic mode; others are only partially functional.

Note that the Show Desktop When in Background and Check Disk if Computer Was Shut Down Improperly options are disabled.

Control Strip Modules

The Control Strip was originally designed to provide quick and easy access to frequently used commands for PowerBook users. Both the Control Strip Modules folder and the Contextual Menu Items folder contain items installed by the Mac OS, as well as modules installed by other applications. Although the Control Strip is not functional under Mac OS 9.x when in Classic mode, it is available when booting directly into Mac OS 9.x.

The Extensions Folder

Extensions, printer drivers, and network drivers are major contributors to System Folder overcrowding. These files have found a home in the Extensions folder since System 7. Your Extensions folder may still become quite crowded, depending on how many of your Classic applications add files and subfolders to it. Most Extensions add features to the Mac OS, thereby extending its capabilities—hence the name Extensions. Drivers extend system software capabilities in a less dramatic, albeit important, way.

During startup, the Mac OS looks in the Extensions folder and loads all its contents. Extensions and Control Panels that aren't stored in the Extensions or Control Panels folders will not execute at startup —nor will they operate properly —until they're correctly positioned and Classic is restarted. The icons of some (but not all) Extensions will appear at the bottom of your screen during startup, as will the icons of some Control Panels.

Favorites

In both Mac OS 9.x and OS X, the Favorites folder serves as a storage bin for shortcuts to your favorite documents, applications, folders, disks, file servers, and Internet location documents. You can add items to the Favorites folder from within Mac OS 9.x-savvy applications (such as the Network Browser) by selecting an item in the Finder and choosing File|Add To Favorites, or by activating the contextual menu (Control+click) and choosing Add To Favorites. Alternatively, you can add items by manually dragging them into the Favorites folder. Mac OS X provides a Favorites folder for each user. Figure 4.9 shows the contents of the Favorites folders in Mac OS 9.x (top) and Mac OS X (bottom).

Finder

The role of the Classic Finder is usurped by the Finder in Mac OS X, although the roles of the two Finders are similar. You cannot activate the Classic Finder from

Figure 4.9
The Favorites folder contains shortcuts to frequently accessed files, folders, applications, documents, and Internet location documents.

within the Classic environment; selecting the Finder from the application menu will bring the Mac OS X Finder to the front instead.

Fonts

Support for a wide range of typefaces continues to be an important characteristic of the Macintosh. Apple uses different locations for storing fonts in Mac OS 9.x and Mac OS X. Whereas each version of the OS has a Fonts folder, Mac OS X allows you to store fonts for specific users. Chapter 10, "Managing Fonts and Printers," covers fonts and printing in Mac OS X, including its ability to access Mac OS 9.x fonts in addition to fonts installed by Mac OS X.

Help

The Help folder contains the Help Viewer application and its associated HTML-style Help documents. It also contains sample AppleScripts and Balloon Help files—none of which you'll probably ever need to access except through the Help Viewer application. Although Mac OS X provides tool tips, it doesn't support Balloon Help. This feature will continue to work for Classic applications for which it has been enabled. Refer to Appendix A for a detailed explanation of how to use the Help Viewer application.

Internet Search Sites

The Internet Search Sites folder houses the plug-ins Sherlock uses to search particular Internet sites, such as AltaVista or Apple's Tech Info Library. The contents of the Internet Search Sites folder is organized into several subfolders, such as Files, News, and Shopping, for easier searching of your favorite categories. Because Sherlock is available as a Mac OS X application under Mac OS X, you might consider just using this version rather than updating the Internet Search Sites folder in Mac OS 9.x.

Language & Region Support

The Language & Region Support folder contains files required to provide support for languages such as Chinese, Nederlander, Finnish, and Swedish. The Mac OS is extremely flexible in terms of language support; see Appendix E, "*Installing and Upgrading Mac OS 9.x and Mac OS X,*" for information about installing additional language support for Mac OS 9.x and Mac OS X.

Launcher Items

The Launcher Items folder contains aliases and folders used by the Launcher Control Panel to assist with the organization of frequently used items. The Launcher's functionality has been taken over by the Dock in Mac OS X; nevertheless, it is still utilized by many users.

Login

The Login file, used by the Multiple Users feature in Mac OS 9.x, is not supported in the Classic environment because of the true multiuser capabilities of Mac OS X. See the previous chapter for more information about customizing your computer to work with multiple users.

MacTCP DNR

The MacTCP DNR file is a holdover from the days when MacTCP (instead of Open Transport) was the primary networking software for the Mac. Its presence ensures backward compatibility with applications that require MacTCP. Although you'll never need to worry about what it does or whether you'll ever use it, don't delete it—doing so could cause problems down the road.

MS Preferences Panels

Microsoft Internet Explorer (IE) is part of the default installation of Mac OS 9.x. The MS Preferences Panels folder contains 20 or so files that are used by IE to configure such things as downloading options, security, and user passwords.

Note Pad File

Although similar to the Scrapbook, the Note Pad File can hold only textual data, not sounds or pictures. Mac OS X offers no counterpart to the Note Pad, but several software developers have come forward with data management utilities that greatly exceed the abilities of Note Pad. These products include iOrganize (**www.brunoblondeau.com**), OmniOutliner (**www.omnigroup.com**), and Sticky Brain (**chronos.iserver.net**).

Panels

The Panels file, part of the Multiple Users feature, presents users with a panel-style interface instead of the traditional Desktop. Much of the Multiple Users interface is derived from At Ease, Apple's popular security application. Similarities are apparent between Multiple Users and the Capabilities feature in Mac OS X , both of which restrict user access to applications and folders.

Preferences

Mac OS 9.x and the Classic application environment store the preferences files created by Classic applications in the Preferences folder. As a user, you shouldn't have to do anything to the Preferences folder or its files. Your applications should create and maintain these files automatically.

PrintMonitor Documents

The PrintMonitor application handle sprinting tasks in the background, whereas the PrintMonitor Documents folder is a temporary storage area for documents that are to be printed (sometimes referred to as *print jobs*). Once a document has been printed by the PrintMonitor, it will be deleted from this folder. In Mac OS X version 10.2, however, the PrintMonitor Documents may not be accessible.

Scrapbook File

The Scrapbook File stores various types of data, including text, images, and sounds, that are accessible via the Scrapbook utility. Mac OS 9.x installs samples of the various types of data that may be stored in the Scrapbook. You can easily modify the Scrapbook's contents with the Cut and Paste commands.

Scripting Additions and Scripts

The Scripting Additions folder contains several files that AppleScript uses to enable certain Classic operations, such as File Sharing. Other applications may install items in this folder in order to enable close collaboration with AppleScript. As with other special folders within the System Folder, a scripting addition that is dropped onto the closed System Folder (when you have booted the computer directly into Mac OS 9.x) will be automatically placed in the Scripting Additions folder by the Mac OS.

The Scripts folder, a relatively new addition to the Mac OS, stores AppleScripts in a central location. In earlier versions of the Mac OS, scripts could be stored wherever you liked. The addition of the Scripts folder has proved to be a great help in organizing various scripts. See Chapter 11, "*Scripting Mac OS X*," for more information about AppleScript in Mac OS X and how your scripts may (or may not)be used in Mac OS 9.x.

Shutdown

The contents of the Shutdown Items folder are activated as the last step when you restart or shut down the computer when booted directly into Mac OS 9.x. When the Classic environment is stopped or restarted, the contents of this folder are activated as well. This feature is especially helpful if you want to sweep your hard drive for viruses prior to restarting or shutting down. For example, if you have an application that can quickly scan your hard drive for viruses, just make an alias to that application and place it in the Shutdown Items folder.

Startup Items

Applications, documents, folders, and volumes in the Startup Items folder are automatically run (or opened) whenever Classic is started or restarted. As with the Apple Menu Items folder, most of the icons in the Startup Items folder will probably be aliases. If you rely on several Classic applications on a regular basis and want them to be launched automatically whenever Classic is activated, just add their aliases to the Startup Items folder.

System Suitcase and System Resources

The System file (technically it's a special type of Finder item called a suitcase) is one of the most critical elements in the Mac OS 9.x System Folder. The System suitcase oversees all basic Mac OS activities and assists every application and utility that runs on the Macintosh. The System Resources file, also a critical file, contains data that is utilized by various elements of the Finder, System suitcase, and the Mac OS in general. As a user, you can remain blissfully ignorant of most of the work performed by the System suitcase. The System suitcase's traditional role as home to sounds and keyboard resources does require some user interaction; now, however, it is only accessible when you boot into Mac OS 9.x directly and not from within the Classic environment. Most other types of data stored in the System suitcase are hidden from view and are inaccessible to the user.

The System Resources file, a critical part of Mac OS 9.x, is required to boot the computer into Classic mode or directly into Mac OS 9.x.

Text Encodings

The Text Encodings folder stores conversion files used by the Mac OS to translate data among languages such as Chinese, Hebrew, and Korean. You won't need to interact with the contents of this folder yourself, but certain applications may not work if the proper translator isn't located in this folder.

Managing and Optimizing Classic

The System Folder and its subfolders are created by the Installer when you first install Mac OS 9.x. At that time, all system software files are placed in their proper locations. The System Folder is constantly modified, however, as you install other software applications and perform common tasks on your Macintosh.

After the initial installation, several types of files are added to the System Folder. These files include fonts and sounds, system Extensions (which add functionality to the Mac OS, applications, and utilities), and miscellaneous files that enable other software applications to function properly.

Several features, including Extensions, Control Panels, and printer or network drivers, allow you to modify the way the system software works and extend the features it provides. Default Folder and ACTION Utilities are two examples of the hundreds of Control Panels, Extensions, and drivers that modify your system software. You've probably already added files of this type to your System Folder.

Many applications store miscellaneous files—files that don't interact directly with the system software—in the System Folder. They're placed in the System Folder for the following reasons:

- *Reliability*—The System Folder is the only "common ground" on a hard drive that applications can rely on in every configuration.

- *Simplicity*—The Macintosh operating system can easily find the System Folder, regardless of what it's called and where it's located. This gives applications quick access to files stored in the System Folder.

- *Security*—The System Folder is a safe place for applications to store files because most users are not likely to disturb files in their System Folder.

Some of the many application-related files (or folders) that use your System Folder as a safe storage place are Microsoft Word's temporary (temp) files, PageMaker and StuffIt's encryption engines, translators, Claris translators, and viewers.

Adding Files to the System Folder

After Mac OS 9.x has been installed or upgraded, files may be added to the System Folder in several ways during the normal course of using your computer. In fact, changes are made to the System Folder every time you use the computer, but sometimes significant updates, additions, and modifications are performed:

■ *By the Mac OS Installer*—To add printer drivers, network drivers, or keyboards, you can run the Mac OS Installer application at any time after booting directly into Mac OS 9.x, but not from within Classic. The Installer installs the selected files to your System Folder and places them in the proper subfolders.

■ *By application software installers*—Many software applications use installation programs that copy the software and its associated files to your hard drive. Installers that have been specifically written or updated for compatibility with Mac OS 9.x can place files correctly into the System Folder or its subfolders.

Older installer applications often place all files directly in the root level of the System Folder, ignoring the subfolder structure. In these cases, the application may require that the files remain as positioned by the installer. However, most Extensions belong in the Extensions folder, and Control Panels belong in the Control Panels folder—regardless of how they were originally positioned. Remember, only properly located files in the System Folder will be loaded at startup.

■ *By software applications*—Many software applications read and write temporary and preferences files to the System Folder. Others use the System Folder for dictionaries and other ancillary files. Some applications, such as Microsoft Internet Explorer and Microsoft Office, even reinstall missing portions of the application if they're accidentally deleted. My experience has been that most applications, including Microsoft Office 2001, are not confused about how to add required files to the System Folder when in Classic mode.

Older applications not updated for Mac OS 9.x may not use the proper subfolders found in the System Folder, such as the Scripting Additions and Scripts folders. Files placed directly in the System Folder may not be accessed properly and could cause problems for your system software or other programs.

■ *By you, the Macintosh user*—Because some programs and utilities don't use installer applications, many files must be placed into the System Folder manually. These files can be dragged onto the System Folder icon or into an open System Folder window from within Classic mode or while booting from Mac OS 9.x.

Most files that are dragged onto the closed System Folder are placed automatically in the correct subfolder, such as the Control Panels or Extensions folder. This helps you add files to the System Folder correctly, even if you know nothing about the System

Folder structure. After booting directly into Mac OS 9.x, the OS informs you how it's positioning your files, but Mac OS X only tells you that files need to be placed in specific locations within the System Folder, examples of which are shown in Figure 4.10.

Once files are in the System Folder, you can reposition them freely. The "helping hand" feature of the Mac OS will not affect the repositioning of files moved from within the System Folder.

Deleting Files from the System Folder

For the most part, files in the System Folder can be deleted just like any other file—by dragging them into the Trash or by selecting the files and then choosing File|Move To Trash. However, some files cannot be deleted because they're "in use." These files include the System file, the Finder, any Extensions or Control Panels that were loaded at startup, fonts, open Control Panels, and any temporary or preferences files used by open applications.

To delete the System file or Finder (but you wouldn't ever want to do this, would you?), you must restart the Macintosh using another boot disk. To delete an in-use Extension or Control Panel, move the file out of the Extensions or Control Panels folder, restart the Mac, and then delete the file. To delete open Control Panels or temporary or preferences files of open applications, simply close the Control Panel or application and drag the file to the Trash.

Figure 4.10
When booting directly into Mac OS 9.x, the OS gives you detailed information about the placement of system files (top), whereas Mac OS X only provides a summary (bottom).

Optimizing Classic

Once you're comfortable with the concepts of managing Mac OS 9.x and the Classic environment, there are a few things you can do to optimize Mac OS 9.x to run in the Classic environment. Granted, Mac OS X version 10.2 makes the startup time for Classic so short (as low as seven seconds on a dual-1Ghz G4) that *optimization* may mean only shaving one more second of the startup time, but each computer is a different situation that calls for different optimization techniques. Consider trying these approaches to optimize Classic:

- Perform a clean installation of Mac OS 9.x to eliminate the possibility of Extension conflicts and corrupt Control Panels.

- Maintain two separate System Folders, a minimized System Folder for use in Classic and another for use when booting directly into Mac OS 9.x, containing customized Extensions, System Extensions, Control Panels, and drivers.

- Use the Extension Manager to create multiple sets of Extensions and Control Panels, one for use in Classic and another for booting directly into Mac OS 9.x.

Because two computers rarely contain exactly the same System Folder elements, there is no single best way to optimize Classic, nor is there a way to predict that your System Folder would be similar to another held up as an example. The best—and safest—way to explore optimizing the System Folder on your computer is to:

1. Perform a clean installation of Mac OS 9.x (see Appendix E, "*Installing and Updating Mac OS 9.x and Mac OS X*" for details).

2. Use the Extension Manager to turn off and on various components of the System Folder to see if your selections have a positive effect on the performance of Classic (see the next section for details on using the Extension Manager).

3. Return to using your default System Folder if your optimization experiments go horribly wrong.

4. Upgrade or replace Classic applications with Mac OS X-native applications to eliminate the need to use the Classic environment.

The next section offers a few tips on how to troubleshoot the Classic environment.

Troubleshooting Classic

Because Extensions and Control Panels modify or enhance the Mac OS at startup, a newly installed Extension or Control Panel may cause your Macintosh to crash when booting into Classic or directly into Mac OS 9.x. If you 're starting up Classic and a conflict occurs, only Classic will crash; the rest of Mac OS X will not be affected.

Crashes can occur if the item is incompatible with the OS, another Extension or Control Panel, a certain combination of Extensions and Control Panels, or even an application.

If you experience a compatibility problem, such as sudden or unexplained freezes or crashes, suspect an Extension conflict first. To test the theory, try turning off your Extensions by using the Turn Off Extension command in the Advanced tab of the Classic System Preferences (described earlier in this chapter). This will disable all but the most essential Extensions and allow you to remove the incompatible file from the System Folder. When you restart or start up with Extensions off, the words "Extensions Off" will appear under "Welcome to Mac OS" during startup.

Various third-party utilities were introduced to automate the process of turning Extensions on and off, changing the loading order, or creating Extension sets. The best-known of these products is Cassidy & Green's Conflict Catcher, which you should purchase if you're having a significant startup problem or otherwise suspect an Extension conflict. If the problem is particularly bad, change the Startup Disk option in the System Preferences to boot from the hard drive containing Mac OS 9.x. You may find it easier to resolve an Extension conflict while in Mac OS 9.x directly, and not while in Classic mode in Mac OS X.

TIP: The Mac OS loads Extensions first, then Control Panels, then the contents (if any) of the Startup Items folder. All items are loaded alphabetically.

In Mac OS 9.x, the number of Extensions was so overwhelming that Apple expanded the capabilities of the Extensions Manager Control Panel from previous versions as a means of taming the System Folder. For example, Figure 4.11 shows the Extension Manager used to manage a set called My Settings, which is sorted to show the contents of the System Folder by Package. The selected item belongs to the Classic Compatibility Environment version 1.7.

To use the Extension Manager, follow these steps:

1. Launch Classic using one of the many methods described previously in the chapter.

2. Open the Extension Manager Control Panel from the System Folder that was used to start Classic.

3. Choose one of the default sets, such as Mac OS 9.x All, Mac OS 9.x Base, or My Settings from the Select Set menu.

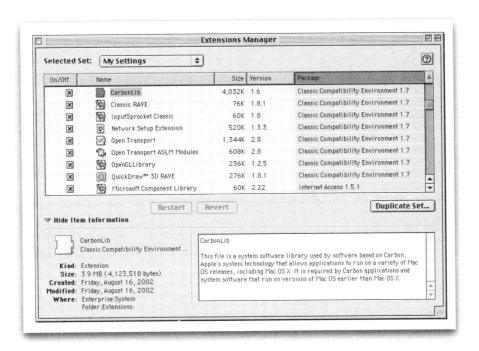

Figure 4.11
Use the Extension Manager to active and deactivate various elements of the System Folder to troubleshoot Classic startup and compatibility issues.

4. Check or uncheck an item in the On/Off column to activate or deactivate it. If you are using one of the default sets such as Mac OS 9.x All or Mac OS 9.x Base (indicated by a small icon of a padlock), you'll need to choose File|Duplicate Set before being able to modify the set.

5. Quit the Extension Manager and restart the Classic environment.

Clicking the checkmark off to remove an Extension, System Extension (one found in the System Folder, not the Extension folder), Control Panel, or Startup Item for the first time creates one of the following folders and places the item in the appropriate folder:

■ Control Panels (Disabled)

■ Extensions (Disabled)

■ Shutdown Items (Disabled)

■ Startup Items (Disabled)

■ System Extensions (Disabled)

Trial and error will usually tell you if what you've changed is an effective method of solving your problem or enhancing the Classic environment. If you disable one of the following items that is required for use by the Classic environment—but not when booting directly into Mac OS 9.x—and you subsequently launch the Classic environment, Mac OS X will ask if it may reinstall the items. You must allow these items to be reinstalled in order to use Mac OS 9.x in the Classic environment:

- Classic
- Classic Support
- Classic Support UI
- ProxyApp

As a final measure in troubleshooting Classic, you may be required to update Mac OS 9.x from time to time to ensure the highest level of compatibility. Like Mac OS X, Mac OS 9.x has the ability to update itself automatically over the Internet via the Software Update feature—but not from within Classic. Because the Mac OS is modular, various components of the OS may be upgraded independently of the Mac OS as a whole. This is a real timesaver, considering how long upgrading the entire OS over the Internet would take! You don't have to update the Mac OS, but you would be wise to check the Apple Web site (**www.apple.com**) often for a new version of the OS that may potentially add new features, increase the speed of the OS, or fix a bug or incompatibility issue.

You can manually check for software updates, or configure the Software Update Control Panel to check automatically. To check manually for new versions of Mac OS components:

1. Boot into Mac OS 9.x.

2. Open the Software Update Control Panel, shown in Figure 4.12.

3. Click the Update Now button.

4. A dialog box will appear asking you for permission to proceed.

If no updates are found for your particular model or versions of installed Mac OS components, another dialog box will appear informing you that no updates are necessary.

You can also check for updates on a schedule that is convenient for you, which frees you from having to remember to do it manually. However, this feature will not function if you are running Mac OS 9.x in the Classic environment instead of booting directly into Mac OS 9.x. To configure an automated update after booting into Mac OS 9.x:

1. Open the Software Update Control Panel.

2. Check the Update Software Automatically checkbox.

Figure 4.12
The Software Update feature of Mac OS 9.x.

3. Click on the Schedule button and choose a schedule for the update.

4. Decide whether you want to be asked by the Mac OS before downloading and installing the updates, and then check (or not, depending on your preference) the option entitled Ask Me Before Installing New Software. I recommend that you always check a reliable Mac-related news Web site before introducing a significant change to any version of the Mac OS because even a minor update could render a beloved application unusable. See **www.macosbook.com/favorites.html** for links to the Web sites I use most frequently to learn about Mac OS, application, and hardware compatibility issues.

5. Close the Software Update Control Panel.

6. Click on OK and then Agree when presented with the Apple Software License Agreement.

At the appropriate time, the Software Update Control Panel will automatically launch itself and begin searching for updated versions of the Mac OS. If no updates are found, then nothing will be installed. If an update is found, you will be presented with an option similar to the one shown in Figure 4.13. In this example, several components for Mac OS 9.x are available for updating.

If you select a software package to update, you may be required to restart your computer to complete the updating process. Also, keep in mind that some update packages may be several MB in size and could take more than an hour to download, depending on the speed of your Internet access.

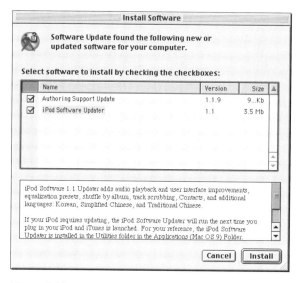

Figure 4.13
Selecting software to update in Mac OS 9.x.

Wrapping Up

Mac OS X offers two approaches to working with Mac OS 9.x—you can run it in Classic mode from within Mac OS X or boot directly into Mac OS 9.x. For the most part, you'll interact less with the contents of the System Folder when in Classic mode because several features are disabled. You'll probably want to work with Carbon and Cocoa applications as much as possible anyway because of the advanced features provided by Mac OS X when using non-Classic applications. Keep in mind that the OS is very particular about the location of its files, so don't muck around too much. In this chapter, we've discussed:

- Using the Startup Disk Control Panel and System Preferences pane to select a hard drive to boot into Mac OS 9.x or Mac OS X.

- Using the Classic System Preferences pane to select and configure startup options for a valid System Folder for use in the Classic environment.

- The various methods for starting and stopping Classic.

- How to store a limited, but essential, number of Mac OS 9.x preferences in a user's home folder to better share the Classic environment among multiple users in Mac OS X.

- The contents and purpose of the Mac OS 9.x System Folder.

- How to manage, optimize, troubleshoot, and update Mac OS 9.x and the Classic environment.

In the next chapter, we'll look at the various ways you can manage the many, many files on your hard drive.

Organizing Your Data

As you've seen in earlier chapters, Mac OS X provides several commands and features that help you manage disks and files. Other than a few rules relating to directory permissions for multiple users, Mac OS X does not require that you organize your data in any particular way. It's up to you to decide how to arrange your files, folders, and applications within your home folder or other areas for which you have permission to create files and folders. The challenge of file management is to design a logical arrangement that allows you to quickly locate the files you need while balancing the amount of available storage space and the quantity and size of your files.

Mac OS X provides several data management tools, including the Make Alias command, the Find command, and the ability to append comments to items in the Finder, to help you meet this challenge. You can use these tools to manage data on your hard drive as well as on removable media, network file servers, or any other removable or remote storage devices. In this chapter, we'll take a look at these organizational tools and how they can help you manage your data efficiently. We'll also look at a couple of third-party utilities designed to help you manage and secure the thousands of files and folders on your computer.

Exploring the Mac OS X File System

What makes Mac OS X's file structure radically different from earlier versions of the operating system? First, the OS itself is completely different from earlier versions of the Mac OS and contains distinct categories of files and subfolders that are stored in new places. For example, the System Folder no longer exists, but a similar type of folder is available for storing system-related resources. Several of the more familiar folders reappear in Mac OS X in new locations, such as the Favorites. Second, Mac OS X is a true multiuser operating system. Each user account is created using a standard template of folders not found (for the most part) in earlier versions of the Mac OS. The basic components of the new file structure are:

- *Applications*—The default set of user applications installed by Mac OS X, including the Address Book, Internet Explorer, and TextEdit.

- *Library*—Resources used by the Mac OS or shared among multiple applications, including ColorSync, printer resources, and screen savers.

- *System*—The majority of the operating system files. The Mach portion of the operating system, located in the root level of the hard drive, is invisible.

- *Users*—A set of folders created for each user account on your computer.

Additional folders may be created at the root level of your hard drive by the OS itself, or by applications whose installation programs don't know to locate files and folders in more appropriate locations (such as the Applications folder or somewhere in your home folder). For example, I have one application that created a log file at the root level of my hard drive with permission settings that made deleting the file difficult. If you choose the Archive and Install option when upgrading to Mac OS X version 10.2, the Mac OS will create a folder called Previous Systems at the root level of your boot drive; various parts of your previous operating system will be stored there. Although having folders other than the four default folders at the root level of a drive isn't necessarily a bad thing, it is counter-intuitive to Mac OS X's goal of a simplified and streamlined file system.

From the perspective of long-time Mac OS users, the biggest change in the file structure is the addition of user-specific "home" folders. Home folders are created alike, initially varying only by the user's access privileges—the goal being to protect personal files while granting read and write access to others. As the home folder's owner, you are free to create and delete subfolders like the ones shown in Figure 5.1. The Library folder is an exception, however—because it's reserved for your application preferences and OS-related files and folders, you should steer clear of it.

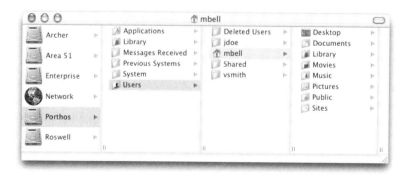

Figure 5.1
Mac OS X provides each user with a home folder for storing personal files such as documents, music, and pictures.

The top-level folders created by Mac OS X in your home folder include:

- Desktop
- Documents
- Library
- Movies
- Music
- Pictures
- Public
- Sites

Although your home folder is created with a suggested set of subfolders, you aren't required to store documents in the Documents folder, music in the Music folder, and so on. The Desktop folder is a little different, however—if you want to see your items displayed on the Desktop, you actually have to store them in the Desktop folder. In Mac OS X, you can view and manipulate the contents of your Desktop from the Desktop itself, or open the Desktop folder in an Icon, List, or Column view. This is very different in previous versions of the OS, in which there is only one Desktop folder for each volume.

If you have multiple user accounts on your computer, most of the subfolders in each user's home folder will be inaccessible to the other users. Although administrative and non-administrative users have the same access restrictions to other users' home folders, it's possible to customize access when creating new folders. See Chapter 16, "Sharing Internet Services," for more information on manipulating permissions.

Working with Aliases

Wouldn't it be nice to be in several places at one time? Imagine, for example, that while you're hard at work earning your paycheck, you could also be lying on a beach enjoying the sun. And if being in two places at once sounds appealing, how would you like to be in any number of places at one time?

Through a feature called *aliasing*, Mac OS X makes it possible for your electronic files to be in many places at the same time without actually using the amount of space that true duplicates would gobble up. For example, Mac OS X takes advantage of aliasing in conjunction with the Favorites folder, as we've seen in earlier chapters. Whenever you add a file, folder, or application using the Favorites menu or toolbar shortcut, you're really just adding that item's alias to the Favorites folder.

Basic Aliasing Concepts

In simple terms, an alias is a special kind of copy of a file, folder, or volume. Unlike copies you create with the Duplicate command, an alias is only a copy of the icon that represents the file, folder, or volume, and not of the item itself.

To understand this distinction, think of an icon as a door; the file represented by the icon is the room behind the door. Each room normally has just one door (just as each file has one icon), and opening that door (the icon) is the only way to enter the room. Creating an alias is like adding an additional door to the room—it presents another entrance to the same place.

The concept of aliasing is not new. Aliasing exists in several earlier versions of the Mac OS as well as in other types of operating systems, including various Unix operating systems, in which they are called *symbolic links*. In Microsoft Windows 3.1 and later operating systems, they are called *shortcuts*. Because Mac OS X is a Unix-style operating system that can utilize multiple types of file systems, it supports both aliases and symbolic links. Let's leave out any talk of symbolic links, however, because that's way too technical for the scope of this book. For example, Figure 5.2 shows an example in which a folder and the Desktop contain an alias to the same file, **index.html**. The original file resides in the Sites folder, and the aliases reside in the Favorites folder and on the Desktop.

An alias can be moved to any folder on the same volume without affecting the relationship between the alias and its original file. In fact, the link between an alias and its original file is maintained even if both files are moved or renamed, feats which would confuse and

Figure 5.2
Aliases in the Favorites folder and on the Desktop point to the original file (index.html) in the Sites folder.

break a symbolic link. The amount of disk space required by an alias is determined by the type and location of the original file, as well as the format of the hard drive. A typical alias is approximately 4KB in size. Aliases can be as large as 50KB, however.

TIP: The differences between aliases and symbolic links aren't important for the average user. Most Mac OS X users will utilize the Mac OS Extended (HFS+) file format instead of the Unix File System (UFS) for their hard drives. Symbolic links are used only in UFS volumes, and only advanced users, system administrators, or network servers are likely to employ the UFS format. So, for the purposes of this book, when I refer to an alias I really mean an alias instead of a symbolic link.

Details about these and other aspects of aliases are provided later in this chapter. But before getting too far into the technical aspects, let's take a quick look at a few practical ways to use aliases:

5

■ *To launch applications easily*—You can launch an application simply by double-clicking on its alias. For example, if you keep one alias of your word processor on the Desktop and another in a folder full of word processing data files, you could then launch the word processor by double-clicking the alias icon that's most convenient at the moment. Figure 5.3 shows a folder containing aliases to some of my frequently used applications, which can be stored anywhere on my computer, including the Dock, Favorites folder, or on the Desktop, for easy access.

Figure 5.3
Create customized groups of application aliases for easy access to frequently needed applications.

■ *To organize data files more effectively*—A data file may contain information that's relevant to several different areas of interest. For example, if you keep a spreadsheet file relating to your income taxes in a folder along with all the other spreadsheets you've created during that year, you may also want to keep aliases of that same spreadsheet in a personal finance folder, a tax folder, and a general accounting folder.

Storing aliases in multiple locations makes it easier to locate a file quickly because you can find it in several places. Placing alias files near other files of related content also increases efficiency because you don't have to look in multiple locations to access the files directly.

■ *To simplify access to files stored on removable media*—Keeping aliases of files from removable storage media (floppy disks, removable hard drives, and CD-ROMs) on your local hard drive allows you to locate those files quickly. For example, clip art collections often have dozens of categories of files, such as business, art, and logos, spread across multiple CD-ROMs. If you create a folder of aliases to the original categories you'll have quick access to them, as well as to the archived folders. When you double-click on an alias whose original is located on a removable media, the Mac OS will ask you to insert the media containing the original.

■ *To simplify access to files stored on network servers*—Placing aliases of files from network file servers on your local hard drive is another way to promptly locate the files, no matter where they're stored. When an alias of a file stored on the network server is opened, the Finder automatically connects to the server and asks you for the necessary password, if it isn't located in the Keychain (see Chapter 15, "Accessing Internet Services," for more information on storing passwords in the Keychain).

Creating and Using Aliases

Creating aliases is almost as easy as falling off a log. To create an alias for a file, folder, or volume, switch to the Finder and select the item's icon. Then use one of the following methods to make an alias:

■ Choose the Make Alias command from the File menu.

■ Press Command+L.

■ Press Control while clicking the mouse on the icon; then select Make Alias from the contextual menu.

■ Use Command+Option+drag to move the icon anywhere—even to the same folder or the Desktop.

The first alias created in the same location as the original will appear with the same file name and icon as the original, and with the word *alias* on the end. Additional aliases in the same location will append a space and a number to the end of the file name following the word *alias*, indicating that it is the second, third, or fourth alias to the same file, as shown in Figure 5.4. This is similar to aliases in Mac OS 9.x, in which the file names of aliases are italicized and followed by a space and the word *alias*.

For the most part, alias icons look and act just like other files, folders, or volumes. You can change the file name of an alias at any time without breaking the link between the alias and its original file. Changing the file name of an alias is like changing the sign on a door—it doesn't change the contents of the room behind the door.

Alias icons are differentiated from original icons by a small arrow that points up and to the right (these can be hard to see). The arrow usually appears when aliased files and folders are viewed in Open and Save dialog boxes, and when they're listed in a Finder window. Figure 5.5 shows an example of an application icon that takes full advantage of Mac OS X's ability to display 128x128-pixel, high-definition icons. The alias arrow is unusually easy to spot in this example.

 TIP: To make aliases more visibly distinguishable, consider adding the word "alias" at the end of the filename.

As mentioned earlier, alias icons can be moved to any available folder on the same volume without losing the link they maintain to the original file. This is the magic of aliases and the key to their utility. No matter where files are moved on the volume, the links are maintained.

Figure 5.4
Alias file names that include a number indicate that multiple aliases to the same item exist in the same location.

Figure 5.5
A well-designed application icon, such as the one for Sherlock, makes it easy to distinguish an alias from the original.

Original files can also be moved, as long as they remain on the same volume, and they can be renamed without breaking the link with their aliases. When the alias icon is opened, the Mac OS finds and opens the original file.

To illustrate how this automatic linkage is maintained, create an empty folder called *BigFiles* in your Desktop folder. Next, create an alias of this folder, move the alias into the Documents folder, and rename the alias *SmallFiles*.

Later, you decide that this folder will contain only medium-sized files so you change the name of the original folder from *BigFiles* to *MediumFiles* and move the folder to the Sites folder. Now, despite renaming and moving both the original folder *and* the alias to the folder, double-clicking on the *SmallFiles* alias in the Documents folder will open the *MediumFiles* folder in the Sites folder.

Advanced Aliasing Concepts

So now you understand the basic concepts of aliases. When you begin using aliases, however, questions may arise, such as: How many aliases can one file have? Is it possible to alias an alias? What happens when an alias's original file is deleted? The answers to these and other questions are as follows:

- *Multiple Aliases*—You can create an unlimited number of aliases from a single file, folder, or volume.

- *Aliasing Aliases*—It is possible to create an alias of an alias. In previous versions of Mac OS X, this could have caused problems because the second alias became orphaned if the first alias was deleted.

- *Fixing Orphaned Aliases*—When you try to open an orphaned alias and the original, or parent, file cannot be found, you'll get an error message like the one shown in Figure 5.6. When this happens, you can create a new parent and restore the link to the file by selecting the Fix Alias button and selecting the file. If you move the parent alias to the Trash, the child alias will be inaccessible, whether or not the Trash is emptied.

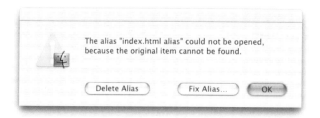

Figure 5.6
Orphaned aliases may be fixed by choosing the Fix Alias button.

- *Deleting Aliases*—You can delete aliases just as you delete normal files:

  - By dragging the alias to the Trash.

  - By selecting the alias and pressing Command+Delete, and then choosing the Empty Trash command (or Shift+Command+Delete).

  Deleting an alias has no effect on the original file, folder, or volume. To access the parent item of the deleted alias, however, you'll have to locate it manually or create another alias.

- *Moving Original Files*—Moving an original file within a single volume does not affect the link between that file and its alias. However, copying the original file to a new volume and then deleting the original file from the first volume destroys the link. In other words, you can't transfer the alias link from an original file to a copy of the original file.

  If you move a parent file from one volume to another and delete the original file, all aliases created from that file become invalid.

- *Deleting Original Files*—Deleting an original file has no immediate effect—you don't even get a warning about breaking the link between the file and its alias. When you try to open the alias of a file that's been deleted, however, a dialog box informs you that the original file cannot be found (see Figure 5.6).

- *Finding Original Files*—In order to accomplish tasks such as deleting the original file or copying the original onto a removable disk or cartridge, you'll first need to find the original file. To locate the original file for any alias, select the alias in the Finder and choose one of the following options:

  - Select Show Original from the Finder's File menu.

  - Press Command+R.

  - Press Command+I or select File|Get Info and view the path to the original item, or click the Select New Original button in the General Information section of the Info window. Figure 5.7 shows the path information for an original item— not the alias itself—as seen through the alias's Info window. If the selected item is an alias of an alias, the Mac OS will find the original file, not the alias used to create the current alias.

- *Replacing Alias Icons*—A new icon can be pasted into the Info window for any file, including an aliased file. Replacing the icon of an alias has no effect on the icon of the original file.

Figure 5.7
The Get Info window reveals the original location of an alias.

Aliasing Folders or Volumes

If you can create aliases for files and applications, you'll have no problem creating aliases for folders and volumes. Folder aliases are created, renamed, repositioned, deleted, and linked to their originals in exactly the same way as the file aliases previously described:

■ Aliasing a folder creates a new folder icon with the same name as the original.

■ The name of an aliased folder appears with a small arrow when viewed on the Desktop, in a Finder window, or in a dialog box.

■ Folder aliases can be renamed at any time; only one alias can have the same name as an original while in the same folder or on the Desktop.

■ Folder aliases can be located inside any other folder.

■ When an aliased folder is double-clicked, the original folder is opened in a Finder window. Aliasing a folder does not alias the folder's content. For this reason, the original folder must be available whenever the folder alias is opened. If the original folder is located on a volume that's not currently mounted, the Mac OS will attempt to mount the volume over the network.

■ Deleting a folder alias does not delete the original folder or any of its contents.

Folder aliases have a few unique aspects, however:

■ When a folder alias is displayed within a list window, it cannot be opened hierarchically (no triangle appears to its left) because, strictly speaking, the folder alias has no content to display. You can open the folder alias in a new Finder window by double-clicking on it, however.

■ When viewed as a column, an aliased folder displays its contents as if it were a folder, not an alias. Furthermore, if the name of the alias has been changed, it will display the name of the original folder in the title bar of the Finder window. Figure 5.8 illustrates the differences between an alias in a List view (top) and a Column view (bottom); note how the original name of the aliased folder is revealed instead of the name of the alias.

■ Anything put into a folder alias—including files, folders, and other aliases—is actually placed into the original folder. The folder alias has no real contents; it's just another "door" to the original folder.

Figure 5.8
Aliased folders displayed in a List view (top) and a Column view (bottom) have slightly different behavior when viewed in the Finder.

Volume aliases are similar to file aliases, but have some of the same characteristics as folder aliases:

■ Opening a volume alias mounts the original volume. If the original volume is not already mounted, Mac OS X will attempt to mount it.

■ Opening a volume alias displays a Finder window of the actual volume.

■ Aliasing a volume aliases the *icon* of the volume itself—not the contents of the volume.

Using Aliases

Aliases have a multitude of uses as shortcuts. The following are some of the more interesting possibilities:

■ *Alias Applications*—The easiest way to launch an application is to double-click on its icon. Some applications are stored in folders containing a morass of ancillary files, such as dictionaries, color palettes, Help files, and printer descriptions. Amid all this clutter, it's difficult to locate the application icon in order to launch it. The most straightforward way to simplify application launching is to collect aliases for each of your applications in a folder, and then drag that folder to the Dock. You can then launch an application by simply choosing its alias from the Dock. You can also put aliases to frequently used applications, documents, folders, volumes, and file servers in the Toolbar for easy access to groups of items.

■ *Multiple Data File Aliases*—Use aliases to store each data file in as many places as it logically fits—anywhere you might look for the file when you need it later.

■ *Removable Cartridge Maps*—Create a folder for each removable cartridge, drive, or floppy disk. Alias the entire contents of these volumes and store the aliases in the volume's folder. Then you can "browse" these volumes without mounting them. You may also want to keep other aliases of files from these volumes in other locations on your drive.

■ *Network File Server Volume Maps*—Create a folder called Servers and place an alias of each remote volume in it. You can then log on to any remote volume by simply double-clicking on the volume's alias. This eliminates the need to access the Connect To Server command and locate the file server and volume every time you want to use the volume. Of course, you'll be prompted for any required passwords.

Aliases have many uses and can provide valuable shortcuts, including the following:

■ You can alias any file, folder, volume.

■ To create an alias, select the desired icon and choose Make Alias from the Finder's File menu; press Command+L; choose Make Alias from the contextual pop-up menu; or drag and drop an icon while holding down the Option and Command keys.

■ An alias takes the same name as its original file unless multiple copies of the same target file are created in the same folder on the Desktop.

■ Alias names no longer appear in italics, but continue to use a small arrow as a visual clue.

- Aliases can be renamed at any time. The same naming limitations apply to aliases as to files and folders (a maximum of 256 characters).

- Aliases can be moved to any location on the same volume.

- An alias is initially given the same icon as its original. The icon can be changed in the Get Info window.

- An alias requires a very small amount of storage space.

- The link between an alias and its original is maintained even when the original is renamed or repositioned, but not when it is moved to another volume.

- Deleting an alias icon has no effect on its original file, folder, or volume.

- Copying an alias to a new location on the current drive (by holding down the Option key while dragging) is the same as creating a new alias of the original file—it does not create an alias of an alias.

- To locate its original, press Command+R after selecting an alias, or choose Show Original from the File menu.

- Opening a folder alias opens the window of the original folder.

- Opening a volume alias opens the window of the original volume.

Searching for Files and Folders

Regardless of how well organized your electronic filing system is, it's sometimes impossible to remember where specific files are located because many Macs have tens of thousands of files in addition to the 90,000 or so files created as part of the default Mac OS X installation. To solve this problem in the past, Apple provided the Find File desk accessory to enable you to search for files—by file name—on any mounted volume. Find File located the files and listed them in a section of its window. Once a file was found, selecting the file name revealed the path of the file along with other basic file information. Sherlock, introduced in Mac OS 8.5, was a dramatic improvement. In Mac OS X versions 0 through 1.1.5, Sherlock continued to evolve into a more powerful application that allows you to find much more than just files on your hard drive. In Mac OS X version 2, Sherlock's purpose has been changed to search for information over the Internet, and the Find command has returned as the tool for searching local and remote file servers, including your iDisk.

Basic Find Commands

Accessed via the File menu, the Find command is part of the Finder, and therefore is multithreaded—meaning that you can execute multiple Find commands at the same time. The Find command functions very much as it did in Mac OS 8.5 and earlier, and allows you to perform two types of searches:

■ Finding files on local or networked volumes using customized search criteria.

■ Finding words and phrases in locally indexed volumes or folders (commonly referred to as a full-text search).

The Find command is launched by selecting File|Find or pressing Command+F, which opens a Find window similar to the one in Figure 5.9. The Find command's most basic type of search is the traditional search by file name, which I'll discuss in detail a little later.

 TIP: The Find command opens the results of each search in separate window.

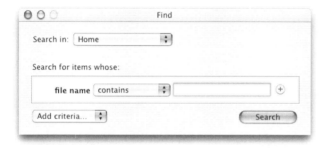

Figure 5.9 The Find command's most basic search window.

Searching for Files

The Find command defaults to a "simple search" window, which allows you to search for files with names containing the characters in the text entry field. You can also use the Find command to do a very complex search. I'll get into that in just a moment—for now let's start with the basics. Using the basic File Name Contains option to locate files or folders by name, you can enter the complete name or any portion of the name for the item that you feel will return a small list of results.

To search for items by name using the Find command, follow these steps:

1. Click on the Desktop or any open Finder window.

2. Press Command+F or choose File|Find.

3. Select a location to search.

4. Select File Name *Contains*.

5. Enter a string of characters in the search field.

6. Click on the Search button or press the Return key.

Let's take a closer look at a few of the main search options.

Select a Location to Search

Use the Search In menu to select the locations you'd like to search, which can include all sources available to the Finder at any given time. If you are logged in to a file server, then you can search the server. If you have more than one volume on your computer, you can search one or all of them using the Find command. The locations for searching include:

- *Everywhere*—Searches all local and networked volumes that are currently visible in the Finder.

- *Local Disks*—Searches only local volumes, including hard drives, Zip disks, and CD-ROMs, if inserted in the computer.

- *Home*—Searches *your* home folder only, and not the home folders of any other users.

- *Specific Places*—Lets you select the volumes or folders to search.

If you want to search just a specific folder, such as your Applications folder, open your home folder and drag the Applications folder to the section of the Find command window listing the available sources, then check only the Applications folder. You may also select a specific location using the Add button to the right of the Search In menu. For example, Figure 5.10 show the Find command window (top) and two search results windows, one for a search of the term acrobat in a volume (bottom left) and the other for same search term, but limited to the Applications folder (bottom right). Note the different views of the path to the selected item in the lower half of the search results windows.

Enter a Term to Search

If you know the complete name of the item you're looking for, enter it into the search field. Bear in mind that the correct file may not be found if you make even a slight error in spelling the file name. Alternatively, enter only the first portion of a name. Entering the first few characters of the title you're searching for is the most common—and usually the most efficient—file name search method. This locates all files whose names contain the characters you've specified. The exact number of characters you should enter will depend on the circumstances; the goal is to enter enough characters to narrow the search, but not so many that you risk a spelling error and therefore risk missing the file.

Figure 5.10
The results of two searches.

For example, if the file you wanted to locate is named *Archaeology Report*, specifying only the letter A would yield a huge number of files to sort through. On the other hand, entering six or seven characters could allow file names with spelling errors, such as Archio or Arhcae, to escape the search. Decide on the number of characters according to how common the first few characters are among your files, and how well you remember the file name. In this example, searching for files starting with Arc would probably be the best strategy. The search term is not case sensitive—both *Apple* and *apple* are returned in the results window.

After specifying the search criteria, click the Search button to start the search. The search begins with the first source selected and proceeds to search any other sources you specify (more on that in a minute). The search results are displayed in results windows like those shown in Figure 5.10. A new search results window will appear for each click of the Search button.

Results windows are divided into two parts. The upper part lists the search results, which may be sorted by whatever columns you decide to view. Clicking on a column will sort or reverse-sort the contents of the search results window; as in any Finder window, all the columns except the Name column may be reordered according to the procedure described in Chapter 2, "Working with the Finder and Desktop." To select the columns you'd like to show in a search results window, follow these steps:

1. Perform a search.

2. Click once on the search results window.

3. Press Command+J or select View|Show View Options, the result of which is shown in Figure 5.11.

4. Select the columns and information you would like to show. This procedure is similar to selecting the columns to view in other Finder windows. Search results windows cannot be displayed in Icon or Column view; the options include Date Modified, Date Created, Size, Kind, Version, and Comments. You can also resize the columns to make them wider or narrower.

5. Close the Search Results View Options window.

The path to an item is displayed in the lower half of the results window in one of two ways, both of which are demonstrated in Figure 5.10. When the results window is large enough to display more than one row of information in the path section, the path to the selected item is shown in hierarchical format. If the window is scrunched to show only

Figure 5.11
Use the Show View Options command in the View menu to select the columns to view in a search results window.

one row, if will display the path to the selected item in a horizontal fashion (which is helpful for users with smaller screens, such as iBook and older PowerBook users).

To open an item after it has been found, just double-click on it in either the upper or lower portion of the results window, or click on the file and press Command+O. After you've executed a search, you can also use the File command and drag-and-drop capabilities of the Mac OS to accomplish various tasks relating to the contents of the Found Items dialog box. These tasks include:

- *Opening the item's window*—Press Command+R to open the item's enclosing folder, or select the Open Enclosing Folder command from the File menu.

- *Moving the file*—Drag the file or folder name to a new location. The item actually moves to where you've dragged it. However, when you drag the item to another disk, it is copied rather than actually relocated.

- *Opening the file*—Double-clicking on a folder, or pressing Command+O with a folder selected, opens the folder. The same actions will open a selected file if the application that created the file is available. You can also drag the file name to an application. If the application isn't already running—and if it can open this type of file—the application will launch itself and then open the file.

- *Get Info for the file*—Press the familiar Command+I combination to open the Get Info window for the item to view its properties.

If the selected file is not the one you wanted, or if after modifying the selected file you want to continue searching for the next file that matches the search criteria, choose Command+F to return to the Find File window.

TIP: Once you have completed a search, the results windows will remain open until you individually close the windows, even if the Find window is closed first.

Advanced File Searches

With the new Find command, you can create custom searches using a wide variety of criteria, but unfortunately, you can no longer save a custom search for later use as you could in versions of Sherlock prior to Mac OS X version 10.2. Saved searches allowed you to easily locate certain types of files without having to remember exactly how the search was constructed, which was a real time-saver. The following search criteria can be used individually or in combination to create highly advanced custom searches on an ad hoc basis in Mac OS X Version 10.2 using the Find command:

- File Name Contains, Starts With, Ends With, Is, Is Not, or Doesn't Contain *XYZ*

- Content Includes *XYZ* (more on content searches in a minute)

- Date Modified Is Today, Is Within, Is Before, Is After, or Is Exactly *XYZ*

- Date Created Is Today, Is Within, Is Before, Is After, or Is Exactly *XYZ*

- Kind Is or Is Not Alias, Application, Clipping File, and so on

- Size Is Less Than or Greater Than *XYZ*

- Extension Is *XYZ*

- Visibility Is On, Off, or All

A final option for several of these criteria is No Value, which means that the selected criteria is lacking from the items for which you want to search. In other words, there may be a file or folder that lacks a modification date, and the Find command lets you look for these as well. However, several valuable search criteria that were present in the previous version of Sherlock are no longer available in the new Find command, including:

- File Type Is or Is Not *XYZ*

- Creator Is or Is Not *XYZ*

- Version Is or Is Not *XYZ*

- Folder Is or Is Not Empty, Shared, or Mounted

- File/Folder Is Locked or Unlocked

- Name/Icon Is Locked or Unlocked

- Has a Custom Icon or No Custom Icon

- Is Invisible or Visible

However, despite these limitations you can customize searches in at least three main ways:

- Simple conditional searches, which include a single search criteria with multiple variations, such as files whose names begin with A and end in B.

- Complex conditional searches, which include multiple search criteria and complex conditional rules, such as those with certain file names and creation dates.

- Full-text searches of document contents.

Let's look at a quick example of each of these three types of custom searches using the new Find command.

Simple Conditional Searches

A conditional search allows you to apply two or more rules, such as filenames that begin with one string of characters and end in another, to a single search criteria. Because some of the possible search criteria do not need or allow multiple conditions to be attached, this type of search is not available with all eight search criteria.

To create a simple conditional search, follow these steps:

1. Click on the Desktop or any open Finder window.

2. Press Command+F or choose File|Find.

3. Select a location to search.

4. From the Add Criteria menu, select an item that contains a rounded plus sign, or click the plus sign to the right of the File Name field to reveal additional conditions, as illustrated in Figure 5.12.

5. Add more search conditions for this particular search criteria by clicking the plus sign again.

6. Delete search conditions for this particular search criteria by clicking the minus sign.

7. Populate the fields as necessary.

8. Click on the Search button or press the Return key.

Complex Conditional Searches

A complex conditional search allows you to apply two or more rules to two or more search criteria, such as files whose name begins with one string of characters and contains another, and whose creation date us between 2001 and 2002. Not all the

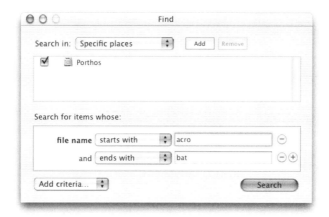

Figure 5.12
An example of a simple search using a single criteria, but with multiple conditions.

possible search criteria need or allow multiple conditions to be attached, so this type of search is not possible with all eight search criteria.

To create a simple conditional search, follow these steps:

1. Click on the Desktop or any open Finder window.

2. Press Command+F or choose File|Find.

3. Select a location to search.

4. Select items from the Add Criteria menu that contains a rounded plus sign, or click the plus sign to the right of the File Name field to reveal additional conditions.

5. Add more search conditions to the search criteria by clicking the plus sign again.

6. Delete search conditions from the search criteria by clicking the minus sign.

7. Populate the fields as necessary.

8. Click on the Search button or press the Return key.

For example, Figure 5.13 shows a search using four criteria (File Name, Date Created, Kind, and Size), but which contain a total of six conditions. Using this type of search really lets you narrow a search to find exactly what you want. The trick is in understanding the eight search terms and their various conditions, so to reduce any possible

Figure 5.13
An example of a complex search using multiple search criteria and multiple conditions.

frustration with the new Find command, experiment until you feel comfortable with the command before you really, really need to find that important file.

Full-text Searches

You can search a volume or a folder for specific words *within* documents—not just in the name of a document itself. Commonly referred to as a full-text search, this approach is helpful in more ways than you might think. For example, how else could you find a specific piece of information without opening every document on your computer? Before you can perform a full-text search, you must index the contents you want to search. This can take a long time, depending on the size of the location being searched.

Mac OS X Version 10.2 automatically indexes local hard drives, but you can also manually select locations you want to index or reindex by following these steps:

1. Select an item in the Finder and choose Command+I or File|Get Info.

2. Expand the Content Index section by clicking the disclosure triangle.

3. Click the Index Now button to begin indexing the selection, as shown in Figure 5.14.

4. Close the Get Info window once the indexing has been completed.

5. Select the Delete Index button to remove the indexed file, which is stored in the home folder of the user who initiated the indexing session.

6. Repeat these steps to reindex the selection.

Figure 5.14
Manually updating the index of a selected folder.

As I mentioned in Chapter 2, "Working With the Finder and Desktop," you can speed up the search process and cut down on the disk space required for the indexes by reducing the number of languages you intend to search. Applications may contain support for multiple languages, and you can index only the language support files you actually need by following these steps:

1. Select the Finder from the Dock.

2. Choose Finder|Preferences.

3. In the bottom section of the Finder Preferences window entitled Languages for Searching File Contents, click the Select button; Figure 5.15 shows the result of this action.

4. Select only the languages you want to include in your search.

5. Click the OK button to return to the Finder Preferences.

6. Close the Finder Preferences window by pressing Command+W or clicking the Close button on the Finder Preferences window.

Although Mac OS X version 10.2 does not allow the automatic updating of indexes, as Sherlock did in earlier versions of the Mac OS, I expect this feature will be added in future releases of Mac OS X.

To search for a word or phrase by content, follow these steps:

1. Click on the Desktop or any open Finder window.

2. Press Command+F or choose File|Find.

3. Select a location to search.

4. Select Content from the Add Criteria menu; remove other criteria as needed by clicking the rounded minus sign beside that criteria.

5. Enter the search criteria in the Content Includes field.

6. Click on the Search button or press the Return key.

The results window looks a bit different for full-text searches because it adds a Relevance column. For example, Figure 5.16 shows a search for the term sharing in my home folder (top) and the results window containing the new Relevance column (bottom), which can be sorted and reordered like other Finder and results windows.

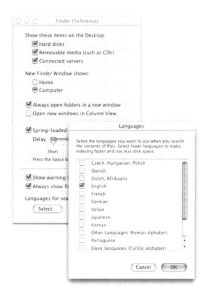

Figure 5.15
To create smaller index files and faster searches, reduce the number of languages to be included.

Figure 5.16
An example of a full-text search using the new Find command.

Tips for Effective Searches

Once you get the hang of it, the new Find command is easy to use. Here are a few tips to help you create effective search:

■ *You can use Find to locate aliases as well as original items.* Aliases will appear with the small arrow in the Found Items window and will be listed as *alias* in the Kind column.

■ *Find also locates folders and volumes.* Like any other file, folders and volumes matching the specified search criteria will be found.

■ *Create a custom search to locate all data files created by one specific application or with a particular file extension.* For instance, you can find all your HTML documents by creating a search for files ending in .html.

■ *Use Find to do quick backups.* After you've used the Find command to locate all files modified after a certain date, you can drag those files to a removable volume for a "quick-and-dirty" backup. Of course, this procedure shouldn't replace a reliable backup utility—but you can never have too many backups.

■ *Use a custom search to perform multiple-criteria searches.* For example, the Find command can locate all file names beginning with S that are less than 32KB in size and that are documents (or any other set of multiple criteria).

■ *Use the content search feature to search your computer for detailed information, such as names and addresses of friends or business contacts sent to you by email.* Mac OS X will index the data of almost all the popular email clients, such as Mail and Eudora, as well as documents belonging to the most frequently used sources, such as AppleWorks, Microsoft Word, and Adobe Acrobat.

Using Comments

A comment is a string of text that you can enter, by way of the Get Info command, for most items in the Finder. Earlier versions of the Mac OS allowed users to assign Finder labels as well as comments; because Mac OS X does not support labels, comments are the only way for you to categorize files and folders as well as sort them from within list-style windows using a customized set of criteria. The Comments column option, found in the View|Show View Options preferences, enables you to show or hide comments in list windows. When selected, the Comments column will display in Finder windows viewed as lists (but not as icons or columns). Comments can also serve as a notes field in which you can jot down a few words describing the item.

You'll discover a variety of productive ways to apply the comment features. Using comments as cues is one possibility—in the form of keywords or phrases, comments can provide data (such as client names, project titles, and names of related documents) beyond what is already included in the standard information about a file (file name, date, kind, and so on). Many shareware developers design their programs to automatically add a comment, including the author's URL, to any file created with their products.

In Mac OS 9.x, for example, I often assigned the numbers one through seven to Finder labels so that I could sort the contents of a folder according to my own preferences rather than by the usual options (name, date modified, size, and so on). In Mac OS X, I can assign a comment to files in the form of the numbers one through seven (or higher) to achieve the same effect. Figure 5.17 shows a folder containing several Lasso documents before I've assigned comments (left) and after comments have been added and the list window sorted by comment (right).

Using this method, I can easily group certain files together and pick them out of a list at a glance.

Compressing and Encrypting Files

Even with today's multigigibyte hard drives, compressing files is still a necessity because many files must be compressed before they travel over the Internet. This is especially true if you want to send a folder containing several files; sending all of the files in the form of one compressed medium-sized file is more efficient than sending numerous small files. Because many files that are stored on Hierarchical File System Plus (HFS+) volumes contain both a data fork and a resource fork, it's easy for the files to get "munged" by alien operating systems that don't know what to do with the resource fork. File compression can help eliminate the issue of a resource fork by encoding your data into a flat file with only one fork.

Like compressing, encrypting files is a valuable skill to possess in today's computing environment. If your Mac is ever connected to the Internet, you will expose yourself to at least some risk of being hacked.

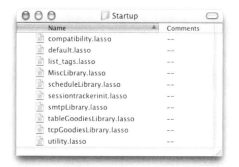 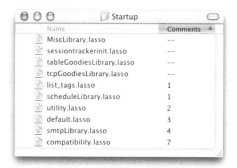

Figure 5.17
Use Finder comments to add more sorting options to Finder windows.

The initial version of Mac OS X lacked the ability to encrypt files; fortunately, Aladdin Systems' venerable StuffIt line of tools was ready to fill the void. Whereas Mac OS X version 10.2 adds the ability to create encrypted disk images using the Disk Copy application found in the Utilities folder, DropStuff and StuffIt Deluxe offer quite a few more options for securing files. DropStuff is an inexpensive utility for encrypting and compressing files into a variety of formats; StuffIt Expander is the freeware decompression utility that is installed automatically as part of Mac OS X. If you want even greater capabilities, you can purchase the complete StuffIt Deluxe package, which includes:

- StuffIt Deluxe application (compression, decompression, encryption, and so on)

- DropStuff (compression)

- StuffIt Expander (decompression)

- DropZip (compression for Microsoft Windows operating systems)

If you have limited compression needs, you can probably get by with DropStuff and StuffIt Expander. For the intermediate to advanced user, however, StuffIt Deluxe is an essential tool.

Compressing and Encrypting Files with DropStuff

Because DropStuff fully supports drag and drop, you can select items for compression and/or encryption by dropping them onto the DropStuff application or alias. Of course, you can also use the Stuff command from the File menu. Before compressing or encrypting any files it's a good idea to review the DropStuff|Preferences options first. Figure 5.18 illustrates my preferred configuration of DropStuff for everyday use.

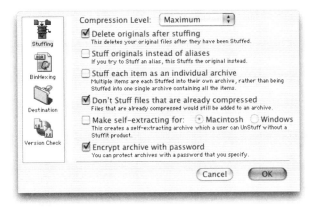

Figure 5.18
Review DropStuff's preferences before using it to compress or encrypt files.

The Stuffing section of the DropStuff preferences allows you to select several features, including the option Delete Originals After Stuffing. This keeps you from ending up with two versions—compressed and uncompressed—of a file or group of files.

To encrypt a file with a password, check the Encrypt Archive With Password option; the next time you compress a file, a password dialog box will appear. Once you enter or generate a password using the Generate Random button, you will be prompted to reenter the password as a safety measure. The other preferences for DropStuff allow you to BinHex a file for safe passage across single-forked file systems; specify the location for storing files once they've been compressed and encrypted; and automatically check for new versions of DropStuff.

Decompressing and Decrypting Files with StuffIt Expander

Mac OS X installs StuffIt Expander in the Utilities folder. StuffIt Expander performs the reverse duties of DropStuff, allowing compressed and encrypted files to be expanded and decrypted, resource fork and all. It has several additional preferences that specify what types of files may be processed and how compressed files should be handled. Figure 5.19 shows a few of the many configuration options for StuffIt Expander.

StuffIt Expander, which is capable of decompressing about a zillion file formats, is probably the only decompression tool you'll ever need. In addition to the native StuffIt format files (.sit and .sea), StuffIt Expander is also capable of decompressing the following formats:

- A to B (.btoa)

- AppleLink Package (.pkg)

- AppleSingle (.as)

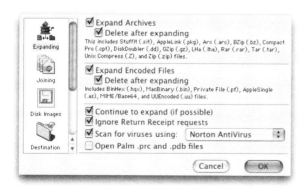

Figure 5.19
Use StuffIt Expander to expand and decrypt files.

- Arc (.arc)

- BinHex (.hqx)

- Bzip (.bzip)

- Compact Pro (.cpt)

- Disk Images (.img and .smi)

- DiskDoubler (.dd)

- GZip (.gz and .tgz)

- LHa (.lha, .lzh)

- MacBinary (.bin)

- MIME/Base 64 (.mime)

- Private File (.pf)

- RAR (.rar)

- TAR (.tar)

- Unix Compress (.z and .taz)

- UU (.uu, .uue, and .enc)

- Zip (.zip)

Like DropStuff, StuffIt Expander is capable of automatically checking for application updates to keep your software up to date. If you like these two applications, check out StuffIt Deluxe. It adds many features and several helper applications; my favorite features are the addition of a contextual menu and keyboard shortcuts that allow me to Control+click on an item in the Finder to compress or decompress it, or select the item in the Finder and choose Command+S to compress the item(s) or Command+U to decompress the items in the Finder.

Creating Encrypted Disk Images with Disk Copy

Disk Copy adds a few basic encryption options to its ability to create disk images. While not earth shattering, the encryption routine is a 128-bit algorithm called Advanced Encryption Standard (AES) based on the standard adopted by the U.S. government's National Institute of Standards and Technology (**http://csrc.nist.gov**); the routine is exportable to foreign countries. To use Disk Copy to create an encrypted disk image, follow these steps:

1. Launch Disk Copy from the Utilities folder.

2. Choose Preferences from the Disk Copy menu, or press Command+; to open the window shown in Figure 5.20.

3. In the Creating tab, select AES-128 (recommended) from the Encryption section.

4. Configure any additional options in this and other areas of the Disk Copy Preferences, then close the Preferences window.

5. Choose Command+N or choose File|New|Disk Image, an example of which is shown in Figure 5.21.

6. In the Encryption section, make sure AES-128 (recommended) is selected.

7. Choose the Create button to create the disk image.

8. When prompted, enter and verify a password.

9. The disk image will be created; you can add and delete items in the disk image once the correct password has been entered and the image has been mounted on the Desktop.

Since disk images are the native format for packaging software in Mac OS X, using Disk Copy to create and encrypt disk images will become a familiar task once you get the hang of it. If you have a recordable CD-ROM or other storage device attached to your computer, you should get into the habit of regularly archiving your important files and settings, just in case your hard drive dies, your computer goes up in smoke (or is damaged by a hurricane, in my case), or is stolen. Encrypting your archived files will prevent unauthorized access and give you peace of mind.

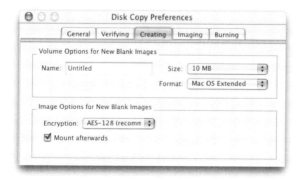

Figure 5.20
Review the Disk Copy encryption preferences before creating disk images.

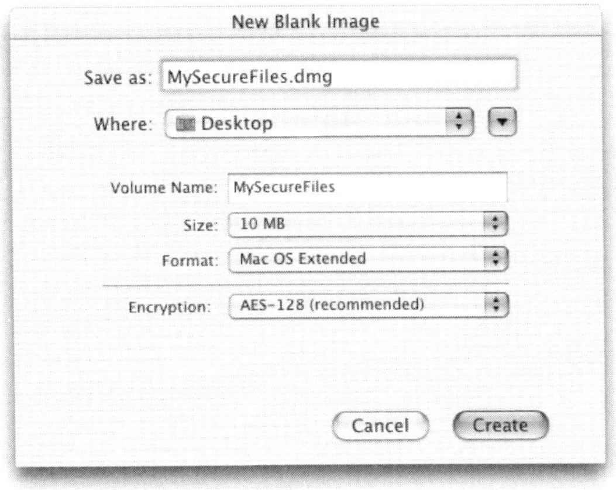

Figure 5.21
Encrypted disk image are easily configured.

Wrapping Up

Everyone suffers from info-glut. With so many files, folders, and applications crowding our hard drives, we need all the organizational help we can get. To make shortcuts and search and organize our data, Mac OS X version 2 offers several useful options and features, including:

- A file structure designed with multiple users in mind.

- Aliases help you locate and launch files, and allow you to access network data quickly and easily.

- The new Find command search engine will solve your "where is that file?" problem.

- Comments remind you of details about the contents of a particular file or folder, and make it possible to organize your files in highly customizable sorting orders.

- DropStuff, StuffIt Expander, and Disk Copy enable you to compress and password-encrypt your files.

Next, we'll look at the special software and features available for users who are running Mac OS X on PowerBooks and iBooks.

Mac OS X for PowerBooks and iBooks

Mac OS X is the first Unix-based operating system designed to be used equally by workstations, servers, and portable computers. If you're accustomed to working with Mac OS X on an iMac, for example, you'd be equally comfortable using the same operating system on a PowerBook or iBook. Whereas the hardware in PowerBooks and iBooks still differs considerably from desktop hardware, the components of the OS itself are pretty much the same from machine to machine. This consistency makes it easier for users of different Mac models to learn the operating system. In fact, as far as mobile users are concerned, the only down side to Mac OS X is the loss of a few minor PowerBook user interface features that were part of previous versions of the Mac OS. Fortunately, Mac OS X software developers have created some useful applications to fill the void.

In the early days of the PowerBook, Apple provided a suite of simple utilities for controlling basic functions, such as screen display, battery longevity, and processor cycling. Sensing an opportunity, many vendors rushed in and substantially improved upon Apple's meager offerings with packages like Claris's Power To Go, Connectix's CPU, Norton's Essentials for the PowerBook, and Inline Design's PBTools, to name a few. Some of these improvements, such as the Control Strip, were eventually incorporated into the Mac OS as a standard feature for all Mac users. If you have a late-model PowerBook or iBook, rest assured that you'll be able to get by with the standard features of Mac OS X; however, the addition of third-party utilities could make your computing life even better.

TIP: Mac OS X will run on any PowerBook or iBook introduced after September 1998. See **www.info.apple.com/applespec/applespec.taf** for a database of all Apple hardware that includes information on the date each product was introduced.

What's Missing in Mac OS X?

A few small features of Mac OS 9.x that were of particular importance for PowerBook and iBook users didn't make it into Mac OS X. These missing features addressed such concerns as conserving battery life and working with a small screen. Although the newer portables narrow the performance and usability gap between portable and non-portable Macs, the loss of the following features (formerly provided by various Control Panels and keyboard shortcuts) is noticeable. In parentheses beside the name of each missing feature is the name of the Mac OS 9.x Control Panel or item that provided the feature:

- Control Strip (Control Strip)

- Separate settings for battery and power adapter (Energy Saver)

- Processor cycling (Energy Saver)

- Reducing processor speed (Energy Saver)

- Remounting servers upon waking (Energy Saver)

- Screen dimming instead of sleep (Energy Saver)

- Turning off power to inactive PCMCIA cards (Energy Saver)

- File synchronization (File Synchronization)

- Infrared networking (Infrared)

- Launcher (Launcher)

- RAM disk (Memory)

- Password protection (Password Security)

- SCSI support (PowerBook SCSI Setup)

Mac OS X provides some new features to make up for the loss of at least a few components of earlier versions of the Mac OS. For example, Mac OS 9.x's Location Manager, Modem, and Remote Access Control Panels have been replaced in functionality by the Networking System Preferences pane. The Battery Monitor is now located in the menu bar, and the configuration options found in the old Trackpad Control Panel are now in the Mouse System Preferences pane. Workarounds for a few other missing features, such as password protection and the Control Strip, are discussed later in this chapter.

Portability Issues

Beginning with the Apple Portable (1989) and then the Apple PowerBook 100 (1991)—the most successful introduction of any family of portable computers of its time—Apple has had a string of successes with virtually all of its PowerBooks, especially with the Titanium PowerBook. The PowerBook has replaced the desktop machine as the computer of choice for millions of Macintosh users. Over the years, system software support for the PowerBook series has been fortified; now, with the iBook or PowerBook, laptop users can enjoy the same benefits from Mac OS X that desktop users do.

Because of issues relating to mobility and the special features found in their computers, users of portable Macintoshes have several unique needs that set them apart from users of workstations and servers. Although Mac OS X is essentially the same on a laptop as it is on a desktop computer, portable users face the following needs:

- *Battery Recharging*—Portables can run on AC power or rechargeable batteries. To reduce power consumption and thereby extend use, Mac OS X supports several energy-saving capabilities, including reducing screen brightness, spinning down the hard drive, and putting the entire computer to sleep.

- *Presentation Services*—Portables can easily connect to external displays, ranging from monitors to a variety of projectors or presentation devices. A video output port is a standard feature of many models, as is video mirroring.

- *Saving Print Documents for Later Printing*—For most Carbon and Cocoa applications, you can save a document as a PDF document for later printing.

- *Support for Device Input*—Keyboards, trackballs, trackpads, and other input devices are supported, as with any desktop Mac.

There are numerous PowerBook- and iBook-specific Web sites where you can find information on the latest hardware, software, and gadgets to make your portable computing experience more rewarding. Check out the following URLs for good information about portable computing and links to additional resources::

- Apple Computer's iBook site—**www.apple.com/ibook**

- Apple Computer's PowerBook site—**www.apple.com/powerbook**

- Jason O'Grady's PowerPage—**www.powerpage.org**

- PowerBook Army—**www.powerbook.org** (outdated, but good archives)

- The PowerBook Guy—**www.powerbookguy.com**

- The PowerBook Source—**www.pbsource.com**

Managing Power and Performance

Some PowerBooks and iBooks consume more power than others, depending largely on differences in processor speed and the type and size of the display. The power consumption of portable Macs is a major portability issue, particularly for users with CD-ROM and DVD-ROM drives (which consume more battery power). Fortunately, Mac OS X includes several techniques for reducing power consumption through the Energy Saver System Preferences pane, which is accessed from the Apple menu. The default configuration of the Energy Saver is shown in Figure 6.1.

At the top of the Energy Saver pane, two new features allow you to make some basic configuration changes. First, the Optimize Energy Settings menu allows you to choose from the following pre-configured sets of Energy Saver settings:

- *Automatic*—Strikes a balance between the power that is available (AC or battery) and adjusts the energy-saving features of the computer accordingly.

- *Highest Performance*—Powers the computer's components with minimal concern for energy-saving.

- *Longest Battery Life*—Uses maximum energy-saving features to prolong battery life.

- *DVD Playback*—Optimizes the computer's components for optimal DVD movie viewing, which is determined to be three hours.

- *Presentations*—Configures the energy-saving features when the computer is used to give a PowerPoint presentation, multimedia slide show, or other type of presentation.

- *Custom*—Allows you to configure the individual preferences to your liking, the options for which are discussed blow.

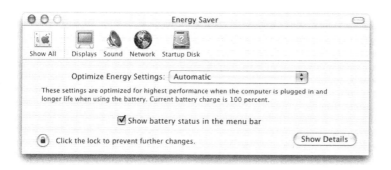

Figure 6.1
The Energy Saver has several new features in Mac OS X version 10.2.

The energy-saving settings are designed to go into effect when the computer has not detected any keyboard input or mouse activity for a certain number of minutes. Parents traveling with kids will appreciate the DVD Playback settings, which prevent the computer from inadvertently going to sleep or turning off the display during the best part of a movie. Business users will appreciate the Presentations setting, which prevent the CEO's presentation from stopping just before the Board has a chance to hear how she'll save the company from a hostile takeover.

In previous releases of Mac OS X, the Energy Saver can't distinguish between when your computer is running on battery—when energy conservation is most important—and when it is plugged into the AC adapter. This was possible in Mac OS 9.x, and is a welcome return to Mac OS X version 10.2. To switch between the two settings, activate the Settings For menu and select one of the following:

■ Power Adapter

■ Battery Power

The pre-configured settings are the same for each source of power (AC adapter or battery); however, the Custom setting enables you to configure your own set of criteria for activating the energy-saving features of your computer. To explore these options, click the Show Details button, which opens the window shown in Figure 6.2.

Figure 6.2
The Details view of the Energy Saver pane reveals the configuration options.

The Sleep tab offers the following options for configuring a custom set of Energy Saver preferences:

■ *Put the Computer to Sleep When It Is Inactive for*—Puts the entire computer to sleep, including the monitor, hard drive(s), processor, and network interfaces, after it has been inactive for a designated period of time.

■ *Use Separate Time to Put the Display to Sleep*—Determines the time limit for putting the display to sleep. If this option remains unchecked, the display will go to sleep (turning itself off, instead of just dimming the screen) at the same designated time as the computer.

■ *Put the Hard Disk to Sleep When Possible*—Spins down the hard drive if it is not in use by an application or essential component of the OS. In Mac OS X version 10.2, the hard disk cannot be configured to sleep independently from the system and monitor sleep settings.

■ *Show Battery Status in Menu Bar*—Enables a battery status monitor in the menu bar, which can be configured to display either the battery power level or estimated time remaining.

The Options tab of the Energy Saver System Preferences pane contains several options, depending on your particular model of Mac portable. Most all models will have an option entitled Wake When the Modem Detects a Ring, which brings the computer out of sleep mode if the modem is called by another modem or telephone while plugged into a phone line. Other options include, Wake for Network Administrator Access, which brings the computer out of sleep mode when certain administrative applications want to connect, and Restart Automatically After a Power Failure, which causes the computer to restart once AC poser has been lost, the battery has been drained, and AC power has been restored.

Although there are no "correct" settings for the Energy Saver configuration options, the following suggestions make help you optimize your settings:

■ Mac OS X allows a computer in sleep mode to "wake up" very quickly, usually in just a few seconds. My PowerBook wakes up in under three seconds, so it's convenient to put the whole system—not just the monitor and/or hard disk—to sleep.

■ Network connectivity is lost when the entire system goes to sleep, and Mac OS X makes no provision for servers to be remounted upon waking.

■ Some applications will not function properly if the whole system or parts of the system are in sleep mode. For example, applications (such as calendars) that issue reminders may not work because the internal clock is disabled while asleep. Also, if the monitor is in sleep mode, you will not be able to see any information on screen, although you might hear an alert if the sound is not muted.

■ If you have enabled Personal File or Web Sharing, avoid putting the whole system or the disk to sleep. Doing so will disrupt your computer's ability to serve these tasks efficiently.

■ Disable speech recognition (in the Speech System Preferences pane) and your screen saver (in the Screen Effects System Preferences pane) to further minimize power consumption.

■ To completely prevent your computer from going to sleep, configure the Energy Saver System Preferences pane by unchecking all the checkboxes and moving all the sliders over to Never.

Experiment with the various options in the Energy Saver to determine the settings that are best for you. To help gauge your power consumption, you can monitor your battery's performance by viewing the battery status in the menu bar, as shown in Figure 6.3. The battery status icon, which provides a general overview of the level of power in your battery, can be configured to show (when clicked) the amount of time remaining on the battery or the percentage of power remaining in the battery. If the computer is connected to the AC adapter, the icon will read "Plugged In" when the Show Time option is selected. As for the Time Remaining option, the system of measuring voltage levels is accurate and reliable—as far as it goes. What voltage measurements don't tell you, though, is *exactly* how much time your battery has left. For that indicator, you need to know the lowest voltage level your battery will drop to, your instantaneous power consumption, and your history of power consumption. Variables such as which battery you're using, memory effects, and unusual power consumption activities make learning about your battery's longevity a difficult proposition. So bear in mind that the power warnings only estimate voltage levels, not how much energy remains in a battery or exactly how long you have before you run out of juice.

Accurate measurement of battery life is so desirable that some batteries contain a small, dedicated microprocessor to help calculate battery performance and give more

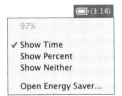

Figure 6.3
Use the battery status feature to show how much life is in the battery.

accurate measurements in the battery status menu. The PowerPC processor itself uses about 25 percent of your battery's current. The display is another major power draw; depending on its type, it can consume anywhere from 20 percent to 50 percent of your power supply. Display issues are covered in the next section of this chapter, "Managing Displays."

During sleep, your hard drive spins down, your screen is powered off, and your micro-processor is in a comatose-like state. You can safely transport your portable, or store it for short periods of time, while it is asleep. Depending on the model, your PowerBook or iBook can retain the contents of its short-term memory for two weeks in this state. However, the amount of memory that needs to be refreshed is a major variable in this equation; large amounts of RAM require additional battery power to maintain memory contents during sleep.

In Mac OS X, you have several ways of manually putting your PowerBook or iBook to sleep:

- Choose the Sleep command from the Apple menu.

- Set the period of inactivity necessary for automatic sleep mode in the Sleep tab of the Energy Saver System Preferences pane.

- Press the Power key on the keyboard and click the Sleep button (or press the letter S on the keyboard).

- Close the cover.

To wake up your Macintosh, press any key other than the Caps Lock key, or open the cover (if closed). Most portables have a small LED light that blinks or pulses when the computer is in sleep mode.

Your hard drive consumes, on average, about 15 percent of your battery power. You can improve the hard drive's power consumption by:

- Using memory-resident (RAM) applications that don't require much I/O.

- Selecting the Put the Hard Drive to Sleep When Possible option in the Energy Saver System Preferences pane.

Don't get too carried away with worrying about the hard drive spinning down. The energy expended in spinning up a hard drive is equivalent to something like 30 to 60 seconds of the hard drive spinning at its rated speed. For the spin-down feature to be valuable, you would need to be in situations in which you don't access the disk more often than every two or three minutes. Also, since Mac OS X uses persistent virtual memory (i.e., it cannot be turned off), if you only have 128MB of memory in your computer, the OS itself may never let the hard drive spin down because it is needed to page information to and from the disk.

Furthermore, because AppleTalk perpetually polls the selected port (usually an Ethernet port) for activity, keeping it active while your computer is asleep may also drain power. You can turn AppleTalk on and off in the AppleTalk section of the Network System Preferences pane, but this is only an option if you aren't planning to connect to AppleTalk-based network devices such as printers.

Managing Displays

The capacity for connecting an external monitor is one of the best features of a PowerBook. (iBooks do not support external video at this time.) In conjunction with LCD projectors, multiple or external monitors are especially useful for making presentations with your PowerBook. Alternatively, you can make your presentation with a larger monitor, often in conjunction with an external mouse and keyboard. Furthermore, you can augment your PowerBook with a "docking" station that allows you to keep an external monitor, keyboard, and mouse plugged into the computer; this option ensures that your computer recognizes the external monitor automatically when you plug the PowerBook into the dock and then boot up.

Most PowerBook models have built-in video, as well as support for various video output ports signified by the TV-like icon on the back of the PowerBook. The possible types of video-out include:

- S-video—A round connector with seven small pinholes.

- SVGA—A four-sided, 15-pin video output port, which is the standard for Windows-based PCs. An SVGA-to-Mac video adapter that will enable you to connect the video output port to an external Apple-style monitor is supplied with some PowerBooks.

- DVI—The latest type of connector that enables Apple-brand LCD displays to connect to PowerBook or iBook computers.

You can plug in a monitor during sleep or at shutdown. When you start up your PowerBook, make sure the external monitor is already powered up. After the startup icons appear on your PowerBook, the Desktop should appear on the external monitor as well as the PowerBook's built-in LCD display. If the Desktop does not appear, shut down the computer, restart after reconnecting the external monitor, and then open the Displays System Preferences pane and make the appropriate selections. When the external monitor is successfully detected, only one of the two displays will contain the Mac OS X menu bar at the top of the screen. Each screen will have its own configuration options, however, because each display will be physically different from the other and have different display characteristics, such as resolution and bit depth capabilities.

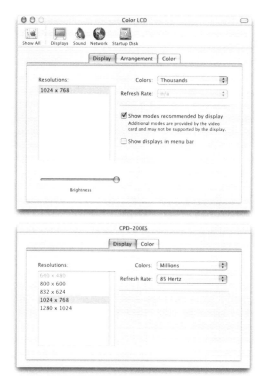

Figure 6.4
The Display settings for the built-in LCD display of a PowerBook (top) and an external display (bottom).

For example, Figure 6.4 shows the differences in the Display System Preferences pane for the built-in LCD display of a PowerBook (top) and a Sony 200ES 17-inch multiscan display (bottom).

When multiple monitors are in use, only one will have the menu bar. You can decide which display will have the menu bar and serve as the "main" screen by following these steps:

1. Open the System Preferences from the Dock or Apple menu.

2. Choose the Displays pane.

3. Select the Arrangement tab, as illustrated in Figure 6.5.

4. Make any desired changes to the relative positions of the monitors and quit the System Preferences.

The concept of arranging the two displays is a bit tricky, and even more so to describe here, but let me give it a shot. From your perspective sitting in front of a PowerBook with an external display attached, the two displays can be arranged side-by-side to

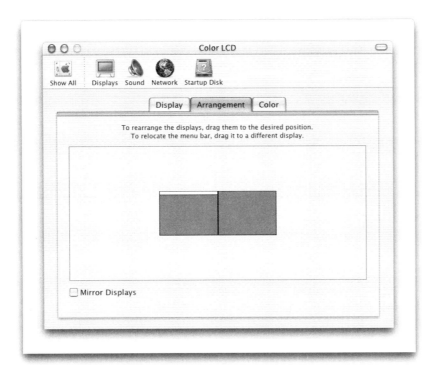

Figure 6.5
Arrange the relative position of an external monitor attached to a PowerBook using the Arrangement tab of the Displays System Preferences pane.

give the effect of being a single, very wide Desktop on which the mouse can be moved from the far right to the far left. In Figure 6.5, the displays are arranged in this way, with the built-in LCD display on the left side of the figure and the external monitor's display on the right side of the figure. The menu bar is positioned on the internal display.

You may reverse the order of the displays by dragging one to the opposite side, or you can even arrange them in a staggered fashion, as in Figure 6.6. The Displays System Preferences pane will not allow you to arrange them as freely as you might like, so you'll have to experiment with repositioning the displays until you come up with a comfortable arrangement.

When working in presentation mode, you may find it convenient to have the display on your external monitor match the one that appears on your PowerBook. This process is called *video mirroring*. To turn on video mirroring:

1. Open the System Preferences from the Dock or Apple menu.

2. Choose the Displays pane.

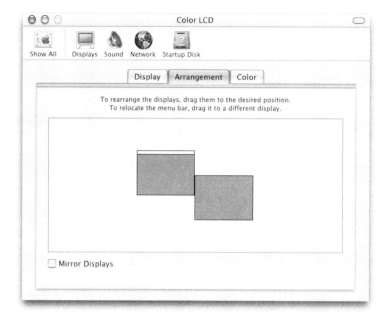

Figure 6.6
Rearrange your displays using the features found in the Arrange tab.

3. Configure the resolution and bit depth to be the same for each display, such as 1024x768 pixels and thousands of colors.

4. Check the Mirror Displays option, as shown in Figure 6.7, and quit the System Preferences.

If the Mirror Displays option is not available, then your PowerBook (or desktop Mac, if a second display card and monitor are available) isn't capable of supporting video mirroring due to a hardware conflict or because the resolution and bit depth are not compatible enough for Mac OS X to support video mirroring.

Finally, you can put your PowerBook into sleep mode when an external monitor is in use only if the external monitor is Energy Star compliant. When the computer is in sleep mode, the external monitor will go to sleep as well. Monitors that are not compliant will not power down, although the PowerBook's processor and hard drive will.

Changing Locations

As you've noticed, your portable Mac has a plethora of controls, and many of them change depending on how you are connected to a network. For instance, your office uses an Ethernet-based TCP/IP Internet connection, while at home you use PPP and a dial-up account or TCP/IP and a broadband DSL or cable modem.

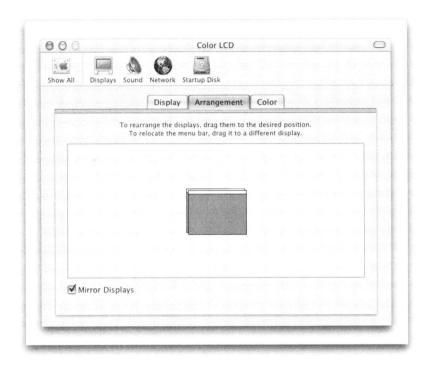

Figure 6.7
Use the video mirroring option to display the same view of the Desktop and Finder on both displays.

Because changing all of these settings just to go between office and home can be a major pain, Apple includes the Locations feature in the Network section of the System Preferences so you can easily switch between settings. The Locations feature, the Mac OS X equivalent of the Location Manager in Mac OS 9.x, lets you create a snapshot of only the network settings you use at particular locations—and not for the many other aspects of the Mac OS handled by the old Location Manager. These settings include:

- AppleTalk & TCP/IP
- Auto-Open Items
- Default Printer
- Extension Set
- File Sharing State
- Internet Set
- QuickTime Speed

- Remote Access

- Sound Level

- Time Zone

Even though the Locations features aren't nearly as robust as they were in the old Location Manager, they still allow you to easily switch between locations without requiring a reboot. The Location submenu, found in the Apple menu, is always visible, no matter what application is open. The options under the Location menu (shown in Figure 6.8) enable you to change locations or open the Network System Preferences to edit, add, or delete a location.

Figure 6.8
Use the Location menu to easily change network locations.

The Location menu also provides a shortcut to the Network System Preferences, where you can edit your network settings, such as a dial-up location for your PowerBook or iBook's internal modem. Because most Macs—not just PowerBooks and iBooks—come with an internal modem, please refer to Chapter 14, "Connecting to the Internet," for information on connecting your laptop or desktop computer to the Internet using the Location feature of the Network System Preferences.

Laptop Security

If there's a downside to owning a portable Macintosh, it's that everyone wants to get their grubby paws on yours. Because PowerBooks and iBooks are so fun and cool, it seems that everyone wants to borrow yours—sometimes without asking!

To forestall anyone who tries to boot your computer and poke around, Mac OS X provides a framework around which developers may add authentication services that provide very secure access to network-based lists of users, as well as encryption for passwords traveling across the network. On many corporate and campus networks, for example, the Kerberos authentication method is the preferred way to authenticate users. Mac OS X has a built-in Kerberos module that can be configured to work with many Kerberos-based network environments to match up large lists of user names and passwords and allow only authorized users to log into a PowerBook, iBook, workstation, or server running Mac OS X.

By configuring a few of the features found in the Accounts and Screen Effects System Preferences, you can provide a moderate level of protection for your portable Mac. Of course, these tips aren't fool-proof if other users have accounts on your computer, or if your PowerBook or iBook has an alternative means of booting, such as a CD-ROM drive or an external FireWire drive. If an additional boot source is present, it's possible to restart the computer and hold down the C or Option key at startup to command the computer to boot from another version of the OS on the CD-ROM or FireWire drive. Once this is accomplished, all your files are vulnerable to inspection, modification, or deletion.

 TIP: See http://docs.info.apple.com/article.html?artnum=106482 for information about using a firmware password to protect your laptop.

Because Mac OS X is a multi-user operating system that provides individual usernames and passwords, you can provide some security by following these steps:

1. Open the System Preferences from the Dock or the Apple menu.

2. Switch to the Accounts pane.

3. Choose the Users tab.

4. Disable the Log In Automatically As option.

5. Select the Login Options tab.

6. Choose Display Login Window As: Name and Password.

7. Select the Hide Restart And Shut Down Buttons option.

When your computer is restarted from the internal hard drive (and until you reenable these options), you will be prompted to enter a username and password at startup, and the Restart and Shut Down buttons will be disabled.

If you think you may forget your password, enter a hint in the Password Hint section of your user account information, which is accessed via the Users System Preferences pane. Include only as much information as you're willing to reveal to potential viewers. Avoid hints that are anything like your password—a creative hacker could guess your password based on the hint you have provided. Also, requiring a username and password at startup will protect the list of user accounts from being known by potential hackers. If they know the usernames, then half the battle is over and they can get to work on cracking a password.

You can also add an additional layer of security by requiring a password whenever your computer wakes from screen effect mode. Depending on the frequency with which the screen effect is set to activate, this could be irritating for some users. On the other hand, it could help keep prying eyes away from sensitive data. To require a password to unlock a screen effect:

1. Open the System Preferences from the Dock or the Apple menu.

2. Switch to the Screen Effects pane.

3. Choose a screen effect.

4. Choose the Activation tab, shown in Figure 6.9.

5. Select a value from the Time Until Screen Effect Starts section.

6. Choose Use My User Account Password from the section entitled Password To Use When Waking The Screen Effect.

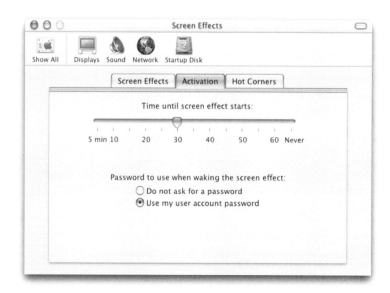

Figure 6.9
Requiring a username and password to wake a screen effect can increase your laptop's security.

Whenever your computer is in screen effect mode and the mouse, trackpad, or keyboard is moved, the password will be required to exit the screen effect and use the computer. To help conserve battery power, use the Basic screen effect that comes with Mac OS X. It is not graphic-intensive and is therefore not as power-hungry as screen effect images that are read into memory.

 TIP: See http://homepage.mac.com/sweetcocoa/ for information on LapCop, a stealth utility that can help you recover your laptop if it has been stolen.

Power Shortcuts

Despite the disappearance of several key features like the Control Strip and Launcher, Mac OS X offers a few shortcuts that can make your laptop easier to use. Eventually, software developers will create more utilities with PowerBook and iBook users in mind. For now, my favorites include the trackpad's several clicking features, MenuStrip, and QuicKeys for remapping my PowerBook's keyboard.

Using Trackpad Shortcuts

The PowerBook was one of the very first portable computers to utilize a sensitive electronic surface—the trackpad—in place of a rolling mouse. At first, many users complained about the trackpad—not so much because it was harder to use, but because it was different. Now, however, most people accept the trackpad as a vast improvement over the roller ball "technology" of past years. Because the trackpad is an all-electronic solution, it has another added benefit: the ability to act as a clicking device as well as a cursor. Again, some people hate this feature, especially when they sit down to use a PowerBook or iBook without realizing that this feature is enabled.

In addition to moving the cursor around the screen, Mac OS X supports the following options in the trackpad (shown in Figure 6.10):

- *Clicking*—Allows a single- or double-tap on the trackpad to emulate single- or double-clicking the mouse.

- *Dragging*—Allows a selected object to be dragged using the trackpad.

- *Drag Lock*—Allows your finger to be raised and moved again across the trackpad when dragging objects. Tapping the trackpad a second time will release the selected object.

- *Ignore Trackpad While Typing*—Renders the trackpad inactive when you're typing on the keyboard, which helps prevent accidental clicking on the trackpad.

- *Ignore Trackpad When Mouse is Present*—Causes the trackpad to be deactivated if you have connected an external mouse.

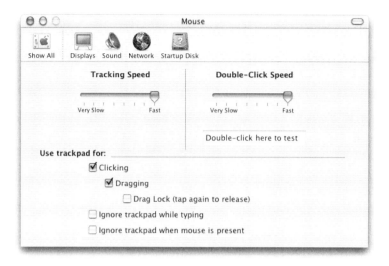

Figure 6.10
Use the Trackpad for clicking and dragging, as well as pointing.

NOTE: *For more tips and tricks on customizing Mac OS X's user interface, see Chapter 3, "Customizing Mac OS X." Using MenuStrip.*

MenuStrip is a great utility for managing your PowerBook or iBook's Desktop "real estate" by managing windows and providing easy access to a few of the features that disappeared with the old Control Strip (MenuStrip uses plug-ins similar to the old Control Strip modules). For about $12, MenuStrip is a terrific deal and works as either a menu extra or a floating window, examples of which are shown in Figure 6.11.

To download the latest version, visit **www.MacPowerUser.com**. After you have followed the installation instructions for the latest version, follow these steps to take advantage of MenuStrip's shortcuts:

Figure 6.11
Try MenuStrip on your laptop as a replacement for the venerable Control Strip.

1. Open the System Preferences from the Apple menu or the Dock.

2. Select MenuStrip from the Other category of panes in the System Preferences.

3. Choose the General tab to start and stop MenuStrip, whether you want to have MenuStrip startup automatically at login, and if you what MenuStrip to appear in the menu bar or as a floating window.

4. Click the Edit Preferences button in the Plugin Settings section and configure the various plugin settings, which are described below. Figure 6.12 shows both the MenuStrip System Preferences pane (top) and the plugin settings (bottom).

MenuStrip's plugins provide multiple features and are organized into several tabs. The general tab controls the following features:

■ *AppSwitcher*—Provides a small icon to help identify the current application, which also serves as a drop-down menu to reveal all running applications.

■ *Clock*—Displays the time and date, similar to the clock in Mac OS X.

6

Figure 6.12
MenuStrip provides several handy shortcuts in the menu bar, as well as a more highly configurable clock.

- *Drag Bar*—Repositions the MenuStrip in the menu bar when dragged to the right or left.

- *Hide All*—Hides all applications other than the Finder.

- *HideToggle*—Hides all applications except the application in the foreground, which brings all an application's windows together in a so-called single-app mode.

- *Monitor Controls*—Changes the resolution and color settings for the display.

- *Show All*—Shows all applications (the same as selecting Show All from the Finder application menu).

- *Volume Control*—Increases, decreases, or mutes the system volume for your computer.

The Hide All, Show All, and HideToggle options make life with the smaller screen of a portable much more livable. Users of PowerBooks and iBooks will appreciate the ability to focus on the Finder or a single application, thereby clearing the clutter of multiple, layered windows. Whereas the Dock doesn't contain a shortcut to the Sound System Preferences, the shortcut provided by MenuStrip is a welcomed feature.

MenuStrip's other configuration tabs manage the remaining configuration options:

- *Clock Settings*—Enables you to configure the highly functional time and date options for the clock, including alarm clock settings.

- *Hide All*—Allows you to identify applications that are not to be hidden when the Hide All and Single App Mode buttons are selected.

- *HideToggle* —Allows you to choose applications that, when active, do not automatically hide other applications when the HideToggle option is enabled. An example that is given by MenuStrip is StuffIt Expander, which typically becomes active for a few seconds at a time as it decompresses an archived file and then quits. If not selected in this configuration tab, it would cause all other applications to hide themselves as it decompresses a file, which may be a little unnecessary for many users.

Give MenuStrip a try on your laptop; the shortcuts and enhancements it provides are very well thought out and highly usable.

QuicKeys

QuicKeys from CE Software (**www.cesoft.com**) is the premier utility for creating simple and complex keyboard shortcuts, which I've mentioned in earlier chapters. Although it isn't what I'd call an inexpensive utility (at about $99), it is essential for anyone with repetitive motion injuries or have difficulty working with computer keyboards. Laptops may present new challenges for these users because the keyboard is not only abbreviated when compared to a standard, fill-sized keyboard, the keys are often smaller and closer together. This combination can make computer life rough!

I use QuicKeys to reduce the number of keystrokes I have to execute in a number of ways, including the following keystroke combination shortcuts that are especially welcome when working on my PowerBook's tiny keyboard:

- F5 for Command+X
- F6 for Command+C
- F7 for Command+V
- F8 for Command+G
- F9 through F14 to launch my favorite applications
- F15 to launch the System Preferences
- Command+Option+Control to hide all applications other than the front-most application
- Control+7 through 9 to insert various e-mail signatures
- Control+P to activate the ubiquitous Print Preview menu option for applications that lack a keyboard shortcut for this feature
- Command+Option+Control+C, I, or L to switch the current Finder window to a Column, Icon, or List view

Shortcuts may be single- or multi-stepped with pauses inserted to ensure the Mac OS has time to complete the first step before moving onto the second. Figure 6.13 shows a single-step shortcut that looks for an option called "Print Preview" in the File menu, which saves my right hand from using the trackpad to manually manipulate the File menu.

Virtual Desktops

Long-time Unix users have probably come across the concept of virtual desktops at one time or another, a concept that Mac OS X laptop users will also appreciate. Virtual desktops allow you to have multiple sets of Desktops and associated Finder and application windows that "stick" to a given virtual desktop window. Since laptops typically have small displays, one could use a highly configurable and feature-rich commercial application such as VirtualDesktop from CodeTek (**www.codetek.com**) to provide virtual desktops, or a limited but useful freeware utility such as Space from Riley Lynch (**space.sourceforge.net**). Space is freeware and allows you to navigate your virtual desktops using a floating palette such as the one shown in the lower-right

Figure 6.13
QuicKeys is a wonderful keyboard shortcut utility, especially for PowerBook and iBook users.

corner of Figure 6.14. In this example, I have four virtual desktops: *Apps*, *Utils*, *Web* (the active virtual desktop), and *sticky*.

You can configure the number of virtual Desktops you want to use, as well as the shape, transparency, and placement of the palette. Each virtual desktop can be assigned a custom name and keyboard shortcuts for navigating among the virtual desktops. It takes just a little getting used to before you're a Unix professional, too!

Wrapping Up

Although mobile computing offers different ways of working with your Macintosh, the freedom of portability comes with a few limitations and risks. In this chapter, you learned:

■ What is lacking in Mac OS X in comparison to Mac OS 9.x

■ How to make your PowerBook or iBook last longer on a battery charge by configuring the Energy Saver settings

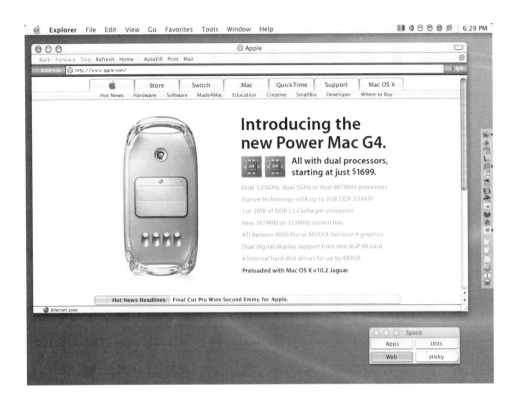

Figure 6.14
Use an application such as Space to provide multiple virtual workspaces, or Desktops.

■ How to connect an external monitor to your portable computer

■ How to select Internet "Locations"

■ How to make your computer more secure using login and Screen Effects passwords

■ How to take advantage of shortcuts using the trackpad, MenuStrip, QuicKeys, and Space

This chapter concludes the first part of this book. In the next section, I'll look at the broad issue of applications in Mac OS X. In the first chapter of Part II, I'll examine how Mac OS X version 2 works with Classic, Carbon and Cocoa applications. Then I'll discuss fonts, printing, and scripting, as well as Java and troubleshooting Mac OS X in the chapters that follow.

Working with Mac OS X Applications

Thus far, I've discussed the Mac OS X features that change the way you organize and manipulate data files at the OS level. As important as the OS is, however, it's not the reason you use a Macintosh. You use the Mac because of its applications—word processors, spreadsheets, databases, graphics programs, and so on. These applications help you accomplish your work effectively.

In this chapter, I'll look at some of the ways that Mac OS X affects applications, beginning with the important issue of compatibility. Then, I'll review the standard applications that are installed by Mac OS X, as well as the applications that are not installed by Mac OS X but that are worth your consideration. I'll also cover the many ways you can launch your applications, how to create and use stationery documents with some of the more popular applications, and details on two important features of Mac OS X–compatible applications—layered windows and attached sheets. In the remaining chapters of this section of the book, I'll discuss other major changes and enhancements that affect Mac OS X and your applications, including using Classic applications, multimedia, fonts, printing, scripting applications, Java, and trouble-shooting applications and Mac OS X.

Mac OS X Compatibility

A new software upgrade is always exciting—it introduces more features, better performance, and an easier-to-use interface. As seasoned computer users know, however, software upgrades often introduce bugs and incompatibilities along with improvements and solutions. Because Macintosh applications are heavily dependent on the operating system, they're particularly susceptible to upgrade-compatibility problems. Each application must be fine-tuned to function smoothly with the OS. The relationship between the Mac OS and an application is like that of two juggling partners, each throwing balls in the air that the other is expected to catch. When the OS is upgraded, a new partner replaces a familiar one; the routine may stay the same, but there's no time to practice and no room for error.

The introduction of Mac OS X brought the biggest change in Mac OS application programming since the migration from the old 68000 family of microprocessors to the PowerPC family in 1994. Although I covered the basics of Classic, Carbon, and Cocoa applications in Chapter 1, the subject bears repeating here because of the importance of the change and because the applications discussed in the following sections are all Carbon or Cocoa applications. Chapter 8 discusses how to use and configure Classic applications within Mac OS X, and Chapter 12, "Using Java," looks at how you can install and run Java-based applications.

Mac OS X-native applications come in two basic forms, Carbon or Cocoa applications. To make their existing products Mac OS X-compatible, application developers sometimes jettisoned sections of code that were not usable under Mac OS X and reworked the remaining code to create a Carbon application. This process is commonly referred to as *Carbonizing* an application. Carbon applications can be Mac OS X-only, or they can be used in both Mac OS X and Mac OS 9.x. These applications are sometimes referred to as "dual-OS applications", and some allow you to choose if you want to open the application in Mac OS X or in the Classic environment. The options and procedures for using dual-OS applications are discussed in the following chapter. Of course, most applications that are not Mac OS X compatible can still be run in the Classic compatibility environment, and you can boot directly into Mac OS 9 x to use applications that are not compatible with the Classic environment. For example, some Classic applications, such as those that rely on Extensions and/or Control Panels, may function partially—or not at all—when run in the Classic environment. However, Apple will eventually discontinue the ability to boot computers into Mac OS 9.x sometime in the year 2003, but the Classic environment will continue to be supported.

Applications written using the Cocoa Application Programming Interface (API) typically contain little code from legacy applications and enable programmers to take advantage of all of Mac OS X's advanced features. Cocoa applications cannot be used in the Classic environment because the Cocoa APIs lack the infrastructure required by Mac OS 9.x, so they cannot also be used as dual-OS applications. Classic applications may be rewritten using Cocoa APIs as well as Carbon APIs, but programmers who want to leave the Classic world behind often choose to switch to using only Cocoa APIs and sacrifice Classic compatibility.

Choosing a Default Application

Mac OS X accurately chooses the appropriate application to open a particular type of document. In the days of Mac OS 9.x, users would have to occasionally "rebuild" the Desktop to reassociate documents and their application types by holding down the

Command+Option keys at startup. Mac OS X doesn't experience this type of problem because the Desktop database isn't used to associate documents and applications in this way, but it is possible to manually change the preferred application for opening a particular type of document. Specifically, Mac OS X can assign an application to open a specific type of document, such as PDF or TEXT, or a document with a particular filename extension, such as .pdf or .txt.

By default, Mac OS X assigns one of its pre-installed applications to open as many types of documents as possible. For example, Preview is used to open not only Portable Document Format (PDF) documents, but any image file format you're likely to encounter when using the Mac OS. However, with one or more applications such as Adobe Acrobat Reader for viewing PDF documents, and Photoshop or GraphicConverter for image files. You can still use Preview to open these types of documents, of course, and it is very easy to switch between applications used by default to open these documents.

To choose a default application for a particular type of document, follow these steps:

1. Select an example document in the Finder and choose Get Info from the File menu. Then, press Command+I or Control+click on the document and choose Get Info from the contextual menu.

2. Expand the Open With section of the Get Info window, which you can see in Figure 7.1.

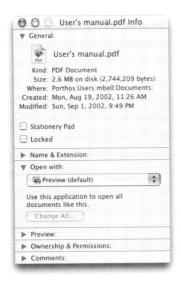

Figure 7.1
Use the Get Info command to change the default application for opening documents.

3. Activate the drop-down menu and select from the list of applications in the menu.

4. Choose the Change All button to always use this application to open documents with this file extension. Otherwise, only the document selected in the Get Info window will be assigned to this alternative application.

If you don't find the correct application in the Open With menu but you know of another application that you'd like to use to open this type of document, repeat steps one and two above, then follow these steps:

1. Choose the last option in the Open With drop-down menu entitled "Other."

2. In the selection window that is presented, choose Show Recommend Applications to let Mac OS X filter out inappropriate applications. Otherwise, choose Show All Applications, but beware that you will be allowed to select an application that will not open the document.

3. Navigate to the location of the application in question using the Choose Other Application navigation and selection window, an example of which is shown in Figure 7.2.

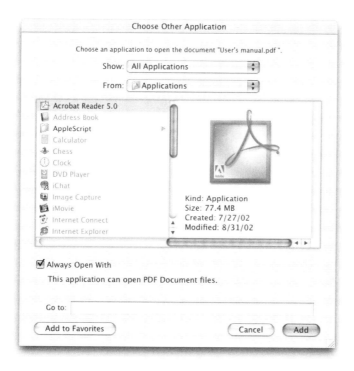

Figure 7.2
Select your own application to open a specific type of document.

4. Select the application.

5. Check the Always Open With button to always use this application when opening documents with this file extension. Otherwise, only the document selected in
   the Get Info window will be assigned to this alternative application.

6. Click the Add button.

Many documents do not have filenames that end with a particular, or even proper, file
extension. So, how does Mac OS X handle this situation? Documents or the Mac OS
Extended file system can store tiny pieces of information about a document that help
categorize it into one of a small number of file types. The information created and
stored by this process is what allows Mac OS X to choose the default application to
open the document. If a document has no file extension, you can use the Change All ,
command and Mac OS X will change the default application for all documents of this
type instead of with a particular *file extension*, as was the case in the examples above.

If you want to explore the nuts and bolts of Mac OS file types and creator codes,
check out these great utilities:

■ *A Better Finder Creators & Types* from publicspace.net (**www.publicspace.net**)

■ *File Buddy 7* from Sky Tag Software (**www.skytag.com**)

■ *Super Get Info* from Bare Bones Software (**www.barebones.com**)

It is possible to get yourself into trouble by misassigning creator types and codes, so be
sure to read the documentation for these applications thoroughly before using them to
make changes on your computer.

Mac OS X Applications

Mac OS X version 10.2 includes dozens of applications and utilities that are either
installed by default or are located on the CDs that accompany the of installation CDs.
In fact, there are too many applications provided to give you a full explanation of each
but I'll provide you with a quick rundown to give you a better idea of the breadth of
applications. Most of the following applications will be discussed in more detail in
other chapters, including the Script Editor (Chapter 11), Disk Utility (Chapter 13),
and Internet Connect (Chapter 14). By default, the Mac OS creates two folders that
house the standard set of applications, Applications and Utilities. Each user can store
applications in his or her home folder as well, but these applications will not be
available to other users on the computer unless the applications are stored in a folder
with the proper access privileges. (See Chapter 16 for more information on sharing
folders.) Table 7.1 provides an alphabetical list of applications that are available as

with the default installation of Mac OS X Version 10.2 or are available on the installation CDs or downloadable from the Apple.com Web site.

Table 7.1   Applications Available in the Applications and Utilities Folder.

Application	Description
Acrobat Reader 5.0	Application from Adobe (**www.adobe.com**) for viewing PDF documents.
Address Book	Application for storing contact information or accessing information from Lightweight Directory Access Protocol (LDAP) servers. The Address Book has a customizable toolbar as well as user-defined categories that allow you to group entries. You can also attach an image to an entry, and access entries from other applications that are Address Book -aware..
Airport Admin Utility	Utility for manually administering AirPort base stations for creating wireless networks.
Airport Setup Assistant	Utility for configuring AirPort base stations with step-by-step assistance.
Apple System Profiler	Utility for gathering important information about your computer for use with technical support issues.
AppleScript Studio	A programming environment for creating robust AppleScript applications.
Applet Launcher	A utility for launching Java applets without the assistance of a Java-enabled Web browser such as Internet Explorer.
Art Directors Toolkit	Application from Code Line Communications (**www.code-line.com**) for graphics and multimedia developers, included with several models of computers from Apple.
Asia Text Extras	A folder of several utilities for managing Asian fonts.
Audio MIDI Setup	A utility for configuring audio interfaces on your computer, including MIDI devices such as keyboards.
Bluetooth File Exchange	A utility for exchanging files with Bluetooth-enabled devices such as cell phones and Personal Digital Assistants.
Calculator	A utility for basic mathematical calculations.
Chess	An application for playing chess against the computer or watching the computer play against itself.
Clock	An application for displaying a digital or analog clock on the Desktop or in the Dock. When viewed on the Desktop, you can set the level of transparency from opaque to very transparent.
ColorSync Utility	A utility for verifying and repairing color profiles used to match color output to screens and printers.

(continued)

Table 7.1   Applications Available in the Applications and Utilities Folder (continued).

Application	Description
Console	A utility for displaying highly technical information about both the Mac OS and Mac OS X–compatible applications; used by developers to troubleshoot (debug) programming errors. This utility can also be used to examine OS X log files, which is useful for verifying the security of your machine, and log application crashes, which is helpful when troubleshooting applications.
CPU Monitor	A utility for displaying processor activity in one of several graphical formats. On dual-processor machines, the CPU Monitor uses two indicators to show the processor usage levels of each processor.
DigitalColor Meter	A utility for sampling the color of any pixel that is visible on your display.
Directory Access	A utility for configuring directory services using Apple's NetInfo services as well as the Lightweight Directory Access Protocol (LDAP). This utility, known as Directory Setup in previous versions of Mac OS X, should be used by system administrators only.
Disk Copy	A utility for mounting and creating disk images. A disk image is a format in which software developers commonly package their applications for downloading over the Web.
Disk Utility	A utility for formatting, partitioning, verifying, and repairing hard disks.
Display Calibrator	A utility for creating ColorSync color profiles and calibrating monitors, used to more accurately match colors for use in documents on other computers and printers.
DVD Player	Application for playing DVD discs, such as commercial movies or home-made iDVD movies.
Earthlink	30-day trial version for Internet access through Earthlink (**www.earthlink.net**).
FAXsft X	Utility from Smith Micro (**www.smithmicro.com**) for faxing documents using your computer's modem.
FileMaker Pro	Trial version of the popular database application from FileMaker, Inc. (**www.filemaker.com**)
gcc Compiler	Utility for programmers to compile source code into executable applications.
Grab	A utility for capturing screenshots of your display.
GraphicConverter	Application from Lemke Software (www.lemkesoft.com) for creating, opening, converting, and manipulating graphic images in over 160 formats.
iChat	Application for instant messaging using a .Mac or AOL Instant Messenger account.

7

(continued)

Table 7.1 Applications Available in the Applications and Utilities Folder (continued).

Application	Description
iDVD	Application for creating movies in DVD format.
Image Capture	An application for downloading images from digital cameras and camcorders.
iMovie	Application for creating digital movies for hard disk or CD storage.
Installer	A utility used by software developers to assist in the installation of software on your computer.
Interface Builder	Application for creating user interface elements for application developers.
Internet Connect	An application for connecting to the Internet using a dial-up connection to an Internet Service Provider (ISP). Internet Connect replaces the Remote Access Control Panel in Mac OS 9.x.
Internet Explorer	Application from Microsoft (**www.microsoft.com**) for browsing the Web.
iPhoto	Application for publishing, organizing, and sharing digital photo graphs from disc or a digital camera to your .Mac account's Web site or to print.
iTunes	Application for playing MP3 music from disc, CD, or the Internet, as well as converting CDs to MP3 format and burning CDs from MP3.
Java Plugin Settings	Utility for configuring various Java settings.
Java Web Start	Utility for easy access to Java applets.
Key Caps	A utility for previewing fonts and using the keyboard.
Keychain Access	A utility for managing passwords to frequently used network resources such as file servers and email accounts.
Mail	An application for sending and receiving email, with integrated support for the Address Book.
NetInfo Manager	A utility for system administrators to manage network resources and root-level access to computers.
Network Utility	A utility for probing and scanning networks, used by system administrators.
ODBC Administrator	Utility for configuring access to Open Database Connector-compliant databases.
OmniGraffle	Application from The Omni Group (**www.omnigroup.com**) for diagramming and flowcharting.
OmniOutliner	Application from The Omni Group (**www.omnigroup.com**) for creating and organizing outlines.

(continued)

Table 7.1   Applications Available in the Applications and Utilities Folder.

Application	Description
PixelNhance	Application from Caffeine software (**www.caffeineSoft.com**) for enhancing digital images.
Preview	An application for viewing documents in the Portable Document Format (PDF), as well as many popular image file formats. Preview replaces the functionality of the QuickTime PictureViewer application in Mac OS 9.x.
Print Center	A utility for adding, modifying, and deleting printers. Print Center replaces the Chooser found in earlier versions of the Mac OS.
ProcessViewer	A utility for system administrators and computer geeks to monitor various Mac OS components and applications. The ProcessViewer displays technical information about processor usage and memory consumption for assistance in diagnostics and troubleshooting.
QuickTime Player	An application used to view and listen to multimedia broadcasts over the Internet as well as from local sources such as CD-ROMs. The standard version of QuickTime 6 is installed by Mac OS X, but you can upgrade to the professional version to add multiple features.
Script Editor	An application for creating and editing AppleScripts.
Script Runner	An application for managing AppleScripts.
SetupAssistant	A utility used by the Mac OS to initially configure your computer's various settings, such as time, date, and user account.
Sherlock	An application for searching the Internet.
Snapz Pro X	Utility from Ambrosia Software (**www.ambrosiasw.com**)for capturing screenshots.
Stickies	An application for writing notes and brief messages.
StuffIt Expander	Utility from Aladdin Systems for decompressing and/or decrypting files.
System Preferences	An application for configuring various aspects of your computer, such as display, sound, date, and time settings.
Terminal	A utility for displaying information, launching applications, and executing commands using a command-line interface instead of clicking on icons and using a mouse. Access to Darwin, the foundation layer of the Mac OS X operating system, is accomplished via Terminal.
TextEdit	An application for creating and editing text documents in Rich Text Format (RTF), plain ASCII, or Unicode.

7

Mac OS X includes hundred of applications for the Unix environment that are executed using the Terminal application, and all but a few are way beyond the scope of this book. For more information on Terminal and executing applications from the "command line," see Appendix C, "Learning Unix Shell Commands."

Launching Applications

Double-click, double-click, double-click—that's how most Macintosh users launch their applications. Two clicks to open the drive or volume, two to open the application folder, and two on the application icon to launch the software.

This method can quickly grow wearisome when it means clicking through many volumes and folder layers to reach the icon you want. A wide range of application launching utilities—including DragThing and Drop Drawers—have emerged as alternatives. With these utilities, you can launch applications by selecting their names from a list or group of buttons instead of searching through folders for icons. Two- and four-button mice, now available for the Mac OS, allow you to assign button combinations to certain processes so that a function normally commanded by a double-click can be activated by a single click. And as we've seen, Mac OS X will allow you to place a shortcut to an application in the Dock—and all Dock items are opened with a single click.

The different ways you can open documents or launch applications with Mac OS X include:

■ *Double-click an application icon or its alias*—You can double-click an application icon or its alias to launch that application.

■ *Double-click a document icon or its alias*—Double-clicking a document will launch the application that Mac OS X associates with that particular document or all documents that have the same file extension or file type.

■ *Double-click a stationery document or its alias*—A stationery document is a template that automatically creates an untitled new document when opened. (I'll provide more information on stationery documents in the section entitled "Working with Stationery Documents," later in this chapter.)

■ *Drag a document icon onto an application icon*—This method of launching will work only when the document is dragged onto the icon of the application that created it, or an application that is capable of opening the same document type. You'll know whether an application is going to launch—its icon will be highlighted when the document icon is dragged onto it, as shown in Figure 7.3.

Adobe Photoshop 7.0

Figure 7.3
Application icons are highlighted when you drag compatible documents over them.

7

- *Add applications or documents to the Login Items System Preferences pane*—To automatically launch an application or open a document and its application at startup, add the application or document to the Startup Items pane of the System Preferences. The application or document will be launched automatically at startup or when you log in to the computer. The Login Items pane is configured for each user of your computer, so if someone else logs in, your selections will not be opened or launched.

- *Choose an application or document from the Dock*—After you place an application or document in the Dock by dragging the icon to the Dock, the application or document can then be accessed by single-clicking it in the Dock.

- *Choose an application or document from a Finder Window toolbar*—Place frequently accessed documents and applications in the customizable Finder window toolbar for single-click access.

- *Choose an application or document name from the Recent Documents or Recent Applications submenus of the Apple\Recent Items menu*—Mac OS X tracks the most recently used documents and applications in the Recent Items menu, a feature that can be configured via the General pane of the System Preferences.

- *Choose an item from the Favorites menu*—Choose an item (file, folder, volume, or application) from the Favorites folder within the Open or Save dialog boxes, or from a Finder window.

The best way to launch applications is the method that works best for you. You'll probably find that a combination approach is the most efficient. Keep the following launching tips in mind:

- *Dock individual icons*—Add individual applications and documents you use most frequently to the Dock. Documents or programs that you use daily will probably stay in the Recent Applications or Recent Documents submenu, so you may not need to put them in the Dock. In any case, consider your work patterns and personal preferences when organizing your Dock.

- *Dock folders of aliases*—Assemble groups of application aliases into folders. Then, place these folders in the Dock. You can choose the item from the Dock via the pop-up list that appears when you click on the docked item, as shown in Figure 7.4.

- *Double-click icons*—When you're browsing in Finder windows to locate specific files, use the tried-and-true double-click method to launch applications, aliases, documents, or stationery icons.

- *Drag icons onto applications*—If you store documents and applications or their aliases in the same folder, or if you place application icons or aliases on the Desktop, dragging icons onto applications (or drop launching) may prove useful. Drop launching is especially useful for opening multiple documents by dragging a group of documents onto an application.

- *Favorites folder*—You can add applications, as well as URLs, documents, and volumes, to the Favorites folder and then access these items in Open and Save dialog boxes or via Finder windows. Most Carbon or Cocoa applications will contain the Add to Favorites button when opening or saving documents.

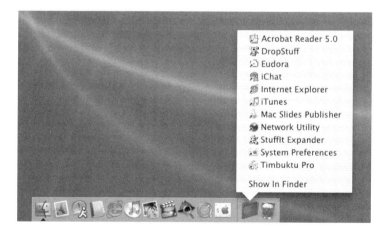

Figure 7.4
Applications are easier to launch when they've been organized into folders in the Dock.

Working with Stationery Documents

The stationery document is another useful feature supported by Mac OS X. A stationery document allows you to quickly turn an existing document into a template. Templates, as you may know, give you a head start in creating new documents by standardizing the basic features of a document.

For example, the documents in your word processing program probably fall into a handful of specific formats—letters, reports, memos, and so on. Rather than start each new document from scratch, you can use the stationery document for a letter, which provides the date, salutation, paragraph formatting, correct margins, and other basic formatting. Template support has been available in numerous Macintosh applications for some time. By including the stationery documents feature in Mac OS X, Apple makes templates available in every software package you use to create documents.

Creating Stationery Documents

Stationery documents are supported in different ways, depending on the application. Some applications, such as Microsoft Internet Explorer, have no need for stationery documents because they are not used to create Web pages. However, for those that do, a stationery document is usually created in three steps:

1. Find an existing example of a document that you create on a regular basis, or start from scratch and make a new document upon which future documents will be based.

2. Modify the example document to make it a good generic representation for future documents, such as form letters or email messages you send on a regular basis. Be sure to remove references to specific names and dates.

3. Save the document As Stationery if possible; if not, select the Stationery option in the file's Get Info window, which is demonstrated below.

For example, create a stationery document for letters by opening an existing letter and modifying it to your liking. Before you save the stationery document, it's a good idea to edit the text in all placeholders, such as greetings, salutations, and dates, with nonsensical data (*greeking*). This ensures that no placeholder elements are accidentally used in finished documents. For example, instead of inserting an actual date and salutation in a stationery document, use 00/00/0000 and Dear Recipient instead.

After you edit the document, use the Save As command to save the template document to disk. Assign a file name that is easily identified in Finder windows and dialog boxes. For example, I like to add the letters *stny* to the end of each stationery file name. Although the

Mac doesn't require the use of naming conventions, distinct file names are easier to spot when you're scanning large collections of files for a particular document. For example, Figure 7.5 shows the folder created by Eudora for the specific purpose of storing stationery documents, which I use to quickly create pre-formatted messages.

Some applications will not allow you to save documents as stationery, however. To try making a stationery document with this kind of application, follow these steps:

1. Create a document and save it.

2. Go to the Finder and select the document's icon.

3. Choose the Get Info command from the File menu.

4. Check the Stationery Pad checkbox in the lower-left corner of the General section of the Get Info window to make this document a stationery document, as shown in Figure 7.6. The icon inside the Get Info window may change to show that the document is now a stationery document; however, not all applications support custom icons for stationery documents.

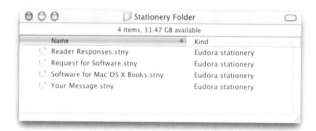

Figure 7.5
A folder containing Eudora stationery documents for easily composing email messages using four different templates.

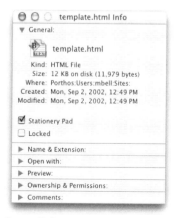

Figure 7.6
Use the Get Info command to manually configure a document as a stationery one.

5. After you close the Get Info window, the conversion is complete.

Some applications, such as BBEdit and Apple Works, give you the option of saving your documents in stationery documents format. Saving this way may be simpler than digging up the Get Info window and manually creating a stationery document.

Using Stationery Documents

After you've created a stationery document, you can open it with the appropriate application, just as you would any other document. When you launch a stationery document, one of two things will happen. Some applications will open a new document with the name of *Untitled*, *Untitled2*, *Untitled3*, and so on, and won't create a new document on your hard drive until you choose Save from the File menu. Other applications first copy the document in the Finder and then open it, creating documents entitled *Untitled copy.doc*, *Untitled copy 1.doc*, *Untitled copy 2.doc*, and so on. Either way, you can create, edit, and save the documents you wish using a stationery document as a template. In such a case the application won't save or it will delete the unwanted documents.

Stationery Tips

Because using stationery documents may be a new concept to you, let's review several tips that may be helpful:

- *Stationery document aliases*— The alias of a stationery document accesses the stationery document normally, whether the alias was created before or after the Stationery Documents option was set.

- *Stationery documents folder*—For easy access to stationery documents, create a stationery or templates folder to house the aliases of all your stationery documents. If you use the aliases frequently, you may want to also put an alias of this folder in the Dock. Some applications are created with stationery documents in mind and offer folders or menu options for storing and accessing stationery documents, including Eudora and the Microsoft Office X suite of applications.

- *Opening stationery documents with the Open command*—When you open stationery documents using the Open command, be sure to assign a new file name using the Save As command. This prevents you from accidentally overwriting your stationery document.

- *Editing stationery documents*—Unchecking the Stationery Pad option in the General section of the Get Info window will turn any stationery document back into a "normal" document. You can then edit the document—think of this as modifying your master template. After editing and saving this document, reselect the Stationery Pad option in the Get Info window to turn the file back into a stationery document.

Working with Multiple Applications

With Mac OS X, you can work with multiple applications simultaneously in many of the same ways you have become accustomed to in Mac OS 9.x and earlier, including switching between foreground and background applications, hiding applications, and using keyboard shortcuts to cycle between applications. In addition to the Dock, Mac OS X utilizes two additional concepts for dealing with application windows that need further attention—layered windows and attached sheets.

Managing Layered Windows

Layered windows, a feature introduced by Mac OS X version 1.0, make it possible for multiple windows of the same application to be interleaved, or layered, with the windows of other applications. In previous versions of the Mac OS, all windows belonging to an application were visible at the same time. For example, if you had two Web browser windows open at the same time, one was the front-most window and the other window would have been right behind it, obscuring all the other windows of your applications. In Mac OS X, however, you can minimize some of the application's windows in the Dock while leaving others visible and interleaved among the windows of other applications.

Layering windows makes keeping track of information more challenging at times, and I often rely on the assistance of third-party applications such as DragThing or Menu Strip to force all the windows of an application to stay together. This concept is a bit tricky to explain without an example, so I'll give it a try using Figure 7.7. In this example, I have three applications open at the same time: Internet Explorer (two windows), BBEdit (one window), and GraphicConverter (one window). Although Internet Explorer is the front-most application, you can see in this figure that one BBEdit and one GraphicConverter window are visible between the two Internet Explorer windows. In addition to the two visible Internet Explorer windows, two more Internet Explorer windows, which I've minimized, are in the Dock. You can't see them—or the Dock, for that matter—because I've hidden the Dock. As you can see, layered windows can be a bit tricky to manage.

Mac OS X applications can help you manage the chaotic effects of layered windowing in at least two ways. However, not all applications support these features, and some applications will not allow their windows to be layered. For the applications that do allow layered windows, here are a couple of solutions to the chaos:

- *Choose Window|Bring All To Front*—Groups all windows of the selected application in front of windows belonging to other applications.

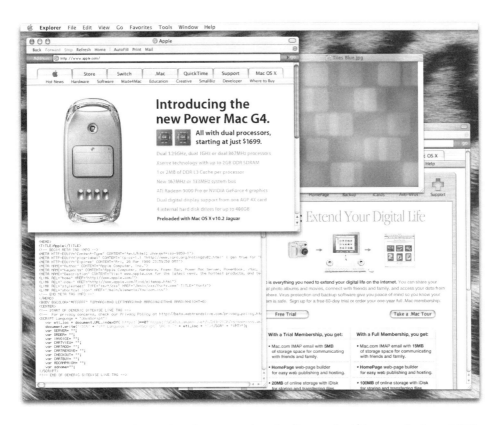

Figure 7.7 An example of layered application windows for (front to back) Internet Explorer, BBEdit, GraphicConverter, and Internet Explorer again.

- *File|Hide Others*—Hides all other applications except the active application (the keyboard shortcut for this feature is Command+Option+H).

If you want to disable the layering of windows, try DragThing from TLA Systems (**www.tla-systems.co.uk**) and select the Bring All Windows to the Front When Switching option in the Switching tab of the Preferences. MenuStrip from MacPowerUser.com (**www.MacPowerUser.com**) provides another type of workaround with its HideToggle feature, which hides all other application windows except those of the front-most application.

Attached Sheets

Most Cocoa applications for Mac OS X utilize Open and Save dialog boxes that are actually attached to a particular window, instead of existing as standalone modal dialog boxes that make it impossible to continue working with the computer until the dialog box had been dismissed. This was the state of things in Mac OS 9.x and earlier, and it was a multitasker's nightmare. Attached sheets, sometimes referred to as just *sheets*, allow you to continue working with other documents and applications while the attached sheets are expanded, as illustrated in Figure 7.8.

Some software developers prefer not to implement attached sheets, whereas others may not have enabled this feature in an effort to quickly Carbonize an existing Classic application for use in Mac OS X. Applications that do not employ attached sheets will probably use the secondary form of Open and Save dialog boxes found in Mac OS X that are displayed as floating windows that may or may not allow you to continue working with the application until the window is dismissed.

Wrapping Up

In many ways, Mac OS X applications are unique compared to applications written for earlier versions of the Mac OS. In this chapter, you've learned about several aspects of Mac OS X applications, including:

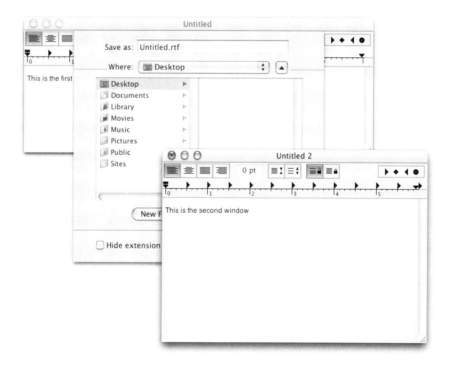

Figure 7.8
An example of how an attached sheet (Untitled.rtf) can be obscured by other windows without disrupting the application.

- Compatibility of Mac OS X applications

- How to select the default application for opening documents with a particular filename extension or a particular document type

- Applications and utilities installed by, or included with, Mac OS X

- Application launching methods and strategies

- Creating and using stationery documents

- Layered windows and attached sheets

In the next chapter, I'll look at a few special issues concerning memory allocation in Mac OS 9.x and how to best work with your Classic applications from within Mac OS X.

7

Part  II

Applications

Working with Classic Applications

Until your favorite programs are available as Carbon or Cocoa applications for Mac OS X, you have two options for using them—running them in Classic mode or booting directly into Mac OS 9.x. When your computer is booted directly into Mac OS 9.x, Classic applications operate no differently from any other applications. You can launch them, use them, and quit them just as you have been doing before upgrading to Mac OS X. But when you're running these applications in Classic mode *within* Mac OS X, they require a little more attention to make sure they run smoothly. With Mac OS X, the amount of physical RAM installed in your Mac is no longer the total measure of memory or the only important memory issue, although it is still important. I have not met a computer with too much RAM!

This chapter looks at the differences between running Classic applications in Classic mode in Mac OS X and when booting directly into Mac OS 9.x. You'll also learn about memory issues, the About This Mac and About This Computer windows, ways you can configure applications to use memory most efficiently in Mac OS 9.x, and a few tools to help you better monitor your Mac's memory usage. Refer to Chapter 4, "Configuring the Classic Environment," for the many options associated with configuring and managing Classic from within Mac OS X.

Memory vs. Storage

Before I jump into how the Mac OS uses memory and the implications for running Classic applications, let's clarify the difference between random access memory (RAM)—frequently termed plain old "memory"—and storage (disk space). This distinction may be clear to experienced Mac users; however, if you're not sure of the difference, please read this section carefully.

In the simplest terms, memory consists of the chips in your computer where data is *temporarily* stored while it is being used by the Mac OS and your applications. This is in contrast to your hard disk, CDs, and other storage devices where data is stored for prolonged periods of time, or when your Macintosh is not using it.

Although both RAM and storage hold data including applications, system software, and data files, the similarities end there. Because RAM stores data electronically on a set of chips, these chips "forget" their contents as soon as the flow of electricity is interrupted (when the Mac is turned off or restarted). Storage devices such as hard drives and CDs, which operate magnetically or by optical technology, are not affected by changes in the power supply. They "forget" information only if it's intentionally erased or becomes corrupted during the writing process. In other words, information stored in RAM is short-lived, whereas information saved to a storage device can hang around for years.

Furthermore, the Mac OS can only work with data stored in RAM; it cannot directly manipulate data on any storage device. Therefore, in order to open an application or file, the data must be read from storage and written into memory. Once the data is in memory, the application can be executed or the file can be modified. To make these changes permanent, however, the information in RAM must be written back out to the storage device—this is what happens when you choose the Save command in an application and convert the data from RAM into storage on a disk.

How the Mac OS Uses Memory

One of the realities Mac users must face is the finite amount of memory available in their computers. Today's software seems to have an insatiable appetite for RAM, and technologies—including multitasking, 24-bit color and sound, and particularly the Web and Web browsers—intensify the problem. The quest for additional memory has always been subject to certain roadblocks: the OS's limited ability to address the need for large amounts of memory, the computer's physical limitations, and the cost of memory chips.

One of the most significant differences between Mac OS X and Mac OS 9.x is in the use of virtual memory, which is the use of hard disk space to emulate RAM. Before Mac OS X, users could enable, adjust, or disable virtual memory by way of the Memory Control Panel. In Mac OS X, however, virtual memory is "always on" and cannot be adjusted. Mac OS 9.x is programmed so that virtual memory is turned off when in Classic mode, and the total amount of memory installed on your computer is always available to your Classic applications. Since Mac OS X uses virtual memory, it can always use hard disk storage space to emulate additional RAM as needed.

On the other hand, when booting directly into Mac OS 9.x, virtual memory issues are important because the OS must be configured to optimize the performance of your

Classic applications. In previous versions of the Mac OS, the appearance of the Memory Control Panel differed according to which model of Macintosh (or Macintosh clone) you owned. With Mac OS 9.x, however, each model has the same three sections in the Memory Control Panel:

■ Disk Cache

■ Virtual Memory

■ RAM Disk

The settings for these three options are not important when using Mac OS 9.x in Classic mode because the Memory Control Panel is disabled, but they are very significant when you boot directly into Mac OS 9.x (see Figure 8.1 for an example). Let's explore these options for a moment.

Disk Cache

The disk cache is a small section of RAM set aside to store a copy of the most recent data read from disk (or volume) into memory. Most operating systems, including Mac OS 9.x and Mac OS X, have a disk cache. Most hard drives also have a RAM chip installed within the drive enclosure that serves as a disk cache; the proximity of the RAM chip decreases the time it takes to access frequently used information. A good hard drive will have at least 2MB of disk cache—some have as much as 4MB. In addition to caching documents and applications, portions of the Mac OS (such as

8

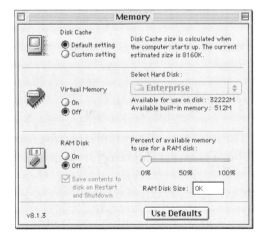

Figure 8.1
The Memory Control Panel has several important configuration options, which are accessible only when booting directly into Mac OS 9.x.

menus) are also cached so that they are displayed immediately whenever one is pulled down. Because menu performance varies with CPU speed, this difference will be most apparent to users with slower machines and video cards with small amounts of RAM.

The disk cache portion of the Memory Control Panel was reworked in Mac OS 8.5 to provide two types of cache settings, both of which exist in Mac OS 9.x as well:

■ Default setting

■ Custom setting

Mac OS X uses roughly 32KB of cache for every 1MB of RAM installed in your computer. If you have 128MB of RAM, for example, then the default cache setting would be 4,096KB. Clicking the Default button will allow the OS to select the setting that is best for most users according to this formula. Don't reduce the cache below its default setting unless you have significant memory limitations and need to free up more RAM—the small amount of memory the cache consumes delivers a big return by significantly improving your computer's performance.

Conversely, it's usually a bad idea to increase the size of your cache too much. Settings greater than 32KB per 1MB of installed RAM should be used only in very specific situations where a large cache allocation can aid performance; your Classic application's documentation should advise you on how to handle this. For example, Adobe's Type Manager can use large cache allocations when it's rendering several fonts for a document. Some software, such as graphics applications, use their own internal disk caching scheme, rather than relying on the Mac OS's cache for performance enhancement.

To use a custom cache setting (i.e., one that is smaller or larger than the default) after booting into Mac OS 9.x, follow these steps:

1. Open the Memory Control Panel and click the Custom button to reveal an information/warning dialog box, and then select the Custom button.

2. Increase or decrease the cache size. The minimum size is 128K, and the maximum size allowed by Mac OS 9.x is 32,736K. Figure 8.2 shows a custom disk cache set to almost 16MB.

The perfect disk cache size is a matter of great debate even among the most technically knowledgeable Mac users. Variables such as your Mac hardware and software configurations and the types of applications you use significantly influence your optimal setting. Trial and error is really the only way to find what works best for you.

TIP: The Disk Cache option is always on in Mac OS 9.x; you may adjust its size downward or upward, but you cannot turn it off.

Figure 8.2
Custom disk cache settings in Mac OS 9.x.

Virtual Memory

As mentioned earlier, virtual memory is actually a hardware trick. It uses space on your hard drive to "fool" the Mac OS into thinking that the available amount of physical memory is greater than it really is. Using virtual memory, a Mac with only 128MB of physical RAM can operate similarly to one that has 256MB or more. In fact, virtual memory can provide your Mac with almost 1GB (990MB, to be precise) of memory when booted directly into Mac OS 9.x. Because virtual memory substitutes hard disk space for RAM, and hard drive space is generally much less expensive than actual RAM, virtual memory offers an obvious financial benefit. However, Macs with 1GB of RAM cannot utilize virtual memory under Mac OS 9.x.

Using virtual memory has two major drawbacks. First, performance is slower than with real RAM. The mechanical actions required of your hard drive are much slower than the electronic speed of RAM chips, which have no moving parts. Second, virtual memory appropriates hard disk space normally available for other activities. If you have a fast drive (7,200 to 10,000 RPM), you'll probably notice less of a difference in overall speed while using virtual memory than if your machine has a slower drive. Drives with an onboard hard drive disk cache (RAM installed on the hard drive itself, discussed earlier in this section) can greatly improve virtual memory performance.

Enabling Virtual Memory

To enable virtual memory, go to the Virtual Memory section of the Memory Control Panel after booting into Mac OS 9.x and follow these steps:

1. Select the On button, at which time the Select Hard Disk option becomes available. From the pop-up menu, choose the hard disk volume on which the virtual memory file will be created and stored. If you have only one hard drive, the menu will offer only one option.

2. Indicate the total amount of memory you want to have after the computer has
    been restarted.

The amount of available space on the selected hard disk is displayed below the hard disk
pop-up menu; it will indicate the amount of space available. The amount of free space
available partially determines the amount of virtual memory that can be configured. The
second determining factor is the maximum amount of memory Mac OS 9.x will allow,
which is 990MB. Based on the total amount of memory available, a virtual memory file
will be created and placed on the selected disk.. In other words, if your Mac has 128MB
of physical RAM, and you want to reach 512MB by using an additional 384MB of
virtual memory, a 512MB virtual memory storage file must be created on the selected
volume. Here's another example: You have 128B of RAM, and you want to turn virtual
memory on but use as little disk space as possible for this purpose. In this case, you
would add 1MB of additional memory for a total of 129MB, thereby creating an
invisible 129MB storage file called VM Storage on the selected volume.

Below the Available For Use On Disk option is the Available Built-in Memory field,
which tells you how much physical RAM is installed and recognized by the Mac OS.
If you increase the amount of virtual memory to be used, a field labeled After Restart
will appear. The After Restart option indicates the amount of memory specified,
including actual RAM and virtual memory. Click on the arrows to modify this
specification. If the After Restart option is not visible, click one of the arrows until it
appears. Figure 8.3 illustrates the differences in the Virtual Memory section of the
Memory Control Panel before (top) and after (bottom) virtual memory has been
enabled under Mac OS 9.x.

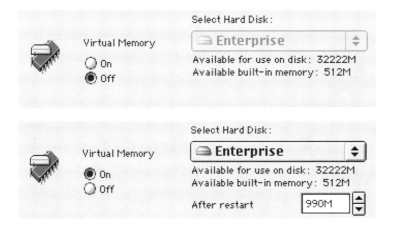

Figure 8.3
Configuring virtual memory under Mac OS 9.x.

Any changes made to the Virtual Memory option will not take effect until you restart your computer. To verify that virtual memory is on, choose the About This Computer command to display the current memory status. (You'll find more information on this command in the "About This Computer/About This Mac" section, later in this chapter.)

TIP: It's possible to have more RAM installed than is recognized by your computer. The RAM that is not recognized is either installed improperly or is not the right type of chip for your particular model of Macintosh. If your computer will not boot after updating the firmware, the firmware update process could have disabled your RAM chip(s). Consult your computer's documentation for the correct RAM specifications, and contact Apple via telephone or email for a local Apple-authorized repair center for expert technical assistance.

Virtual Memory Performance in Mac OS 9.x

Virtual memory works by moving information between a disk-based swap file and the RAM inside the computer. Even when virtual memory is being used, the Mac OS communicates only with the real RAM. This movement of data between hard disk and RAM, technically known as *paging*, causes the Mac to perform at a slower speed than it does when using actual RAM only.

The amount of paging slowdown depends on how much actual RAM is available and how virtual memory is being used. The more available RAM, the less paging interference. The type of activity you're performing also affects paging—working on multi-megabyte data files and frequent switching between open applications usually requires more paging and therefore decreases performance. Virtual memory problems manifest themselves as poor performance in animation, video, and sound. Games and multimedia content that require manipulation of large amounts of data are the first to suffer. Frequent hard disk activity associated with virtual memory is a prime energy drain for PowerBooks and iBooks because of the electricity required to keep the disk drive spinning.

A good rule of thumb in determining your own RAM/virtual memory mix is that you should have enough actual RAM to cover your normal memory needs and enough supplemental virtual memory to handle occasional, large requirements. If you find that approximately 128MB of RAM lets you work comfortably in the three or four open applications you use regularly, but you occasionally need another 128MB to open additional applications or work with large data files, then 128MB of real RAM and a combined total of 256MB of RAM and virtual memory would probably be adequate. However, if you don't need an additional 128MB of virtual memory on top of your 128MB of physical memory, use just one additional megabyte of virtual memory instead. This will help speed up things a bit and, as with using any amount of virtual memory, your applications won't ask for as much RAM.

Why is this, you ask? The presence of virtual memory allows only the PowerPC-native code necessary for launch to be read into memory when the application is opened. The remaining code used by an application is loaded only when needed. This allows for a quicker launch; however, when you actually use the program, it may be slower to operate than if you weren't using virtual memory because not all the code was loaded in the beginning. This trade-off is an inevitable part of using virtual memory: applications launch faster, but any speed gained in the beginning may be lost as you continue to use the application. This is only true for PowerPC-native applications, however. Applications written for the older Motorola 68K family of processors do not behave in this way.

Similar to the disk cache debate, the appropriate ratio of real to virtual memory has long been the subject of speculation. Ultimately, the question will become irrelevant as older versions of the Mac OS fade out of existence because Mac OS X uses persistent virtual memory—it cannot be turned off. One benefit of this approach is that you will never get an "out of memory" error message like in previous versions of the Mac OS. However, the answer for Classic Mac OS users is to use as much virtual memory as is practical and efficacious. Physical RAM is fairly cheap these days (less than $1/megabyte for most models of Macintosh computers), and you must have at least 128MB to run Mac OS X. Bear in mind that most entry-level Macs ship with 128MB now—and some ship with 512MB of RAM. My personal preference is to have no less than 256MB of RAM and not to use virtual memory at all when booting into Mac OS 9.x. With this amount of physical RAM, the disk cache defaults to the maximum of 8,160K, which is adequate for all my needs.

Virtual Memory Advantages in Mac OS 9.x

I've discussed how PowerPC-native applications may be partially loaded into memory at startup if virtual memory is turned on. But what about the impact virtual memory has on the memory requirements of an application? Figure 8.4 gives you an idea of how this works. On the left side of the figure is the memory section of the Get Info window for Microsoft Word with virtual memory turned on, which is the default setting for Mac OS 9.x. Observe that the Note section points out the application may require 7,532K of additional memory to run if virtual memory is turned off. The right side of the figure shows the same dialog box once the computer has been restarted with virtual memory turned off. The reverse is now true: the Note section says the application may require 7,532KB less memory if virtual memory is turned on.

Another benefit to using virtual memory (in addition to a quicker launch time for applications) is that you'll have more room to launch additional applications. The amount of virtual memory your computer is using doesn't matter, however; the

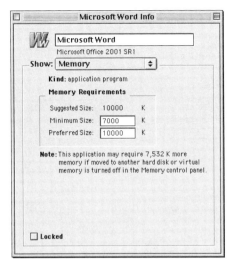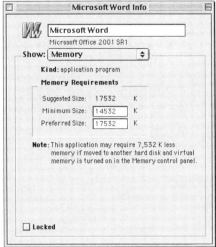

Figure 8.4

A comparison of memory requirements with virtual memory turned on (left) and off (right) for the same application.

changes in an application's memory requirements will never vary in proportion to how much virtual memory is in use. It will only change if it is in use at all.

Disabling Virtual Memory

Virtual memory can be disabled by clicking the Off button in the Virtual Memory area of the Memory Control Panel and restarting your computer directly into Mac OS 9.x. After disabling virtual memory, the invisible virtual memory storage file (VM Storage) is deleted from your hard drive automatically, and the space it occupied becomes available to the Mac OS and your files. The Mac OS is said to launch applications more slowly with virtual memory disabled, whereas the overall speed of an application is said to increase.

Memory Control Panel Tips

Here are a few tips to keep in mind when configuring the Mac OS to use both physical and virtual memory in Mac OS 9.x:

■ *Use at least the minimum recommended disk cache as defined by the Default setting.* Because the disk cache speeds up operation, you should set it to at least 32KB for every megabyte of RAM installed in your Mac (that means 4,096KB for 128MB of RAM).

■ *Install enough physical RAM in your Macintosh.* Physical RAM chips should provide enough memory to cover your normal daily memory needs—at least 128MB, and in many cases for multimedia developers, up to 512MB. Although virtual memory can provide inexpensive additional memory, 80 percent of your memory needs should be covered by real RAM. The relatively small amount of money saved does not justify the performance drawbacks of relying too heavily on virtual memory.

■ *Extend your available memory with virtual memory.* Once you've installed enough RAM to satisfy your everyday needs, use the virtual memory when special situations (such as working with large color images, animation, or more than the usual number of simultaneously open programs) demand extra memory.

■ *Some applications, especially multimedia games, movies, and audio programs, just don't like virtual memory.* If these types of programs don't behave properly, check with their instructions for information about possible virtual memory incompatibilities.

TIP: Turn off virtual memory when you experience performance problems. Some programs, such as games and graphics programs, execute considerable data input/output. Virtual memory can degrade performance, and rapid paging can lead to system crashes.

RAM Disk

A RAM disk is a chunk of RAM set aside to emulate a hard disk. When running in Classic mode within Mac OS X, the RAM disk feature is not available; when you boot directly into Mac OS 9.x, however, you can set aside a certain amount of memory to use as a RAM disk, which functions just like a hard disk in many respects. You can add, delete, edit, and save files on a RAM disk. The chief advantage of using a RAM disk is speed. Unlike a hard drive, a RAM disk has no moving parts, which makes working with large files on a RAM disk significantly faster. The chief drawback, however, is that the amount of RAM set aside as a RAM disk is not available to the rest of the Mac OS or your applications.

To create a RAM disk, open the Memory Control Panel; select the On button in the RAM Disk section, and select the amount of RAM to set aside as a RAM disk. When you reboot the computer into Mac OS 9.x, the RAM disk will appear on the Desktop. You can read and write data to the RAM disk, as well as delete files. To remove the RAM disk, select the Off button in the Memory Control Panel and reboot.

Controlling Memory for Classic Applications

After you have determined how much memory you need and made it available to Mac OS 9.x (by installing RAM and by using virtual memory), you'll want to manage that memory wisely and use it economically. Managing your Mac's memory ensures that each application has enough RAM to operate properly and that enough total memory is available to open as many different applications as necessary. This is possible for

Classic applications under Mac OS 9.x because they are allocated memory on an application-by-application basis that is determined by preferences set by the software programmer and the user. Carbon and Cocoa applications do not allow such changes because Mac OS X handles all aspects of memory management, and the result is that you'll never get memory error messages in Mac OS X.

The Classic environment provides two excellent tools for memory management—the About This Computer command and the Get Info window. In this section, we'll look at both of these tools in conjunction with their Mac OS X counterparts.

About This Computer/About This Mac

Starting with Mac OS 8, the familiar About This Macintosh command was changed to About This Computer, and the dialog box associated with it was improved. The About This Computer command provides information about the Mac you're using, including the system software version, installed and available memory, and the amount of memory used by each open application. Figure 8.5 shows an example of the About This Computer window in Mac OS 9.x with multiple applications open.

The upper section of the window shown in Figure 8.5 gives the version of the operating system that is currently in use as well as the following data regarding the available memory:

■ *Built-in Memory—512MB*. Displays the amount of physical RAM installed in this particular Macintosh, exclusive of virtual memory.

Figure 8.5
The result of executing the About This Computer command when booting directly into Mac OS 9.x.

■ *Virtual Memory—Off.* States the total memory available in your Macintosh, including installed RAM plus available virtual memory, if enabled. The name of the hard disk storing the virtual memory file and the amount of hard drive space being used are listed to the right of the Virtual Memory field. Virtual memory and hard drive designations are set via the Memory Control Panel, described earlier in this chapter.

■ *Largest Unused Block—380.4MB.* Calculates the largest contiguous section of memory currently not being used by open software applications. This number is important because it determines both the number and size of additional software applications you can open. In some cases, the largest unused block will not equal the amount of total memory available minus the size of all open applications. This is the result of memory fragmentation—the formation of gaps between sections of memory that are used and those that are available. To defragment your memory and create larger unused blocks, quit all open applications and then relaunch them. As they're relaunched, applications will use available memory sequentially, leaving the largest possible unused block.

Each application requires a particular amount of memory to open successfully. The amount of memory is documented and can be controlled in the Memory section of the Get Info window, as described later in this chapter. When a program is launched, it cannot be opened if its memory requirement is larger than the largest unused block. Therefore, it's important to know approximately how much memory an application needs.

TIP: If you get an out-of-memory alert box when plenty of memory should be available, you could have a fragmented memory situation. This occurs when you launch and quit programs repeatedly. You can avoid this problem by leaving open programs you'll most likely use again instead of quitting them as soon as you've finished. If you have a fragmented memory problem, first try quitting programs in the reverse order in which they were launched. If that doesn't do the trick, you'll have to restart to flush your computer's memory.

The lower portion of the About This Computer window displays information about the memory used by the Mac OS as well as information about each open application:

■ *Application icon and name*—Each open application, preceded by a small version of its icon, is listed in alphabetical order.

■ *Amount of memory used*—In most cases, only a portion of an application's total allocated memory is used immediately upon opening it. Usually, some of the memory is used by the application itself, some is used to hold open document files, and some is left over for use by the software's commands and features. Only the memory currently being used appears as the filled-in percentage of the memory allocation bar.

■ *Amount of memory allocated*—The total amount of memory allocated to the program opened is displayed in a bar graph. The graph also shows the allocated amount in relation to amounts used by other open applications. The entire bar represents total allocated memory. The filled portion of the bar represents the portion of allocated memory currently in use.

 TIP: Double-clicking on the name of an application in the About This Computer window will bring that application to the foreground.

Holding down the Option key when choosing the About This Computer command changes the command and brings up About The Finder. Choosing About The Finder brings up a copyright screen that first appeared in Finder 1.0 in 1984 (if you wait a bit, you'll see a message about the Finder scrolling across the screen).

■ The About This Computer command changed its name to About This Mac in Mac OS X, an example of which is shown in Figure 8.6. Since memory usage is not as big an issue in Mac OS X, About This Mac does not offer you as many details regarding memory allocation. However, it still provides information about the operating system version, the amount of physical RAM installed, and the type of and number of processors.

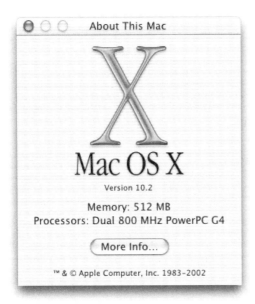

Figure 8.6
The About This Mac command in Mac OS X.

Clicking on the version number in the About This Mac window will reveal the *build* number, which refers to a specific compilation of the entire operating system; clicking a second time will reveal your computer's serial number. Information about running applications can be obtained by other utilities such as the Process Viewer, which is discussed in Chapter 13, "Troubleshooting Mac OS X."

Mac OS X Version 10.2 introduces a new feature in the Classic System Preferences pane that (when booting directly into Mac OS 9.x) provides some of the same memory allocation information found in the About This Mac command. To see information about what Classic applications are running in the Classic environment, following these steps:

1. Start Classic and launch a few applications.

2. Open the System Preferences and select the Classic pane.

3. Choose the Memory/Versions tab.

4. Check the Show Background Processes checkbox to see which background processes are running, in addition to any open Classic applications.

For example, Figure 8.7 shows a machine booted directly into Mac OS 9.x. The Memory/Versions tab shows the machine running the same six applications shown in Figure 8.5. Both the About This Computer and the Memory/Versions tab list the version of Mac OS 9.x, running applications, the amount of RAM in use, and the maximum amount of RAM available to each application. The Memory/Versions tab also displays the version and build number of the Classic environment, including Classic Support, and Classic Enabler. The version and build number of the Classic Environment aren't pieces of information you need to know on a daily basis, but they might come in handy if you ever have to troubleshoot Mac OS X and the Classic environment.

Using Get Info for Classic Applications

All files, folders, and applications have information properties that can be viewed using a simple command called Get Info, which is discussed in detail in previous chapters. The Memory section of the Get Info window allows you to take charge of your Classic applications' memory consumption (additional information about which is provided in the About This Computer window discussed earlier in this chapter). To minimize problems related to memory shortages, or to better allocate your available RAM to the different applications you want to open simultaneously, you can adjust the amount of memory each program uses with the Get Info command.

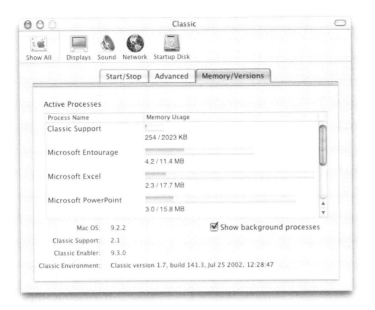

Figure 8.7
The Memory/Versions tab (found in the Classic System Preferences pane) and the About This Mac command in Mac OS 9.x. provide similar information.

Memory Section of Get Info/Show Info

The Memory section of the Get Info window provides greater control over how your applications use memory. The Get Info window's options in Mac OS 9.x (as in System 7.6 and later) also eliminate the need to change settings for different memory situations; they allow you to set options that determine how much memory will be used depending on the amount of memory available at launch time. Now, however, these memory requirements are set in the Memory section of the Get Info window, which is activated by following these steps:

1. From the Finder, navigate to an application icon such as Microsoft Word and select the icon by clicking on it once. Keep in mind that your application must not be currently running if you want to change its memory requirements.

2. Press Command+I or choose File|Get Info.

3. Select the Memory section of the Get Info window, examples of which are shown in Figure 8.4 (in Mac OS 9.x) and Figure 8.8 (Mac OS X).

In Mac OS 9.x, the Memory section of the Get Info command includes four main parts—Suggested Size, Minimum Size, Preferred Size, and Note, which are explained as follows.

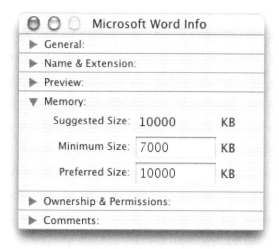

Figure 8.8
Use the Get Info command to configure memory settings for Classic applications from within Mac OS X, as well as Mac OS 9.x.

■ *Suggested Size*—Lists the amount of RAM needed to properly run the application. This option cannot be modified; it serves as a reminder of the memory requirements as defined by the application developer.

■ *Minimum Size*—Designates the smallest amount of RAM required for the application to run properly. Although you can change this option by entering a new value, your application may become unstable as a result.

■ *Preferred Size*—Specifies the actual amount of RAM that the application will request when it's launched. You can change the amount of memory that will be allocated by entering a new value in this option and then closing the Get Info window.

■ *Note*—Informs you how much additional memory may be required if virtual memory is turned on.

In Mac OS X, the Get Info command lacks the Notes section. This may seem a little confusing because you can actually view and change memory allocation for Classic applications from within Mac OS X. The impact of the changes is the same, however. When an application is launched, the program requests the amount of memory specified in the Preferred Size option. If this amount is available in a contiguous, unused memory block, the memory is allocated and the program is opened. You can check the size of the largest available block in the About This Computer/About This Mac window, as described earlier.

If the amount of memory requested by the Preferred Size option is not available, but more memory is available than the Minimum Size option, the application will launch using all available memory. If the amount of RAM specified in the Minimum Size option is unavailable, and you have booted directly into Mac OS 9.x, a dialog box will appear offering advice on quitting other applications. This should free enough memory to complete the launch. If you are running the application while in Classic mode from within Mac OS X, the application simply will not launch and you are unlikely to receive an error message.

Setting Memory Options for Classic Applications

Although you can modify a Classic application's memory parameters from either Mac OS 9.x or Mac OS X, you can only determine how active applications are using memory in Mac OS 9.x.. Optimally, 15 to 25 percent of the space in the memory allocation bar (displayed next to an application name in the About This Computer window) should remain open (or unused) while the application is running. (As explained earlier, the bar illustrates total allocated RAM in gray and the portion of memory actually being used in blue. These are the default colors.)

Some applications do not use all of their allocated memory at all times—usage may vary as commands and features are executed. Other applications, however, automatically grab all of their allocated memory. Therefore, if you want to determine the actual, average, and maximum amount of memory used, keep the About This Computer window open in the lower half of the screen so that you can monitor the applications' memory usage,, as illustrated in Figure 8.8.

Given that 15 to 25 percent unused space is the goal, watching the amount of actual memory used will tell you if the current memory allocation is too low, too high, or about right. You may discover that you need to increase a program's memory allocation, or you may be able to decrease it. Either of these modifications is made via the Size options.

Increasing memory allocation provides additional memory that, in many cases, can improve application performance, allow larger and more complete document files to be opened, and reduce or eliminate the possibility of memory-related crashes. For example, I often open numerous large HTML documents in BBEdit, and I often change its memory requirements to accomplish a specific set of tasks. These benefits are hardly surprising when you consider how an application uses its allocated memory: It must control and manage its own code, in addition to data from any open document files and all data manipulations performed by its commands and features. And it must do all this with an allocated memory that's less than the total size of the application program and its data files, let alone what it needs to manipulate its data. As a result, software must constantly shift parts of its own code and data from open documents

8

back and forth between disk-storage memory and real memory. Providing additional memory minimizes this activity and allows the program to concentrate on operating efficiently.

For most programs, increasing the Current Size or Preferred Size option by 20 to 25 percent is optimal. If you experience frequent "out of memory" errors in any software application, however, continue increasing the amount of memory until these errors are eliminated. Increasing the amount of memory will sometimes fix problems associated with launching applications, even if a specific error is not presented by the Mac OS.

Decreasing memory allocation allows you to successfully launch applications using less memory and run more programs simultaneously. Although this practice is generally not recommended, in many cases software can operate successfully using less RAM than suggested by the developer.

The true minimum, although it will rarely be more than 20 percent smaller than the suggested size, cannot easily be determined. Don't be afraid to try, however—just be sure to test the application in this configuration before working on important data, and save frequently once you begin working. Start by reducing the Current or Minimum Size option by just 5 to 10 percent; if you find that the About This Computer window shows large amounts of unused space, you may be able to reduce the allocation even more.

With the low price of RAM and the availability of virtual memory, the need for most Mac users to reduce memory allocation should become less common. Even if you have only 128MB of RAM installed, using virtual memory is preferable to reducing the Current or Minimum Size options when you boot directly into Mac OS 9.x. You're less likely to experience crashes or loss of data with virtual memory than with a reduced Current Size. (See the discussion of virtual memory earlier in this chapter.) Of course, the best long-range solution is to add enough RAM to your Mac so you won't have to depend on either virtual memory or Memory Requirements reductions.

Configuring Dual-OS Applications

Some application programmers choose to create a Carbon-based application that can be opened in Mac OS 9.x as well as Mac OS X, a so-called "dual-OS application". The advantage of this approach is that they only have to maintain one distribution of the application, and the advantage for you is that you only have to install, configure, and maintain one version of the application. As more developers and Apple itself move toward Mac OS X and away from Mac OS 9.x, you're less likely to see this type of application as time goes by. If you do have a dual-OS application, you can force it to open in the Classic environment by following these steps:

1. Select the application in the Finder.

2. Choose Get Info from the File menu or press Command+I.

3. Look in the General section and check the option entitled Open in the Classic Environment, which you can see in Figure 8.9.

If you don't choose the Open In the Classic Environment, the application will automatically open in Mac OS X.

Figure 8.9
Dual-OS applications such as this one can be opened in either Mac OS X or using Mac OS 9.x and the Classic environment.

Managing Classic Applications

Mac users have had multitasking—the ability to run multiple applications at the same time—for many years. Mac OS 9.x features cooperative multitasking, a type of multitasking that requires individual application programmers to request and yield the computer's processor cooperatively. Without cooperative multitasking, for example, program A is allowed to hog the processor, forcing programs B, C, and D to suffer until program A quits. Cooperative multitasking has become the standard for desktop operating systems such as Mac OS 9.x, Windows 98, and Windows ME.

In Mac OS X, Classic applications still multitask cooperatively within the Classic environment. Mac OS X has taken the process one step further, and utilizes the most sophisticated (and stable) type of multitasking — preemptive multitasking. What this means is that the Classic environment is treated as just another application, the only difference being that the Classic environment is actually running Mac OS 9.x, the Classic Finder, and one or more Classic applications. So, if you are working with Classic application within the Classic environment or if you're booting directly into Mac OS 9.x, there are several things to keep in mind above and beyond the memory requirements of Classic applications.

Multitasking in Mac OS 9.x

Believe it or not, there are some computer users who only run one application at a time. I think of these people as "multitasking-challenged", and their productivity is not as high as it could be. Multitasking refers to the ability to run your word processor, Web browser, and graphics package at the same time and switch among them freely without jeopardizing performance. In fact, one application can continue processing information while you're using another application. Cooperative multitasking is actually an old feature; Macintosh users have been familiar with it for over ten years. Cooperative multitasking allows you to:

■ Run multiple applications simultaneously

■ Switch among open applications as necessary

■ Leave one program working while you switch to another

■ Copy multiple items concurrently and return to the Finder (or another application) while the items are being copied in the background

The most obvious benefit of multitasking is that it enables you to use two or more applications together to complete a single project. To prepare a mail merge, for example, you can export data from your database manager, prepare the merge lists, and execute the merge into a word processing document. In most cases, the raw data exported from your database will require some cleaning up before it's ready to be merged, and often you'll encounter a minor formatting problem that requires you to repeat the whole process. By using multitasking, however, you avoid the delay and frustration of quitting the word processor, returning to the database, quitting the database, and returning to the word processor.

Suppose you need to read reports and view database or spreadsheet data while preparing presentation graphics, update graphic illustrations in a drawing package before importing them into a page layout, or use an optical character recognition package to scan articles for storage in a database. In situations like these, switching from one application to another and using the Cut, Copy, and Paste commands makes it possible to transfer information between applications that otherwise could not share data.

Another benefit of multitasking is one that yields the greatest productivity gains: multitasking, as well as cooperative multitasking, supports background processing. This means that an open application can continue to process data even when you switch away from that application to work in another. Tasks that tie up your computer, such as printing, downloading files from the Internet, making large spreadsheet calculations, and generating database reports are likely to benefit from background processing. Examples of background processing and techniques for taking advantage of it are discussed later in this chapter in the section entitled "Background Processing."

Multitasking and Classic Applications in Mac OS X

Mac OS X utilizes preemptive multitasking and is one of the first desktop operating systems to provide such an advanced feature. With preemptive multitasking, the kernel portion of Mac OS X plays the role of traffic cop, allowing each program to have as much processor time as needed without denying other programs or the operating system itself the processor time they require. "Balance and share" is the motto of preemptive multitasking. As far as access to multiple applications is concerned, multitasking in Mac OS X is no different from multitasking in Mac OS 9.x. However, Mac OS X does a much better job of sharing processor time among all applications and dividing up requests for processor time among multiple processors, if available. If you run Mac OS 9.x applications in Classic mode instead of booting directly into Mac OS 9.x, you get the best of both worlds.

In Mac OS X, each Carbon or Cocoa application launched has a main thread (or process); other subthreads may be spawned by the application. These threads are managed preemptively because they are written for Mac OS X, but they may also be managed cooperatively as well. On the other hand, when Mac OS 9.x is running in Classic mode within Mac OS X, it too is considered a thread, and Classic applications are processes within this thread. If you boot directly into Mac OS 9.x, all applications are managed cooperatively instead of preemptively and therefore are still vulnerable to processor hogging and cascading failure that can bring down the whole system. But because Classic is running as an application environment within Mac OS X, if an application were to crash, the worst-case scenario is that only the main Classic thread will crash, and Mac OS X and all your Carbon and Cocoa applications will survive unscathed. To summarize, although Classic applications still rely on cooperative multitasking even when in Classic mode, the entire computer will not crash if a Classic application misbehaves.

Managing Multiple Applications

When you first start using multiple applications simultaneously, the sight of several windows open at the same time may be a little disconcerting. As you learn to arrange and manipulate these windows and enjoy the benefits of multiple open applications, you'll soon find yourself wondering how you ever got along using just one program at a time. The number of applications you can launch simultaneously is practically unlimited in Mac OS X, because virtual memory can provide hundreds of gigabytes of emulated RAM for your applications, but under Mac OS 9.x the number of applications is limited by the amount of memory available to your computer.

Foreground and Background Applications

Although more than one program can be open at once, only one program can be active at any one time. This is true for applications in Mac OS 9.x, Classic mode, and Mac OS X. The active program is known as the *foreground application*; other open but inactive applications are called *background applications*, even if you can see portions of their windows or if they're simultaneously processing tasks. For example, Figure 8.10 shows one Classic application (Microsoft Excel) and one Mac OS X application ((Microsoft Word) running at the same time, but only one can be the front-most application.

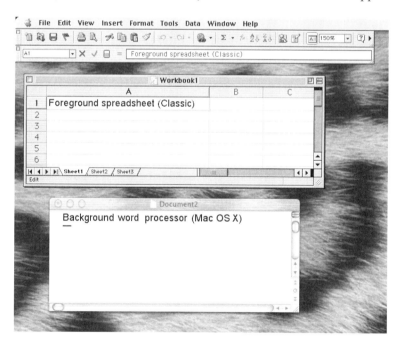

Figure 8.10

The concept of foreground and background applications applies to applications in Mac OS 9.x and Mac OS X, and only one application can be in the foreground at any time.

Under Mac OS X, you can identify the currently active program in several ways:

■ The menu bar displays the menu commands of the active program.

■ The title of the application is shown in the menu bar.

■ The icon is displayed with a small triangle in the Dock (although the Dock doesn't indicate which is the front-most application if more than one application is running).

■ The active program window overlaps other visible windows or elements.

■ The active program window's close, minimize, and zoom buttons are displayed in color (although you can change them all to shades of gray in the Appearance section of the General System Preferences pane), and the background applications are translucent and monochromatic.

Mac OS 9.x offers additional ways to identify foreground applications, including:

■ The active program's icon appears at the top of the Application menu.

■ The active program name is checked in the Application menu.

■ The first item in the Apple menu says About Program A instead of About This Mac.

■ The Application Switcher will highlight the most active application.

Switching Among Classic and Carbon/Cocoa Applications

Because only one program can be in the foreground, it's important to be able to switch quickly and easily from one program to another. Switching between applications is commonly referred to as "sending to the back" and "bringing to the front." You can switch between open applications in at least five ways:

■ *Use the Dock*—Located in the bottom, left, or right of the screen, the Dock lists the icons of all applications currently running with a small triangle underneath the icon, as well as bookmarked files, folders, and applications. Select the icon of the application you want to switch to, and its menu bar and windows will be brought to the front.

■ *Use the keyboard shortcut*—Press Command+Tab to cycle through the open applications one at a time, whether in Mac OS 9.x or Mac OS X. Press Shift+Command+Tab to cycle in reverse. Each application icon in the Dock will be highlighted as it is selected, and if the Dock is minimized, the dock will become visible as you press Command+Tab or Shift+Command+Tab.

■ *Click any visible window*—Clicking any visible element of the application brings the application to the front. For example, while working in your word processor, if you can still see the icons on the Desktop, clicking one of them will bring the

Finder to the front, making it the current application. You can then return to the word processor by clicking in its window.

■ *Use the Recent Items/Applications menu*—Select an application by name from the Recent Items submenu of the Apple menu (Mac OS X) or the Recent Applications submenu (Mac OS 9.x).

See Chapter 3, "Customizing Mac OS X," for utilities from third-party developers that list foreground and background applications that enhance many other facets of the user experience.

Finally, you can launch multiple Classic, Carbon, and Cocoa applications and easily switch among them by clicking on the appropriate window. However, since application windows in Mac OS 9.x are grouped together by application instead of layered, as they are in Mac OS X, when you click a Classic application that has multiple windows, all the windows will be placed in front of the windows of all other applications. The windows belonging to Mac OS X applications will remain layered amongst one another.

Background Processing

You can bring any application to the foreground, thereby sending any other applications to the background, at any time—except when dialog boxes that are not Navigational Services-savvy are open in Mac OS 9.x. Classic Mac OS applications that have the new Navigational Services (i.e., Open and Save) dialog boxes open can be moved safely into the background even if one of those dialog boxes is active. In fact, you can have multiple Navigational Services windows open for different Classic applications, even if they are intermingled with Carbon and Cocoa applications windows. However, you should be aware that many Classic applications do not implement Navigational Services; when an Open or Save dialog box for such an application is open, you may not be able to continue working with any of your open Classic applications until you have dismissed the window. These types of windows are often referred to as modal windows. The sheets feature, described in the previous chapter, eliminates modal dialog boxes, enabling you to continue working even if an Open or Save window is open for a Carbon or Cocoa application.

You can send most applications to the background while they're processing data, and they will continue to calculate or process. Background processing brings to light an entirely new dimension of using multiple open applications simultaneously.

If you could use multiple open applications only sequentially (one after the other), the increase in productivity would be limited to the time you saved by avoiding repeated opening and quitting of applications. Background processing, however, lets you print a newsletter, calculate a spreadsheet, and download files from the Internet at the same time. This capacity is the ultimate in computer productivity, but keep this in mind: the efficiency of background processing depends on your Mac's power and the number and requirements of the background tasks being performed. Classic applications will suffer the most because they share system resources cooperatively; Carbon and Cocoa applications will benefit from preemptive multitasking.

 TIP: Using virtual memory can emphasize slowness when switching between applications while in Mac OS 9.x.

The Mac OS will notify you if your attention is needed for a task running in the background, or when a task has been completed.

Hiding Applications

Running several applications concurrently can result in an onscreen clutter of windows. To alleviate this problem, the Mac OS lets you "hide" open application windows and the Desktop, thus removing them from the screen without changing their status or the background work they're doing. Hiding applications instead of quitting them is an important point to remember because of the way the Mac OS allocates memory. If you've booted directly into Mac OS 9.x and decide to quit an application out of the sequence in which it was launched, you can potentially cause problems down the road. The memory used by that application may not be reclaimed until you reboot the computer, and this delay could lead to memory fragmentation and pollution of the System Heap. So, when working with multiple applications, leave them open until you are either ready to quit all the applications or reboot. In fact, I recommend adding aliases for each of the frequently used applications to your Startup Items folder so that they will launch automatically. Quit these applications only when you are ready to shut down the computer; in the meantime, just hide them. Your system, whether in Mac OS 9.x or Classic mode, will be more stable, and you won't have to relaunch the applications.

You can hide an application at the time you leave it to switch to another application, or while it's running in the background. Mac OS 9.x and the Classic application environment feature commands that can also be used to hide and show applications. Mac OS 9.x provides three commands in the Application menu (at the upper-right corner of your screen) for these purposes, and Mac OS X places the same commands in the application menu for each program (between the Apple and File menus in the upper left corner of your screen). The commands are Hide *Current Application* (*Current Application* being the name of the current foreground application), Hide Others, and Show All:

■ *Hide Current Application*—Removes all windows of the current application from the screen. The next-most recently used application is brought to the front when this command is selected. The icon of a hidden application is dimmed in the Application or Application Switcher menu (in Mac OS 9.x) to signify that it has been hidden. Unfortunately, the Dock cannot distinguish between hidden and unhidden applications. To unhide the application, select its name from the Application menu, Application Switcher menu, or Dock, or choose the Show All command.

■ *Hide Others*—Removes all windows from the screen except those of the currently active application. This is useful when onscreen clutter is bothersome, or if you're accidentally clicking the windows of background applications and bringing them forward. After the Hide Others command has been used, the icons of all open applications—except those of the foreground application—are dimmed in the Application menu as a visual reminder that these applications are hidden.

■ *Show All*—Makes all current applications visible. When you choose the Show All command, the current foreground application remains in the foreground and the windows of hidden background applications become visible.

Figure 8.11 illustrates the similarities between the hide and show options for Mac OS X (left) and Mac OS 9.x while in Classic mode (right).

While an application is hidden, it continues to operate in exactly the same way it would if it were running as a visible background application. If an application normally performs tasks in the background, hiding the application will not interfere with its ability to perform these tasks. In fact, because of the effort saved by not having to upgrade the screen display, the background operation of some tasks is faster when their parent application is hidden.

Figure 8.11
Note the similarities in the Hide and Show commands between Mac OS X (left) and Mac OS 9.x (right).

To hide the current foreground application completely when you send it to the background, hold down the Option key while clicking on the Desktop or bringing another application forward (either by choosing its name from the Application menu, Application Switcher menu, the Dock, or by clicking the mouse in one of its windows). You can retrieve applications hidden in this manner by using the Show All command or by selecting their dimmed icons from the Application menu or Application Switcher menu, as well as the Dock.

Hiding the Desktop in Mac OS 9.x

A potential problem lies in wait for novices who are working with multiple applications at the same time. If you inadvertently click the Desktop, you switch into the Finder and out of your current program. Suddenly you've lost your place, and the menus have changed. Because the old Performa series was built for the home market (and for novices), Apple included in System 7.0.1P and 7.1P a feature called Finder hiding that prevented users from switching to the Finder by inadvertently clicking on the desktop.

 TIP: Some users simply close all of an application's windows and mistakenly believe that the application has therefore been quit. Some applications will automatically quit after the last window has been closed, but most will continue to run until "Quit" has been selected from the File menu.

Voluntary Desktop hiding first appeared in System 7.5 and continues to be a useful option in Mac OS 9.x. A modified form of this feature can be replicated in Mac OS X as well. With Desktop hiding, when you switch into an application other than the Finder, the Desktop disappears (not unlike the way things worked before System 7—the difference is that this hiding is by choice). You can't click in the background and switch out of your application. You turn on Desktop hiding by disabling the Show Desktop When In Background checkbox in the General Controls Control Panel. Therefore, if you're working in an application and you can't see your hard disk, Trash, or file and folder icons, blame Desktop hiding. Figure 8.12 shows an example of iTunes with the Desktop hidden.

 TIP: For the ultimate way to focus on a single application, hide the Desktop and all other applications to reduce the number of visual distractions on your screen.

Hiding the Desktop in Mac OS X

Mac OS X allows you to mimic some of the Hide Desktop feature of Mac OS 9.x through the Finder Preferences instead of System Preferences. To hide disk icons for file servers, hard drives, CD-ROMs, and other removable media:

Figure 8.12
Hiding the Desktop in Mac OS 9.x can help users focus on using applications.

1. Switch to the Finder and select Finder Preferences from the Application menu.

2. Uncheck all the options under the Show These Items on the Desktop (Hard Disks, Removable Media (such As CDs), and Connected Servers).

3. Close the Finder Preferences.

4. Manually remove the other items on the Desktop such as aliases, files, folders, applications, and Internet downloads.

To hide the Desktop in Mac OS X more like you can in Mac OS 9.x, try DeskShade Plus from MacRabbit.com (**www.macrabbit.com/deskshadesplus/**). For about $7, you can use DeskShade Plus to:

■ Hide everything on the Desktop.

■ Use a keyboard shortcut to toggle between showing and hiding the Desktop.

■ Require a password to unlock the Desktop.

■ Select a QuickTime movie instead of an image to use as a Desktop background.

■ Redirect items dropped onto the Desktop to a different folder on your hard drive.

You might not think of showing and hiding the Desktop as a useful feature, but if you download or store tons of files on the Desktop, you'll appreciate DeskShade Plus.

Classic Multitasking Tips

When you start using the Hide commands to reduce screen clutter when in Classic mode or when booting directly into Mac OS 9.x, you should be comfortable working with multiple open applications. The following tips can help:

- *Saving before switching or printing*—Before bringing another application to the foreground or printing a document, save your work in the application you're using in Classic mode; if Classic crashes, you won't lose your work.

- *Saving before printing*— I can't tell you how many users have been burned by sending a job to print before saving it only to see the computer freeze. So before you print a document you've been working on for a while, first save it to ensure it won't have to be recreated.

- *Resuming after crashing*—Some applications use scratch space or create temporary files, such as Microsoft Word, and when the application is restarted, will attempt to recover your document after a crash.

- *Shutting down or restarting*—Selecting the Shut Down or Restart commands from the Apple menu while multiple Classic, Carbon, or Cocoa applications are open will cause all open applications to quit (even if an application hasn't been properly programmed to accept the Quit command using Apple Events). If any Classic documents contain changes that haven't been saved, the parent application will be brought to the foreground and you'll be asked whether you want to save those changes before the Classic environment is terminated.

- *Maintaining efficiency for background applications*—Remember that because Classic applications rely on cooperative multithreading while in Classic mode, processor-hungry applications in the foreground will slow down other Classic applications considerably. Try hiding these applications when not in use.

Wrapping Up

Working with Classic applications is slightly different when booting directly into Mac OS 9.x than when in Classic mode under Mac OS X, especially in the area of memory management. The amount of memory available on your Macintosh determines, in large measure, what you can do with your computer. As we've seen in this chapter, Mac OS X introduces dramatic changes in memory management, although most of the old methods of managing memory are still alive and well thanks to the Classic environment. These improvements were designed to give you much more control over memory availability and how that memory is utilized. This chapter has covered many aspects of working with Classic applications which are important to note:

■ Virtual memory lets you "create" memory by using space on your hard drive as if it were RAM. In Mac OS 9.x it is optional; in Mac OS X it is always on.

■ The About This Computer and About This Mac windows provide useful information about how your Mac's memory is being allocated.

■ The Memory section of the Get Info window helps you control the amount of memory an application uses while in Mac OS 9.x or Classic mode.

■ You can launch as many different applications as your available memory permits.

■ Many applications can continue to process data while they're running in the background.

■ Hiding open applications reduces onscreen clutter without affecting the operation of the applications.

Because Classic is probably going to be around for several years while developers port their applications to Mac OS X, it's a good idea to have an adequate understanding of how Mac OS 9.x and Mac OS X interact. In the next chapter we'll explore Mac OS X multimedia capabilities.

Exploring Multimedia

The definition of multimedia varies from person to person and era to era. When QuickTime was first released by Apple (11 years ago), it helped introduce and popularize the concept of watching movies on your computer—the latest in multimedia technology at the time. Today, on the other hand, watching videos with a Web browser, converting CDs into MP3 format, and burning them on a CD-ROM constitute examples of multimedia. As times change, so does the relevance of multimedia. What will we think of as multimedia ten years from now?

Technically speaking, multimedia refers to the combination of sounds and images in digital format on a computer. In the past few years, the definition of multimedia has expanded to encompass QuickTime movies, Musical Instrument Digital Interface (MIDI), virtual reality, 3D rendering, and Moving Picture Experts Group Layer-3 (MPEG-3 or MP3). Mac OS X supports all of the multimedia capabilities of Mac OS 9.x, and I'll demonstrate how you can use Mac OS X to implement the following multimedia applications:

- QuickTime, for playing QuickTime, QuickTime VR, and streaming QuickTime movies

- Preview, for opening and exporting images

- Text-to-speech and speech-to-text

- iTunes, for listening to MP3s and burning custom CDs

- iMovie and iDVD, for creating professional-looking movies

- iPhoto, for importing, organizing, and sharing digital images

Together, these components give you a high-performance multimedia computer that can play movies, sounds, and MIDI files, and even speak back to you using a variety of voices. Captain Archer would be proud of our progress, don't you think?

QuickTime

For years, the Mac has led the way for personal computers in typography, graphics, sound, and high-resolution color. Version 6 of QuickTime, which ships with Mac OS X, continues this tradition, and takes video and audio capabilities to the next level. The multimedia framework of QuickTime converts moving images and sounds into basic types of Macintosh data. All kinds of applications—word processors, databases, presentation graphics packages, page-layout programs—can incorporate these moving images as easily as standard graphics.

QuickTime is now an essential component of the Mac OS, and is also an option for users of Windows 95, 98, ME, NT, 2000, and XP. QuickTime for Java enables any computer running Java to use QuickTime features, regardless of whether the computer is Mac or runs the Windows platform. The consumer version of QuickTime is available at no charge and is distributed in a number of different formats and channels:

■ QuickTime is included as part of Mac OS X.

■ QuickTime can be downloaded from Apple's QuickTime Web site (**www.apple.com/quicktime/**).

■ Many QuickTime-dependent applications include QuickTime on their distribution CDs.

Actually, QuickTime comes in two versions: QuickTime and QuickTime Pro. QuickTime is free and comes with Mac OS X. QuickTime Pro, on the other hand, costs around $30 and is enhanced with many additional features. These features allow you to::

■ Create new QuickTime movies from existing movies

■ Edit QuickTime movies, including individual tracks within a movie

■ Play or export more than 50 types of multimedia file formats

■ View almost all of the multimedia types on the Web with the QuickTime plug-in

■ Create slide shows

Although the standard version is fine if you are simply going to view movies over the Web, the Pro version gives you more access to the world of multimedia.

What's New in QuickTime 6

Many of QuickTime 6's new features are performance-related or enable additional file formats to be opened or saved. Depending on your computer's processor and video card capabilities, movies can be comfortably played from 240x180 pixels at 1fps (frames per second) to full-screen at 30fps. The QuickTime Player application replaces SimplePlayer, which shipped with earlier versions of QuickTime. In addition, the following features of QuickTime have undergone improvement or have been added in version 6:

- *Motion Picture Exports Group Level 4 (MPEG-4) support*—The latest digital movie authoring and viewing format.

- *Motion Picture Exports Group Level 2 (MPEG-2) playback capability*—Access broadcast-quality professional video with the purchase of the MPEG-2 Playback Component from Apple.

- *AAC (Advanced Audio Coding) support*—Audio CD quality encoding and "instant-on" playback.

- *QuickTime Broadcaster and Streaming Server*—Server software to broadcast live or pre-recorded QuickTime movies over the Internet.

These are only a small fraction of the total improvements and capabilities of QuickTime—I could easily write an entire book covering QuickTime's capabilities and features. Instead, let me describe some of the basic features of QuickTime that you're most likely to utilize.

9

QuickTime Basics

QuickTime has hundreds of features and numerous capabilities, but at its most basic level QuickTime enables you to perform the following three types of tasks:

- Play movies

- Navigate QuickTime VR panoramas

- Play audio

The basic QuickTime movie file format is called Movie. The file extension is .mov and the file type is MooV. Like other file formats, such as PICT, EPS, or TIFF, the Movie file format saves a certain kind of data—in this case, moving video, animation, or sound (or all of these)—in a way that can be viewed at a specified rate and quality.

By defining this file format at the system level, Apple makes it easy for application developers to support QuickTime. Developers are encouraged to create sophisticated special effects, clickable hotspots to other movies, or even Web pages. The major file import and export formats supported by QuickTime 6 are shown in Table 9.1.

Table 9.1   QuickTime 6 import/export file formats.

File Format	Import?	Export?	Application
3DMF	Yes	No	QuickTime
AIFF	Yes	Yes	QuickTime
AU	Yes	Yes	QuickTime
Audio CD Data	Yes	No	QuickTime
AVI	Yes	Yes	QuickTime
BMP	Yes	Yes	Preview
Cubic VR	Yes	Yes	QuickTime
DLS	Yes	No	QuickTime
DV	Yes	Yes	QuickTime
DV Stream	No	Yes	QuickTime
FlashPix	Yes	No	QuickTime
FLC	Yes	Yes	QuickTime
GIF	Yes	No	QuickTime
JPEG/JFIF	Yes	Yes	Preview
Karaoke	Yes	No	QuickTime
M3U (playlist for MP3)	Yes	No	QuickTime
MacPaint	Yes	Yes	Preview
Macromedia Flash 5	Yes	No	QuickTime
MIDI	Yes	Yes	QuickTime
MPEG-1	Yes	No	QuickTime
MPEG-2	Yes	No	QuickTime
MPEG-4	Yes	Yes	QuickTime
MP3	Yes	No	QuickTime
Photoshop	Yes	Yes	Preview
PICS	Yes	No	QuickTime
PICT	Yes	Yes	Preview
PLS	Yes	No	QuickTime

(continued)

Table 9.1   QuickTime 6 import/export file formats (continued).

File Format	Import?	Export?	Application
PNG	Yes	Yes	Preview
QuickTime Image File	Yes	Yes	Preview
QuickTime Movie	Yes	Yes	QuickTime
SF2	Yes	No	QuickTime
SGI	Yes	Yes	Preview
System 7 Sound	Yes	Yes	QuickTime
TARGA	Yes	Yes	Preview
Text	Yes	Yes	QuickTime
TIFF	Yes	Yes	Preview
TIFF Fax	Yes	No	Preview
Virtual Reality	Yes	No	QuickTime
WAV	Yes	Yes	QuickTime

Table Note: A QuickTime movie acts much as any other text or graphic element—you can select, cut, copy, or paste it either within or between QuickTime-savvy applications. When you select a movie, the QuickTime Player displays a set of controls that enables you to adjust the volume (if it has sound) and play the movie, as well as fast forward, reverse, or jump to specific scenes. For example, Figure 9.1 shows a QuickTime movie embedded in a Web page, with its controllers shown at the bottom of the movie. HTML authors can choose whether or not to show QuickTime movie controllers, depending on the design and purpose of the Web page.

The image you see in the QuickTime Player window when the movie itself isn't playing is called a *poster frame*. The poster frame is a selected image from the movie. Because it's often not the first frame of the movie, you'll see the image of the poster jump to another image when the movie begins.

A *preview* is a moving representation of the movie. Although not all movies have previews, most longer ones do. A preview gives you a quick look at the movie highlights. A series of standard file dialog boxes lets you choose whether to see the poster or a preview before you open a movie.

As in previous versions of the Mac OS, all these features are available whether you are viewing QuickTime files in a Web browser using the QuickTime plug-in (Figure 9.1) or through the QuickTime Player application, shown in Figure 9.2.

Configuring QuickTime

QuickTime's main configuration is accomplished through the QuickTime System Preferences pane, shown in Figure 9.3. However, because QuickTime is also an application and a Web browser plug-in, there are shortcuts in each to configure QuickTime's preferences. The Preferences screen contains the following options:

Figure 9.1
A QuickTime movie embedded in a Web page.

Figure 9.2
Use the QuickTime Player application to view QuickTime movies.

■ *Plug-In tab*—Configure the QuickTime Web browser plug-in to play movies automatically when loaded, save the movie and sound files in the browser's cache

Figure 9.3
Configure QuickTime using the QuickTime System Preferences pane.

file on the hard drive, and enable a kiosk mode, which is designed to prevent users from saving movies to disk. The MIME Settings button is used to set which types of data the QuickTime plug-in is allowed to handle from within the Web browser.

■ *Connection tab*—Allows you to tell QuickTime the speed of your network connection. QuickTime uses this information to help download the best file size for movies that have been optimized for various connection speeds. As a general rule, faster connections can handle larger files, and larger files are capable of better image and sound quality. You can also configure streaming transport options, which the QuickTime Player application uses to receive streamed data by way of one of several Internet protocols.

■ *Music tab*—Configures QuickTime to use a particular synthesizer to play MIDI and music data.

■ *Media Keys tab*—Provided by content creators to allow you to access private files.

■ *Update tab*—Allows you to update or install QuickTime and third-party software, as well as check for updates automatically. This feature works independently of the Software Update System Preferences feature.

■ *About QuickTime button*—Displays the version of QuickTime installed on your computer.

■ *Registration button*—The Registration section is where you go to register the Pro version of QuickTime.

In addition to these configuration options, you can also configure Web browsers to use the QuickTime plug-in for various types of multimedia. To configure the QuickTime plug-in, follow these steps:

1. Make sure the QuickTime plug-in named QuickTime Plugin.plugin is in your Internet Plug-ins folder, located in /Macintosh HD/Library/.

2. Review your browser's file helper configuration options to make sure QuickTime is properly defined as a file type. If not, open Explorer|Preferences|File Helpers and configure your settings for the helper application that handles items with the file extension ".mov" like those shown in Figure 9.4.

3. Next, visit the QuickTime home page at **www.apple.com/quicktime/** and load one of the movies listed in the Movie Trailers section. If it won't load, check your browser's preferences and make sure it's configured to view QuickTime files via the QuickTime plug-in.

4. If the QuickTime plug-in is properly recognized by the browser, the movie will begin streaming.

Figure 9.4
Your browser may need a bit of assistance in recognizing QuickTime files, although the presence of the QuickTime plug-in should be sufficient for most Web browsers.

5. To configure the QuickTime plug-in, click on the triangle in the lower-right corner of the controls to reveal a shortcut to several of the QuickTime System Preferences.

6. When you're ready to save a movie or sound file (if you have the Pro version), just Control+click on the movie or click on the triangle again and choose Save As QuickTime Movie, as in Figure 9.5, or Save As Source (to preserve the original file format).

QuickTime and Data Compression

One of QuickTime's most important technological breakthroughs is the real-time compression and decompression it provides to video, animation, and other graphics. QuickTime supports several built-in compression/decompression (codec) schemes and can easily support others as necessary. The built-in compression is a software-only solution, capable of achieving ratios as great as 25:1 without any visible loss in image quality. With specialized hardware, compression ratios as high as 160:1 are possible. Table 9.2 lists the audio and video codices supported by QuickTime 6.

Figure 9.5
Click the small triangle in the lower-right of a movie to save a QuickTime movie from within a Web browser (requires QuickTime Pro).

9

Table 9.2 Audio and video codices supported by QuickTime 6.

Codec	Type
24-bit integer	(audio)
32-bit floating point	(audio)
32-bit integer	(audio)
64-bit floating point	(audio)
AAC	(audio)
ALaw 2:1	(audio)
Animation	(video)
Apple BMP	(video)
Apple Video	(video)
Cinepak	(video)
Component video	(video)
DV and DVC Pro NTSC	(video)
DV PAL	(video)
DVC Pro PAL	(video)
Graphics	(video)
H.261	(video)
H.263	(video)
IMA 4:1	(audio)
JPEG 2000	(video)
MACE 3:1	(audio)
MACE 6:1	(audio)
Microsoft OLE	(video)
Microsoft Video 1	(video)
Motion JPEG A and B	(video)
MPEG-4	(video)
MS ADPCM	(audio)
Photo JPEG	(video)
Planar RGB	(video)
PNG	(video)
QDesign Music 2	(audio)
Qualcomm PureVoice	(audio)
Sorenson Video 2 and 3	(video)

(continued)

Table 9.2   Audio and video codices supported by QuickTime 6 (continued).

Codec	Type
TGA	(video)
TIFF	(video)
ULaw 2:1	(audio)

Compression is particularly important because of all the data needed to generate moving images and accompanying sounds. A good rule of thumb for estimating movie size is that every minute of motion consumes 10MB of disk space. As another example, a seven-minute, full-size, full-resolution movie could consume 200MB in its uncompressed form. Compressed, that same movie might need only 45MB. Of course, most movies are significantly shorter (lasting between 5 and 30 seconds), so files in the 200KB to 1MB range are common.

The actual size of a QuickTime movie depends on many things, including:

- *Frames per second*—Most QuickTime movies are recorded using 10, 12, 15, or 30 frames per second (fps). Without additional hardware for video acceleration, 15fps is the QuickTime standard; 30fps, which is the standard for commercial-quality video, is supported by QuickTime 6, although it will also support 29.97fps (which matches the frame rate of professional video equipment). The higher the frame rate, the larger the resulting movie file.

- *Image size*—Measured in horizontal and vertical pixels, the image size determines how large the movie will appear onscreen. The larger the image, the larger the file.

- *Resolution*—QuickTime supports all of the Mac's color bit depth—from 1 to 32 bit. The higher the resolution, the larger the file.

- *Audio sampling rate*—This rate can be thought of as the "resolution" of the sound. The Macintosh supports 8, 11, 22, or 44kHz audio sampling, although anything higher than 22kHz requires additional hardware. The higher the sampling rate, the larger the sound portion of the file.

- *Compression*—As mentioned earlier, QuickTime supports a number of compression schemes. You can select the degree of compression for each scheme. Increasing compression reduces movie size, but sometimes compromises playback quality. New compression schemes in QuickTime 6 should reduce or eliminate these kinds of problems.

- *Content*—Beyond the previously mentioned technical factors, the actual set of sounds and images contained in a movie is what will ultimately determine its size. This factor makes it difficult to estimate the size of a QuickTime movie based solely on its length or technical characteristics.

9

You can use QuickTime to watch movies (which may be included on CD-ROM disks, obtained from user groups or online services, or come embedded in documents you get from other Mac users), or you can create your own QuickTime movies. It's easy for almost anyone with a Mac to view a QuickTime movie, and with a digital camcorder and iMovie (discussed later in this chapter) just about anyone can create a movie and save it in QuickTime format. Users with DVD-R capabilities can import QuickTime movies and convert them into Digital Video (DV) format and burn them onto DVD using Apple's iDVD software.

Most available QuickTime movies are part of CD-ROM–based information discs that provide education or information on music, history, sports, news, entertainment, or computer-related topics. CD-ROM is the perfect medium for QuickTime because it has huge storage capabilities (650MB), can be inexpensively reproduced, and has access times sufficient to deliver good-quality playback. CD-ROM support for QuickTime has recently been enhanced by faster CD drives and performance improvements included in QuickTime 6.

Using the QuickTime Player

QuickTime Player 6 has been slightly revised for Mac OS X.2 to incorporate more intuitive (i.e., fewer) user controls. It also features QuickTime TV and an area in which you can store your favorite movies. And in addition to the QuickTime System Preferences, a few additional preferences that affect the behavior of the QuickTime Player are accessed via the QuickTime Player|Preferences|Player Preferences menu, including:

- *Open Movies In New Players*—Opens each movie in a new window.

- *Automatically Play Movies When Opened*—Begins playing a movie when opened in the QuickTime Player application.

- *Play Sound In Frontmost Player Only*—Mutes the sound of all movies and sound files except the one in the frontmost window.

- *Play Sound When Application Is In Background*—Continues to play the sound of a movie or sound file when the QuickTime Player is in the background.

- Hot Picks—Chooses whether to automatically play Apple's Hot Picks movie when you open a new QuickTime Player window.

To play a movie, double-click on any movie or sound file with a QuickTime icon, or launch the QuickTime Player application from the Dock. When playing a movie, you'll notice that the QuickTime Player controls look different than in previous versions of the application. Users complained that there were too many controls, and that they were not intuitive. Figure 9.6 illustrates the new controls in version 6 of QuickTime Player.

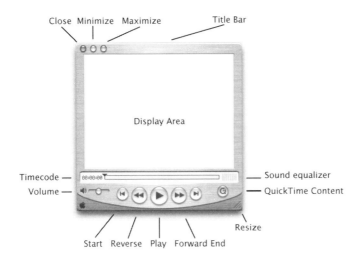

Figure 9.6
The QuickTime Player 6 application controls.

9

Right off the bat, experienced users will notice the Aquafied interface and that the TV button has been renamed Content. Otherwise, the controls are self-explanatory and include volume, start/stop, and directional buttons. The Content button replaces the QuickTime TV button and reveals a collection of QuickTime content channels, shown in Figure 9.7, which are links to QuickTime-enabled Web sites with streaming and downloadable content. For more QuickTime TV channels, see **www.apple.com/quicktime**.

Choosing Favorites|Show Favorites reveals a palette where you can store shortcuts to your favorite QuickTime files or online movies. To add an item located on your hard drive as a favorite, just drag and drop its Finder icon in the Favorites palette. To add any item currently opened in a QuickTime Player window, such as a movie trailer on a remote Web site, choose Command+D or choose Favorites|Add Movie as Favorite. To select a bookmarked favorite, select it from the Favorites palette or choose it from the Favorites menu.

QuickTime 6 Pro allows you to selectively play the audio or video track of a movie, as well as export it as a streaming QuickTime movie, among other formats. Of course, you can also create new movies and sound tracks if you have a digital input device for movies, such as a digital camera, or for sounds, such as a microphone or a CD-ROM.

Figure 9.7
Check out the QuickTime Content channels by clicking the round Content button in the QuickTime Player application.

QuickTime VR

QuickTime VR (QTVR) is a type of QuickTime movie that allows you to actually walk through a movie, spin around, look up and down, and manipulate objects from within the movie. QTVR takes digital images, stitches them together, and makes them appear three dimensional—pretty neat stuff. You can view QTVR movies from within a Web browser, thanks to the QuickTime plug-in, or using the QuickTime Player application.

QTVR movies come in two basic types: one in which you move around within the movie, and another in which an object, such as a book, car, or planet, is manipulated. The difference is whether you're moving, or manipulating an object. A really complex QTVR movie can contain both. Figure 9.8 shows a sample QTVR movie of Grand Central Station in New York City. Notice the controls are a little different when viewing a QTVR movie. Typically, you can zoom in, out, or restart a QTVR movie.

QTVR movies are not too difficult to make. For more information on what you need to create QTVR movies, see the QTVR home page at **www.apple.com/quicktime/qtvr/**.

Figure 9.8
Take a virtual tour using QuickTime VR.

Preview

Older versions of QuickTime included a small helper application called
PictureViewer whose sole purpose was to view images. However, Mac OS X
delegates the viewing and exporting of images to Preview, the application used
primarily for viewing Portable Document Format (PDF) documents. Preview
supports all the same formats as PictureViewer. QuickTime 6 allows Mac OS X to
play many types of movie and sound formats as well, including many of the image
formats supported by Preview, but Preview is the application of choice for opening
and converting images in the following formats:

- BMP (the native, bitmap image format for Microsoft Windows)

- JP2

- Joint Photographic Experts Group (JPEG)

- MacPaint (the original Apple imaging application)

- PDF

- Photoshop

- PICT (the native image format for Mac OS 9.x and earlier)

■ Portable Network Graphics (PNG)

■ QuickTime Image

■ Silicon Graphics (SGI)

■ Tagged Information File Format (TIFF)

■ Targa Graphics Adapter (TGA)

In addition to opening images in these file formats, Preview can export an image or document into another supported format. To export a an item using Preview, follow these steps:

1. Open a document in Preview.

2. Choose Save As from the File menu to save the document in the same format.

3. Choose Export from the File menu and select the desired export format from the Format pop-up menu, an example of which is shown in Figure 9.9.

4. Select the Options button to reveal any compression, color selection, or bit-depth options that are associated with the selected file type. For example, the Option button will reveal a different set of options for exporting images in JPEG format compared to TIFF format.

5. Choose a name and destination for the exported image.

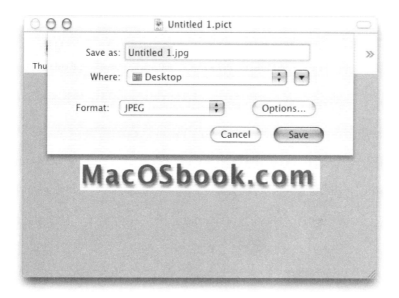

Figure 9.9
Use Preview to convert images from one file format to another.

Since Preview is a very basic application, try the shareware application called GraphicConverter from Thorsten Lemke (www.graphicconverter.net). GraphicConverter is very inexpensive ($30) and can open and save over 160 different image formats. It is truly the Swiss Army knife of image utilities.

Speech Recognition

Computer-generated speech has had an interesting history on the Mac. The very first Mac program of its kind was Macintalk, a text-to-speech generator that could create fairly realistic-sounding speech. At the introduction of the Mac, Steve Jobs pulled a Mac out of a carrying case and the Mac joked, "Thanks, it was hot in there." Ah, progress.

Apple eventually released Macintalk for developers to incorporate into their own programs; few took the opportunity, however, because Macintalk wasn't part of the standard system installation. Eventually, two forms of speech compatibility were incorporated into the Mac OS:

- *Speech recognition*—The ability of the Mac OS to recognize and perform commands spoken through a microphone.

- *Text-to-speech*—The conversion of written text into speech, output through the computer's internal or external speakers

Mac OS X incorporates all of the speech features found in earlier versions of the Mac OS, with a few cosmetic differences and a new set of built-in commands. The following sections describe the basics of these speech capabilities.

9

Recognizing Speech

Mac OS X installs all the software necessary for your computer to listen for and execute a predefined set of commands, as well allowing you to add commands of your own. All you need is a microphone, which is built into most PowerBooks and iBooks, or which can be purchased from a variety of sources. Speech recognition is not enabled by default, however; to get started, open the System Preferences and follow these steps:

1. Switch to the Speech pane, shown in Figure 9.10. Although Apple Speakable Items is the only system available at this time to implement speech recognition in Mac OS X, other systems may be developed or ported to Mac OS X in the future.

2. Enable Apple Speakable Items by selecting the On button in the On/Off section of the window.

3. Click the Helpful Tips button for a few pointers on topics such as how to best position the microphone.

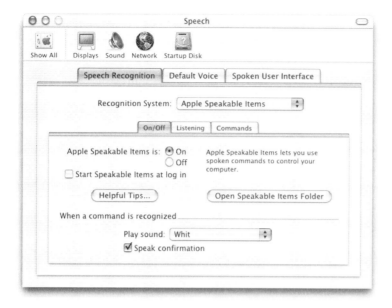

Figure 9.10
Use the Speech Recognition section of the Speech System Preferences pane to configure your computer to execute voice commands.

4. Click the Open Speakable Items Folder button to get a better idea of what commands are available for execution using speech recognition.

5. Choose a feedback sound to play when Speech Recognition has recognized a command; this is helpful because it lets you know that your command has been accepted properly.

6. Click the Speak Confirmation checkbox to have the Mac OS read alerts and dialog boxes to you.

7. Click on the Listening tab of the Speech Recognition section of the Speech System Preferences pane and configure how Mac OS X will listen for your commands. You have two basic options on how to issue commands, which are shown in Figure 9.11:

   ■ *Listen Only While Key Is Pressed*—This option will activate the Listening command only if a key is pressed for one second prior to issuing a spoken command. If you choose this option, select the Change Key button to identify a key on the keyboard, such as the Escape or F12 key, to hold down before the command.

   ■ *Key Toggles Listening On And Off*—Choose this option to use the selected key to turn listening on and off, and enable the Listening command without depressing

Figure 9.11
Configure how your computer should listen for commands.

a key. Instead, toggle speech recognition on and issue a command, name the computer in the Name field, and configure how the name is to be used in the Name Is field. The name can be anything you like, but I suggest that you don't use a monosyllabic name such as *Fred* or *Jane*. Another option is for the name to be completely optional, in which case the computer is constantly listening for commands, which might degrade system performance.

8. Select a microphone from the Microphone drop-down menu at the bottom of the Listening window, then click the Volume button to test a few commands and adjust the microphone volume. This will optimize Mac OS X's ability to hear your spoken commands. Excessive background noise, such as air conditioners and typical office chatter, can make adjusting the microphone volume a necessity, in order to compensate for the distractions.

9. Click the Selecting A Microphone button for a few tips on how Speech Recognition uses microphones to listen for commands.

10. Click the Commands tab in the Speech Recognition tab and choose what types of spoken commands you would like the computer to execute. For example, you can elect to use only the pre-defined commands included with Mac OS X, or activate menu options for the front-most application, whatever that application may be. The use of application-specific commands requires that you enable certain features in the Universal Access System Preferences pane.

11. Select the Default Voice tab in the Speech System Preferences pane and choose a voice for your computer when speaking commands or providing feedback. The options in this tab are:

   ■ *Voice*—The computer-generated voice, such as Fred or Kathy, used by Mac OS X to speak.

   ■ *Rate*—The rate at which the voice speaks. Some of the voices are slow and could use a little speeding up, so play around to configure a voice you'll be comfortable listening to.

12. Finally, select the Spoken User Interface tab in the Speech System Preferences pane and choose if you want alerts spoken out loud, (so-called Talking Alerts). You can also choose to have the Finder alert you when it needs your attention..

13. Quit the System Preferences.

Speech recognition works by matching commands you speak with those contained in the folder /Macintosh HD/Users/username/Library/Speech/Speakable Items, which is created only after you have enabled Speech recognition. This folder contains over 70 items for you to try out, such as *Close this window*, *Get my mail*, and *Reply to sender*. When you activate speech recognition, Mac OS X displays a small floating palette that visually confirms the command. The small round palette (shown in the upper half of Figure 9.12) floats above other windows and displays different information, depending on its status. If you have a listening key selected, such as the Escape key, or have assigned a name for the computer, such as Computer, that information will be displayed while awaiting a command (left). When a command is ready to be executed, the floating palette will become animated and change color (middle). When a command has been accepted, it is displayed above the floating palette (right).

Clicking on the tab at the bottom of the floating palette reveals two shortcuts, one that opens the Speech System Preferences pane and one that lists the commands found in the Speakable Items folder. These shortcuts are very handy while you're learning to use speech recognition. The lower section of Figure 9.12 shows the Speech Commands floating palette.

Finally, you'll probably want to create new, personalized commands rather than be limited by the canned commands installed by the Speech System Preferences. You have two options for creating new commands:

■ Create an alias to an existing Finder item, such as an application or document, and place the alias in the Speakable Items folder.

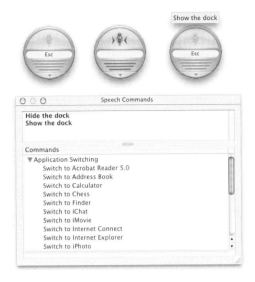

Figure 9.12
Speech recognition uses small floating palettes to provide feedback and shortcuts to the various speech commands and configuration options.

■ Write an AppleScript to execute a command or series of commands, and place the script in the Speakable Items folder.

I'll cover AppleScript in Chapter 11, "Scripting Mac OS X." In the interim, let me give you a quick example that demonstrates how to make a useful command using an alias.

iTunes has quickly become one of the most popular applications for the Mac OS, and the following steps will show you how to open iTunes using speech recognition:

1. Locate the iTunes application in the Finder.

2. Create an alias of iTunes and rename it *Open iTunes*.

3. Open the Speakable Items folder in a Finder window.

4. Drag the alias entitled *Open iTunes* into the Speakable Items folder.

5. Stop and restart Speech Recognition in the On/Off section of the Speech Recognition tab of the Speech System Preferences pane.

To try out your new shortcut, just speak the command *Open iTunes*.

Next, let's look at how to convert text on your computer into spoken words.

Converting Text to Speech

In addition to recognizing certain spoken commands and verbalizing certain elements of the user interface, Mac OS X's speech recognition system allows speech-aware applications to verbalize the contents of documents. TextEdit and Eudora are two applications that have this ability, but not all applications support Mac OS X's speech APIs. You don't need a microphone to use speech recognition because the printed word is the source of input. To configure your Mac to "read" the contents of a document, review the speech recognition options in the previous section, then follow these steps:

1. Open an existing document in TextEdit or create a new document.

2. Choose Edit|Speech|Start Speaking to begin at the top of the document.

3. Select a paragraph of text by highlighting it with the mouse, the choose Edit|Speech|Start Speaking to speak only the selected text, or select a paragraph of text by highlighting it with the mouse. Then, choose Services|Speech|Start Speaking Text from the Application menu to speak only the selected text.

4. To stop speaking, choose Edit|Speech|Stop Speaking, or Services|Speech|Stop Speaking from the application menu.

Figure 9.13 demonstrates the selection of only part of a document which will be read aloud by selecting it, then control+clicking the selected text to reveal the speech options.

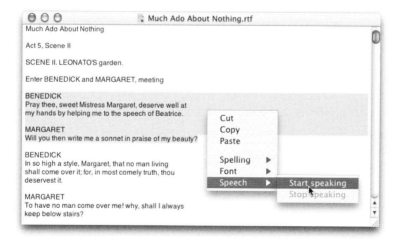

Figure 9.13
Use Mac OS X to read part or all of a document using speech-enabled applications such as TextEdit.

iTunes

The latest craze in the multimedia world is MPEG Audio Layer-3 (abbreviated MP3), an ultra-efficient audio file format that is about 10 times more efficient than the standard CD-ROM. The greatest thing about MP3 is that you can shrink an entire audio CD track, which is usually about 30MB, into a file that's 2 to 3MB in size. This is a very manageable file size for use on the Web, and it opens up new possibilities for artists who want to gain greater exposure, but can't afford the overhead costs of mastering and distributing CDs. In fact, many people believe that the future of music distribution will be in a format similar to MP3, which can be downloaded over the Web instead of purchased in a music store. Unfortunately, recent lawsuits suggest this is farther in the future than most people first thought.

iTunes is a complete application for managing digital audio, allowing you to play, encode, and write audio CDs. If you'd like to take your tunes on the road, iTunes can synchronize your music and playlists to Apple's latest digital lifestyle device, the iPod. iTunes 3 is the latest version, and it sports many useful features. iTunes 3 can:

■ Play audio CDs.

■ Encode audio CDs into MP3 format.

■ Burn audio CDs from MP3.

■ Categorize music by creating custom playlists (i.e., collections of songs).

■ Search for tracks by keyword using a built-in search window.

■ Listen to streaming MP3 Internet radio stations.

■ Adjust audio output with a 10-band equalizer.

■ Create "smart" playlists of your favorite or most frequently used tracks.

■ Synchronize MP3s and playlists on your computer with an iPod.

■ Listen to spoken-word content from Audible.com.

There are too many features to cover in detail here, so let's look at the five most common uses for iTunes: playing CDs, converting audio CDs to MP3, creating playlists, listening to Internet radio, and creating CDs from MP3s.

Playing Audio CDs

iTunes allows users to play the same audio CDs used in a home CD player or in a car stereo—but with numerous additional features. To play a CD:

1. Insert the CD and click on the small icon of the CD in the Source section on the left side of the iTunes window.

2. Click the Play button in the iTunes application window, or press the space bar on the keyboard to toggle between playing and pausing the CD.

If iTunes is already opened, you can configure iTunes to automatically play a CD when inserted by choosing On CD Insert: Begin Playing from the iTunes preferences. You can also configure iTunes to open automatically when an audio CD is inserted by selecting the CDs & DVDs pane in the System Preferences and choosing When You Insert a Music CD: Open iTunes. Also, if you have a connection to the Internet, iTunes will query an online database and attempt to retrieve the playlist for a CD when it is opened in iTunes. If it can't recognize the CD, you can submit the playlist for others to use when they insert the same CD on their computer.

Converting Audio CDs to MP3

iTunes allows you to convert audio CDs into MP3 format and store them on your hard drive. My experience has been that each CD takes up between 35 and 45MB of disk space, and I use a different hard drive than my startup drive to store all my MP3s. By default, iTunes stores your converted CDs in your home folder, but you can customize the location of your MP3s (and change a few encoding options) by following these steps:

1. Open iTunes and choose Preferences from the application menu, or choose Command+Y.

2. Click the Importing button.

3. Choose Import Using MP3 Encoder.

4. Choose a level of encoding quality from the Configuration menu. The higher the quality, the bigger the MP3 files created on your hard drive.

5. Click on the Advanced button and choose the storage location. If multiple people share your computer, it is possible to select the same folder for all users, or let each user store their MP3s in their home folders. In this case, you'll have multiple copies on your hard drive.

Each CD track is converted into a separate file and placed into a folder with the other tracks from the CD; iTunes will try to determine the artist of the CD and group CDs from the same artist into the same folder.

Creating Playlists

MP3 tracks are entered into the Library section of iTunes after they have been converted. You can refer to the Library when creating a playlist for the CD, or you can create a custom playlist using any of the tracks from the Library. To create a playlist, follow these steps:

1. Launch iTunes and choose File|New Playlist or press Command+N.

2. Assign a name to the new playlist, such as My Playlist, then double-click the new playlist to open it into a new window.

3. Open the Library by clicking the Library icon. This will reveal all the available MP3s, from which you can compile your new playlist.

4. Drag and drop the tracks you want from the Library to the new playlist, an example of which is shown in Figure 9.14.

Figure 9.14
Creating a custom playlist from multiple artists.

5. Reorder the tracks by dragging them by their titles and moving them up or down.

6. Close the playlist.

iTunes also lets you create what it calls a smart playlist, which is a playlist based on selection criteria — artist or composer name, genre, or song name, for example. You can use multiple search criteria to create smart playlists, and have them automatically updated. When you encode a CD in the future, tracks will be automatically added if they meet one of the search criteria. To create a smart playlists, follow these steps:

1. Launch iTunes and choose File|New Smart Playlist or press Command+Option+N.

2. Click the Simple or Advanced tab to select the criteria for creating the new smart playlist, an example of which is shown in Figure 9.15.

3. Click the OK button to close the configuration tab and rename the smart playlist.

Listening to Internet Radio

If you have an Internet connection, you can listen to streaming MP3 radio stations over the Internet with iTunes. Apple provides access to a great collection of available Internet radio stations from Live365.com, and you can manually connect to a station if

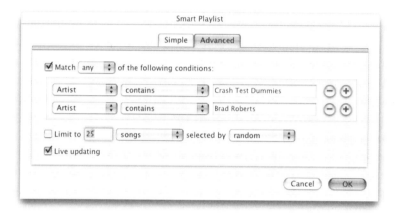

Figure 9.15
Use smart playlist to create dynamic playlists based on simple or complex search criteria.

you know the URL. The quality of playback for each station depends on several factors, including encoded bit depth of the audio stream and network conditions, so the quality of each will vary. To listen to a streaming Internet radio station, follow these steps:

1. Launch iTunes and choose Radio in the Source column.

2. Expand one of the pre-defined music categories (such as Ambient) to reveal the radio stations in this category, an example of which is shown in Figure 9.16. Use the Name and Comment columns to locate a station of interest; use the Bit Rate column to gauge the potential quality of the stream.

3. Double-click a radio station to open a connection and begin listening.

To listen to a radio station which has a known URL:

1. Launch iTunes.

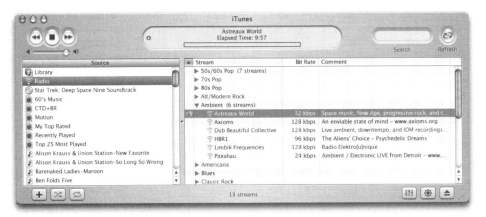

Figure 9.16
Use iTunes to listen to streaming MP3 radio stations over the Internet.

2. Choose Advanced|Open stream or press Command+U.

3. Enter the URL for the site in question, such as **http://152.2.63.108:8000** for the WUNC FM radio station.

For the best results, review the General section of the iTunes Preferences and select Connect to Internet When Needed. Increasing the Streaming Buffer Size to Large will provide quicker and better quality playback.

Creating Audio CDs from MP3s

If you have a CD-R (CD-Record) or CD-RW (CD-Rewrite) drive, iTunes will also allow you to create (or "burn") CDs using the MP3 files on your computer. The great thing about burning your own CDs is that you can mix and match tracks from different artists to create a unique CD to fit any occasion. Blank CDs are fairly inexpensive (less than $1 each). To burn a CD using iTunes, follow these steps:

1. Encode one or more tracks and create a playlist following the steps outlined above.

2. Select the playlist and confirm the total length of the playlist does not exceed the recording length of the CD (which is typically either 74 or 80 minutes). The statistics for each playlist are located at the bottom center of the playlist window.

3. Choose File|Burn Playlist to CD, or click the Burn CD button in the upper right of the playlist.

4. Enter a blank CD and iTunes will begin burning the CD.

Finally, for the latest information about MP3 and links to FAQs and MP3 files, see the MP3.com Web site (**www.mp3.com**). For information about the most popular

CD cataloging resource, see Gracenote (**www.gracenote.com**), formerly known as CDDB. The Gracenote (CDDB) database is a massive database of audio CDs that is used by iTunes and other MP3 players to recognize CDs when they are inserted in your computer, and to display information about the CD's artist, tracks, genre, and so on.

iMovie and iDVD

iMovie, the latest addition to the Apple multimedia family, allows you to create professional-looking movies. iMovie is capable of incorporating QuickTime movies, images, sounds, MP3s, title tracks, and transitional and special effects into a multilayered movie that you can save to disk or, if you have a VHS camcorder, convert to VHS. Figure 9.17 shows a tiny fraction of iMovie's capabilities.

iMovie works with many FireWire-enabled camcorders to acquire video, or you can use existing QuickTime movie and sound tracks as the basis for your new movie. Because the movie files you create can be huge, be wary about saving them to a file. Instead of saving them to a file, you can upload them to VHS through your digital camcorder, burn them to CD or DVD, or upload them (small ones, anyway!) to your .Mac account. For more information about iMovie, and to download the latest version, see **www.apple.com/imovie/**.

Figure 9.17
Use iMovie to import digital audio and video to create movies to share with others using the Internet, CDs, or video tape.

iDVD is geared more for the professional multimedia developer and is not bundled with Mac OS X Version 10.2 unless your computer comes with a DVD-R (SuperDrive). It is available from Apple at **www.apple.com/idvd/**. iDVD provides authors with the ability to create menu-driven multimedia slide shows of still images, and movies that can be read on most set-top DVD players. iDVD lets you apply preset themes to the user interface, or you can create you own look and feel.

The price of digital cameras continues to decline, allowing Mac users to take advantage of iPhoto, an application bundled with Mac OS X for importing, organizing, editing, and sharing photos over the Web or as a printed book. If your model of camera is supported by iPhoto (see www.apple.com/iphoto/ for details), you can shoot photos, connect the camera to your Mac using a USB cable and have iPhoto automatically open when attached, then import the photos with a click of the mouse. If you don't have a digital camera you can import a folder of photos by choosing Import from the File menu and selecting a folder containing the images. Once imported, you can organize them in a similar fashion as you can organize MP3 files in iTunes. For example I have several categories of photos, and some of the photos exist in more than one of the categories, referred to as albums.

iPhoto allows you to easily import and organize digital images into photo albums.Once you have imported and organized photos into an album, you can convert them into a printed book or click the Share button and choose from a variety of options to share your creation. There are many ways to share photos™ including:

■ Print to a local or networked printer

■ Create a digital slide show with an accompanying sound track

■ Send the photos via email

■ Order prints from Kodak

■ Order a professionally printed and hard-bound photo album

■ Publish the photos on the Web using your .Mac account

■ Export photos as Desktop images

■ Export the photos as a screen saver using Mac OS X's Screen Effects

■ Export the photos in TIFF, JPEG, or PNG files, as a local Web page, or as a QuickTime movie with soundtrack

9

Even if you don't have a digital camera, try importing a few photos from the Web using iPhoto and explore some of its many cool features. You'll be a multimedia addict in no time!

Wrapping Up

Mac OS X has many powerful multimedia features that allow you to view, manipulate, and play audio, video, and 3D objects, although not all Macs have CD-R and DVD-R capabilities. The Mac OS is the leader in integrating multimedia into the home computer, and whenever a new technology comes to market, you can be sure that it will make its way into the next version of the Mac OS. In this chapter, you've learned about:

■ Playing video with QuickTime Player and QuickTime-enabled Web browsers

■ Using QuickTime VR to walk through virtual worlds and manipulate objects

■ Viewing and exporting still images with Preview

■ Using speech recognition and text-to-speech

■ Using iTunes to play and encode audio CDs into MP3 format, create custom and "smart" playlist, and listen to Internet radio.

■ The power of iMovie and iDVD to create digital movies and presentations.

The innovative use of fonts and thorough support of printing are among the Mac's greatest strengths. In the next chapter, I'll explore what's new in the realm of fonts and printing in Mac OS X.

Managing Fonts and Printers

A great deal of the Mac's success is due to its graphics and publishing capabilities. In fact, you could say that desktop publishing is the Macintosh's heritage. Drawing on years of experience and technological advances, Mac OS X provides the best font and printing technologies that can be found in a personal computer. In this chapter, we'll look at the ways Mac OS X displays fonts and images on your screen and handles local and networked printers, with special emphasis on fonts and type issues.

Imaging Models

The methods, or models, that Mac OS X employs to generate fonts and images differ according to how the fonts and images will be used--on computer screens or by printers. On screen, the Mac OS displays information at 72 dots per inch (dpi), a much lower resolution than printers, which are capable of resolutions of 2,400 dpi or higher. This disparity in quality between screen and printer output necessitates the use of different imaging models. Over the last 20 years, Apple has invented several imaging models, including QuickDraw, QuickDraw GX, and QuickDraw 3D.

The new imaging model that supplies the 2D, 3D, PDF, and font support in Mac OS X is code–named Quartz Extreme. It replaces QuickDraw , although many QuickDraw features are still present in Mac OS X. Quartz allows Carbon or Cocoa programmers to implement several advanced imaging features, which include:

■ Antialiasing text

■ Creating drop shadows around text and windows

■ Saving documents in PDF format

The distinctive features of Mac OS X's Aqua interface, including the drop shadows and translucent Finder windows, are the result of Quartz Extreme. Aqua is, on the whole, more aesthetically pleasing than the old Platinum interface of Mac OS 9.x. For example, take a look at Figure 10.1, which shows two versions of a BBEdit document in Mac OS X (top) and Mac OS 9.x (bottom). Note the drop shadow around the window and the overall crispness of the Mac OS X version. Also, check out the letter M, which I've enlarged to give you a better view of how text is antialiased, giving images a smoother appearance around the edges and making them easier to read.

Apple has licensed OpenGL, the new standard imaging model, as a replacement for QuickDraw 3D, because of OpenGL's cross-platform appeal. Quartz Extreme also enables applications to create cross-platform PDF documents that can be read on any computer that has Adobe Acrobat Reader or a comparable program. Although Acrobat Reader is still installed as part of Mac OS X, PDF documents can be viewed with the application named Preview, as long as they were created in a Carbon or Cocoa application.

For most users, the components of the Mac OS that generate images and fonts on screen are not as important as the fonts themselves. Let's move on to the issue of fonts supported by Mac OS X.

Mac OS X Fonts

Mac OS X is a powerful desktop publishing platform that offers improved font management as well as maximum backward compatibility. To some users, backward compatibility may be of little importance. However, if you've ever purchased a set of commercial fonts, you know how expensive fonts can be. In fact, Apple claims to include over $1,000 worth of fonts in Mac OS X.

In addition to a high degree of backward compatibility, Mac OS X also allows developers to write font management tools into their applications. Users can create and edit groups of fonts in many different types of documents, such as Web documents or

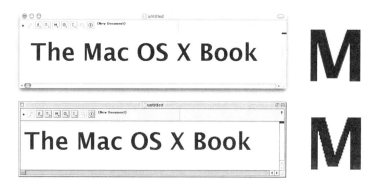

Figure 10.1
The Quartz Extreme imaging model allows for antialiased text in Mac OS X applications such as BBEdit.

word processing documents. Several third-party font utilities, including eBookfaces, FontChecker, and FontExampler, enhance Mac OS X's built-in font management capability and include the following types of fonts:

■ Bitmapped (fixed-size) fonts

■ Type 1 (also called PostScript or variable-size) fonts

■ TrueType (variable-size) fonts

■ OpenType (variable-size) fonts

Let's look at these types of fonts in detail, paying particularly close attention to TrueType fonts, the most popular type of font for the Mac OS.

Bitmapped Fonts

The original Macintosh fonts (New York, Monaco, Geneva, and Chicago) were fixed-width bitmapped fonts—each character was predefined by the series of dots necessary to create that character at a specific point size. Most bitmapped fonts were produced in 10-, 11-, 12-, and 14-point sizes, and were not scalable (meaning each font was incapable of having a variable width).

The original bitmapped fonts, and the many bitmapped fonts that soon followed, were optimized for display on the Macintosh screen and for printing on the Apple ImageWriter (the only printer available at the time). These bitmapped fonts were sometimes difficult to work with. Limitations to their use included:

■ *Dot-matrix bitmapped quality was unacceptable for most business uses.* Although font variety was certainly a welcome improvement, most people still considered the quality of ImageWriter output unacceptable for business use.

■ *Font variety was limited.* Although bitmapped fonts proliferated, almost all were novelty styles with little utility beyond advertisements, invitations, and entertainment.

■ *The 400KB system disks could hold only a limited selection of fonts.* Because hard drives were not generally available at that time, it was necessary to boot the Macintosh from a 400KB floppy disk. After squeezing the System folder and an application or two onto a floppy, only a small amount of room was left for font styles and sizes.

■ *Macintosh applications could support only a limited number of fonts at one time.* When too many fonts were installed in the System file, applications acted strangely, often providing only a random subset of the installed fonts.

New releases of system software, application software, and third-party utility programs helped alleviate these problems. The next big change was not based on software, but hardware. The introduction of the Apple LaserWriter printer included built-in support for the PostScript page description language. Bitmapped fonts are still in use today, but PostScript, TrueType, and other types of fonts are much more popular.

Type 1 Fonts (PostScript)

The introduction of the Apple LaserWriter printer brought a new variety of font to the Macintosh: the Type 1, or PostScript, font. To be more precise, Type 1 fonts are actually a subset of Adobe's PostScript language. The LaserWriter (and all later PostScript printers) required these fonts to ensure that the type could be printed at high resolution. PostScript fonts came to be known by a variety of names, including laser fonts, outline fonts, and Type 1 fonts. Apple traditionally refers to them as PostScript fonts, however.

Each PostScript font consists of two parts: a screen font and a printer font. The screen font replicates the printer font, providing different sizes optimized for on-screen use, rather than one font that is viewable at multiple sizes. Other similarities between the two include:

■ Both are provided in different styles and sizes

■ Both appear in the font menu or Font Panel in most Mac OS X applications

With PostScript fonts, the screen font is only a general representation of the corresponding printer font. The PostScript printer font gives the PostScript printer a mathematical description of each character, as well as other information necessary to create and produce high-resolution output.

Usually, all screen fonts and printer fonts are present in matched pairs. But it isn't imperative that you use all the available screen fonts, because the Mac OS can simulate a missing one. You must, however, have all printer fonts available to the operating system. In other words, you can *view* Helvetica Bold without installing the Helvetica Bold screen font (by using the Helvetica font and the Bold type style), but you cannot *print* Helvetica Bold without the Helvetica Bold printer font.

For a PostScript font to print correctly, the printer font file must be available to the PostScript printer. A font is available when it has been built into the printer's Read Only Memory (ROM) chips, stored on a printer's hard disk, or kept on the Macintosh hard disk and automatically downloaded to the printer. Modern PostScript-enabled printers typically have a hard drive to store fonts and documents, and some have the ability to store additional fonts using software provided by the manufacturer.

PostScript Font Challenges

Using PostScript fonts in the real-world Macintosh environment has never been easy. The difficulties arise because PostScript fonts, as well as the software and hardware environment in which they're utilized, continually evolve. Most of these problems were solved with system software upgrades, new font management utilities, or workaround methods that have become well–known and commonly accepted.

The following list describes many of the challenges presented by PostScript fonts, along with the corresponding solutions:

- *PostScript fonts versus non-PostScript fonts*—Because PostScript screen fonts are not noticeably different from non-PostScript screen fonts, it's difficult for inexperienced users to distinguish between them when creating documents for high-resolution PostScript printers. This problem has been solved, at least partially, by PostScript's dominance in the Macintosh world—most Macintosh users now have access to PostScript printers, and PostScript fonts are now the rule rather than the exception.

- *Screen font availability*—It's a good idea to determine which fonts a document contains to ensure the availability of all necessary screen and printer fonts at print time. This isn't always easy to do, however, especially if the person printing the file did not create it. Individual software vendors have different methods for identifying the screen fonts in a document: PageMaker displays the dimmed names of used but currently unavailable fonts in its Font menu; both PageMaker and QuarkXPress produce a list of fonts used. Adobe has enabled Illustrator to print files correctly even if the screen fonts used to create the file aren't available at the time of printing. Unfortunately, this solution hasn't caught on with all software vendors.

- *Printer font availability*—The most fundamental requirement of PostScript fonts is the need for corresponding screen and printer fonts. This requirement is problematic because of the lack of an automated method of tracking the screen font/printer font correlation.

- *Different fonts with the same names*—As more vendors began producing PostScript fonts, another problem appeared: different vendors created their own versions of the same fonts. This proliferation of fonts caused confusion — which vendor's screen fonts and printer fonts were used. It also made it difficult for service bureaus to know, for instance, if the Garamond specified in a document was the Adobe Garamond, Bitstream Garamond, or some other vendor's version. This point was crucial because font substitutions wouldn't work—and even if they did, character width differences wreaked havoc with the output.

10

■ *The Type 1 font secret*—Because Adobe Systems developed PostScript, they didn't reveal the specifics of the optimized format that came to be known as PostScript Type 1. The Type 1 format embedded "hints" in font outlines that made the fonts look better when produced in small type sizes on 300-dpi laser printers. Because Adobe fonts were compressed and encrypted, other vendors had to reverse-engineer the Type 1 font-hinting scheme to incorporate a comparable feature in their own fonts. Bitstream and others were successful in cloning the functionality of PostScript. Finally, after all the political turmoil surrounding TrueType and the successful cloning of PostScript Type 1 fonts, Adobe unsealed the specifications for Type 1. Today, most other font vendors have upgraded their fonts to the Type 1 format.

Printing PostScript Fonts

When a document containing PostScript fonts is printed to a PostScript printer, the Mac OS queries the printer to determine whether the required fonts are present in the printer's hard drive. These fonts may be built into a printer's ROM chips, or they may have been previously downloaded into the printer's RAM or onto the printer's hard disk. If the fonts are indeed present, the document is sent to the printer for output. If the fonts are not resident, the printer driver checks to see if they're available on the Macintosh hard disk. If they are, they're temporarily downloaded into the printer's RAM. If they are not available, an error message in the Print Status dialog box alerts you to that fact. This message usually states that Courier is being substituted for the missing font, and your document is then printed.

When the document is printed, the PostScript printer uses the printer font information to create each character. The information from the PostScript screen font is translated into printer font characters. The process of creating the printed characters—*rasterization*—is the most complex part of the PostScript printing process. During rasterization, PostScript uses the printer font file's mathematical character descriptions to select the pixels necessary to produce the requested character at the highest possible resolution.

TrueType Fonts

In addition to supporting the same bitmapped and PostScript fonts that Mac users have worked with for years, Mac OS X utilizes a preferred font format that was introduced in System 7. TrueType fonts were designed to appear on the Mac screen at high resolution at any point size and to print at high resolution on virtually any output device.

TrueType was a fundamental shift from bitmapped and PostScript fonts. Each TrueType font exists as a single file that does the work of both the screen font and the printer font. In earlier versions of the Mac OS, TrueType fonts appeared smooth and crisp on screen, no matter what the point size. In Mac OS X, the Quartz Extreme imaging engine smoothes out everything on screen, including fonts.

TrueType's font specifications are published and available for use by a wide variety of vendors. AGFA Compugraphic, Bitstream, International Typeface Corporation, Monotype, and others support it. Microsoft Windows and even IBM's OS/2 support the TrueType standard, ensuring strong cross-platform compatibility. Both Apple and Microsoft now sell or freely distribute many TrueType fonts. You can buy TrueType font packages from most vendors, with the notable exception of Adobe (because of their historical support for Type 1 fonts, and now their support for OpenType fonts— discussed in the next section).

TrueType Technology

TrueType fonts, like PostScript printer fonts, are outline fonts—each character is described mathematically as opposed to the bit-by-bit description used by older screen fonts. TrueType mathematical descriptions are based on quadratic Bézier curve equations rather than PostScript's standard Bézier curve equations. The difference between these equations is in the number of points used to determine the positions of the lines and curves that make up each character. Apple claims TrueType's method creates better-looking characters in a wider range of output and display resolutions.

Because TrueType uses mathematical descriptions for both on-screen and printer font versions, a single file can serve the display and any output devices. As mentioned previously in this chapter, PostScript requires two files—a screen font file and a printer font file—to display or print at full resolution. Although it's easier to manage one font file than two, Adobe claims that putting its screen fonts and printer fonts in separate files is an asset, because either can be updated or enhanced independently at any time without affecting existing documents or printer configurations.

OpenType Fonts

The OpenType font, the newest arrival on the font scene, is a joint venture from Adobe and Microsoft that provides a cross-platform font for the Mac OS and various Windows operating systems. OpenType uses a single, cross-platform font file to perform all the required tasks, including bitmapping, outlining, display, printing, and multilingual support—no small feat. The font files are also designed to be smaller in size to encourage portability between computers and over the Web.

Choosing a Font Standard

In an idealized laboratory environment, the daily use of these systems would be very straightforward from a font-management perspective. Some Macs would use only

PostScript fonts, and some use only TrueType fonts. All documents using PostScript fonts would be created on the PostScript computers, and those using TrueType fonts would be created on the TrueType computers,

Unfortunately, none of us live or work in such a laboratory. Most Macintosh computers are likely to be configured with PostScript fonts, TrueType fonts, and non-PostScript, non-TrueType bitmapped fonts. Most people will have some documents created with only PostScript fonts, some with only bitmapped fonts, some with only TrueType fonts, and many with mixes of TrueType, PostScript, and bitmapped fonts. So how can all this jumble work in the real world?

The answer is: easily! The Quartz Extreme imaging model takes into account all the advances made in the field of typography—therefore, the differences among types of fonts aren't as pronounced as in the days of System 7 and the original Apple LaserWriter. To desktop publishing professionals, this may sound like heresy. As far as the rest of us are concerned, however, we can use the fonts we like best as long as their on-screen appearance and output meet our standards.

Installing and Removing Fonts

In the old days of the Mac OS (prior to System 7.1), all fonts were stored in the System suitcase (located in the System Folder) and were installed using a utility called the Font/DA Mover. The only limitation was that fonts could not be installed while any application other than the Finder was open.. In System 7.1, a folder called Fonts was introduced to store fonts apart from the System suitcase. The concept of the Fonts folder continues in Mac OS X, but with an interesting twist: as a true multi-user operating system, Mac OS X can access fonts stored in multiple locations—not just the main Fonts folder. This approach makes installing new fonts very easy and allows multiple users to keep their fonts separate.

Here's how it works: When a user logs into Mac OS X, the operating system checks local and networked file systems for the types of fonts it is capable of using. The unsupported fonts are ignored. Specifically, Mac OS X looks for fonts in the following locations:

- /Macintosh HD/Library/Fonts/

- /Macintosh HD/Users/*username*/Library/Fonts/

- /Macintosh HD/System Folder /Fonts/

- /Network/Library/Fonts/

- /Network/Users/*username*/Library/Fonts

If you don't have Mac OS 9.x installed on the same computer as Mac OS X, or you are not logged into a Mac OS X Server, only the two local Mac OS X folders will be searched. If Mac OS 9.x and Mac OS X are installed on the same computer, all Mac OS 9.x fonts of the correct type will be available for use in Mac OS X as well. When working with any application that allows you to select fonts, all the fonts will be accessible to the application. This is an interesting change since Mac OS 9.x, in which only the contents of the Fonts folder are searched for fonts.

The number of fonts installed on your Mac in the main Fonts folder will vary depending on the type of installation performed. Lucida Grande is used as the default system font, and to install additional fonts, just copy or move fonts to one of the Fonts folders mentioned above. You may not be able to add fonts to the Fonts folder when applications other than the Finder are running. Also, when you add fonts to one of the Fonts folders, they will not become available to any open applications until you quit and relaunch those programs. In fact, after installing the fonts, it's best to log out and log back in so that the Mac OS will recognize the new fonts. The newly installed fonts will then be available to your Carbon and Cocoa applications.

When you're installing fonts, Mac OS X doesn't display the contents of font suitcases (a family of fonts). Mac OS 9.x, on the other hand, allows you to open font suitcases directly from the Finder by double-clicking them as if they were folders. This action opens a suitcase window that contains individual icons for each screen font in the folder. The icons enable you to distinguish PostScript screen fonts or bitmapped fonts from TrueType fonts. TrueType fonts use an icon with three *A*s, whereas PostScript screen fonts or bitmapped fonts use an icon with a single *A*. Mac OS X doesn't support the telltale icons, which makes managing fonts a little more difficult. For example, Figure 10.2 shows the font Arial viewed in Mac OS X (left), and Arial Narrow (top right) and Adobe Garamond (bottom right) in Mac OS 9.x. Notice that in Mac OS X you cannot double-click an individual screen font to open a font suitcase. The Mac OS X Finder icon does not distinguish between TrueType and bitmapped fonts.

10

Removing fonts is essentially the same as installing them. First, quit all open applications, then move or delete the selected fonts from the Fonts folder. You cannot move fonts that are in use by the Mac OS itself, such as Lucida Grande. To get rid of any other font, you'll need to boot from an alternative startup disk, such as the Mac OS X installation CD-ROM or a drive containing Mac OS 9.x.

Working with the Font Panel

The portion of Quartz Extreme imaging system that controls font detail is known as the *Apple Type Solution (ATS)*. When working with Cocoa applications, ATS provides access to all of your fonts through a feature called the Font Panel. The Font Panel, an

Figure 10.2
Mac OS X and Mac OS 9.x display information about fonts differently.

example of which is shown in Figure 10.3, allows you to group fonts into user-defined categories for easy access from within Font Panel–aware applications such as Mail and TextEdit. (Not all applications provide access to the Font Panel.) This type of coordination is reminiscent of the color picker utility, which provides a similar type of access for color selection in different types of applications.

To access the Font Panel, choose Format|Font|Font Panel (or Command+T) when using TextEdit, Mail, or another application that has been programmed to use the Font Panel feature.

Figure 10.3
The Font Panel provides a unified method of selecting fonts from within applications such as Mail and TextEdit.

In addition to selecting a font family, such as Web, a typeface such as Regular or Bold, or a font size, clicking the drop-down menu called Extras at the bottom of the Font Panel reveals the following options:

■ *Add To Favorites*—Adds the selected font to the font category called Favorites.

■ *Edit Collections*—Opens the Font Collections window (shown in Figure 10.4) in which you can edit, add, and delete categories of fonts.

■ *Edit Sizes*—Allows you to set the minimum and maximum font sizes between which the font slider may be moved.

■ *Show/Hide Preview*—Shows or hides a preview area to view the selected font.

■ *Show Characters*—Displays a floating palette used for viewing and selecting special types of characters, an example of which is shown in Figure 10.5.

■ *Color*—Opens a Mac OS X–style color picker to select the color for a font.

■ *Get Fonts*—Opens your default Web browser to an Apple Web page for information on purchasing fonts.

The Font Panel and color picker are actually floating windows that can be resized to suit your needs. They can be made very small or very large, and will float above your TextEdit or Mail documents. To reduce screen clutter, the floating palettes will disappear when Mail or TextEdit is moved into the background when you launch another application.

Third-Party Font Utilities

Mac OS X's Font Panel and Characters palette are helpful in managing some aspects of your fonts, but there are several third-party utilities available to help you manage your fonts in many more ways. The following utilities are available for download and are either shareware or low-cost commercial applications. Give them a try to see if they meet your font management needs.

Figure 10.4
Use the Font Panel feature to create collections of fonts.

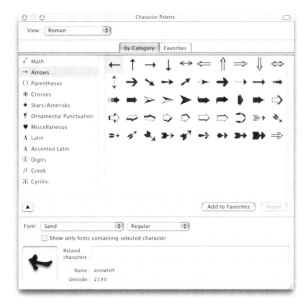

Figure 10.5
The new Show Characters feature helps you select special characters to insert into documents.

eBookfaces
www.corpus-callosum.com/software.html

eBookfaces is a utility for viewing large samples of a font at different sizes. The display area is large enough to provide an excellent preview of a particular font, and a tab to the side of the display area allows you to filter certain styles of fonts. For example, Figure 10.6 shows one of the four fonts on my computer that are bold and narrow.

FontChecker
www.wundermoosen.com/ /wmMacXProducts.html#FC

FontChecker is a utility for previewing a font and displaying technical information about the decimal, Hex, octal, HTML, and key information for a specific character. In Figure 10.7, for example, FontChecker is displaying the capital letter "X" in the Lucida Grand regular font.

FontExampler
www.pixits.com

FontExampler is a handy little utility for seeing what a font looks like. It uses a scrolling list that displays the font name on the left and a sample of the font on the

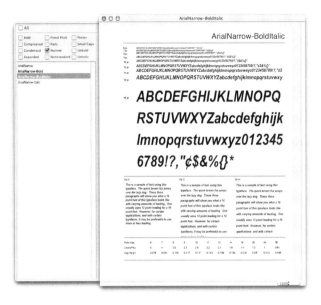

Figure 10.6
eBookfaces allows you to preview all your fonts, or filter them out to view only certain types of fonts.

right of a window. Type the example text in the top portion of the utility. Figure 10.8 shows an example of how easy it is to browse large numbers of fonts with FontExampler.

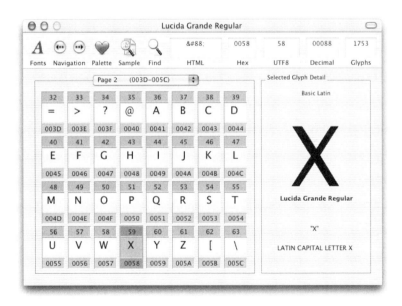

Figure 10.7
FontChecker provides technical information about characters, as well as font types and styles.

Figure 10.8
FontExampler allows you to preview fonts with a user-defined string of text.

Font Reserve
www.fontreserve.com

Font Reserve is one of the most powerful and complete utilities for managing fonts under Mac OS X. Font Reserve consists of several components, including:

■ Font Reserve Settings—Utility for configuring general preferences for Font Reserve.

■ Font Reserve Browser—Utility for browsing, previewing, and managing sets of fonts.

■ Font Reserve Database—Database of information about fonts that can be shared with other users.

■ MyFonts.com—Utility for searching for, and purchasing, fonts online.

You can have Font Reserve search for fonts in specific locations, such as those in the main Mac OS X Fonts folder, as well as fonts used by Mac OS 9.x or on a file server. Once the fonts have been located and entered into the Font Reserve Database, you can use the Font Reserve Browser utility to peruse and group fonts in multiple ways. For example, Figure 10.9 shows the Font Reserve Browser with a specific font opened in a preview window.

Figure 10.9
Use the Font Reserve suite of utilities for powerful font management.

Although other font utilities are available for Mac OS X, they don't really offer any functionality beyond what eBookfaces, FontChecker, FontExampler, and Font Reserve can provide. Keep your eyes peeled for helpful font management utilities such as these, and tens of thousands of fonts by visiting www.myfonts.com and www.macfonts.com.

Printing in Mac OS X

Mac OS X Version 10.2 updates the printing architecture, combining the ease-of-use found in earlier versions of the Mac OS with the established Unix architecture called Common UNIX Printing System (CUPS). By marshalling the features of the old Chooser and Desktop printing into a Finder-independent application called the Print Center, Mac OS X provides a more flexible framework to help developers incorporate printing capabilities into their programs. To you and me, this means a familiar interface for printing documents, and fewer problems relating to large or corrupt print files.

With the new printing architecture comes the introduction of several concepts that may be somewhat familiar to many users. To print a document in Mac OS X, you'll eventually encounter the following concepts:

■ *Print Center*—A new utility for selecting printers.

■ *Page Setup*—The command found in most applications to prepare a document for printing to a specific printer.

■ *Print Preview*—A feature found in many applications that enables you to preview a document before sending it to a printer.

■ *Save As PDF*—A command that allows you to create a PDF document in any Carbon or Cocoa application that has printing capabilities.

Many people will miss the Desktop printer feature found in previous versions of the operating system, which allows users to drag and drop documents onto a Desktop printer icon to print documents, or double-click the printer icon to manage the printer. In my opinion, the faster and more reliable printing features found in Mac OS X more than make up for this inconvenience. Let's take a look at the first step—selecting a printer.

Selecting Printers with Print Center

Print Center is the new application you'll use to select, configure, and delete printers in Mac OS X. Its function is similar to that of the old Desktop Printer Utility in that it offers several methods for adding a printer, including:

■ AppleTalk

■ Directory Services

■ IP Printing, which uses the Transmission Control Protocol/Internet Protocol (TCP/IP)

■ Universal Serial Bus (USB)

Most users will access printers via a USB cable directly connected to the printer, or over a network using AppleTalk or IP Printing. However, because many non-Apple print drivers have yet to be updated for Mac OS X, the number of unsupported printers probably outnumbered those that can be used with Mac OS X until recently.

To connect to a printer through an AppleTalk

network, follow these steps once you have confirmed that AppleTalk has been enabled in the Network System Preferences pane:

1. Launch Print Center from the Utilities folder.

2. Choose the Add Printer from the Printers menu, or click the Add button in the Print Center toolbar if the option to add a printer isn't automatically presented.

3. From the pop-up list visible in Figure 10.10, select the protocol through which the printer will be connected, in this case AppleTalk.

Figure 10.10
When using the Print Center utility to add a printer, select the appropriate protocol in order to locate the printer.

4. In the second pop-up list, select from the various AppleTalk zones available on your network (if it is segmented into zones), or choose Local AppleTalk Zone. If your AppleTalk-enabled printer doesn't appear in the window below the second pop-up list, select AppleTalk Network. If the printer is an AppleTalk-enabled printer, it should appear in a list along with other AppleTalk-enabled printers (provided that AppleTalk is properly enabled in the Network System Preferences pane). Select the printer from the list and click the Add button.

5. Select the printer from the list by clicking it once.

6. In the Printer Model pop-up list, select the model of printer, or choose Auto Select to have Print Center make an educated guess as to the correct model.

7. Click the Add button and wait for Print Center to identify the printer description file that matches the printer you selected.

8. If necessary, Print Center will alert you if the proper printer description file cannot be located, or if there is more than one printer description file that matches your selection. Follow the instructions presented if this is the case.

Once the printer has been added to your list of printers, it will remain in the Print Center's Printer List window, shown in Figure 10.11, until you delete it by selecting

10

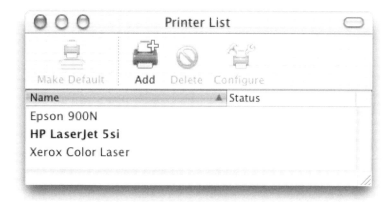

Figure 10.11
The Print Center's Printer List window displays your currently configured printers.

the printer and choosing the Delete button. If you have more than one printer, select a printer in the Printer List and choose Command+D to make it the default printer.

 TIP: PostScript printers rely upon PostScript Printer Description (PPD) files to enable the Mac OS to print. These files contain printer-specific information on such things as the number of trays, printer resolution, and color matching. PPDs are stored deep in the / System/Library/ folder hierarchy.

IP Printing replaces the Line Printer (LPR) option in previous versions of Mac OS X. IP Printing is Unix-speak for a network-enabled printer that uses TCP/IP to communicate with host computers, such as your Mac, a Windows-based computer, or a variety of computers that can print via the same communications protocol. Generally speaking, before you can connect to an IP-based printer you need to know the printer's make, model, and most importantly, its IP address. To connect to an IP printer, follow these steps:

1. Launch Print Center from the Utilities folder.

2. Choose the Add Printer option from the Printers menu, or click the Add button in the Print Center toolbar.

3. Select IP Printing from the pop-up selection list.

4. Provide an IP address or host name for the printer in the Printer's Address field, an example of which is shown in Figure 10.12.

5. Do not uncheck Use Default Queue On Server unless a network administrator gives you the name of an alternative queue to use.

Figure 10.12
Adding a printer using the IP Printer option.

6. Select the make of printer from the Printer Model drop-down list. This reveals the individual printers associated with the particular maker, such as Apple or HP.

7. Select an individual model of printer from the list.

8. Click the Add button to add the printer to the Printer List.

Mac OS X automatically recognizes printers connected via USB when your computer is started up. However, you can manually add a printer that is connected via USB but not recognized by Mac OS X by following these steps:

1. Launch the Print Center from the Utilities folder.

2. Choose the Add Printer option from the Printers menu, or click the Add button in the Print Center toolbar.

3. Select USB from the pop-up selection list.

4. Select the make of printer from the Printer Model drop-down list to reveal the individual printers associated with the particular maker, such as Apple or HP.

5. Select an individual model from the list.

6. Click the Add button to add the printer to the Printer List.

Finally, Directory Services allows you to select any printer available over a network, including printers networked via AppleTalk, TCP/IP (using LPR), Rendezvous or other protocols yet to be incorporated into Mac OS X. To select a printer using Directory Services:

1. Launch the Print Center from the Utilities folder.

2. Choose the Add Printer option from the Printers menu, or click the Add button in the Print Center toolbar.

3. Select Directory Services from the pop-up selection list.

4. In the second pop-up list, select Rendezvous, NetInfo Network, or another type of directory services that may be incorporated in the future.

5. Select the printer from the list by clicking it once.

6. In the Printer Model pop-up list, select the model of printer, or choose Auto Select to have the Print Center make an educated guess as to the correct model.

7. Click the Add button and wait for the Print Center to identify the printer description file that matches the printer you selected.

8. If necessary, the Print Center will alert you if the proper printer description file cannot be located, or if there is more than one printer description file that matches your selection. Follow the instructions presented if this is the case.

Printers that have been added using the Print Center will be available to any Carbon or Cocoa application whose printing capability was programmed with the Mac OS X printing Application Programming Interface (API). See the "Using Page Setup" and "Working with the Print Dialog Box" sections later in this chapter for instructions on changing printers from within a document.

Using Page Setup

The Mac OS X implementation of the Page Setup command, which should be very familiar to any Mac user, is very similar to the same command found in previous versions of the Mac OS. In Mac OS X, the Page Setup window may look different depending on the application, because software developers are able to customize it to suit their products. For the sake of continuity, however, Apple strives to make the basics of Page Setup the same for every application.

The Page Setup command is usually found under the File menu. In some applications, the Page Setup window is presented in the form of an attached sheet (described in several earlier chapters), and in others it resembles a free-floating modal dialog box that must be dismissed before you can use any of the application's other features. For

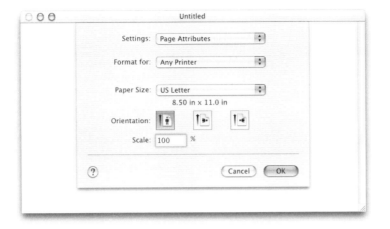

Figure 10.13
The Page Setup command in Mac OS X.

example, Figure 10.13 shows the Page Setup window as it appears in the TextEdit application; it is similar to the Page Setup window in AppleWorks, except the latter uses a free-floating window instead of an attached sheet.

The following options are found in most implementations of the Page Setup window:

■ *Settings*—Select from Page Attributes or Summary. The Summary option just provides an overview of the options that are available in the Page Attributes section.

■ *Format For*—Select a printer using the Print Center utility, or choose Any Printer to make the choices valid for all your printers.

■ *Paper Size*—The size of the paper on which the document will be printed.

■ *Orientation*—The orientation of the document, either portrait (the default), landscape right-to-left, or landscape left-to-right.

■ *Scale*—The scale at which the document is to be printed.

To configure a document for printing, open the Page Setup window, make your selections, and click on the OK button. Your choices will be saved until you use Page Setup to change them.

Previewing and Saving Documents as PDFs

The new printing architecture in Mac OS X is designed so that any document created in a Carbon or Cocoa application can be previewed before printing. Prior to Mac OS X, many applications did not provide this feature. One byproduct of Quartz Extreme is the ability for programmers to easily incorporate it into their applications. To provide the print preview feature, Mac OS X converts a document to PDF format, and then opens a temporary version of it in the Preview application. Converting the document to PDF results in excellent display and print quality, as well as a very high level of cross-platform compatibility. Any document that can be previewed can most likely be saved as a PDF document—a great option, when you consider that PDF is the preferred document format for Web and business use.

Most Carbon or Cocoa applications will allow you to preview a document by following steps similar to these, which describe how to preview a document created using TextEdit:

1. Launch TextEdit and create a document.

2. Choose File|Page Setup; confirm the paper size and orientation, and click the OK button.

3. Choose File|Print and click the Print Preview button.

When previewed, the document will be converted into a PDF file and automatically opened in Preview or Acrobat Reader. For example, Figure 10.14 shows how the PDF document (bottom) looks compared to the original TextEdit document (top).

After a document has been converted to PDF format and is open in the Print Preview feature, you have two additional options. You can save the document in PDF format,

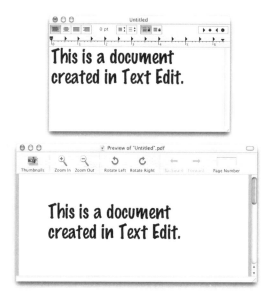

Figure 10.14
Previewing a TextEdit document in PDF format using the Print Preview command.

or as a Tagged Image File Format (TIFF) image file. TIFF format is commonly used in the graphics and publishing industries. You could go on to export the PDF document to numerous other formats, including Graphics Interchange Format (GIF) or Joint Photographic Experts Group (JPEG) for use on the Web.

Working with the Print Dialog Box

Now that you've selected a printer and confirmed your basic options using the Page Setup command, printing a document is just a few clicks away. In most applications, the Print command is located in the File menu, and also can be accessed through the Command+P shortcut, which produces a print dialog box like the one shown in Figure 10.15.

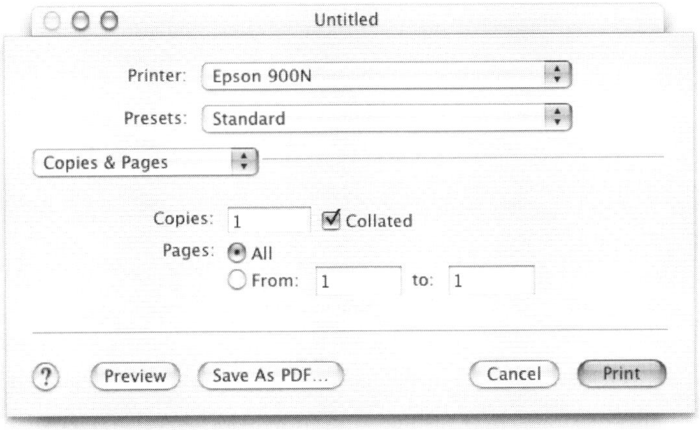

Figure 10.15
A sample print dialog box for TextEdit.

10

The configuration options for a specific print job are easily identified here, but take note of a hidden catch: each application may have additional settings that apply to only that specific application, as is the case with the HTML and text-editing powerhouse BBEdit. Figure 10.16 shows the BBEdit-specific settings in the Print dialog box; these settings offer users the opportunity to select a different set of font and tab settings for printing documents. These font and tab options are different from those used for viewing documents. To determine whether an application has additional printing options, click on the Copies & Pages drop-down menu (see Figure 10.15) for any available options. Otherwise, just enter any necessary information about the printer to which the document should be sent, the number of copies, and so on.

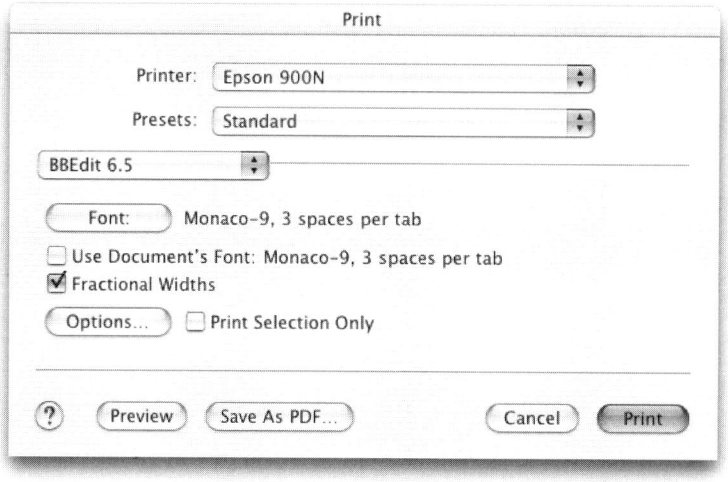

Figure 10.16
Many applications have additional printing options that are accessible via the Print dialog box.

ColorSync and Color Matching

The Mac's proficiency and popularity as a publishing computer is well known. In the past few years, advances in processing power, storage capacities, scanning, and output technology have earned the Mac OS the leading role in even the most demanding high-quality color publishing situations. Publications from *The New Yorker* to *People* are now produced fully or partially on the Mac. Mac OS X continues to support this effort with the latest version of ColorSync.

Despite the overall improvements in color publishing technology, one aspect of color publishing lags behind: matching the onscreen colors to those that are printed on color proofing devices and, finally, to the colors of the finished product, which are usually based on film output. Maintaining the consistency of colors as they move from an onscreen display to different output devices has been difficult for two basic reasons.

First, computer monitors produce colors by adding together differing percentages of red, green, and blue light. This method of mixing light from original sources is called *additive color*. Output devices, on the other hand, work by applying color to a page that selectively absorbs light waves from an external source, such as that from light bulbs or the sun. This method of creating colors is called *subtractive color*. Additive and subtractive colors produce fundamentally different ranges of colors. For this reason, onscreen color (additive) offers bright, highly saturated colors that invariably appear darker when printed (subtractive) on paper or other materials.

Second, variations among printers, monitors, and presses make it impossible for each of them to produce exactly the same range and quality of colors. An inexpensive ink-jet printer has one set of printable colors, a color laser printer another, a dye sublimation printer yet another, a web press another, and a high-quality sheet-fed press another still.

Differences in the color models and technical characteristics of color devices result in device-specific gamuts, or ranges, of colors. To achieve consistent color across different devices, the trick is to map colors from one device to another so that when a file is displayed or produced on each device, the differences between the gamuts are accounted and compensated for and the color remains as consistent as possible.

Apple's ColorSync performs this task using a system of device-specific profiles. With ColorSync, colors are converted from their original definitions into a device-independent definition based on the international CIE XYZ color standard, or color space. (A color space is a three-dimensional mapping of a range of possible colors.) This conversion is done using a device profile, a small file that contains information about the color characteristics and capabilities of the input device or monitor. Once a color is defined in CIE XYZ, it is then translated (by utilizing a set of color matching method (CMM) algorithms) for output using the device profile of the output device.

Apple furnishes device profiles for its own monitors, scanners, and color printers, but the success of ColorSync is dependent upon third-party developers producing and distributing device profiles for their scanners, monitors, and printers. To use ColorSync effectively, you must have device profiles for each of the specific scanners, monitors, and printers you're using for any given project. You can use the ColorSync Utility application to create ColorSync profiles for specific documents, then use the ColorSync pane in the System Preferences to select a default profile when an embedded profile is not available. Let's start with the steps necessary to calibrate a monitor:

1. Launch the System Preferences from the Dock or Apple menu.

2. Select the Displays pane.

3. Select the Color tab.

4. Click the Calibrate button to launch the Display Calibrator Assistant.

5. Advance through the many options, such as the gamma option, shown in Figure 10.17.

6. Give your new profile a name. At this point, the Display Calibrator Assistant will automatically quit, and you will be returned to the ColorSync pane of the System Preferences.

10

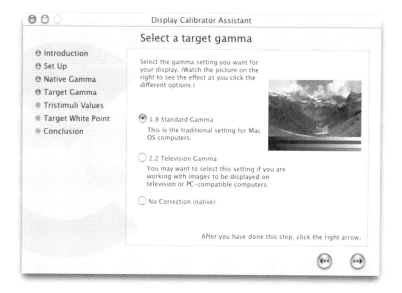

Figure 10.17
Use the ColorSync System Preferences pane to create a ColorSync profile for your display.

8. Select the new profile, or an existing profile, in the Display Profile list.

9. Quit the System Preferences.

To maintain the accuracy of your computer's ColorSync profiles, launch the ColorSync Utility from the Utilities folder and follow these steps:

1. Select the Profile First Aid button at the top of the window.

2. Click the Verify button to evaluate the accuracy of profiles on your computer.

3. Problems will be reported on the right side of the ColorSync Utility window. During the verification process, you can click the repair button to fix these problems.

4. Follow the instructions for additional information or recommended action, if presented.

5. Quit the ColorSync Utility.

ColorSync profiles contain highly detailed information about color values, and you can use the ColorSync Utility to view this information in excruciating detail by launching the ColorSync Utility from the Utilities folder. Then follow these steps:

1. Select the Profile button at the top of the window.

2. Expand the hierarchical list of profiles to locate the profile you want to view, as in Figure 10.18.

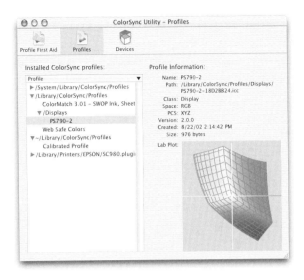

Figure 10.18
Use the ColorSync Utility to view summary information about ColorSync profiles on your computer.

3. Double-click the selected item to reveal more detailed information, as in Figure 10.19.

4. Quit the ColorSync Utility.

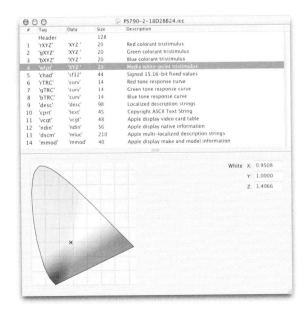

Figure 10.19
A detailed view of a ColorSync profile for a ViewSonic display.

The ColorSync Utility also allows you to view detailed information about ColorSync-aware hardware attached to your computer, including scanners, digital cameras, displays, printers, and color proofing devices. To view this information, launch the ColorSync Utility from the Utilities folder and follow these steps:

1. Select the Devices button at the top of the window.

2. Expand the hierarchical list of devices to reveal a device, an example of which is shown in Figure 10.20.

Figure 10.20
Use the ColorSync profile to view and assign ColorSync profiles to ColorSync-aware hardware associated with your computer.

3. To change the assigned profile, click the Current Profile menu on the right and locate the new color profile.

4. Quit the ColorSync Utility.

When ColorSync translates colors into or out of the CIE XYZ color model, it does so with the goal of providing the best possible match between the original color and the final color. Differences in devices sometimes make an exact match impossible, as explained earlier. The algorithm ColorSync uses to perform this translation was designed for optimum results, but it was also designed to use a small amount of memory and provide good performance. Other companies, such as EFI and Kodak, have developed their own conversion methods—based on look-up tables rather than algorithms—that produce superior results. These methods, however, require far more memory, information, and expertise for each input and output device. Finally, these methods are compatible with ColorSync and can be put to good use by anyone working in high-quality color that desires improved results.

By providing an automated color-matching system, Apple has taken the uncertainty out of using color. What was once tedious work is now handled for you by hardware vendors and software programmers. The quality of this translation will no doubt improve over time.

Wrapping Up

Fonts, printing, and color matching continue to be crucial parts of the Macintosh experience, and as shown in this chapter, font technology remains a source of innovation and complexity. In this chapter, I hope you have learned more about:

- *The Quartz Extreme imaging model*—How Apple's system-level page description language for graphics and type allows for easy development of sophisticated applications.

- *Fonts*—How to select, install, and work with the many types of fonts supported by Mac OS X.

- *The Font Panel*—How to use the Font Panel to easily change font options from within Carbon and Cocoa applications.

- *Font utilities*—How to use several third-party font utilities to view and mange fonts.

- *Color matching*—How ColorSync helps match colors.

In Chapter 11, we'll explore AppleScript's ability to automate tasks and communicate among applications.

10

Scripting Mac OS X

Shortcuts are a way of life for many computer users. They help us save time and effort and are occasionally entertaining, but most importantly, they make us more productive. The Mac OS has a long history of providing shortcuts to applications and the Mac OS itself through key combinations and menus. In fact, it's safe to say that the graphical user interface's raison d'Ítre is to enable the user to execute complex commands with a click of the mouse—perhaps the ultimate shortcut. Macintosh users can create their own shortcuts with AppleScript, a programming language that is unique to the Mac OS. Many elements of the Mac OS are scriptable (meaning that they "understand" AppleScript as a programming language), as are numerous applications that run under Mac OS X, Mac OS 9.x, and earlier.

The ability to control applications, repeat actions, and automate system tasks must originate in the operating system if it is to be successful. AppleScript was designed to provide these essential capabilities as part of an overall strategy to supply automation tools for Macintosh applications. A fully integrated part of the operating system, AppleScript is automatically installed as part of Mac OS X.

AppleScript can be utilized in an impressive variety of ways:

- AppleScript lets you tailor applications to meet your needs.

- AppleScript simplifies the work of developers, systems integrators, and value–added resellers (VARs) by providing custom solutions based on standard Macintosh applications.

- AppleScript allows you to write an application, an intelligent agent, or a smart document that seamlessly integrates small components into larger solutions.

- Software developers can create entirely new products with AppleScript.

Mac OS X includes several new benefits in AppleScript version 1.9:

- Expanded Internet scripting services

- Return of Folder Actions scripting

- Script Menu for quick access to scripts

- Additional scriptable applications

This chapter looks at how AppleScript version 1.9 is implemented in Mac OS X. I'll also show you how to get your programming feet wet with AppleScript and then use your script-writing skills to become more productive.

What Is AppleScript?

Technically speaking, AppleScript is a high-level, object-oriented programming language. As far as programming languages go, AppleScript is the real thing: it can store variables and lists (records or arrays); repeat through looping; make decisions based on cases; do If-Then branching; compare; practice Boolean logic; and manipulate text, numbers, dates, times, and other values. AppleScript can also declare variables, create user-defined commands or subroutines, and store and manipulate data to return values. Of course, this is all meaningless if you're not a real computer geek, which goes to show that underneath the pretty interface, Mac OS X is a complex operating system.

AppleScript is termed an object-oriented programming language because it imposes actions on objects that are defined as part of its programming model. Objects can be applications (the Finder, TextEdit, BBEdit, and so on), files, resources, interface elements (buttons, windows, and so on), or data. In the Finder, objects can be a variety of computers, printers, and even Appletalk zones on a network. Even the objects you see on your Desktop can be manipulated with AppleScript. Mac OS X enables many of its own applications to be scripted, as do authors of many third-party applications.

In AppleScript, objects have two additional characteristics that are part of the programming language: *inheritance* and *encapsulation*. Objects, like applications, can contain other objects (encapsulation); objects derived from other objects share common characteristics (inheritance). AppleScript is an object-oriented programming language, and scriptable applications serve as the objects upon which scripts act. The rules of scriptability from Apple impose regularity on objects by making them behave in ways you expect and come to learn intuitively, like rules of grammar.

AppleScript is different from most other programming languages because it uses *words* and *statements* instead of arcane programming characters and symbols to form a coherent group of commands into a script. Like the English language, AppleScript uses words as nouns (objects), verbs, and modifiers. In AppleScript, verbs are common action commands (such as open, close, print, or delete) that are often derived from standard menu commands. Statements are commands that can be conveyed in the form of messages to objects in other applications. Applications themselves are objects because they can be commanded to do actions. For example, consider the following:

```
tell application "Clock"
    activate
end tell
```

This three-line statement is a complete script that instructs the Finder to launch the Clock application. When viewed in the Script Editor program, located in /Macintosh HD/Applications/AppleScript/, you can see that this type of script uses bolded verbs, plain nouns, and italicized variables to make working with scripts easier than if all the text in the script were plain ASCII text. Often you'll see AppleScripts written in clegic logic (or hierarchical display) format, with indentations for each command structure. You can see an example of this formatting in the **Current Date & Time.scpt** script, which is located in the Scripts folder (discussed later in this chapter) provided by Apple as part of Mac OS X. Figure 11.1 shows what this script looks like in the Script Editor application, as well as the result of the script when the Run button is clicked.

As much as possible, AppleScript is written in a manner similar to the way you normally write and speak—although the syntax is certainly much more precise and

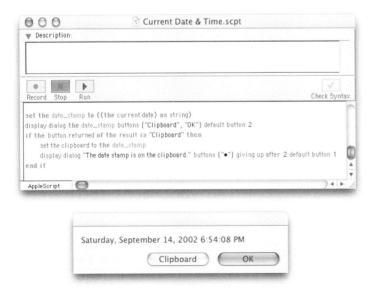

Figure 11.1
Current Date & Time.scpt, shown in the Script Editor (top) and the result of the script when it is run (bottom).

demanding. The intent is to lower the learning curve for AppleScript by employing words, expressions, and modifiers that you use in your everyday life.

Programs written in AppleScript, called *scripts*, are like those written for all other high-level programming languages. Scripts must be *interpreted* or *compiled* to run on your Mac. You can store your script for interpretation at run time or transform it into an interpreted read-only program, which you can then distribute freely to other users. When you compile a script, it is transformed into a dialect-independent format called *Universal AppleScript*. Upon opening a script, you'll see it displayed in the default language of the Mac you're working on—not necessarily the language in which the script was originally written. This means that the script has been translated from Universal AppleScript.

AppleScript isn't just a fixed set of commands. Instead, AppleScript is extensible by the scripting commands contained in the scripting dictionaries of scriptable applications. Each scripting dictionary is composed of commands (verbs), objects (nouns), and modifiers that are accessible via AppleScript for that specific application, such as Mail or even the Finder. You can view the scripting dictionaries of all the scriptable applications on your computer by selecting the File|Open Dictionary command of the Script Editor, which presents the window shown in Figure 11.2.

The ability to see all the scripting dictionaries at once is was a feature first included with AppleScript 1.6 for Mac OS X Version 1.0. However, you can still browse your computer for the scripting dictionary of a specific application by clicking the Browse button in the Open Dictionary window shown in Figure 11.2. You'll be asked to locate the application whose scripting dictionary you're looking for. Figure 11.3 shows

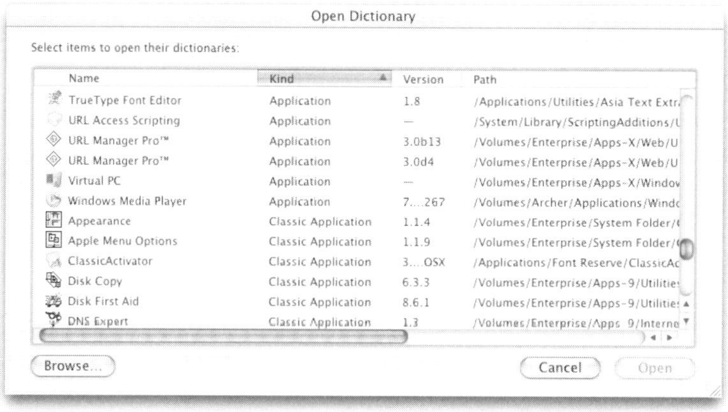

Figure 11.2
Use the Open Dictionary command to browse the scripting commands for scriptable applications.

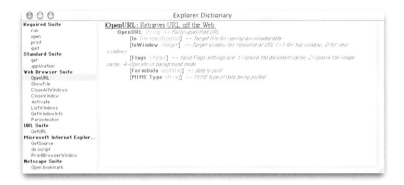

Figure 11.3
The scripting dictionary for Internet Explorer.

an example of one item in the scripting dictionary for Internet Explorer. Although scripting dictionaries share many of the same elements, the dictionary of each scriptable application has at least a few elements all its own.

You can use applications other than Script Editor to write AppleScripts, such as Apple's AppleScript Studio (**www.apple.com/applescript/studio/**), BBEdit from Bare Bones Software (**www.barebones.com**), and Script Debugger from Late Night Software (**www.latenightsw.com**).

The AppleScript Architecture

Most programming languages require that you learn a new language. To minimize this inconvenience, Apple introduced the Open Scripting Architecture (OSA) as a language framework that other software venders could adopt, so that their applications could communicate with each other. A software vendor merely has to follow the OSA specifications to make an application scriptable.

The standards definition phase of OSA began in 1989 and is ongoing. OSA and the Apple Event Registry were released concurrently with System 7 in 1991. This marked the beginning of Interapplication Communication, which is the foundation of the AppleScript architecture. Some key applications that supported AppleScript with the original architecture (such as Excel 4.0, FileMaker Pro 2.0, PageMaker 4.2, and others) were released in 1992. Bundled with System 7 Pro, AppleScript 1.0 premiered as a separate product in 1993; version 1.1 and the Scriptable Finder appeared in System 7.5. The Scriptable Finder, a very important addition to the AppleScript architecture, removed the final advantage of text-based operating systems such as MS-DOS by allowing users to script the operating system. Mac OS X includes the latest version, AppleScript 1.9, and of course it is also highly scriptable using

11

command-line scripts through the Terminal application. See Appendix C for information on learning basic Unix shell commands.

AppleScript is just one expression of OSA. OSA includes AppleEvents, the object model, and a reference library of objects and events that are codified by third parties through Apple. These components form the basis for an open standard that Apple hopes others will build upon in the years to come. AppleScript uses AppleEvents as the messaging medium through which script commands are passed and results returned.

To prevent AppleScript from growing in nonstandard ways, Apple imposes a standard language. Objects in AppleScript are identified by compound names, called *references*. The overall naming scheme is called the *object model*. With this lexicon of references, the language allows you to refer to individual objects in several ways without worrying about how each application prefers to describe an object. Some commands have alternate expressions, as do some objects—fortunately, AppleScript validates both kinds in any application.

A standard syntax is imposed on developers only for common language tasks. Apple has organized events and objects into *event suites*, which are common ways to do tasks based on application categories: text processing, databases and spreadsheets, communications, page layout, and so on. Event suites extend the concept of common menu-command language elements such as *copy* and *paste* to scripting commands such as **delete**, **contain**, **get**, and **set**.

Event suites are evolving as developers register their commands, objects, and suites in the AppleEvent Registry (available from the Apple Developer Connection, or ADC). The event suites in this registry are the approved language for interapplication communication; the registry serves as a standard reference for developers who want to implement AppleScript support within their own applications.

The commands that compose the language of AppleScript are contained in files called OSAX, which stands for Open Scripting Architecture Extension. These files are also called Scripting Additions. In previous versions of the operating system, Scripting Additions were contained in a single file called Standard Additions. This file, and other OSAX files, are now located in /Macintosh HD/System/Library/Scripting Additions/. In addition to this unification, a few of the features that extend a developer's abilities include:

■ *User interaction*—Users can interact with scripts through script-generated dialog boxes, sounds, and text-to-speech.

■ *File commands*—Scripts can request and present files and information about files, disks, folders, and volumes.

- *String commands*—Scripts can manipulate ASCII text, as well as summarize paragraphs or pages of text.

- *Clipboard*—Scripts can now access the data that is contained in the clipboard, set new data, or get information on the data.

- *Delay*—Scripts can incorporate a delay of a certain amount of time, specified in seconds. Scriptwriters use this to give scripts a more natural feel.

- *Choice menus*—A list of items can be presented to users, allowing them to make selections.

- *Timed dialog boxes*—A dialog box can assume a default value if a user does not respond to it within a certain amount of time.

Scripting Basics

AppleScript has been implemented using different components over the years. In earlier versions, AppleScript wasn't a mandatory part of the Mac OS, but eventually it became an integral part of the operating system. Mac OS X installs all the necessary components of AppleScript, including:

- *AppleScript framework*—Contains the AppleScript libraries necessary to interpret scripts for the Mac OS; also passes script commands and data between applications.

- *ScriptingAdditions folder*—Houses scripting additions that have been written to provide additional functionality the basic feature set of AppleScript.

- *Scripts folders*—Two folders for storing scripts. Although AppleScripts can be placed just about anywhere on your computer, it makes sense to keep them in one place. Mac OS X provides two Scripts folders, on in /Macintosh HD/Library/Scripts/ and one in each user's home folder (inside the Library folder).

The AppleScript folder, located in the Applications folder, is the home folder for the three items you'll use most when working with AppleScript. The AppleScript folder includes:

- *Script Editor*—The primary application that enables you to write, record, edit, check the syntax of, compile, and run scripts. Shown earlier in Figure 11.1, the Script Editor is a basic but effective means of manipulating AppleScripts. The Script Editor Help covers the basics of writing AppleScripts and using the Script Editor. Choose Help|Script Editor Help to activate the Help Viewer application.

- *Script Menu.menu*—A new menu extra that provides easy access to the contents of your Scripts folder, which are described in detail a little later in this chapter. The

11

Script Menu replaces the functionality of the Script Runner utility found in previous versions of Mac OS X.

- *Example Scripts*—An alias to the /Macintosh HD/Library/Scripts/ folder, which contains dozens and dozens of example scripts that you can execute or explore with the Script Editor to help teach yourself about AppleScript.

Because AppleScript support is added to an application by its developer, not all applications are scriptable in Mac OS X. Moreover, an application may or may not support each of the three levels of scriptability, which are referred to as:

- *Scriptable*—A scriptable application represents the highest level of AppleScript support. These applications can understand and respond to AppleEvents generated by scripts, and can be controlled by an AppleScript.

- *Recordable*—A recordable application is capable of sending itself AppleEvents (the messaging medium through which script commands are passed and results returned) and reporting user actions to the Apple Event Manager so that a script summarizing these actions can be recorded. When you use the Record button of the Script Editor, recordable applications allow you to create and compile scripts as applications. This is probably the easiest way to create a script, as it requires no knowledge of scripting. For many users, pressing the Record button and then opening an application is easier than typing the corresponding commands into the Script Editor.

- *Attachable*—This type of application can trigger a script as a response to a user action (such as clicking a button or entering a text string). Apple describes an attachable application as "tinkerable." Attachable applications are useful as menus to other applications.

Any combination of these three levels of scriptability is possible—you can have an application that is scriptable and recordable, recordable and attachable, scriptable and attachable, or all three. Apple publishes a Web page entitled Scriptable Applications with a listing of each application's capabilities. To view the list or to add an application to the list, you can visit the Apple Web site at **www.apple.com/ applescript/apps/**.

The Script Editor

The Script Editor, which is located in the Applications/AppleScript folder, is the primary application for opening, running, recording, editing, and saving scripts in various forms. Creating AppleScripts ranges anywhere from falling-off-a-log easy, to highly difficult, so I don't want to give you the impression that you'll be a professional scriptor after you read this chapter! It takes quite a bit of time to become proficient with AppleScript, so I hope the following sections illustrate many of the basic principles used in creating and working with AppleScripts. If you want to learn more about AppleScript, visit **www.apple.com/applescript/resources/**.

Recording a Script

The Script Editor comes with a recorder feature that enables you to create scripts based on your actions. Other scripting programs call this a "watch me" kind of programming. As described previously, applications can be scripted in this way only if they are recordable, and the easiest way to determine recordability is to try it out. To record a script, follow these steps:

1. Launch the Script Editor.

2. Click the Record button to turn on the recording feature, or press Command+D.

3. Switch to the application of your choice, including the Finder.

4. Perform the actions in the sequence in which you want them to be recorded.

5. Switch back to the Script Editor window and click the Stop button, or press Command+. (Command+period).

What if you follow these steps and only some of what you did shows up in the Script Editor window? This means that the actions you attempted to record are not in the scripting dictionary of the application(s) involved in creating your recorded script. For example, Figure 11.4 shows the results of recording a script designed to switch to the application BBEdit, create a new document, and type "Hello world" in the new document.

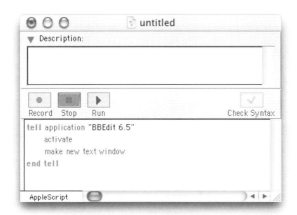

11

Figure 11.4
The Script Editor window with a sample recorded script.

You will notice that the Script Editor has recorded all the commands that correspond to my actions in this example except for the typing of "Hello world" within the BBEdit document. As with other keystroke macro recorders, only certain actions can be captured by the Script Editor: using menu commands, pressing keys, saving files, opening and closing windows and files, and clicking the mouse. Drags and clicks are not captured because they usually don't result in any actions or changes. However, when a click or drag does result in an action, such as activating a button or moving a file to a new folder, that action is recorded. In this example, typing in a BBEdit document is not a recordable action.

 TIP: You can also use the commands in the Control menu of the Script Editor in place of the buttons you see in the Script Editor window.

Finally, because the actions were recorded as a script, the syntax does not require checking—therefore, the Check Syntax option (described later) is not available in the Script Editor window.

Saving a Script

When you stop the recording of a script in the Script Editor, or when you've made changes to an existing script, you can save the script from within the Script Editor via the Save As command, as shown in Figure 11.5. Using Script Editor, you can save your script in any of the following formats:

- *Text*—It's best to save a script as a plain ASCII text file if you intend to use it in programs such as BBEdit, a program that's very popular with application and script authors.

- *Compiled Script*—Scripts saved as compiled scripts are designed to be used from within applications or by other scripts, rather than by you, the user.

- *Application* —A script saved as an application for Mac OS X is capable of running on any computer with Mac OS X that has the same scripting addition, if referenced in the application.

- *Application for Classic*—Scripts can be saved as applications that require the Classic environment. When you double-click on an AppleScript that was saved as a Classic application, the application runs by itself (without the assistance of the Script Editor) in the Classic environment, if Mac OS 9.x is installed on the computer. When you save a script as an application, use the checkboxes in the lower-left corner of the Save dialog box to specify that an AppleScript application be kept open after the script is run (Stay Open), that a preliminary screen asking if you

Figure 11.5
Saving an AppleScript as a compiled script.

want to proceed not be displayed (Never Show Startup Screen), or that the application be opened in the Classic environment (Require the Classic Environment). Figure 11.6 shown these three options in the lower left corner of the window.

TIP: Earlier versions of AppleScript supported various languages, and the compiling operation translated a script from its language of origin into Universal AppleScript, a pseudocode that your Macintosh can read. Since Mac OS 8.6, however, AppleScript has supported English only.

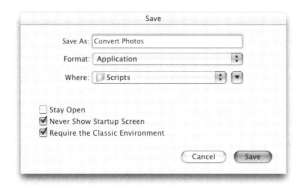

Figure 11.6
Saving an AppleScript as an application for the Classic environment.

You can save an application or compiled script as a *runtime*—or as AppleScript calls it, *run-only*—version of your script. You cannot, however, save text files as run-only. A run-only script is kind of like a compiled application in this respect because you cannot "reverse-engineer" this type of script to see what it looks like in the Script Editor. To save a run-only version of a script, choose the Save As Run-Only command from the File menu. The resulting dialog box will ask you to specify the script's location, name, and format.

 TIP: To save a script in a non-editable format, choose Save As | Run-Only from the File menu.

Finally, when saving scripts, Apple recommends that you use the following file extensions for the various types of AppleScript components:

- *AppleScript applications*—No recommendation

- *Compiled script*—MyScript.scpt

- *Script text*—MyScript.applescript

- *Scripting addition*— MyAdditions.osax

- *Scripting dictionary*—MyScriptDictionary.asdictionary

It isn't required that you follow these naming schemes, but it could come in handy because Mac OS X supports the opening of items based on file name extensions, which is discussed in Chapter 7, "Working with Mac OS X Applications."

Running a Script

Once you have recorded, written, edited, and saved a script, you can run it in several ways, depending on how the script was saved. You can run the script, or you can run an alias to the script as if it were the script itself. Aliasing scripts allows you to access scripts through various locations as well. For example, if you store all your scripts in your Scripts folder, you can still alias certain scripts in other locations as well, such as from within an application's own Scripts folder. The main ways to run a script include:

- Select a script from within applications such as BBEdit and GraphicConverter, each of which has its own script folder for AppleScripts. Figure 11.7 shows the Script menus for BBEdit (left) and GraphicConverter (right).

- Double-click a script saved as an application from within the Finder.

- Open a script in the Script Editor and click the Run button.

Figure 11.7
Many applications have robust support for AppleScript and even have a Script menu for easy access to application-specific scripts.

■ Run a script from within another script or application.

■ Add a script to the Login Items pane of the System Preferences.

■ Use the Script Menu, described in the following section.

When you launch an AppleScript application, a startup screen may appear if you didn't choose the Never Show Startup Screen option (refer to Figure 11.6) in the Save dialog box. Click the Run button or press the Return key to run the script; click the Quit button or press Command+Q to abort the script.

Running a script results in a visible or invisible action. Some scripts return a value or expression based on the results of their actions. If you expect an outcome and want to see it displayed in a window, choose the Show Result command from the Script Editor Control menu. If there is an error in your script, you may see an error message in the Result window.

Scripts also can be saved in the form of a *droplet* (a drag-and-drop-enabled application). This type of script contains a handler that uses the **On Open** command and can be identified by the down-pointing arrow on their icons. To launch an AppleScript droplet, first decide what object will be on the receiving end of the droplet's action. Then simply drag that object's icon over the droplet's icon or alias. (This process is similar to opening a document with a particular application by dragging the document's icon onto the application's icon.) If the droplet supports the object, the action will take place immediately; otherwise, an error message will appear.

Scripts can, of course, be embedded inside other applications or files. Scripts in this form can be called up in many ways. Some embedded (or attached) scripts will be under your control; others will not. You'll often see scripts attached to buttons—when you click the button, the script runs. Other scripts will look for a text string in a field,

11

check a condition, or enact other tasks that may not be obvious to you. These scripts can often run in the background and escape your detection.

Modifying a Script

Scripts recorded in the Script Editor are fully editable in the script window, as is any text document. To begin modifying a script, launch the Script Editor and use the Open Script command from the File menu to open the script by name. Most of the text editing actions in the Script Editor should be familiar to you from your word processor. Just type in your changes and save the results. In addition to simple clicks and drags, you can use the following shortcuts in the Script Editor window:

■ Double-click to select a word; triple-click to select a line.

■ Use the arrow keys to move the insertion point.

■ Use the Command+left arrow or Command+right arrow keystrokes to move to the beginning or end of a line, respectively.

■ Use the Command+up arrow or Command+down arrow keystroke to move to the beginning or end of the script, respectively.

■ Use the Tab key at the beginning of a line to indent it. Tabs typed in the middle of a line are converted to space characters when you apply syntax formatting.

■ Use the Return key at the end of an indented line to apply indenting automatically to the next line.

■ Use the Option+Return keystroke to insert a continuation character (¨) and move to the beginning of the next line. This shortcut lets you work with a line that is too long to fit in the view of the active window. AppleScript ignores the continuation character and treats the lines on either side of it as one line.

■ Use the Shift+Return keystroke to move the insertion point from the end of an indented line to the beginning of a new, unindented line.

The Script Editor has a Check Syntax button for written or modified scripts. This feature will run through a script to check that the syntax of the programming steps is correct. Syntax is the collection of grammar rules for a programming language. For example, if you have a command that requires a companion command, and if you forgot to put it in, you'll get an error when you click on the Check Syntax button. The Check Syntax button will check for errors in construction only, not errors in programming logic.

When applied, the Check Syntax feature returns the first error as selected text. If there is an error in the text, no formatting is applied to the text in the Script Editor window. When the error is corrected, the Script Editor compiles the script, showing it with clegic (indented) formatting and other formatting options.

Some Script Editor features let you set the formatting of the script to make it easier to read. Some programs call this *beautifying* the script. You can change fonts, styles, sizes, and colors that are used in your scripts. Whereas these formatting styles make it easier to read the script and understand it, they have no effect on the operation of the script. To set formatting options, choose the AppleScript Formatting command from the Edit menu; an example of the AppleScript Formatting window is shown in Figure 11.8. Changes you make in this window will affect any script you open from the Script Editor.

Figure 11.8
The AppleScript Formatting preferences window.

The elements of formatting that you can apply, based on the AppleScript formatting window, are as follows:

- *New Text*—Any modifications you make to a script before you check its syntax, run it, or save the results. Formatting these modifications allows you to easily discern your changes from a "wall of text."

- *Operators*—Actions (verbs) applied to objects in AppleScript.

- *Language Keywords*—Commands available as part of the AppleScript language. They are often also actions and verbs.

- *Application Keywords*—Language extensions added to AppleScript by an application referenced from within a script.

■ *Comments*—Explanatory text that you add to a script to make its purpose understandable. Some people add comments to the beginning of a script as a header, to the beginning of a procedure, or even after important lines in a script. Comments in AppleScript are preceded by a double hyphen. Anything on a line to the right of the double hyphen is formatted in italics when compiled and then ignored at execution time or during a syntax check. For a multiline comment, use an asterisk to mark the beginning and end of the comment. Supplying brief yet cogent commenting is an art and the sure sign of a good programmer. For beginners, it's better to over-comment script than under-comment it.

■ *Values*—Data or information, such as names, words, and numbers, used by AppleScript.

■ *Variables*—A phrase you identify that can contain multiple values. Values can change according to conditions.

■ *References*—A pointer to an object. When you describe "window 1 of application BBEdit," AppleScript knows you're referring to the first opened BBEdit window. Reference formatting appears in the Result window, not in the script window.

To change the style of text for a category, select the category by clicking on it once, then select a font from the Font menu, and then a style from the Style menu. To erase your changes and revert to the default styles for all the categories, select the Use Defaults button.

Using the Script Menu

The Script Menu, located in the main AppleScript folder alongside the Script Editor application, replaces the old Script Runner utility as a shortcut for accessing scripts. The Script Menu isn't new, however; it has been an optional download from Apple for some time now, and it is a good addition to the default installation of Mac OS X. The Script Menu provides a drop-down menu in which you can access all of the scripts located in your personal Scripts folder, as well as the system-wide Scripts folder. Figure 11.9 shows an example of the Script Menu once it has been installed.

The Script Menu recognizes individual scripts in the Scripts folder, as well as subfolders of scripts that you can customize. To try out the Script Menu's features, follow these steps to activate it and access the example scripts that come with Mac OS X into your Scripts folders:

1. Open the AppleScript folder located in the Applications folder.

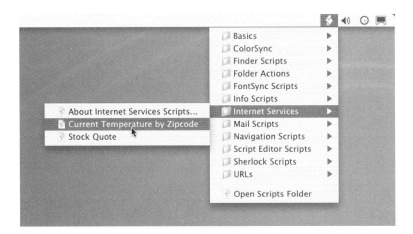

Figure 11.9
The Script Menu provides a shortcut to the scripts stored in your Scripts folders.

2. Drag the folder named Script Menu.menu to the upper-right area of the menu bar. Once the AppleScript icon has appeared in the menu, it has been successfully installed.

3. Press the Command key and drag the AppleScript Menu icon to the right or left to reposition it among any other menu bar icons that might be present, such as those for Sound, Date & Time, or Displays.

4. Press the Command key and drag the AppleScript Menu to the Desktop to remove it from the menu bar.

The Script Menu will display all types of scripts and applications. It will not, however, display scripts saved as text because technically, these are document instead of scripts and cannot be run or launched to perform an action, as can scripts and applications. Items in /Macintosh HD/Library/Scripts/ are displayed first, including the contents of any subfolders in this location. Use the Open Scripts Folder option at the very bottom of the Script Menu to open the Scripts folder in your home folder. Once you have added one or more items to this folder, they will appear in the Script Menu between those in the main Scripts folder at the top, and the Open Scripts Folder option at the bottom. Figure 11.10 illustrates the position of a user's scripts in the Script Menu and a sample Scripts folder in a user's home folder.

Finally, unlike the old Script Runner utility, which wouldn't recognize any new scripts or applications added to one of the Scripts folders until Script Runner was quit and relaunched, changes to the Scripts folders are immediately reflected in the Script Menu.

11

Figure 11.10
The Script Menu displays the contents of a user's Scripts folder toward the bottom of the Script Menu.

Scriptable Applications

Every scriptable application has its own set of terms to add to the AppleScript vocabulary. Those terms are described in the application's scripting dictionary, as mentioned earlier in this chapter. Items, commands, and other verbs that are scriptable by the application are organized into categories called event suites. Because Script Editor recognizes the scripting dictionaries of both Classic and Mac OS X scriptable applications, you need to be careful about selecting the correct scripting dictionary. When you choose File|Open Dictionary in the Script Editor the scripting dictionaries that are available are listed in alphabetical order, but clicking on the Kind column heading will sort them by Mac OS X versus Classic, making it easier to select the correct scripting dictionary (see Figure 11.2 for an example).

In addition to the Finder, several of Mac OS X's applications are scriptable, including:

■ Address Book

■ Apple System Profiler

■ ColorSync

■ Disk Copy

- DVD Player

- iCal

- iDVD

- Image Capture

- Internet Connect

- Internet Explorer

- iTunes

- Keychain

- Mail

- Print Center

- QuickTime Player

- Sherlock

- StuffIt Expander

- System Preferences

- Terminal

- TextEdit

- URL Access Scripting

With former incarnations of AppleScript, scriptwriters complained that the dictionaries of various applications are very hard to understand. The greatest difficulty has been the tendency of the commands that are specific to an application to be presented in a single, unorganized list. While this presentation format is concise, it's difficult for a scriptwriter to find the name of a script command without having some idea of where the command is located alphabetically. In the current version of AppleScript, dictionaries are subdivided into sections that represent different types of functionality. This allows a scriptwriter to narrow a search without previous knowledge of the component, but again, it is up to the application developer to organize the scripting dictionary according to Apple's recommended guidelines.

When you click on a dictionary item, the definition of the command appears in the right panel of the window; click on a category and all the commands for that category

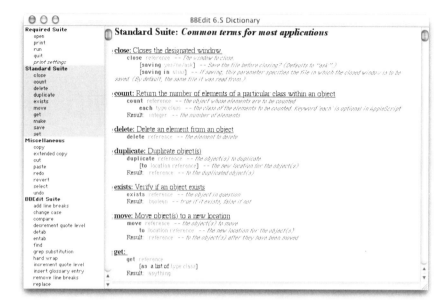

Figure 11.11
The Standard Suite of BBEdit's scripting dictionary.

are displayed, as illustrated in Figure 11.11. You'll also see information about the item, such as the kinds of objects that it acts on, the information or values that it requires, and the results that are returned. Nearly every AppleScript-aware application supports the required and standard suites of commands.

I find that Script Debugger , mentioned earlier in this chapter, does a much better job at displaying the scripting dictionaries of scriptable applications. It allows you to view scripting dictionaries in the traditional hierarchical way of the Script Editor, but it also provides two additional ways of viewing scripting dictionaries, including the Object Model view, shown in Figure 11.12, and the Explorer view. The information is all the same, but viewing it in different ways can be helpful.

Folder Actions

Folder Actions allows a script to be associated with a specific folder on your computer. For example, a script can be designed to run every time a certain folder is opened. The other interactions are closing a folder, adding items to a folder, removing items from a folder, and moving or resizing a folder window. Folder Actions scripts are associated with:

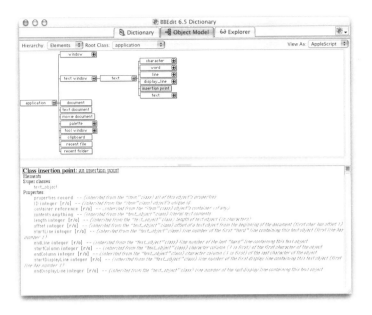

Figure 11.12
A scripting dictionary viewed in Script Debugger.

- Opening a folder

- Closing a folder

- Moving the window of a folder that has been opened

- When you put one or more items in an open folder

- When you remove one or more items from an open folder

Folder Actions were introduced several years ago but it was not supported in Mac OS X until Mac OS X Version 10.2. In the past, Folder Actions scripts were associated with a folder by holding down the Control key while clicking the folder's icon, and selecting "Attach a Folder Action" from the contextual menu, which presented a file selection dialog box in which you selected the desired script to attach to the folder. In Mac OS X, it works differently:

1. Enable the Script Menu using the steps outlined previously in this chapter.

2. Select Folder Actions|Enable Folder Actions in the Script Menu.

11

3. Write a script containing on of the five actions described above, and store the script in /Macintosh HD/Library/Scripts/Folder Actions Scripts/ or /Macintosh HD/Users/username/Scripts/Folder Actions Scripts/, which is created automatically one you enable Folder Actions. Mac OS X installs a few scripts that you can attach to a folder, which are stored in /Macintosh HD/Library/Scripts/Folder Actions Scripts/.

4. Select Folder Actions|Attach Script to Folder in the Script Menu, and choose a script to attach to a folder.

5. When prompted, choose a folder to which a script is to be attached.

Writing your own Folder Actions script is easy. For example, the following easy script beeps and displays the dialog window shown in Figure 11.13 when the folder to which the script is attached is opened:

```
on opening folder this_folder
tell application "Finder"
set this_name to the name of this_folder
end tell
beep
display dialog "The folder named "" & this_name & "" has been opened. Thought
you might want to know!" buttons {"Cool!"} default button 1
end opening folder
```

Figure 11.13
A sample action taken by an Folder Actions script when a designated folder is opened.

To unattach a script, follow these steps:

1. Select Folder Actions|Remove Folder Actions in the Script Menu.

2. Choose a folder from the list of folders to which scripts have been attached, then click the OK button.

3. Choose a script to remove from the folder, then click the OK button.

You may attach more than one folder action to a folder following the same steps outlined above for attaching the first script. If you have more than one script attached to a folder, all the scripts will appear in a list during the removal process, and you will have to repeat the process to remove all the scripts from a folder.

Example Scripts

Mac OS X includes numerous example scripts, which were mentioned earlier in the section entitled "Using the Script Menu." The eighty or so example scripts are divided into the following categories:

- *Basics*—Scripts for working with the Script Editor and getting help

- ColorSync—Scripts for managing ColorSync profiles and devices

- *Finder Scripts*—Scripts for working in the Finder in Mac OS X

- *Folder Actions Scripts*—Scripts for attaching to folders

- *Folder Actions*—Scripts for enabling, disabling, adding and removing Folder Actions scripts

- *FontSync Scripts*—Scripts for synchronizing sets of fonts

- *Info Scripts*—One script for getting the current date and time, and another that creates a sample of all the fonts available to the operating system

- *Internet Ssevices*—Scripts for obtaining information over Internet

- *Mail Scripts*—An example script for the Mail application

- *Navigation Scripts*—Scripts for manipulating Finder windows

- *Script Editor Scripts*—Advanced scripts for manipulating the Script Editor

- *Sherlock Scripts*—Scripts for searching the Internet with Sherlock

- *URLs*—Example scripts for opening URLs in a Web browser

11

In addition to these scripts, you may also download numerous sample scripts and view online tutorials from **www.apple.com/applescript/guidebook/sbrt/**. Some of the scripts found at this site may not be compatible with Mac OS X Version 10.2; nevertheless, many of them contain useful examples and information that can help you understand the fundamentals of scripting. In addition to these sample scripts, the Resources section on the main AppleScript site at **www.apple.com/applescript/resources/** has links to several valuable resources for learning more about AppleScript. And finally, check out your favorite online bookstores for the latest books about AppleScript.

Wrapping Up

AppleScript fulfills a long-standing promise to provide automation capabilities within the Macintosh operating system, and although the Mac OS X version is still playing catch-up, AppleScript is thorough and rigorous in its implementation, laying the groundwork for more important and convenient expressions to come.

In this chapter, you've learned:

- The purpose and basics of the AppleScript architecture

- How to record, run, modify and save scripts using the Script Editor, including Folder Actions

- How to access scripts the Script Menu

- How to identify applications that are AppleScript aware (recordable, scriptable, and attachable)

The next chapter will explore an important, but often overlooked, feature of Mac OS X: Java.

Using Java

It seems that anyone who knows anything about computers these days has heard about Java. Though hailed as the greatest advance in computer programming since the one and the zero, some say that Java has yet to live up to the hype.

Java was developed by Sun Microsystems as a platform-independent language for the Internet. It was originally designed as a language for embedded systems (the tiny computers in your car or VCR, for example), but Sun quickly realized that Java could be used to create software that would perfectly suit the needs of the Internet. Because the majority of users access the Internet over modems and phone lines instead of broadband or Ethernet networks, Internet-based software must be relatively small so that it can be downloaded quickly. It's also essential for Internet-based software to understand TCP/IP, as well as the higher-level applications that use it, such as Web servers and FTP servers. With its small executable files and vast networking capabilities, Java meets these needs.

Many of the programming concepts used in Java are borrowed from other languages; its syntax is very close to C++, and its object orientation is very much like Smalltalk. Many Web sites use Java applets (small applications) to make a page dynamic—so it's more than likely that you've already used Java.

Apple has embraced Java in a big way. Mac OS X Version 10.0 was the first major desktop operating system to ship with Java 2 Standard Edition (J2SE). In fact, Apple expects programmers to move to Java, and is ensuring system software compatibility by including more complete support for both Java and QuickTime within Java applications. Mac OS X also boasts several Java-specific performance enhancements, including multiprocessor support. You can see why you, as an Apple user, should spend some time getting to know Java. This chapter will tell you what Java is and how you can run it on your Macintosh.

Java on the Macintosh

Apple began supporting Java in late 1996, with the introduction of Macintosh Runtime for Java. Now, J2SE is bundled with Mac OS X so that all Macs can run Java programs without needing additional software—or even a Java-enabled Web browser. Java programs are usually referred to as applets because most Java applications are tiny in size and focused on providing a small set of features. However, there's no reason why a full-featured application can't be written in Java—in fact, most software vendors would love to have their applications written in Java. Why? Because a program created in Java could be written and debugged once, and work on any computer, regardless of platform.. Software developers could make more money with less effort, and updates for all platforms would be released more quickly. Eventually, more developers may use Java to create the programs we use every day, because of the many unique features that Java offers, including:

- *Cross-platform compatibility*—Java applets use what's called *byte code*, which any computer can read using a Java Virtual Machine (commonly abbreviated VM). A VM is all any operating system needs to run Java applets. In the case of Mac OS X, HotSpot is the VM. Thanks to the VM, a single Java applet can be run on a Mac, a Windows computer, or a Sun workstation.

- *Apple support*—Apple has, in its infinite wisdom, included Mac Runtime for Java (MRJ) in all versions of the operating system since Mac OS 8.

- *Small*—Because Java is an object-oriented language, applets "inherit" features of the language that reside on the user's computer. These features, therefore, don't need to be downloaded. Java also features built-in compression features so that bitmaps and sounds, for example, can be as small as possible.

- *Security*—Java applets are restricted so that your computer can't be harmed by malicious (or inept) applet programmers.

- *Network-readiness*—Java includes a rich feature set for connection over the Internet. Java applets can connect to Web servers, FTP servers, chat servers, or just about anything else that uses TCP/IP.

- *Performance*—Although the execution speed of many Java programs is slower than programs written for a specific operating system, special technologies such as Just in Time (JIT) and HotSpot compilers are closing this gap. Java also offers other performance benefits, particularly in networked applications. The Java Virtual Machine uses the *garbage collection* technique, which monitors memory use and ensures that Java programs don't suffer from memory leaks. This feature significantly reduces software crashes.

These features make Java a great language for any computer, and especially for the Mac. Over the years, Mac users were often left waiting for developers to port Windows software to the Mac platform. Java eliminates this need, because any Java applet that runs under Windows will run under the Mac OS. As more and more software is created for Java, Mac users will benefit greatly.

Because of Java's crossplatform capabilities, many of the applications written for Java run on the "back end" of large, expensive corporate servers, and provide networking and intraoperating system integration. Java enables mainframe computers to talk with mini computers, workgroup servers, workstations, and even hand-held devices, because they all can speak the same language—Java. However, Java applications are appearing more and more in the form of personal productivity applications and games. For example, Moneydance is a personal accounting application written entirely in Java. Moneydance is not only for use under Mac OS X, but for Mac OS 8 through 9.1, FreeBSD, OS/2, Linux, Solaris, and multiple versions of Microsoft Windows as well. Shown in Figure 12.1, Moneydance has the look, feel, and speed of any Carbon or Cocoa application, and includes features you'd expect to find in the most popular financial management applications, including online banking, stock management, check printing, and account reconciliation.

Java applets are also appropriate for fun and games, and can be used as part of a Web page instead of simply a standalone application. Art Safari, shown in Figure 12.2, is a Java applet used on the Museum of Modern Art (MoMA) website. This Java program, which works on most Java-enabled browsers, offers a palette for young artists to experiment with. Take a look at the Art Safari home page at **www.moma.org/ onlineprojects/artsafari/**. Like all Java programs, Art Safari became available to Mac users as soon as it was available to Windows users.

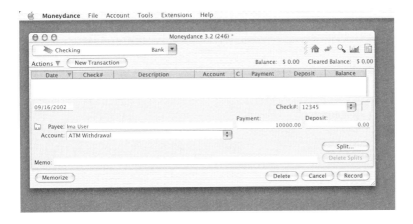

Figure 12.1
Moneydance is a sophisticated application written entirely in Java.

Figure 12.2
The Art Safari applet.

Macintosh Runtime for Java

When you install Mac OS X, Java 2 Standard Edition is installed along with the HotSpot VM and the Java Development Kit. Apple refers to its Java implementation as version 3 of Macintosh Runtime for Java (MRJ 3). MRJ 3 installs three types of frameworks to integrate Java into Mac OS X:

■ *Application framework*—A code base necessary to build Java applets

■ *Development environment*—Tools to create Java applets

■ *Runtime environment*—Resources to execute Java applets

MRJ 3 provides a number of new features and improvements over previous versions of MRJ. MRJ 3 can:

■ Process graphics with the Quartz Extreme imaging model, including antialiasing of text and the ability to use Mac OS X's implementation of OpenGL to render 3D objects

■ Accelerate Java code execution using HotSpot 1.3 VM

■ Support cross-platform Swing implementation

■ Support preemptive multitasking of application threads

- Support Macs with multiple processors

- Utilize the full Java Development Kit (JDK)

- Utilize QuickTime for Java

- Support Unicode language and font support

- Support Apple's WebObjects

- Provide the ability to embed Java applets within Web pages

- Access Java applets over the Internet using Java Web Start

- Configure Java preferences using Java Plugin Settings

Java utilities relocated to /Macintosh HD/Applications/Utilities/Java/. Java is built into the layered framework of Mac OS X (described in Chapter 1), whereas it was an optional installation in earlier versions of the Mac OS. When using Java in Mac OS X, the resources required by your Web browsers and Java-enabled applications are automatically available. Very few configurations are required on your part. The next section explains how to use a few example applets included as part of MRJ 3.

Other Java VMs

Apple isn't the only maker of a Java Virtual Machine for Mac OS X. Because Java is an open standard, any company is welcome—in fact, encouraged—to try its hand at producing Java software. At least one other company makes a Java Virtual Machine and development environment for Mac OS X. Metrowerks (**www.metrowerks.com**) makes CodeWarrior, the premiere programming environment for the Mac, and has created a fast VM that Microsoft included with previous versions of Internet Explorer (i.e., Mac OS 9.1 and earlier).

Unlike HotSpot, third-party Java VMs aren't integrated into Mac OS X and must be installed independently. Earlier versions of the Mac OS often included two different VMs, and not all Java applets worked properly with both. A user would sometimes have to reconfigure the Web browser to select the VM that worked best with a particular applet. This situation may recur with OS X. For now, the HotSpot VM is the only VM demonstrated in this chapter.

Running Java Applets

From a user's perspective, the runtime environment is the most important of the three frameworks that constitute MRJ. The runtime environment provides the interface that allows you to execute Java applets in a number of ways in, including:

12

■ As part of a Carbon or Cocoa application

■ From a command line using the Terminal application

■ As a double-clickable application

■ Using Applet Launcher

■ Using a Web browser

■ Using Java Web Start

Moneydance is an example of a double-clickable application, and Art Safari is a creative example of a Java applet embedded within a Web page. Let's look more closely at the other ways to run Java applets: the Applet Launcher, Web browser, and Java Web Start.

Applet Launcher

The Applet Launcher, a standalone application located in the /Macintosh HD/ Applications/Utilities/Java/ folder, can be used to explore the several example applets that are installed as part of Mac OS X, or any applets that you download from the Web. To run a Java applet:

1. Open the Java folder and double-click the Applet Launcher.

2. Click the Open button, shown in Figure 12.3, or press Command+O.

3. Navigate your hard drive using the dialog box shown in Figure 12.4 and select an applet, typically an HTML file with an embedded applet.

Figure 12.3 The Applet Launcher.

If you're a Unix geek and want to type in the path of an applet, just enter it in the path area of the Applet Launcher .Then you can either click the Launch button or press the Return key. The path should be in the form of a file accessed using a URL, like the one shown in Figure 12.5. Files are accessed using three forward slashes, unlike HTML documents, which require only two slashes.

The Applet Launcher has no preferences or configuration options to speak of, and few interface features with which you'll need to become familiar other than the Open

Figure 12.4
Selecting an HTML document containing a Java applet.

button (Command+O) and the Launch button. However, you can review and configure some aspects of an applet's preferences once the applet has been opened. When an
applet is running, you'll see the following options in the Applet menu:

Figure 12.5 Type the path to a Java applet using the Applet Launcher.

12

■ *Restart*—Forces the applet to start again from the beginning.

■ *Stop*—Pauses the applet.

■ *Save*—Saves the applet to disk.

■ *Start*—Continues a paused applet.

■ *Clone*—Re-creates the applet in a second window.

■ *Tag*—Reveals the HTML code used to embed the applet in an HTML document,
which is useful if you want to see how the code is used.

- *Info*—Displays information and parameters provided by the applet's developer.

- *Edit*—Allows you to edit the applet (if enabled).

- *Character Encoding*—Reveals information about language options used to display the applet.

- *Print*—Prints the window containing the applet.

- *Properties*—Opens the window (shown in Figure 12.6) and enables you to configure how the Applet Launcher accesses a network. You can also determine whether the applet's code is a security risk. The Properties window also allows you to configure the following features:

Figure 12.6
Configuring how the Applet Launcher accesses a network.

- *HTTP Proxy Server*—The Internet address of the proxy server used to access the applet.

- *HTTP Proxy Port*—The TCP/IP port of the HTTP proxy server; the default port for all Web servers is 80.

- *Class Access*—Choose between Restricted and Unrestricted to determine whether applets are allowed to write files to the local file system.

- *Close*—Closes the applet, but does not quit the Applet Launcher.

Each the above options, except for the Properties option, relates to the front-most applet. To affect another applet, launch that applet and review the settings in the Applet menu.

For security purposes, an applet's functionality is usually restricted. For instance, applets usually can't write files to the user's hard disk; this restriction prevents an applet from overwriting important files.

 TIP: Unless you make changes, the default settings ensure that a Java applet cannot cause harm to your system. No other safety measures are necessary.

Java Applets with Web Browsers

Java applets are more frequently encountered as embedded components of a Web page rather than as standalone files. Only two Web browsers were capable of supporting Java when Mac OS X was initially released, but the number continues to grow. With the release of Mac Os X Version 10.2, the following Web browsers are Java-enabled:

- Chimera

- Internet Explorer

- Netscape Navigator (the open-source version is called Mozilla)

- OmniWeb

- Opera

Internet Explorer is installed automatically as part of Mac OS X, and configuring it to access Java applets is a two-step process. First, Java must be enabled in the Web browser itself, and then the settings for the Java plugin should be reviewed using the new Java Plugin Settings utility. To review Internet Explorer's Java settings, follow these steps:

1. Launch Internet Explorer from the Dock or the Applications folder.

2. Choose Explorer|Preferences and select the Java section..

3. Check the Enable Java option in the Java Options section. The other options in this section are not necessary to enable Java. They merely enable alerts to errors and logging options, such as the Log Java Exceptions option I have checked in this example.

4. The Security section provides a way for you to protect the Java code that is executed on your computer. The Byte-Code Verification option tells Internet Explorer to check the code of local applets only, all Java code accessed over a network, or not to check code at all. The Network Access options control how an applet in a Web page connects to the Internet, with three options to choose from:

   - *No Network Access*—The applet can't use the network at all.

   - *Applet Host Access*—The applet can use the restricted network access provided for applets.

   - *Unrestricted*—The applet can use the network in any way it wishes.

5. Check the option entitled Restrict Access To Non-Java Class Files to prevent applets from accessing files that are not part of Java, such as operating system files, documents, or other applications.

6. Click the OK button.

Using the Java Plugin Settings Utility

The Java Plugin Settings utility is new to Mac OS X, and allows users to configure various technical aspects of Java. The preferences file created by the Java Plugin Settings utility is stored in your Preferences folder, which is located in the Library folder. The Library folder resides in your home folder, so each user's settings are stored separately. To configure your Java settings, launch Java Plugin Settings from the Java folder and review the information in the following four configuration tabs:

- *Basic*—Enables or disables the basic features of Java in Mac OS X, as shown in Figure 12.7.

Figure 12.7
Use the Java Plugin Settings utility to review your Java settings.

- *Cache*—Allows you to clear the Java cache file.

- *Certificates*—Lets you view and remove Web site certificates, which provide security information about trusted Web sites.

- *About*—Displays the version information about Java installed on your computer.

Now you're ready to visit a Web site that uses Java, such as the Art Safari Web site mentioned earlier, or one of the many example applets located on the official Java Web site at http://java.sun.com/applets/.

Java Web Start

Java Web Start is an application from Sun Microsystems (**http://java.sun.com/products/javawebstart/**) used for launching Java applets and applications over the Internet. The primary benefit for users is that full-featured Java programs can be accessed using a single point of reference. Software developers share this benefit, because it provides a unified method for delivering applications to existing and potential consumers. Java Web Start automatically checks for program updates every time it is launched so you don't have to worry about updating it manually. Java Web Start also stores the Java class files and libraries on your computer's hard drive for future use with individual Java programs. To access Java programs over the Internet using Java Web Start, follow these steps:

1. Launch Java Web Start from the Java folder.

2. Click the Start button to connect to the Apple Java Web Start home page. The URL for the Welcome to Web Start button is displayed in the lower half of the window, and can also be clicked to open the URL in your default Web browser.

3. Select the Welcome to Web Start link at the bottom of the Web page to download an applet, which will be automatically launched by the Java Web Start utility after several seconds. Figure 12.8 shows the applet that will be launched, which serves as an introduction to the Java Web Start implementation on Mac OS X.

4. Visit **http://java.sun.com/products/javawebstart/demos.html** to try more demo applets. Once an applet has been run, it will appear in the Downloaded Applications section of the Java Web Start utility, an example of which is shown in Figure 12.9.

5. Java Web Start and any open Java applets are quit independently of one another.

Java Web Start applets and applications are designed to download and run using a special type of HTML document, a link to which is embedded in a Web page. When you click on such a link, like the Welcome to Web Start link on the Apple Web site

Figure 12.8
The Welcome to Web Start link opens this Java applet.

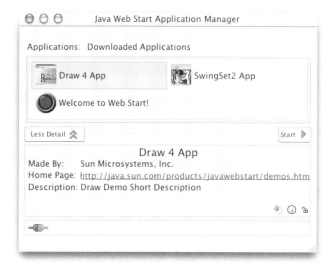

Figure 12.9
The View | Remote Applications menu opens the Application Manager window where you can launch Java applets and applications.

mentioned above, (**http://developer.apple.com/java/javawebstart/apps/welcome/ JWS_Demo.jnlp**), it is opened using Java Web Start. If your Web browser does not automatically open documents ending in .jnlp using Java Web Start, review your browser's settings using the settings shown in Figure 12.10. Each browser that supports Java will have different settings, however, so you may need to reference the documentation and help system provided by your browser.

The Look of Cross-Platform Programs

From the beginning, Java programs were designed to blend seamlessly with other programs on each operating system. When a Java program contains a button and the program is run on a Macintosh, the button appears to be a Mac button. When the same Java program is run on a Windows computer, the button looks like a Windows button. The person who writes the program has no control over this—it's an inherent element of Java. Swing is a special type of Java code that allows an applet to take on the appearance of the host operating system. For example, Figure 12.11 shows two examples of an applet that implements the Swing class to give the contents of the applet the appropriate look and feel for Mac OS X (left) and Windows (right).

Although in some ways it's desirable to have your applets automatically assume the look of an operating system, some definite disadvantages exist:

Figure 12.10
Review your Web browser's settings if it cannot automatically send Java Web Start applets to the Java Web Start application.

- *Excessive need for testing*—A program that will use different components on different platforms must be tested on each platform to make sure that it looks correct.

- *Limited number of components*—This mechanism imposes a limit on the number of components that could exist in Java. The only components that can be used are components that are available on all platforms.

12

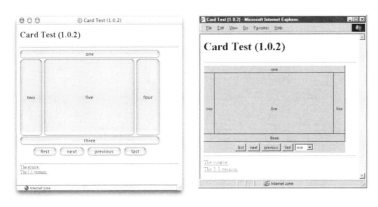

Figure 12.11
Swing allows Java developers to deliver the look and feel of the host operating system, such as Mac OS X (left) and Microsoft Windows (right).

■ *Loss of control*—In the software business, it's never good to completely remove options. A developer should have ultimate control over how a component will look.

The SwingSet applet shown in Figure 12.12 is an example of how themes can be switched "on the fly," without having to restart the applet or the computer. The windowing look and feel in this example is called Motif, a popular windowing system on various Unix operating systems.

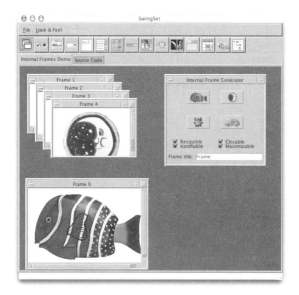

Figure 12.12
Swing can change the look and feel of an applet on the fly.

When Sun and other companies realized these limitations, writing the components completely in the Java language became the solution. In Java Foundation Classes (JFCs), developers were taught to use the Java language to overcome the problems described above.

Note: Swing was the original code name for the Java Foundation Classes. One of the Sun creators of JFC was a big fan of Duke Ellington, who popularized a song containing the lyric, "It don't mean a thing if it ain't got that swing." He assigned the Ellington reference as a temporary name for the evolving JFCs, which were so eagerly anticipated even before their release that the code name became a common term.

To sum things up, Swing and the Java Foundation Classes not only give developers the option to use more components, but also the ability to determine exactly how each component will look.

Wrapping Up

Mac OS X includes robust support for J2SE, the latest version of Java. The most significant characteristic of Java is that it allows computer programmers to write one version of a program, such as a money management application, which can then be run on many different types of computer operating systems without modification. Programmers refer to this as the "write once, run anywhere" capability. Developers no longer have to choose a target platform when writing software. The popularity of Java means that Java applets can debut for the Mac at the same time they debut on other operating systems. With Java-written software available for every platform at once, users will be free to choose the operating system that is most comfortable, and businesses will choose the OS that is easiest (and cheapest) to support.

This chapter has demonstrated several aspects of J2SE on Mac OS X, including:

■ Macintosh Runtime for Java (MRJ)

■ How to run Java applets using the Applet Launcher, Web browser, and Java Web Start

■ How Java can emulate the look and feel of just about any operating system

The next chapter will wrap up this section of the book by looking at ways to prevent problems with your Mac and how to troubleshoot problems when they arise.

12

Troubleshooting Mac OS X

Every computer and operating system has its own quirks and challenges, and Mac OS X is no exception. In fact, Mac OS X introduces a number of new support issues because it is unfamiliar to many Mac users. Many of the issues that faced users of Mac OS 9.x and previous versions simply do not exist in Mac OS X, although they do relate to troubleshooting in the Classic environment. In earlier versions of the Mac OS, you could troubleshoot the operating system by disabling certain Extensions and Control Panels. Troubleshooting Mac OS X, on the other hand, is more about tweaking applications and user configuration features, because the components of Mac OS X cannot be modified easily by the typical user. Solutions to the kinds of problems Mac users were once able to fix on their own are more likely to be found in updates of the operating system from Apple.

Using a handful of tools for Mac OS X and Mac OS 9.x, however, you can help prevent—and even troubleshoot—some of the most common problems in Mac OS X. In this chapter, we'll discuss prevention and treatment, as well as list a select number of online resources you can use to research technical problems and locate solutions from third-party developers.

Preventing Problems

Problems are a fact of computing life, but you can take several steps to prevent these problems. These steps don't guarantee that you'll never have problems—instead, think of them as vaccinations that help ward off problems. Many problems are in fact not problems at all, but new features or procedures that are unrecognized, and sometimes become frustrating. The only cure for these types of problems is to get your feet wet, and then learn to swim. In the meantime, you should consider the following measures as a first line of defense towards preventing problems:

- *Back up your data*—It's a good idea to perform full backups on a regular basis, and perform incremental backups in between. At a minimum, back up your home folder and keep the installation disks and CDs handy in the event you have to reinstall the

Mac OS and/or your applications. Check out the following backup solutions to protect your data:

- Backup (Apple)— **www.mac.com**

- FolderSynchronizerX (softoBe)—**www.softobe.com**

- iMsafe (SweatCocoa)—**http://homepage.mac.com/sweetcocoa/**)

- Personal Backup (Intego)—**www.intego.com**

- Retrospect Client (Dantz)—**www.dantz.com**

- SwitchBack (Glendower)— **www.glendower.co.nz**

- Synchronize! (Qdea)—**www.qdea.com**

- Synk X (Randall Voth)— **http://hyperarchive.lcs.mit.edu/HyperArchive/ Archive/disk/synk-401.hqx**

- *Remove unneeded documents*—The fewer large documents on your drives, the easier (and faster) it will be for the Mac OS to manage your file systems. If you really need to keep large documents, such as iMovie and iDVD files, for long periods of time, consider purchasing a CD recorder to create archival copies of important collections of folders and documents. Use the Find command to search for large documents to archive, or for documents that are no longer accessed.

- *Keep a record of important settings*—If your disk crashes and you must reinstall all your software, how will you be able to reconfigure your Internet settings? Periodically write down or print out any critical settings. information This will get you up and running more quickly after a catastrophic event such as a drive failure, lightning strike, or theft.

- *Retain all software installers*—Keep all your software installation CDs handy in case you have to reinstall Mac OS X or your third-party applications and utilities.

- *Read installation notes*—Because Mac OS X version 10.2 is a relatively new operating system, I encourage you to read all the installation notes for Mac OS X and your applications before loading or updating software. Mac OS X is very particular about how and where many applications are installed!

Common Problems and Their Solutions

The vast majority of problems you're likely to encounter with Mac OS X involve a handful of common scenarios that are easily resolved. You might encounter some of the following problems on more than one occasion, and never see others. Take a look at each of the following scenarios so that you'll at least be familiar with each problem, its possible cause, and the likely solutions. For more information on problem solving, see the following section entitled "Useful Tools for Mac OS X" later in this chapter. Appendix A, "Getting Help," also helps you learn where to go to solve application-specific questions that are too numerous to cover in this chapter.

Computer Won't Start Up

On startup or restart, the computer won't start at all. The screen displays no activity, and/or you don't hear anything coming from the central processing unit (CPU).

Cause

Power is not flowing to the computer and/or the monitor, or the power isn't reaching the CPU or monitor. The first of these scenarios is much easier to detect than the second.

Solution

Be sure that the computer is plugged into a surge-protected outlet that is itself receiving power. If your monitor is plugged in through the courtesy outlet on the back of the CPU, make sure that the connection is secure. If it isn't, the CPU may be receiving power but isn't passing it on to the monitor, even though the monitor is turned on. To test the outlet for power, plug in a lamp or other device and turn it on. If it works, the outlet is receiving power.

If your computer is plugged into a surge protector (and it should be!), check to see if the surge protector is turned on. Most surge protectors have an On/Off switch. If the surge protector has a Reset button, try it; a power surge may have tripped it. Finally, if your surge protector has a fuse, shut down everything that's plugged into it, unplug the surge protector from the outlet, and check the fuse.

If your computer is receiving power but still doesn't start up, two possible explanations remain—but both require the services of an Apple-authorized repair center. First, the power supply in your CPU may be damaged. The power supply converts the current received from an outlet into a form that the computer can use. It's not uncommon for a power supply to go bad, especially if the computer is left on for extended periods of time. The minimal life span for a power supply that's left on 24 hours per day should be several years—I own a Mac Classic whose power supply is still going after eleven years! The worst-case scenario requires replacing the logic board because it can no longer transfer the power received from the outlet to the necessary components of the computer. PowerBooks are especially susceptible to simultaneous power supply and logic board failure because of the way the power cord plugs into the back of many older models.

13

Blinking Question Mark on Startup

On startup, the CPU and monitor receive power, but a blinking question mark appears on screen and no further startup activity occurs.

Cause

The computer cannot detect a startup disk containing the Mac OS. Either the drive is bad, or one or more of the essential components is missing.

Solution

Approximately half of the infamous blinking question mark's appearances are due to the computer's inability to locate the designated startup disk. Most Macs only have one hard drive, and many computers have a booting utility built into the Read-Only Memory (ROM) chip. This chip resides on the motherboard, and allows you to see what drives are available for booting before the booting routine actually begins. If the designated disk can't be found, the computer looks for additional disks containing the Mac OS. To use the boot utility to select a disk containing Mac OS X:

1. Restart the computer.

2. Hold down the Option key until the boot menu appears.

3. Select the drive containing Mac OS X, and click the Continue button.

If the boot utility doesn't appear when holding down the Option key, then your computer doesn't support this feature and you'll have to boot from the Mac OS installation CD-ROM. Run the Disk Utility from the CD to check the startup disk for errors, which is explained below.

The next line of defense is to reset, or *zap*, the computer's parameter RAM (PRAM), which is kind of like giving the computer a loud wakeup call to restart and behave! To zap the PRAM:

1. Restart the computer by pressing Control+Command+Power key (also known as a hard restart, a hard boot, or a three-finger salute), or by pressing the restart button on your computer. The restart button is identified in your computer's documentation, and the exact location varies with different models of Mac, iMac, Cube, PowerBook, iBook, or Xserve. If your computer doesn't have an easily accessible Restart button (like the Cube), press the round On button for about six seconds to force the computer to switch itself off. Wait 20 seconds and press the On button again to start the computer.

2. Hold down the Option+Command+P+R keys while the Caps Lock key is *not* depressed.

3. Keep holding down these keys until you hear the startup chime a second time, then release.

If you have Mac OS 9.x installed on your computer and it boots into Mac OS 9.x instead of Mac OS X, the computer probably cannot find all the Mac OS X components (such as the mach.sym or mach_kernel files) that are necessary to boot properly. In this case, allow the computer to boot into Mac OS 9.x and follow these steps:

1. Download and install the latest version of the Startup Disk Control Panel using the Software Update Control Panel, or by visiting the Apple Support Web site (**www.apple.com/support/**). At this time, version 9.2.1 and later is required to properly boot into Mac OS X.

2. Restart into Mac OS 9.x and open the Startup Disk Control Panel.

3. Select the volume containing Mac OS X and click the Restart button.

If you cannot boot into Mac OS X or Mac OS 9.x on your hard drive, you'll have to boot from an alternative source of Mac OS 9.x or Mac OS X, such as an installation CD-ROM. When a Mac boots up, it looks for a valid operating system in the following order:

1. Hard drive designated in the Startup Disk System Preferences (Mac OS X) or the Startup Disk Control Panel (Mac OS 9.x)

2. Additional hard drives

3. CD-ROM drive

The most common method is to start up from a bootable CD-ROM, which you can do in two easy steps:

1. Insert the CD-ROM.

2. Restart while holding down the C key until the computer boots from the CD-ROM.

Once the computer has restarted from CD-ROM, the Installer program will automatically run. However, instead of reinstalling Mac OS X at this point, follow these steps to run the Disk Utility to verify and/or repair the startup disk:

1. Choose Open Disk Utility from the Installer menu.

2. Select a volume or partition in the left side of the utility.

3. Select the First Aid tab containing Mac OS X.

13

Figure 13.1
Checking a drive for errors using Disk Utility while booting from the Mac OS X installation CD.

4. Click the Verify button to verify the integrity of the drive or the Repair button to scan for and repair problems   automatically. Figure 13.1 shows the Disk Utility repairing a drive partition named Archer.

5. Follow any on-screen instructions and choose Quit Disk Utility (Command+Q) from the Disk Utility menu to return to the Installer.

6. If you believe the repair was successful, choose Quit Installer from the Installer menu and then click the Restart button in the Installer window. If you doubt that the Disk Utility was successful in repairing your drive, reinstall Mac OS X by choosing the Continue button—and be prepared to reinstall the entire operating system.

Reinstalling Mac OS X is a last-ditch effort. If all else fails and you must reinstall Mac OS X, be   sure that all the necessary operating system application installation CDs are handy. Of course, if you've backed up all the important files on your computer regularly, reinstalling won't be too much of an inconvenience.

Application Crashes

An application crashes periodically, or consistently.

Cause

The application may have a bug or may conflict with the Mac OS or another application.

Solution

Applications crash for many mysterious reasons. Fortunately, Mac OS X prevents wayward applications from taking down other applications or the operating system itself. If you can re-create the same error a second or third time, the problem is most likely related to the application's preferences file, or the application itself, rather than Mac OS X. To remedy a problem with an application, follow these steps:

1. Check the documentation for any mention of known internal problems orcompatibility issues.

2. Check the software creator's Web site to see if any new information or updates to the application have been posted. If the software in question is from Apple, run the Software Update to see if a newer version is available.

3. Delete the application's preference file, typically located in /Macintosh HD/ Users/*username*/Library/Preferences. Apple encourages software developers to incorporate their company domain name into a program's preference file. This practice ensures that all preference files for that company's products are grouped together. For example, Figure 13.2 shows the preference file for the Print Center utility grouped with all the other application preference files for Apple products.

4. Restart the computer to make sure all the log and preferences files for the application have been closed and are not part of the problem.

5. Reinstall the application as a last resort.

Of course, if you delete a preference file or reinstall an application, you risk losing the application registration or serial number, settings, custom dictionaries, and other

Figure 13.2
Try deleting the preference file of a troublesome application to prevent the application from crashing.

information that is commonly stored in a preference list (.plist) file, so be prepared to reenter this information.

Application Stalls During Use

An application stalls during use and displays an error message, or will not return control to the user.

Cause

The application performs an illegal operation or contains a programming error.

Solution

Application programming is an extremely sophisticated business, and sometimes programmers make mistakes that lead to an application's failure during use. Because Mac OS X uses protected memory, the offending application should not cause other applications or the Mac OS itself to crash. If the application doesn't automatically terminate itself and just hangs there without allowing you to quit, follow these steps to *force quit* the application:

1. Press Command+Option+Escape simultaneously or choose Force Quit from the Apple menu

2. Select which application to force quit from the window shown in Figure 13.3.

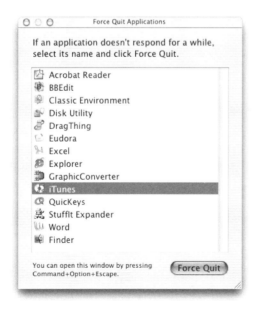

Figure 13.3
Choose Option+Command+Escape to force quit an application that is misbehaving.

3. Click the Force Quit button. If the Finder is selected in the list of applications, the button will be named Relaunch instead of Force Quit.

4. Dismiss the Force Quit window by clicking the close button.

Forcing an application to quit no longer requires a complete restart.   In the past, a complete restart was necessary to prevent a cascading affect with other applications. If the misbehaving application is the Finder, relaunch it, but if the problem persists, try logging out, then restart the computer by choosing restart from the Apple menu.

Computer Won't Restart or Shut Down
The Mac OS won't respond to the Restart or Shut Down commands.

Cause
The Mac OS or an application is preventing the partial or full execution of the Restart Shut Down commands.

Solution
When you select Restart or Shut Down, the Mac OS issues an AppleEvent instructing all open applications to quit before executing the actual Restart or Shut Down command. If an application doesn't receive the AppleEvent or cannot interpret it properly, the Mac OS will not comply with the final steps of the process. The first solution is to retry the command. If that fails, manually quit any applications that have not responded to the AppleEvent. If all the applications do indeed quit, leaving only the Finder open, initiate a relaunch of the Finder, or restart the computer according to the steps outlined previously in this chapter . If all else fails, unplug the computer. If you have a PowerBook or iBook, you may also need to eject the battery after disconnecting the power cord to deprive the computer of all sources of power, and then wait a moment for all power to dissipate.

Restart the computer and run the Disk Utility to check for, and repair, any disk errors that may have occurred.

Kernel Panic
The computer freezes or a strange looking, white-lettered screen appears.

Cause
The Mach kernel has crashed, commonly referred to as a kernel panic.

Solution
Sometimes, Mac OS X cannot handle an instruction from an application or a hardware device, causing the core element of the Mac OS (called the Mach kernel) to crash. The only solution is to restart the computer.   Note which applications were

13

open   when the Mach kernel crashed, and what hardware devices were connected. It could be that an application or hardware device (such as a keyboard or printer) is sending catastrophic commands to the kernel that cannot be properly interpreted. If the problem reoccurs and you can identify the offender, try upgrading the application or replacing the device. The final solution is to not use the application or device.

Drive Not Recognized

One or more hard drives are not recognized during startup (they don't appear on the Desktop or you are asked to initialize the startup drive).

Cause

The Mac OS cannot find a boot partition or driver.

Solution

If the Mac OS cannot find a hard drive, follow the steps outlined earlier in the section entitled "Blinking Question Mark on Startup" and boot from the Mac OS X installation CD. After the Installer has launched, follow these steps:

1. Choose Open Disk Utility from the Installer menu.

2. Select the problematic volume or partition in the left side of the utility.

3. Select the Information tab, an example of which is shown in Figure 13.4.

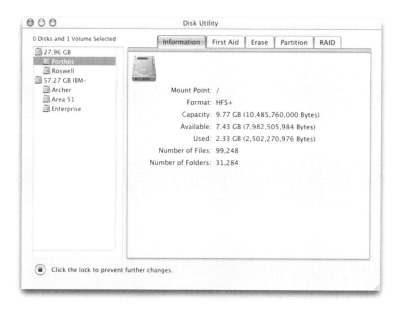

Figure 13.4
Reviewing the information about a drive partition using the Disk Utility application.

4. Review the information and make sure the drive name is recognized. If the drive is significantly corrupted, the drive name and information in the Information tab may not be available. In this case, you may need to erase the drive or partition and reinstall Mac OS X from scratch. However, don't attempt to erase or repartition the drive until you have confirmed that you are unable to repair the drive or recover your applications, documents, and Preferences using after reading the "Useful tools for Mac OS X" section later in this chapter.

Every hard drive contains a special partition, or section of the drive, called the *boot partition*. To load the drivers and information required for mounting the disk on startup, the OS must be able to access the boot partition. If the boot partition is corrupted or the driver information is unreadable, the drive will not be mounted until it has been repaired. The partition containing the files used by the operating system, applications and documents may be intact, however, and therefore recoverable, so don't act too quickly and erase files that may be recoverable.

If the problem stems from an internal hard drive that came installed in your computer from Apple, the First Aid section of the Disk Utility application described earlier is the best solution to try first. If this doesn't work, however, you can't go wrong purchasing a commercial utility that specializes in disk storage, if you can afford it. In the worst-case scenario— you cannot reinstall the proper driver for a drive or repair it— you may have to reformat the drive, which will cause all of your data to be lost.

If the problematic drive is a secondary drive (i.e., not the original, internal hard drive that came with your computer), the problem could be a Small Computer Serial Interface (SCSI) ID conflict, or an Integrated Drive Electronics (IDE) master/slave configuration error. Each SCSI disk must have a unique ID; if it shares the ID of an existing drive, it will not boot. IDE drives have a similar problem, but they allow for only two drives on each Advanced Technology Attachment (ATA) bus—a master and a slave—whereas SCSI buses allow for seven IDs. Macs can have multiple SCSI and ATA buses, which can cause confusion when you're trying to assign IDs and configure multiple drives. Firewire drives do not have these limitations. Use the Apple System Profiler's Devices and Volumes tab for a detailed listing of all the SCSI, ATA, and USB devices connected to your computer (discussed later in this chapter).

Can't Connect to a Network/Internet

Computer cannot connect to AppleTalk devices over the network or access the Internet.

Cause

Your computer has been physically disconnected from the network or a software error has occurred. Also, the network may be down, in which case your Mac is not the problem.

Solution

The first solution with a network problem is to reboot the computer and let Mac OS X try to reestablish a network connection automatically. If this doesn't help, check with your Internet Service Provider (ISP) to see if there is a known network problem, especially if you're connected via cable modem or a Digital Subscriber Line (DSL) connection. Network failures are common, and may be diagnosed fairly quickly. Look at your cable or DSL modem and determine if the diagnostic or informational lights are properly illuminated. For example, my cable modem has all green or orange lights; anytime I see a red light, I know there is a connectivity problem that is beyond my control. The only solution is to call my ISP and report the problem once you have followed any troubleshooting instructions from your ISP, such as rebooting the cable modem prior to calling for assistance.

If your ISP isn't the problem, make sure that your Ethernet or modem cable is properly connected. Network cables and hardware devices such as Ethernet cards and modems rarely go bad, but it does happen from time to time. If you are using a traditional modem to dial into an ISP such as Earthlink or America Online, you're connected using a traditional phone line. If you are connected to the Internet through a Local Area Network (LAN), cable modem, or a DSL connection, you are using an Ethernet cable. Traditional phone lines can by purchased in numerous locations, such as computer, grocery, and hardware stores. Ethernet cables may be a little harder to find. Most electronics stores, such as Best Buy, Circuit City, or CompUSA will carry these. Try replacing the cable if you suspect your cable has been damaged.

Next, check your Network System Preferences. To confirm that your network settings have not been altered, follow these steps:

1. Choose System Preferences from the Apple menu or the Dock.

2. Select the Network pane.

3. Make sure that the proper Location, such as Home or Work, is selected.

4. Determine whether the proper type of interface, such as Built-in Ethernet or Modem Port, is selected in the Connection section.

5. If you are on a local area network, review the TCP/IP settings for accuracy.

6. If you are dialing into an Internet service provider (ISP) using a modem, check the Point-to-Point Protocol (PPP) settings.

7. If you are using any proxy servers to connect to the Web or other Internet resources, check the Proxy section.

8. If you are dialing into an ISP using a modem, check the Modem section to make sure that the proper modem is selected.

Modem errors are usually related to configuration errors in the PPP and Modem sections of the Network System Preferences. Dial-up connections are often very difficult to troubleshoot because of the hardware and software conflicts between an ISP's modem, and those found in Apple computers. Make sure that your ISP supports the type and speed of your Mac's modem. Some ISPs do not support the 56Kbps V.90 modem, which is found in most Apple computers.

If you have a hub, router, or switch to share the Internet connection with other computers on your network, check these devices as well. Refer to the next chapter for details on using various technologies for connecting to the Internet.

Mouse and Keyboard Won't Work

The mouse and/or keyboard won't work.

Cause

The Apple Desktop Bus (ADB) or Universal Serial Bus (USB) cables connecting the mouse and keyboard to the CPU have become disconnected, or the mouse or keyboard is broken.

Solution

In about 70 percent of cases, the answer to this problem is simple — the cables connecting the mouse or keyboard have become disconnected. All pre-iMac and G4 computers use the ADB-style cable to connect the mouse to the keyboard and the keyboard to the CPU. In some of these computers, the ADB cable passes through the monitor, connecting the mouse and keyboard independently to the monitor, which is then connected to the CPU. First, check to see if any of these cables are loose, especially if your keyboard has ADB connectors on either side (these are notorious for becoming bent and broken). If all cables are connected properly and the problem persists, you could have a bad mouse or keyboard. Try borrowing a similar mouse or keyboard from a coworker or friend before buying a new one—you can quickly determine if the mouse or keyboard is the problem.

For iMacs, Cubes, and G4s, the USB cable may have become crimped or disconnected. Although the USB connectors are a great improvement over ADB connectors and are much less prone to failure, you should be aware of one issue. USB hubs connect USB mice, keyboards, and peripherals. These hubs either don't have a power supply, or are powered by an external power supply, and some USB devices draw more power than can be provided by an un-powered USB hub. So, if you intend to connect multiple USB devices and are in need of a hub, consider purchasing a hub with its own external power supply to ensure that your peripherals get enough juice.

13

TIP: Whenever possible, shut down the computer before connecting and disconnecting ADB cables. USB cables may be freely connected and disconnected at any time,.

PowerBooks and iBooks can have an external ADB or USB keyboard, but the internal keyboard is always connected using an internal ribbon cable that is not exposed. The ribbon cable cannot be damaged or disconnected unless the keyboard has been removed for cleaning, a RAM upgrade is performed, or for general maintenance. Of course, dropping or spilling a liquid on any portable computer can cause the keyboard to fail, in which case you should turn it off, unplug it, remove the battery and take it to an Apple-authorized service center for repair. Continuing to use an obviously damaged keyboard can cause further damage, including complete failure of the logic board.

Colors Won't Display Properly

Colors displayed on screen looks odd, especially when browsing the Web.

Cause

A loose connection or erroneous Monitor settings.

Solution

Color problems are typically due to one of two causes. First, make sure your monitor cable is not loose. A loose monitor cable can prevent one or more of the pins in the cable from making a good connection. This results in a display with an unusual color balance, such as a green or amber wash over the entire screen. Securing the cable will usually take care of this problem. If the problem persists, it could indicate a bad monitor or a malfunctioning video card. PowerBooks, iBooks, and iMacs do not have external video cables for the primary display, so a loose cable cannot be the cause unless a cable is used to connect a second display.

Second, open the Displays System Preferences and check the color depth and resolution settings. As a rule of thumb, configure your computer's display as follows:

- Select as many colors as possible.

- Select the highest resolution you're comfortable with.

- Choose a refresh rate of 75Hz or higher.

The color depth setting is especially important, because it controls the quality with which Web images are displayed.

 TIP: If looking at your monitor makes you queasy, check the refresh rate to make sure that it's set to 75Hz or higher (I prefer 85Hz). Accountants, graphic designers, and others who sit at their computers all day have been known to become nauseous if the refresh rate is too low.

Computer Won't Print

Computer won't print to the connected printer.

Cause

Printer is physically disconnected, Network System Preferences are misconfigured, print driver is improperly selected via the Print Center, or the Preferences file is corrupt.

Solution

If you're connected locally to the printer, check your printer cable to ensure connectivity. Both ends of the cable should be tightly connected, and the cable should not be crimped. If you're using a networked printer, check the network connectivity between your computer and the printer. Are they both available on the network? Physical printer connectivity problems are usually pretty easy to troubleshoot:

1. Shut down the Mac and the printer.

2. Start the printer. Once the printer is online, start the Mac.

If you're certain that the printer is connected properly and have reviewed your network settings in the Network pane of the System Preferences, open the Print Center from the Utilities folder and look for the printer—it should be listed under its proper connection method, such as USB or AppleTalk. You can also try removing the Print Center preferences file and reconnecting to the printer from scratch (removing the preferences file will delete all your printers from the Print Center's Printer List window). Refer to Chapter 10, "Managing Fonts and Printers," for instructions on selecting a printer using the Print Center.

Document Won't Open

A document won't open, even though you're using the appropriate application.

Cause

An incomplete application database or file extension mapping.

Solution

Mac OS X opens application-specific documents differently than Mac OS 9.x and earlier. Mac OS 9.x and prior versions of the Mac OS used a "Desktop" database for each volume.   Different volumes were   used by Mac OS 9.x to keep track of applications and their assigned document types. Mac OS X allows software developers to incorporate this type of tracking mechanism in their applications, but encourages the use of file extensions as the preferred means of assigning documents to applications. Developers are continually debating the best way to manage the document/application

13

relationship, and there could be changes made in future versions of the Mac OS in this respect.

It's not unusual for a computer to contain tens of thousands of files—no wonder the Mac OS gets a bit confused about which documents were created with what application. If you're using a previous version of the Mac OS, the solution to this problem is to "rebuild the Desktop." This process involves holding down the Command+Option keys at startup. A dialog box appears and asks if you want to rebuild the Desktop database, which will reassociate all applications with the appropriate documents. This is also possible when starting up theClassic environment, or by selecting the Rebuild Desktop button in the Advanced tab of the Classic System Preferences pane.

Mac OS X does not use the same type of volume-wide database as Mac OS 9.x. Instead, Mac OS X allows programmers to include file types (such as TEXT) and creator codes (such as "R*ch" for BBEdit or "MSIE" for Microsoft Internet Explorer) that are "bound" to specific applications on a per-user basis instead of a per-volume basis. Straight out of the box, Mac OS X assigns default applications to certain document types, and although you cannot manually rebuild the application database in Mac OS X, you can follow these steps to refresh the information available to the operating system:

1. Restart the computer and log in to your account.

2. Open a Finder window in column view and navigate to the folders containing your applications.

3. Try opening the document again.

Mac OS X refreshes the application database for each user at startup, and whenever a folder containing one or more applications is opened in a Finder window. It does not search for every application on the entire hard drive, as in previous versions of the Mac OS. Instead, Mac OS X looks in the Applications and Utilities folders and records the information about each application's type and creator codes.   If this information exists (not all Cocoa applications have creator types and codes), it will determine the types of documents an application can open. When a document is double-clicked, Mac OS X attempts to match the Finder attributes of that document with all applications associated with that user. If a matching application is found, the OS opens the document with the appropriate application. If a match cannot be made, the Finder responds with a dialog box to inform you that the correct application is not available.

To search for an application to open the document:

1. Select the document in the Finder, choose File|Get Info (Command+I), and expand the Open With section, shown in the left of Figure 13.5.

2. Select the Open With menu and select the option entitled Other.

3. Choose Show Recommended Applications (shown in the right of Figure 13.5), which allows the Finder to weed out inappropriate applications. Recommended applications are chosen on the basis of the Finder type and creator codes stored in your application database.

4. Choose Show All Applications to attempt to open the document with a non-recommended application.

5. Choose the location for the recommended application, such as the Applications folder, or browse your hard drive for additional applications.

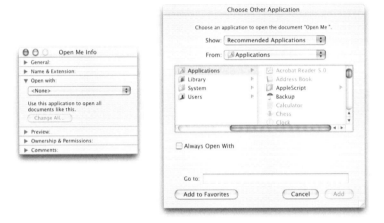

Figure 13.5
Searching for an application to open a document.

6. Select an application and click the Add button.

7. Click the Change All button to instruct Mac OS X to open all documents with the same creator type, if desired.

8. Close the Info window and try double-clicking the document again.

If the document still won't open, try choosing an appropriate application and open the document from within that application, rather than letting the Mac choose for you.). If that fails, too, you can assume that either the document is corrupt, or you truly don't have the appropriate application for the job.

Forgot Password

Cannot log in to Mac OS X using the usual password.

Cause

Forgot password.

Solution

Ask the owner or anyone else with administrative access to reset your password. If you are the only administrator, you'll need to boot the computer using the Mac OS X installation CD and follow these steps:

1. Choose Reset Password from the Installer menu.

2. Select the volume containing your home folder.

3. Select your username from the pop-up menu of users with accounts on the selected volume.

4. Enter and reenter the new password.

5. Click the Save button and choose Command+Q to quit the Reset Password application and return to the Installer application once a confirmation window has appeared letting you know the password has been successfully changed..

6. Choose Command+Q to quit the Installer application.

7. Choose Restart to restart the computer.

In the next section, we'll look at the best tools to diagnose and repair the most common hardware and software problems.

Useful Tools for Mac OS X

Mac OS X includes several helpful tools for gathering information, monitoring, and repairing   your computer's resources. In addition to these tools, several third-party applications and utilities are available to help you troubleshoot Mac OS X. The following list describes some of the more frequently used tools that you should consider adding to your troubleshooting tool kit, and tells you where you can get the latest versions. For those of you who rely on Classic mode, a handful of the most essential Mac OS 9.x utilities are listed as well.

Software Update

Apple is constantly working on updates to Mac OS X to enhance performance, resolveproblems, enhance security, and incorporate new features. You can use the System Preferences' Software Update feature to manually check for updates to software installed by Mac OS X , or on a daily, weekly, or monthly schedule. Appendix E, "Installing and Updating Mac OS 9.x and Mac OS X," contains detailed information on how to update Mac OS X using the Software Update feature, as well as how to download the updates from the Apple Web site.

Get Mac OS X Software

Instead of banging your head against a virtual wall when an application misbehaves, look for an updated version of the application. Make sure you read the application's release notes first (they should be located on your hard drive). New and updated applications for Mac OS X are being released every day, and Apple has made it as easy as possible for you to stay abreast of all the news about the latest software. To connect to Mac OS X Downloads, Apple's news and software download site, choose Get Mac OS X Software from the Apple menu, which opens the Web site shown in Figure 13.6. The applications are well categorized, so it's easy to find the type of software you're looking for, and the most popular downloads are featured on the first page of the site. Developers can easily update or add new descriptions of their software on the Mac OS X Downloads site.

Mac Help

Mac Help is an essential resource when troubleshooting Mac OS X or an application. The Help information for an application is written by the same author or company as the application, but it is not up to Apple to provide third-party software assistance for applications other than those bundled with Mac OS X (or Apple-branded software

Figure 13.6
The Get Mac OS X Software command from the Apple menu gives you easy access to the latest applications for Mac OS X.

downloaded from Apple.com). Also, the format and type of help may vary from application to application, so you shouldn't expect the same level of assistance from every application. For additional information on getting help from the Mac OS and its applications, see Appendix A, "Getting Help."

Apple System Profiler

The Apple System Profiler utility is a great tool for learning about   Mac OS X resources and devices that are connected to your computer. The Apple System Profiler, located in the Utilities folder, catalogs your computer's hardware and software attributes for reference and use by trained support professionals. It records just about every conceivable aspect of your Mac, including hardware specifications, Mac OS version, and what frameworks, extensions, and applications are installed on your computer. For example, Figure 13.7 shows the Devices and Volumes tab for a dual-processor G4, which I can use to quickly determine if all my hard drives and peripherals are recognized by Mac OS X.

Console

The Console, a somewhat geeky utility, displays a variety of error messages from the operating system that may prove useful to some users. The Console logs all types of anomalies about Finder operations, networking errors, printer communication problems, and errors about communications with other peripheral devices, such as the mouse and keyboard. You can also configure Console to immediately open the log file for an application that crashes, which may be helpful in tracking down the cause of a

Figure 13.7
The Apple System Profiler tracks a great deal of information about your computer's hardware and software.

problem. Figure 13.8 shows the Console preference options necessary to automatically open the crash log, as well as a sample log entry.

CPU Monitor

Sometimes your computer might seem a little sluggish, especially when you're running several applications at the same time. You can use the CPU Monitor utility to track processor resources and make sure the processor isn't causing the sluggish performance. You can display the activity levels of your processors in a variety of ways. For example, Figure 13.9 shows the CPU Monitor in Standard (top left), Floating (top right), and Expanded (bottom) views for a dual-processor G4. Select CPU Monitor|Preferences to configure the monitor's on-screen display, including colors and level of transparency. My preference is to display the Floating version with slight transparency to minimize the distraction caused by the CPU Monitor.

ProcessViewer

The ProcessViewer, a companion utility for the CPU Monitor, provides detailed information about the processes and applications running on your computer. Most Unix operating systems provide this utility so that system administrators can closely monitor the performance of mission-critical computers and keep track of processor resources. You can view all processes in a window like the one shown in Figure 13.10, or only those processes belonging to the current user, administrative processes (used

13

Figure 13.8
Use Console to log problems with application crashes.

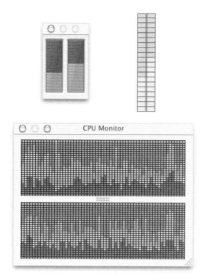

Figure 13.9
Monitor the load on your processor(s) using one of three views of the CPU Monitor.

by the operating system), or processes belonging to the NetBoot feature. Even if you are not using a NetBoot server to boot your computer over a network, a few NetBoot processes will be running, so don't be alarmed.

To get information about a particular process, select it from the list of processes in the upper half of the window. The Process ID and Statistics tabs in the lower half of the window provide some rather technical information about the process you've selected, which you can also terminate from within the ProcessViewer by selecting Process|Quit Process (or Command+Option+Q). If you ever doubted that Mac OS X is really a Unix operating system (albeit with a very friendly user interface), doubt no more!

Disk Utility

The Disk Utility was described earlier in this chapter in the context of booting from the Mac OS X installation CD-ROM to troubleshoot and partition hard drives. However, you may also launch Disk Utility from the Utilities folder when the computer has finished booting from the hard drive, as long as the drive containins the Disk Utility instead of an external boot source (such as a CD-ROM or Mac OS 9.x disk). However, you cannot repair a disk that has been used as the startup disk, a locked disk (such as a CD-ROM), or a disk containing open files. You can verify these disks, but not repair them. You can also use the Disk Utility to erase a volume, as well as divide a volume into multiple partitions, or create a Redundant Array of Inexpensive Disks (RAID).

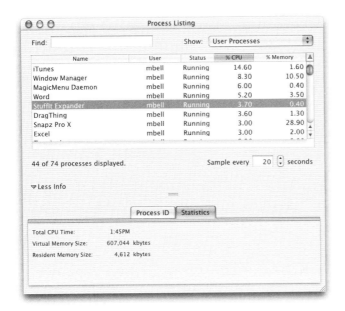

Figure 13.10
The ProcessViewer shows detailed information about the many processes running under Mac OS X.

Third-party Utilities

There are numerous utilities for maintaining, protecting, and repairing the contents of your Mac OS X computer, most of which are locatable using the Web sites listed in the "Useful Resources" section presented later in this chapter. These utilities come in the form of freeware, shareware, and commercial packages that range in price from a few dollars to over one hundred dollars. I'm constantly reviewing utilities that perform various maintenance, troubleshooting, and security tasks, and here are the utilities I'm using on a daily basis:

■ Backup: iMsafe (**http://homepage.mac.com/sweetcocoa/**)

■ Disk repair and maintenance: Norton Utilities (**www.norton.com/nu/nu_mac/**)

■ Finder permissions: Super Get Info (**www.barebones.com**)

■ Finder types and creator codes: File Buddy (**http://skytag.com/filebuddy/7/**)

■ Virus protection: Norton AntiVirus (**www.norton.com/nav/nav_mac/**)

I'm particularly fond of Norton SystemWorks, which bundles several utilities and features into one suite, including:

■ Aladdin Spring Cleaning, for cleaning up and removing redundant files

■ Alsoft DiskWarrior, a Classic application for repairing hard drives

13

- Dantz Retrospect Express, for backing up files

- FileSaver, for tracking deleted files

- Norton Antivirus, for virus protection

- Norton Disk Doctor, for repairing hard drives

- Speed Disk, for defragmenting and optimizing hard drives

- UnErase, for recovering deleted files

Norton SystemWorks has good support, can be scheduled to perform certain tasks, and can update itself over the Internet, so you have the latest versions of many of its components and its virus definitions.

Useful Tools for Mac OS 9.x

Because Mac OS 9.x will continue to be a part of the Mac experience for the foreseeable future, consider the following utilities for use with your computer when booting directly into Mac OS 9.x. Some of these utilities may work from within Classic mode, but I strongly recommend that you boot into Mac OS 9.x if you're attempting to repair a drive or resolve especially difficult startup problems. Many of the utilities mentioned here are in the process of being Carbonized for use in Mac OS X, so keep checking for new versions.

Disk First Aid

The Disk First Aid utility comes bundled with the Mac OS, and is an essential tool for diagnosing and repairing Apple hard drives, much like the Disk Utility for Mac OS X. It can verify the physical integrity of a disk, as well as make some repairs.

Drive Setup

The Drive Setup utility is   the companion tool to Disk First Aid., It is used to format and initialize drives, and can partition, perform low-level formatting functions, and update disk drivers. The Disk First Aid and Drive Setup utilities are included on the Mac OS 9.x CD-ROM.

Extension Manager

As you've seen in previous chapters, Mac OS 9.x relies on Extensions to provide essential functionality for your computer. The Extensions Manager is the best way to manage these Extensions, and can also manage Control Panels and Startup Items.

Extension Overload

www.extensionoverload.com

Extension Overload from Teng Chou Ming and Peter Hardman is an award-winning utility that helps users manage the dozens of Extensions in the System Folder. In fact, this utility contains information on over 1,200 items! Extension Overload provides detailed information about each item and offers a searchable interface to help you locate a specific Extension or Control Panel.

Conflict Catcher

www.casadyg.com

Conflict Catcher helps resolve Extension conflicts and startup problems by identifying offending items. It works by cataloging your System Folder and performing a series of restarts, identifying problems along the way.

FWB Hard Disk Toolkit

www.fwb.com

FWB Hard Disk Toolkit is a powerful application that specializes in the formatting, performance optimization, and repair of hard drives. In addition to individual drives, it supports RAID (Redundant Array of Inexpensive Disks) drives as well.

Useful Resources

Many new Web sites are devoted to helping you troubleshoot problems and provide software solutions for Mac OS X. Several of these sites will be familiar to the experienced Mac user, because they've been around for years and are regarded as reliable. For additional information about where to go for help with Mac OS X, refer to Appendix A, "Getting Help."

AppleCare Service and Support

www.apple.com/support/

The Apple support Web site provides excellent information about all of Apple's hardware and software products, including Mac OS X. The site has several subsections, including a new Knowledge Base search engine. AppleCare also allows registered users to customize several aspects of the support page, an example of which is shown in Figure 13.11. The Knowledge Base search allows you to select a broad topic, such as Mac OS X, and then narrow the search to a subcategory (such as configuration), and then type in the search term for that subcategory. You can further

Figure 13.11
Apple's support site allows you to register and customize your own support page.

narrow the search to a specific type of computer, such as iMac, iBook, PowerBook, or Desktop, or expand the search to include all of these Macs.

You can also perform an advanced search using natural language and Boolean logic, such as "Mac and OS and X and installation," as well as search the Tech Info Library or browse the AppleSpec database for technical information about your particular model of Mac.

MacNN

www.macnn.com

The MacNN Web site is my site of choice for news about Mac OS X, applications, and discussion forums. Their slogan is ReadMe First for a good reason!

Macintouch

www.macintouch.com

Macintouch is less organized than MacNN, but it is nevertheless a great resource because of the sophisticated level of information contributed by loyal Macintouch readers.

MacCentral

maccentral.macworld.com

MacCentral is the news service of *Macworld* magazine, perhaps the largest and best-known monthly print magazine covering Apple hardware and software. News stories are easy to browse and are searchable, and many reviews are available for popular hardware and software.

MacFixIt

www.macfixit.com

MacFixIt is the most thorough site for troubleshooting Mac OS software and hardware. It has a great forum for discussing technical issues and troubleshooting tips, as well as a good search engine to look for tips in their archive of information (requires a small annual fee).

Mac OS X Apps

www.macosxapps.com

Mac OS X Apps tracks new and updated Mac OS X applications, which are organized in numerous subcategories such as Docklets, Games, Productivity, Security, and Utilities. It also has a good search engine and links to news stories.

Version Tracker: Mac OS X

www.versiontracker.com/macosx/

Version Tracker, which is similar to Mac OS Apps, has a membership section that allows you (for a fee) to be notified of changes to certain applications and utilities. Between Mac OS X Apps and Version Tracker, you'll have the most up-to-date information on Mac OS X software.

Mac OS X Hints

www.macosxhints.com

Mac OS X Hints is a really cool site that organizes readers' hints, tips, and tricks about Mac OS X into different categories: Applications, Classic Environment, Desktop, Help Requests, Install, Internet, Networking, Site News, System, and Unix. The search engine allows you to search for hints by keyword, such as Dock, and returns entries in all the above categories.

13

macosxlabs.org
www. macosxlabs.org

Macosxlabs.org is a Web site dedicated to discussion and resources for system administrators who install and maintain Mac OS X in large clusters in education environments. The Mac OS has long been a significant part of academic computing, and this site is a great resource for Mac OS X know-how in this type of setting.

Wrapping Up

Troubleshooting the Mac OS is fairly easy when compared to other operating systems—but this observation won't do you much good if you're the one trying to resolve a problem! Don't underestimate the effectiveness of preventative maintenance, however, and above all else, *back up your data on a regular basis*. Your number *will* come up one of these days! If you do have a problem, keep in mind the most common problems and their solutions discussed in this chapter, including:

- Tips for preventing problems

- Startup and shutdown problems

- Application freezing and crashing problems

- Hard drive-related problems

- Networking difficulties

- Mouse and keyboard issues

- Problems with displays

- Printing problems

- Problems opening documents

- How to reset passwords

- Mac OS X diagnostic and repair tools

- Mac OS 9.x diagnostic and repair tools

- Web sites for Mac OS X troubleshooting and applications

In the next section, we'll look at the many networking-related tasks and applications you're likely to encounter when using Mac OS X on a variety of networks, starting with connecting your computer to the Internet.

Part 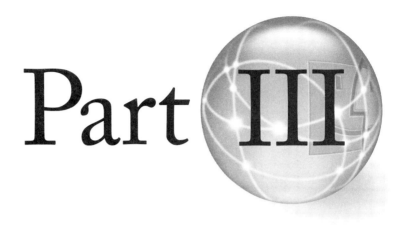 III

Networking

Connecting to the Internet

If the big story of the eighties was the advent of affordable personal computers, then the big story of the nineties was the Internet and the World Wide Web. Now the story is about super-fast Internet access via cable modem and various versions of digital subscriber line (DSL). The Net is still a hot news topic, of course, and in just a few years the World Wide Web has grown from a handful of university pages to a massive conglomeration of commercial, personal, governmental, and educational sites. The Web provides an easy-to-use interface to the Internet's interconnectivity in much the same way that the Mac OS serves as an interface to powerful and complex computer hardware.

If you've ever used other computers to work on the Web, you know that a Mac is the best way to get online. The Mac OS—a superior multimedia platform—is the perfect complement to the Net's combination of text, sound, images, and movies. The people at Apple realized this, and have integrated Internet connectivity into the operating system itself. In addition, they included everything you need to connect to the Net as part of the basic installation of Mac OS X.

Each of the major applications and utilities you need to master the Internet and the Web is already installed on your machine; I'll discuss these applications and utilities in Chapter 17, "Mastering Internet Applications and Utilities." But first, let's talk about how Mac OS X can help you quickly get online using a cable-, DSL-, or dial-up modem.

Getting Connected: LAN vs. Modem

Connecting to the Internet requires, first and foremost, an Internet service provider (ISP). As far as most users are concerned, there are essentially two main types of ISPs: a private local area network (LAN) or a commercial provider. Most LAN users connect via a corporate or educational LAN. LANs use various forms of wireless or Ethernet network cabling, as well as other types of cabling and protocols such as Token Ring, that are not supported by Mac OS X. Moreover, many large colleges and universities use their LANs to provide Internet access for their faculty, staff, and students while on campus, as well as dial-up access to their resources from off campus. Most people connecting to an ISP from home use one of several types of modems (dial-up, cable, or DSL) to establish a connection. Although the vast majority of home users still use a dial-up modem, the number of cable and DSL (both commonly referred to as *broadband*) subscribers is expected to increase, along with the number of commercial ISPs that offer both dial-up and broadband access.

LAN Access

More businesses than ever use LANs to connect the various computers throughout an office or group of offices. LANs come in several varieties. For example, a group of LANs connected together makes up what is referred to as a *wide area network (WAN)*. An *intranet* is any private network that is accessible to the employees of an organization over a LAN or WAN. LANs, WANs, and intranets use communications software such as email clients, Web browsers, and collaboration software that utilize the same protocols as the Internet, so Mac OS X runs as smoothly on any type of LAN as it does on the Internet.

For novice users, connecting to the Internet through a LAN is generally less confusing than connecting through a modem. The steps that are necessary to connect to the Net by way of a LAN are extraordinarily easy, and most businesses with large networks have full-time computer and networking professionals on staff to take care of all the configuration details. The Mac OS X has streamlined the connectivity process to such a degree that most people will be able to set themselves up on a LAN with little effort.

Modem Access

Mac OS X users who access the Internet from home connect to their ISP with a modem and software installed by the operating system. No additional software is required, whereas in older versions of the Mac OS, third-party connectivity software was sometimes necessary. Although modems can still be tricky, all computers that support Mac OS X come with modems that are compatible with the modems of the major ISPs. In fact, Apple has teamed up with Earthlink, naming it the preferred Macintosh ISP, to ensure that the modems installed in Apple computers have the highest level of compatibility with Earthlink modems.

The greater availability of broadband cable and DSL modems presents new opportunities for Mac OS X users—and fortunately, these types of connections are easy to establish and maintain, compared to dial-up modems. In fact, broadband connections more closely resemble LAN connections than dial-up connections in terms of configuration and troubleshooting. The following sections describe how to use the Network System Preferences to configure your Ethernet and modem ports to communicate over the Internet.

Ports and Protocols

Some people may get confused when confronted with the various selection options for configuring Internet access. I believe the key to understanding how to configure the Network System Preferences and connect to any network is this: most computers have multiple ports through which data flows, and each port may accept one or more protocols, or languages. The secret to configuring Mac OS X for Internet access is to select the right protocols for the right ports.

TIP: Modem connections make use of two sets of rules, called *protocols*: Transmission Control Protocol and Internet Protocol, commonly referred to as TCP/IP. The first determines how information is split into smaller parts and then reassembled at the destination, and the second determines the best path for the information to travel.

One of the great things about Mac OS X is the Location feature, which allows you to take the management of ports and protocols one step further. The Location feature lets you create sets of ports and protocols, and easily switch among them from the Apple menu. Like Open Transport in Mac OS 9.x, the networking layer of Mac OS X allows you to switch between Locations without restarting the computer, and use more than one type of network port or protocol at the same time. For example, Mac OS X enables you to use AppleTalk to communicate with a network printer while using TCP/IP to connect to the Internet.

Configuring Network System Preferences

As I've mentioned in several earlier chapters, the Network System Preferences pane (which replaces the old AppleTalk and TCP/IP Control Panels in Mac OS 9.x) is used to configure all the features essential to getting your computer on the Internet. In addition to the TCP/IP, AppleTalk, and modem settings, the Network System Preferences also supports several features of the old Location Manager. You can create multiple locations that allow you to easily switch between network configuration preferences—a feature that PowerBook and iBook users will find especially helpful when connecting on the road using a dial-up modem, and switching to Ethernet when in the office. Locations are helpful for other users as well, but the primary benefit is for mobile users. Let's start by looking at the Locations feature.

Managing Locations

The first option in the Network System Preferences is the Location field, which is shown in the top center of Figure 14.1. In the Location section, you can create, edit, and delete locations that identify what protocols are active on which ports on your computer. For example, you could have one location called "Earthlink" or "AOL" for

14

Figure 14.1
Use the Location feature to configure multiple collections of ports and protocols.

your dial-up account, and another called "LAN" for your Ethernet connection when in the office. Locations can be named whatever you wish. You can easily switch among locations from within the Network System Preferences or via the Apple menu.

To add a new location, open the Network pane of the System Preferences and then follow these steps:

1. Select the Location pop-up menu.

2. Choose New Location and give the location a name when prompted.

3. Select and configure the ports and protocols outlined in the next section.

You can add, delete, or rename a location at any time by following these steps:

1. Select Edit Location from the Location pop-up menu.

2. Select an existing location from the list of locations.

3. Click the Duplicate, Rename, or Delete button.

4. Choose Cancel to abort the process, or choose Done when finished.

If you have only one port for accessing the Internet or a LAN, such as an Ethernet connection, multiple locations may be unnecessary. However, you can also use locations to easily change network settings for the same port. For example, you can create one location called "AT-On" that has the AppleTalk protocol enabled, and another called "AT-Off" that disables AppleTalk. This makes changing between the two settings a simple matter. Once you've configured multiple locations, for whatever purpose, you can switch between them by following these steps:

1. While using any application, activate the Location section of the Apple menu, as shown in Figure 14.2.

2. Select a location from the alphabetized list.

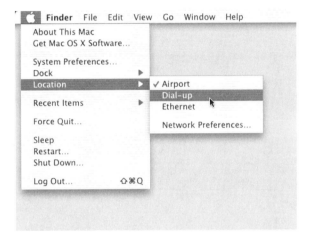

Figure 14.2
You can easily switch among network configurations without having to reboot using the Location section of the Apple menu.

Locations may also be selected from within the Network System Preferences by choosing Network Preferences from the Location pop-up menu.

Configuring Network Ports

You can configure the communications ports on your computer, as well as the protocols that flow through these ports, in the Configure section of the Network System Preferences. Most Macs have two ports, a built-in Ethernet port and an internal modem port, although it is possible to add additional ports for Ethernet, modem, and wireless devices. To make things a bit more interesting, Mac OS X also allows you to configure ports in two interesting ways:

■ Selectively enable or disable each port to show or hide the port in a location.

■ Prioritize each port within a particular location as a means of locating a port to connect to a network.

14

For example, let's create a configuration called Ethernet that uses the Built-in Ethernet port as the primary Internet access port. My computer has a wireless Airport card and a standard 56K modem, in addition to the Built-in Ethernet port. In the Port Configurations listing of the Configure menu, shown in Figure 14.3, I've selectively enabled the Airport and Ethernet ports, but disabled the modem port because I don't want it to be involved in connecting to my LAN. The Ethernet port is the third port found by the Mac OS, and I want to move it up to the first position so that it, instead of the Airport port, will be used as the primary networking device. The Airport card will serve as a secondary port in case the primary port becomes unavailable.

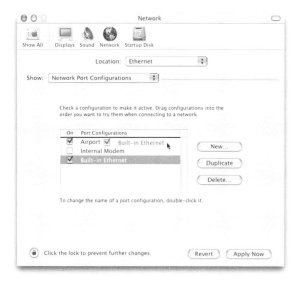

Figure 14.3
Mac OS X can prioritize selected ports for network communication to increase reliability and customize locations.

To select and prioritize ports, open the Network System Preferences and follow these steps:

1. Click the Show pop-up menu and choose the Network Port Configurations option.

2. Place a check beside the ports you wish to enable. I recommend disabling unwanted ports—this decreases the amount of energy your computer consumes managing ports and networking resources.

3. Drag the enabled ports to the desired location in the list to prioritize the ports, as in Figure 14.3.

4. Click the Apply Now button.

5. Click the Show pop-up menu again and choose a port to configure.

When configuring the ports, you can rename the ports by double-clicking on the name of the port and typing a new name, or click the New button and create a new port.

Because different types of ports have different protocol configuration options, each port needs to be configured separately for the various protocols it supports. For example, Ethernet cards typically support the AppleTalk protocol for communicating over a LAN, but modems do not because they're not designed for LAN use. However, Ethernet and modem ports do share certain protocol configuration options, including some TCP/IP and proxy settings. The possible configuration options for the ports on a typical desktop Macintosh are described in the following sections.

Connecting to the Internet Using Ethernet

Ethernet has been the standard networking protocol for the Macintosh for many years. All Macs capable of supporting Mac OS X have an Ethernet port built into the motherboard of the computer, and an additional Ethernet and AirPort card can be installed as well. The following protocols are typically found on any Mac with a built-in Ethernet port; an example configuration is shown in Figure 14.4.

TCP/IP

The Internet relies on the TCP/IP suite of protocols to connect the hundreds of millions of computers around the world. Fortunately, Mac OS X is based on the NeXTStep/OpenSTEP operating system, upon which Tim Berners-Lee invented the

Figure 14.4
Most Macs have a built-in Ethernet port for connecting to an Ethernet network.

World Wide Web in 1990 (see **www.w3.org/People/Berners-Lee/ WorldWideWeb.html** for more information and a few screen shots of the very first Web browser). The TCP/IP section of the Network System Preferences has multiple configuration options that relate to how your Mac obtains an IP address—manually or dynamically. Manually assigned IP addresses are managed by a system administrator who gives your computer an IP address that sticks with your computer for a long period of time. Dynamically assigned addresses are issued by a special type of server, firewall, or a router, and can be used by your computer typically for a fixed period of time. Dynamic IP addressing is commonplace in large network environments with thousands of users, such as dial-up ISPs, broadband networks, and college campuses. Dynamically assigned IP addressing enables unused IP addresses to be reclaimed when not in use, and distributed to other computers, thereby decreasing the overall number of addresses in use at any one time. IP addresses are in short supply around the world because only a limited number of them exist, whereas an unlimited number of computers are able to connect to the Internet.

The main ways in which Mac OS X obtains an IP address include the following methods, one of which must be selected in the Configure pop-up menu in the TCP/IP tab:

■ *Manually*—You or a system administrator manually enter the IP address. Additional configuration options, which are described below, must be completed when the IP address is configured manually.

■ *Using DHCP With Manual IP Address*—Many of the network settings are assigned automatically by a Dynamic Host Configuration Protocol (DHCP) server, such as the subnet mask and router settings, but the IP address is entered manually. This option is typically used by computers on a commercial network who need a static IP address. A monthly fee is usually charged.

■ *Using DHCP*—The IP address is assigned by a DHCP server. This method is typically used when connecting via cable or DSL modem, or on networks that are so large it would be impractical to manually assign IP addresses to tens of thousands of computers (such as colleges and universities). The IP address assigned using this method is typically "released" when the computer is shut down, and a new address is assigned when the computer is restarted. However, DHCP servers can also be configured to give the same IP address to a specific computer by looking at the computer's unique Ethernet hardware address.

■ *Using BootP*—The IP address is assigned dynamically by a Bootstrap Protocol (BootP) server. Use of Bootstrap Protocol servers is declining in favor of the DHCP server.

Whether your Mac obtains an IP address statically or dynamically, the networking layer of the operating system needs to know the IP addresses of several other types of servers in order to connect to a TCP/IP-based network, such as the Internet. When selecting one of the four configuration options just described, the following information may be required:

- *IP Address*—Entered either manually (by you or your system administrator), or dynamically (by a server). IP addresses are always four segments in length, with each segment containing one to three characters.

- *Subnet Mask*—Tells the Mac OS the type of sub-network it is connected to for IP addressing purposes. You can think of the Internet as the main network, and your ISP as a sub-network with special settings.

- *Router Address*—The IP address of your ISP's router, which connects and routes IP traffic between subnets and to the Internet.

- *Domain Name Servers*—Enter one or more DNS server addresses here. However, the addresses may be assigned dynamically when choosing DHCP, in which case you may not be required to enter information in this section.

- *Search Domains*—Enter the names of other domains you would like to connect to without having to type the entire URL in the Address field of a Web browser. For example, if you add apple.com as a search domain and type "www" in the Address field, the Network System Preferences tells the Web browser to append *apple.com* onto *www* to search for the address **www.apple.com**. It is not important to enter anything into this field unless instructed to do so by your ISP.

- *DHCP Client ID*—When connecting via DHCP, you may be required to enter a username assigned by your ISP.

Finally, your computer's Ethernet hardware address is also displayed in the TCP/IP section of the Network System Preferences. Each Ethernet adapter should have a unique hardware address, in the same way that each computer has a unique IP address. This helps simplify network management. Your ISP may record your Ethernet adapter's hardware address and the physical location of your computer as a security precaution. Security devices, such as firewalls, are sometimes capable of reporting your Ethernet hardware address to a system administrator if it thinks network violation has occurred. Knowing the location of the corresponding Ethernet adapter will help them fix the problem.

14

PPPoE

The Point-to-Point Protocol Over Ethernet (PPPoE) is a relatively new protocol used by wireless networks and broadband ISPs. PPPoE combines the Point-to-Point

Protocol (PPP) with standard Ethernet wiring. Apple's AirPort wireless base station, (which is attached to a network via Ethernet or modem), and broadband connections, (which rely on cable and DSL modems), sometimes use PPPoE as a means of dynamically assigning IP address information and performing user authentication. The main PPPoE configuration options, shown in Figure 14.5, include the following:

- *Connect Using PPPoE*—Click this option if your ISP requires a PPPoE connection in order to access their services. If checked, the following options become available:

  - *Service Provider (Optional)*—The name provided by your ISP.

  - *Account Name*—The username of your account.

  - *Password*—The password for your dial-up or broadband account.

  - *PPPoE Service Name (Optional)*—The name of the PPPoE service, also provided by your ISP.

  - PPPoE Options—Additional configuration options, which are described below.

  - *Save Password*—Check to save your password.

  - *Show PPPoE Status in the Menu Bar*—Displays a menu in the upper right area of the menu bar for quick access to PPPoE status and network settings.

If you select PPPoE, several related protocol settings will be affected . For example, your TCP/IP settings will be modified to obtain an IP address via PPP (instead of

Figure 14.5
The PPPoE configuration section of a built-in Ethernet port.

Manually, Using DHCP, Using DHCP With Manual IP Address, or Using BootP)
because PPP and PPPoE obtain IP addresses dynamically using a PPP server. Also,
the AppleTalk protocol, discussed in the next section, is automatically disabled when
PPPoE is being used on the same port. However, it's possible to create a new port and
run AppleTalk on that port (this option is also discussed in the following section). To
complete the configuration of the PPPoE protocol, click the PPPoE Options button
and review the following settings:

- *Connect Automatically When Needed*—Initiates a connection to your ISP whenever
  an Internet application such as Mail or Internet Explorer is launched and attempts
  to connect to a remote server.

- *Prompt Every __ Minutes To Maintain Connection* —Issues a reminder to remain
  connected to the ISP after a certain amount of time, which is helpful if you're
  paying by the minute.

- *Disconnect If Idle For __ Minutes*—Releases the connection if you haven't touched
  the mouse or keyboard for a certain amount of time.

- *Disconnect When User Logs Out*—Terminates the network connection when you
  choose Log Out from the Apple menu.

- *Send PPP Echo Packets*—Enhances the way Mac OS X communicates with your
  ISP's routers to ensure connectivity to the network.

- *Use Verbose Logging*—Increases the details entered into the Connection Log of the
  Internet Connect application when accessing an ISP by PPPoE, modem, or AirPort.

- *Cancel*—Cancels changes made to the PPPoE Options settings.

- *OK*—Approves changes made to the PPPoE Options settings.

AppleTalk
The AppleTalk tab of the Built-in Ethernet port, shown in Figure 14.6, is where you
can configure your computer to send and receive AppleTalk data over a network.
Although it is not the preferred protocol in Mac OS X, AppleTalk is still useful for
certain tasks such as network printing. Like the IP address of the TCP/IP protocol,
the AppleTalk protocol identifies computers on a network by a unique number called
a Node ID. Zone names and Network ID numbers identify different segments of
AppleTalk networks. You can tell the computer to assign these numbers automatically,
or you can assign them yourself (although I don't recommend it). Depending on how
you've chosen to obtain these numbers, your configuration choices may differ from
those in Figure 14.6. If the Mac OS assigns the numbers automatically, your configuration choices will include:

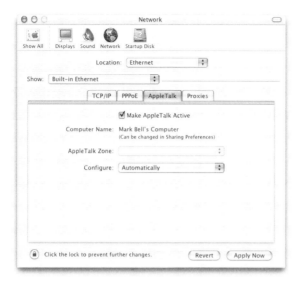

Figure 14.6
The AppleTalk section of the Network System Preferences.

- *Make AppleTalk Active*—Enables AppleTalk.

- *Computer Name*—Displays the name that your computer broadcasts over an AppleTalk network. To change the name, go to the Sharing pane of the System Preferences, as outlined in Chapter 16, "Sharing Internet Services".

- *AppleTalk Zone*—Choose the Zone to which your Mac should belong. Zones are simply smaller networks within AppleTalk's larger network. If your network's routers are not configured to segment AppleTalk networks into zones, your Mac will belong to the Default zone and you will be unable to make any changes for this setting.

- *Configure*—Choose to configure the Node and Network IDs automatically or manually. You should attempt to manually configure these settings only if you are told to do so by a system administrator. If you do choose Manually, the following two options are displayed:

    - *Node ID*—The numerical address of your computer, using a number between 1 and 253.

    - *Network ID*—The numerical address of an AppleTalk network, using a number between 1 and 65534.

Proxies

The Proxies tab of the Built-in Ethernet port, shown in Figure 14.7, allows you to configure proxy access to five of the most popular Internet protocols. When using a

Figure 14.7
Proxy settings for the Built-in Ethernet port.

proxy server, your computer connects to a proxy server for a particular type of service, and the proxy server accesses that service on your behalf—hence the term *proxy*. This type of arrangement is widely used in corporate and university settings to keep unwanted users from accessing online resources, such as an online catalog or journal subscription. Proxy servers can also serve as part of a firewall, through which a Web browser must pass to gain access to a network. Finally, proxy servers can cache frequently accessed Web pages, increasing the download speed of these pages. For example, if 10 people on the same network access the Apple home page (**www.apple.com**) simultaneously without the use of a proxy server, the apple.com page is downloaded over the Internet 10 times. If everyone goes through a proxy server that is cached, however, the first user's request is fulfilled over the Internet and the remaining nine users obtain the apple.com page from the proxy server.

Your network system administrator or ISP will tell you whether you need to use a proxy server to access an Internet protocol. The following protocols are handled via the Proxy section of the Network System Preferences:

- *FTP Proxy*—For downloading files via FTP.

- *Web Proxy (HTTP)*—For access to the World Wide Web.

- *Secure Web Proxy*—For access to the World Wide Web using a Secure Sockets Layer (SSL) connection.

14

- *Streaming Proxy (RTSP)*—For access to Real Time Streaming Protocol (RTSP) servers for QuickTime and other streaming multimedia.

- *Gopher Proxy*—For access to Gopher servers, which are becoming increasingly rare.

- *SOCKS Firewall*—For access through a SOCKS firewall to access Internet services on the other side of the firewall.

For each of these protocols, you'll be required to enter the following information:

- *Domain Name or IP Address*—The IP address or domain name for the proxy server.

- *Port*—The TCP/IP port number over which a protocol flows. Typically, a proxy server will often require that you use a non-standard port number, such as 8080 instead of 80 for Web proxy access.

In addition to these settings, the Proxy section of the Built-in Ethernet port provides two other options:

- *Use Passive FTP Mode (PASV)*—Check this option to enable Passive FTP, a more secure mode of FTP. In passive FTP mode, the FTP client software makes all the requests to the server, unlike normal FTP, in which the FTP server sends data to the client via a pre-negotiated communications channel. Although passive FTP can prevent certain types of attacks upon an FTP server, non-passive FTP is still the normal way for FTP clients and servers to communicate. Don't enable this option unless your network administrator tells you to.

- *Bypass Proxy Settings For These Hosts & Domains*—Enter the names of any domains to bypass when using a protocol for which a proxy has been configured. For example, you may need to use a proxy server for Web access, but there is one Web site whose firewall will not work properly through the proxy server. To bypass the proxy server for this domain, enter the root level of the domain, such as **macosbook.com** or **apple.com**, in this area, or the host name of the particular Web server, such as **www.macosbook.com** or **www.apple.com**.

These are pretty much all the settings you'll encounter for a typical Built-in Ethernet port. Let's take a look at the protocol settings for a typical modem port.

Connecting to the Internet Using a Modem

Although modems and Ethernet adapters utilize many of the same communications protocols, modems need additional protocols to communicate with the modem hardware. This is where things get a little tricky because of the vast array of modems available to the ISPs and consumers. Before you can configure a modem to work properly, you have to get Mac OS X to recognize and communicate with the modem—and then hope the modem works well with the ISP's modem on the other end of the telephone line. Fortunately, Mac OS X supports a wide array of modems using one of over 150 *modem scripts*. Modem scripts are small files that tell the operating system how to communicate with a particular modem. Each modem script defines everything from getting the attention of the modem and dialing a telephone number to negotiating the speed of the modem port. One modem script for each supported modem is located in /Macintosh HD/Library/Modem Scripts/. A modem script contains up to several hundred lines of instructions that look something like this:

```
ifstr 5 1 "0"
serreset 115200, 0, 8, 1
jump 2
!
@LABEL 1
serreset 57600, 0, 8, 1
!
@LABEL 2
hsreset 0 0 0 0 0 0
settries 0
```

In most Mac OS X-capable computers, a modem has been installed on the motherboard, but modems can also be installed in a PCI slot or externally via a USB port. If the modem is installed correctly and the proper modem script is available, you should be able to connect to the Internet as soon as you have an ISP account that offers a compatible modem. Check your modem's documentation and the support section of your ISP's Web site for information about modem incompatibilities. Some ISPs will give specific telephone numbers to dial for a specific type of modem.

Although the TCP/IP and Proxy settings are similar to those used when connecting to an Ethernet port and the PPP section is similar to the PPPoE section, the Modems section is unique. I'll point out the similarities and differences below. The following protocol settings should be reviewed and configured when using a modem to connect to an ISP by selecting a modem in the Show menu.

TCP/IP

The TCP/IP section of the Network System Preferences pane has a different set of options when using a modem instead of an Ethernet port. Modems and Ethernet ports both use TCP/IP as the protocol to communicate over the Internet, but the ways in which these two devices are configured differ in several ways. When you select a modem and then choose the TCP/IP tab, you'll see the following options:

14

■ *Manually*—Allows you to manually configure many of the same network settings as an Ethernet port, including IP address, DNS servers, and search domains. Typically, your ISP must configure the subnet mask and router addresswhen you establish a connection, so these options are not modifiable.

■ *Using PPP*—Allows you to only configure DNS servers and search domains; all the remaining options are configured by the ISP. Some PPP connections will also automatically enter the DNS server information as well.

■ *AOL Dialup*—Provides the same configuration choices as the Using PPP option above, and is included by Mac OS X to assist AOL users in selecting the right configuration options for America Online accounts.

PPP

PPP has made the old Serial Line Internet Protocol (SLIP) all but obsolete. In the PPP tab of the Network System Preferences (shown in Figure 14.8), you can configure how Mac OS X communicates with a PPP server using the following options:

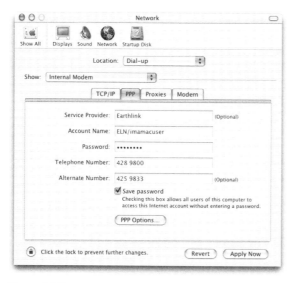

Figure 14.8
The PPP section of a modem connection in the Network System Preferences.

■ *Service Provider (Optional)*—The name of your ISP, which is displayed in the Internet Connect utility when connecting to the Internet.

■ *Account Name*—The username for your dialup account, provided by your ISP.

■ *Password*—The password for your dial-up or broadband account.

- *Telephone Number*—The primary telephone number dialed by your modem to connect to your ISP. Prefix this number with any additional numbers required to make a connection, such as 9 to access an outside line, or *70 to disable call waiting.

- *Alternate Number (Optional)*—A secondary telephone number to access your ISP.

- *Save Password*—Check to save your password.

Like the PPPoE Options button described earlier, clicking the PPP Options button reveals the following PPP-specific options:

- *Connect Automatically When Needed*—Initiates a connection to your ISP whenever an Internet application such as Mail or Internet Explorer is launched. This option used to be called *Connect Automatically When Starting TCP/IP Applications.*

- *Prompt Every __ Minutes To Maintain Connection* —Issues a reminder to remain connected to the ISP after a certain amount of time, which is helpful if you're paying by the minute.

- *Disconnect If Idle For __ Minutes*—Releases the connection if you haven't touched the mouse or keyboard after a certain amount of time.

- *Disconnect When User Logs Out*—Automatically disconnects the modem from the ISP when the logs out using the Log Out command from the Apple menu. Of course, the connection will also be terminated if the user restarts the computer or chooses Shut Down instead of Log Out.

- *Redial If Busy*—Tells the Internet Connect application how many times to redial the main or alternative number to establish a connection, as well as how long to wait between tries. This feature is very handy if you frequently receive a busy signal when trying to dial in to your ISP.

- *Terminal Script*—Select a script from this pop-up menu to execute the shell commands contained in the script (a new feature in Mac OS X Version 10.2). Terminal shell scripts are not installed by default, but if you or your ISP add any scripts, they should be stored in /Macintosh HD/Library/Terminal Scripts/, which you will have to manually create (this folder should not be created in the Library folder in your home folder).

- *Send PPP Echo Packets*—Enhances the way Mac OS X communicates with your ISP's routers to ensure network connectivity.

- *Use TCP Header Compression*—Speeds up the connection by telling the modem to compress the header information in TCP/IP packets as they are sent to the

14

receiving modem. Not all modems support this feature, so try disabling this option if you have trouble connecting to an ISP.

■ *Connect Using A Terminal Window (Command Line)*—Opens a Terminal window and requires that you manually initiate the connection. Occasionally, your ISP may ask you to enable this feature to troubleshoot a connection problem. It enables the ISP rep to see the exact steps your computer is following,and the response from the PPP server.

■ *Use Verbose Logging*—Increases the details entered into the Connection Log of the Internet Connect application when accessing an ISP by PPPoE, PPP, or AirPort.

■ *Cancel*—Cancels changes made to the PPP Options settings.

■ *OK*—Approves changes made to the PPP Options settings.

Proxies

The Proxies tab provides exactly the same options described in the Built-in Ethernet section above. Many dial-up ISPs require that you access certain services using one of their own proxy servers as a security measure.

Modem

The Modem protocol tab, which is shown in Figure 14.9, is very easy to configure. Each modem script located in /Macintosh HD/Library/Modem Scripts/ appears as an option in this section, so if you're not sure which modem is installed in your

Figure 14.9
Configure your modem using the Modem tab of an internal modem in the Network System Preferences.

computer, check the computer's documentation. If the documentation is not available, check the Support section of the Apple Web site (**www.apple.com/support/**)for assistance. Otherwise, start with the Apple-brand modems.

Use the following settings to configure your modem:

- *Modem*—Select one of the many modems from the Modem pop-up list.

- *Enable Error Correction and Compression in Modem*—Check this option to attempt a connection to your ISP to enable a faster connection, but disable it as a troubleshooting measure if necessary.

- *Wait For Dial Tone Before Dialing*—Tells the Internet Connect application to confirm a dial tone before initiating a connection. This helps to confirm whether any prefixes, such as *70 for call waiting, were entered correctly in the Telephone Number section of the PPP section,and whether a dial tone is present.

- *Dialing*—Choose between tone or pulse dialing; tone dialing is by far the most common of the two.

- *Sound*—Turn the modem's sound on or off. Many people resent the squelching and squawking sounds of modems,and prefer to disable this option.

- *Country Setting*—Displays the country as configured in the Time & Date System Preferences pane. Click the change button to change this setting.

- *Show Modem Status in Menu Bar*—Places a menu extra in the menu bar that provides quick access to connection information and the Internet Connect utility for initiating and disconnecting connections to your ISP.

When all the protocols have been reviewed and configured, you're ready to launch the Internet Connect application and connect to your dial-up ISP.

Dialing Into an ISP with Internet Connect

Connecting to a network via Ethernet is typically a "configure-it-and-forget-it" operation. Unless your computer needs to change locations while on a network, you'll probably never have to revisit the configuration options. Dialing into an ISP via modem, on the other hand, requires that you use the Internet Connect application to initiate a session,unless you selected the Connect Automatically When Needed option described in the PPPoE and PPP sections earlier in the chapter.

14

After you've configured the ports and protocols outlined in the preceding sections, choose a location containing a modem, such as the Earthlink location shown in Figure 14.8, using the Location shortcut in the Apple menu. Then launch the Internet

Connect application from the Applications folder or from the Modem Status option in the menu bar. Figure 14.10 shows Internet Connect in a collapsed (left) and expanded view (right).

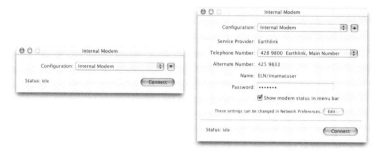

Figure 14.10
Use the Internet Connect application to initiate a dial-up connection to your ISP.

The name in the title bar of the Internet Connect window will reflect the name given in the Show field for the selected network port and not the location, which may be confusing to some users. To collapse or expand the window, click the disclosure triangle to the far right of the Configuration pop-up menu. The information in the Internet Connect application is retrieved from the settings you entered in the PPP tab discussed earlier.

To connect to your ISP, click the Connect button and monitor the Status section of the window, until you see information that confirms a connection has been made. Once the connection has been established, the Internet Connect utility (shown in Figure 14.11) reveals the following details in its lower section when viewed in the expanded format:

Figure 14.11
Two views of the Internet Connect utility once a connection has been established to an ISP.

- *Status: Connected To*—The IP address of the PPP server to which your computer is connected.

- *Send*—The level of information flowing from your computer.

- *Receive*—The level of information flowing to your computer.

- *Connect Time*—The amount of time your computer has been connected to the ISP.

- *IP Address*—The IP address assigned to your computer.

Once connected, you can minimize the connection window; or, if you want to monitor your connection while online, select the disclosure window to hide all but the most important information about your connection, also shown in Figure 14.11. To terminate the connection to your ISP, click the Disconnect button and quit the Internet Connect application.

If you choose to show the Modem Status in the menu bar, you can also connect (and end the connection) to an ISP using a modem without using Internet Connect. Figure 14.12 shows two views of the Modem Status menu, before connecting (left) and after connecting (right). Select a modem (if you have more than one configured) and choose Connect to open a connection to your ISP; select Disconnect to terminate the session.

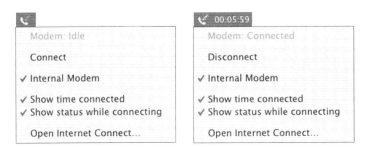

Figure 14.12
Use the Modem Status menu to easily connect and terminate a dial-up connection.

Wrapping Up

The Internet is an important part of modern life, and this chapter has shown you how Mac OS X has taken this fact into account:

- You've learned about the basic differences between connecting to a LAN and connecting to a modem.

14

■ You've seen how to configure and prioritize the ports and protocols in the Network System Preferences to connect to a network.

■ You've learned how to create locations to make switching between Internet access methods as easy as possible.

■ You've seen how to use the Internet Connect application to dial into an ISP using a modem.

Once you've connected to the Internet you're ready to start exploring! In the next chapter, I'll demonstrate several tips and strategies for accessing services over the Internet.

Accessing Internet Services

Mac OS users have long known the benefits of computer networking—the very first Macs were designed to easily connect to a network, and Mac OS X makes it faster, easier, and safer than ever before. Accessing file servers, networked printers, and Web servers is commonplace on almost every computer network. In this chapter, I'll focus on using your Mac to access services and resources over the Internet. Specifically, this chapter explores connecting to other Macs using AppleShare, how to access the many services provided by a .Mac account, how to access File Transfer Protocol (FTP) and Secure Shell (SSH) services, screen and file sharing utilities (such as Apple Remote Desktop, Timbuktu and Virtual Network Computing (VNC)), and how to store passwords to these and many other types of services in your Keychain. You'll learn how to provide these types of services yourself, using your Mac, in the next chapter, and the other Internet-based applications and utilities not mentioned thus far will be discussed in the last chapter. Let's start with connecting to file servers using Mac OS X.

Accessing Network Volumes

A *server* is a computer that is dedicated to serving up files or information to other computers, usually referred to as *clients* or *users*. A *file server* refers to a server that stores files shared among groups of users, typically in a corporate environment. Servers come in numerous shapes and sizes, and Mac OS X lets you connect to most types. A "personal" file server usually refers to someone's personal computer that has enabled one of the many forms of file sharing, including:

- AppleTalk Filing Protocol (AFP, for Macintosh computers)
- Common Internet File System (CIFS, for Microsoft Windows file sharing)
- Hypertext Transfer Protocol (HTTP, for the World Wide Web)
- File Transfer Protocol (FTP, for most computers on the Internet)
- Server Message Block (SMB, for Microsoft Windows file sharing)

In fact, every computer running Mac OS X Version 10.2 can access and serve files using all of these protocols. Other types of servers, including Microsoft Windows, Novell NetWare and IntranetWare, and various Unix-based servers, do exist—they're just not discussed here because Mac OS X allows you to connect to 99% of the types of servers that are out there. In addition to connecting to and serving these protocols, you can also connect to, but not serve, these types of server protocols:

■ Network File System (NFS, used by many Unix computers)

■ SAMBA, an open source version of SMB

■ Web-based Distributed Authoring and Versioning (WebDAV), used by many types of computers to access files directly on a Web server. WebDAV allows you to edit and manage these files without the need of a Web browser.

Before attempting to connect to a file server, make sure your computer is physically connected to a network, and that the Network settings in the System Preferences are properly configured. For detailed information on connecting to the Internet using an Internet service provider (ISP), refer to the previous chapter. Once you're connected, proceed with the instructions that follow. If you don't understand the options as they're presented, talk to a network administrator or see Appendix A, "Getting Help," for more information.

Connecting to a Server

Before you can access network data, you need to issue the Connect To Server command, often referred to simply as Connect. As I've mentioned before, Connect replaces both the Chooser and the Network Browser (found in Mac OS 9.x) as the sole means of connecting to file servers. To issue the Connect To Server command, switch to the Finder and choose Go|Connect To Server, or press Command+K. A window similar to the one shown in Figure 15.1, which is the contracted version of the Connect window, will be displayed. Clicking on the disclosure triangle in the upper-right of this window reveals additional options, which I'll discuss in a moment.

The Connect To Server command provides two ways to access a file server. First, you can enter the IP address or domain name of the server in the Address field (much like a URL in a Web browser). Although it isn't required when using the Connect to Server command, Macintosh File server URLs begin with afp:// (which stands for AppleTalk Filing Protocol), followed by the address of the server, so bother of the following addresses will work just fine:

```
myserver.macosbook.com
afp://myserver.macosbook.com
```

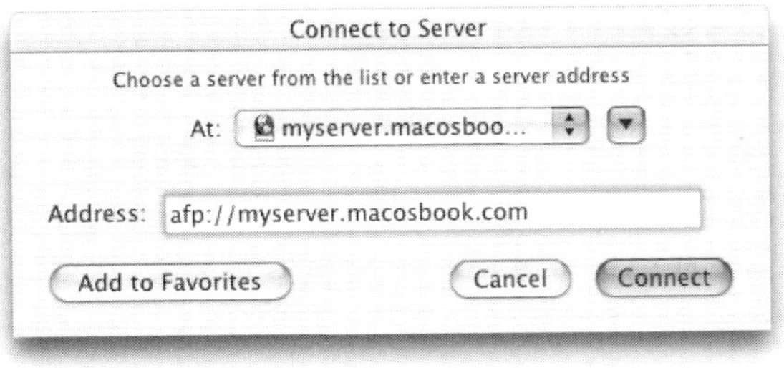

Connect to Server

Choose a server from the list or enter a server address

At: myserver.macosboo...

Address: afp://myserver.macosbook.com

Add to Favorites   Cancel   Connect

Figure 15.1
The Connect To Server window.

The second way is to browse your LAN's server list, and identify those that advertise themselves as AFP servers. This distinction is significant because not all AFP servers advertise on a LAN, and servers cannot advertise themselves across the Internet. AFP servers communicate using the AppleTalk protocol, the TCP/IP protocol, or both, depending on how they're configured. Because AppleTalk is perceived as a "chatty" protocol (one that creates a lot of unwanted traffic on a network), some server administrators only permit connections via TCP/IP, which is not chatty, and allows for speedier file transfers. Figure 15.2 shows the Connect window, expanded to view the Local network option, which is selected and displays several servers on a LAN.

If your computer is on a LAN, you may see several groups of servers in the connect window. In this example, the list of file servers includes a Mac OS X Server, and two Macs using Mac OS X's Personal File Server. From the listing, it's not easy to tell which servers are which. In any case, as a client accessing a server over the network, it makes no difference whether you're accessing data from a dedicated file server or from a Mac that's running File Sharing. Likewise, when you connect to a server over the Internet, the only difference you'll experience when compared to a local server is the speed with which you are able to upload and download files.

When you've located the file server you wish to access, double-click the name of the server (or use a single click, and then click the Connect button) to open a connection

15

Figure 15.2
Browsing a list of servers on a LAN.

to the server. The connection dialog box offers you the option of connecting to the selected file server as a guest or as a registered user:

- *Guest*—Although connecting as a guest is a simple matter, access privileges are severely restricted. Of course, this is your only option if you're not a registered user. To connect as a guest, click the Guest button and then click Connect . If the selected file server does not allow guests to connect, the Guest button will be dimmed. If this is the case, the only way to connect is to contact the server administrator and ask to become a registered user.

- *Registered User*—To connect as a registered user, select the Registered User option in the connection dialog box. The information specified in the Name field of your User System Preferences will be entered for you in the Name field of the connection dialog box.

If you're connecting as a guest, the Options button will be dimmed because, well, you just don't have many options as a guest! If you're a registered user, however, you can select from several preferences.

Configuring Connection Options

If you've connected as a registered user, you can select the Options button to modify several preferences associated with a particular file server. The Options button opens a preferences window, shown in Figure 15.3, that allows you to change the settings or perform the following actions:

- *Add Password To Keychain*—Creates a Keychain entry that associates the username and password (entered in the previous step) with the file server in question. See the

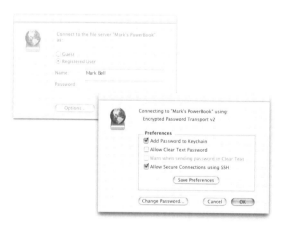

Figure 15.3
The Options button.

section later in the chapter entitled "Storing Passwords in the Keychain" for detailed information.

■ *Allow Clear Text Password*—Permits unencrypted –or, clear text — passwords to be sent across the network, which is a significant security risk. This option and the following option are present in the Options dialog window because not all file servers accept encrypted passwords.

■ *Warn When Sending Password In Clear Text*—Allows a clear text password to be sent, but issues a warning before it's actually transmitted. By warning you about the risk, this option provides some level of security, while still enabling you to connect to the maximum number of servers.

■ *Allow Secure Connection Using SSH*—Allows a connection to be attempted between your Mac and the remote server using a Secure Shell (SSH) connection, which encrypts the password and renders it unreadable to hackers.

■ *Save Preferences*—Saves the previous three settings, which can then be used by the Connect To Server command for subsequent access to all file servers.

■ *Change Password*—Allows you to reset a password to the file server by clicking this option, entering your old password, and then entering a new password. You'll be asked to reenter the new password for verification.

■ *Cancel*—Return to the Connect window.

■ *OK*—Accept the changes and proceed to log in to the remote server.

When you have reviewed the connection settings for a particular server, click the OK button to return to the main Connect dialog box. The next steps are authentication and selection of the volumes you wish to access, described next.

 TIP: Always select the Allow Secure Connection Using SSH option in the Connect to Server Options to increase the level of security on your computer and on your network.

Authentication

After identifying yourself as either Registered User or Guest, click the Connect button to submit your request for access to the server. If you entered an incorrect name or password, an alert dialog box will inform you that your attempt to log in to the server failed for one or more of the following reasons:

■ Unknown user

■ Incorrect password

15

■ Log on disabled

As another security measure, the Connect To Server command doesn't reveal which error caused the failure. For example, if a hacker's attempt to log in to a server is unsuccessful and the server tells the hacker precisely why, then the hacker has just picked up a free clue about how to (or how not to) get into the server. An error message such as "The password you entered is incorrect" reveals that the username, but not the password, used by the hacker was correct. Therefore, the error message is designed to be purposefully vague.

Selecting and Mounting Specific Volumes

After the file server has authenticated your username and password, a volume selection window is presented, in which you choose the volume you want to mount. (In case you're wondering, *mounting* is merely computer jargon for making a file system available to your computer over a network.) Whereas some file servers have only one volume to mount, others have multiple volumes—and quite often, these aren't volumes at all, but something Apple refers to as *mount points*, or folders that the server has designated for sharing. Servers can have anywhere from one to multiple volumes or mount points.

For example, Figure 15.4 shows two views of the same server's mount points. The left view shows the mount points listed when you log in as a guest. This server only permits access to the Public folders of its user accounts. The right view shows the mount points available when you log in to the same computer as a registered user. Note the differences in mount points depending on guest versus registered user access privileges.

 TIP: Because it's usually impossible to differentiate between shared folders and shared volumes, the term *volumes* is used generically to refer to mount points.

Figure 15.4
Two views of a server's mount points, logging in as a guest (left) and as a registered user (right).

To select one or more volumes to mount, click or Command+click on each of the volume names and then click the OK button. The volumes will be mounted on the Desktop, assuming you haven't disabled the Show Connected Servers option in the Finder|Preferences menu. Regardless of whether you've chosen this option, you'll be able to access any mounted network volume by switching to the Finder and selecting Go|Computer, or by pressing Command+Shift+C. To mount additional volumes from the selected file server, repeat the preceding steps. This time, however, you will not be prompted to enter a username or password because your access privileges have already been authenticated. Also, any volumes that you've already mounted will appear grayed out in the volume selection list.

Remote Volumes and Access Privileges

File server volumes are used in the same way as local volumes (those physically connected to your Mac), with one exception: any restrictions imposed by the file server also apply to the volumes. This means that you can't save or copy a file to a volume unless you have Read & Write privileges. In Save dialog boxes, the Save button is dimmed when the selected volume is write-protected in this way, and in the Finder, any attempt to copy or create files brings up an alert telling you that the volume cannot be modified. Finder commands such as File|New Folder are disabled as well.

The Privileges section of the Get Info command (shown in Figure 15.5) contains the access privileges for any volume you're allowed to mount. To view this information, select the volume icon and choose Get Info from the File menu (or press Command+I). When you create a folder on a shared volume, you're automatically designated as the folder's owner, and as the owner, you can use the File menu's Get Info command to reset the access privileges. See the next chapter for more details on reviewing and changing permissions in Mac OS X.

15

Figure 15.5
Use the File|Get Info command to view the sharing privileges for a volume mounted on the Desktop.

Volume Access Shortcuts

Want to avoid going through this lengthy process every time you mount a networked volume? You can create an alias of a volume that appears on your Desktop, and store the alias in a convenient spot on your hard drive, perhaps in your Documents or Favorites folders.

Double-clicking on the network volume alias icon mounts the volume as soon as you supply the necessary passwords. If the username and password are stored in the Keychain, however, the volume will be mounted automatically—no questions asked. How's that for quick and easy?

After you've mounted a network volume, that volume will appear in the Recent Servers list in the At section of the Connect To Server window. Because the Recent Servers section remembers only a few servers at a time, the volume you're interested in may not stay there for long—it depends on how many other servers you've accessed since the last time you accessed the server in question. By way of the Connect To Server window, you can add the server to your Favorites folder and then remove it, if you change your mind. Shortcuts like these are real timesavers when you're working with a frequently accessed network volume.

You can also drag the server's icon to the Dock or a toolbar menu to provide super-quick access to an item, and if you intend to access a server every time you log in to your own computer, follow these steps to automatically log in to a file server:

1. Switch to the Finder and choose Go|Connect to Server or press Command+K.

2. Enter the address of the server, or select it from among the local servers.

3. Enter your username and password.

4. Click the Options button.

5. Choose the Add Password to Keychain and the Allow Secure Connections Using SSH options.

6. Press the OK button.

7. Click the Connect button and choose which volumes you want to mount.

8. Open the System Preferences and select the Login Items pane.

9. Drag the server volume on the Desktop to the Login Items window to add it to the list of items to be opened at login, or choose the Add button and locate the volume.

10. Quit the System Preferences.

Figure 15.6
To automatically log in to a server without being prompted, choose Always Allowed when asked to allow the login window to decrypt the password stored in your keychain.

11. Log out and then log back in again.

12. When prompted by the Keychain Access application, an example of which is shown in Figure 15.6, choose Always Allow when asked if you want to grant access to the password stored in the keychain for the file server.

Anytime you log in to your computer, the server will be automatically mounted. However, this also means that if you enable the Log In Automatically option in the Accounts System Preferences pane, whoever starts up your computer will also have automatic access to the mounted file server volume(s). Be careful with this option — you could expose the data on the remote server to prying eyes.

Disconnecting from Remote Volumes

After you've logged in and mounted one or more remote volumes, you can disconnect a mounted network volume in any of the following four ways:

■ *Trash the volume*—Simply drag the volume icon into the Trash in the same way you would eject a removable disk.

■ *Shut Down or Restart*—All mounted volumes are released when you execute the Restart, Shut Down or Logout command.

■ *Eject*—The File menu's Eject command, or its keyboard equivalent, Command+E, dismounts any selected volumes.

■ *Contextual menu*—Control+click on a volume from within a Finder window or on the Desktop and then choose Eject from the contextual menu.

15

None of these four commands are labeled well. It would be more intuitive if Apple changed the Eject command to Log Out From Server, or something similar.

Accessing .Mac Services

Apple has recently transformed its free iTools service to a fee-based, expanded suite of services called .Mac. For about $100 per year, your .Mac account gives you access to:

- *Email*—Your very own Mac.com email account with 15MB of mail storage, which you can access using a Web browser or popular email clients such as Mail, Eudora, or Microsoft Entourage.

- *iDisk*—Store up to 100MB of files on an Apple-hosted file server, accessible anywhere in the world over the Internet.

- *HomePage*—A Web site creation and storage tool.

- *Backup*—An application from Apple that will back up files to your iDisk, or a local CD or DVD on your Mac.

- *iCards*—Customizable electronic greeting cards.

- *Anti-Virus*—Download and install McAfee Virex.

- *iCal*—Share your iCal calendar over the Web.

- *iSync*—Synchronize your Address Book and iCal calendars among multiple Macs over the Internet, as well as Bluetooth-enabled phones and Personal Digital Assistants (PDAs).

- *Public Slide Show*—Publish your favorite screen effects to your .Mac account, and share them with other .Mac users.

- iPhoto—Publish iPhoto images to your .Mac account using the iPhoto application.

For an additional fee, you can increase the amount of storage space on your iDisk, the number of email accounts, and the amount of email storage space. The entry-level amount of storage space is 100MB; the maximum amount of additional storage space is 1GB for an additional $250 per year. Additional email accounts are $10 per year for each account, and 200MB of email storage space will set you back an additional $90 per year.

To sign up for an .Mac account:

1. Configure your computer to access the Internet.

2. Open the System Preferences from the Dock or the Apple menu.

3. Choose the Internet pane of the System Preferences.

4. Click the Sign Up button to open the registration page in your Web browser, then complete the registration process. A free trial membership is available, but the services are limited when compared to all the features mentioned above.

5. Return to the Internet section of the System Preferences and enter your username and password.

To mount your iDisk once your account has been set up, choose Go|iDisk from the Finder or choose Command+Shift+I. Your iDisk will be mounted like other server volumes, but without the log-in procedures outlined above (provided that the correct username and password are entered in the Internet System Preferences). The name of your iDisk is equal to your .Mac username, and you can log out of your iDisk just as you would from any other file server volume. The iDisk is structured similar to your home folder, so mounting and using your iDisk should be a familiar process. The folders on your iDisk include:

■ Backup

■ Documents

■ Library (one you use iSync)

■ Movies

■ Music

■ Pictures

■ Public

■ Sites

■ Software

To configure access privileges to your iDisk, open the Internet pane of the System Preferences and select the iDisk tab, an example of which is shown in Figure 15.7.

The iDisk tab will display a bar representing the total amount of disk space, as well as how much of that space is available. In the Public Folder Access section, you can choose to grant people read-only or read-write access to your Public folder; you can also require a universal password to access your Public folder for both read-only and write-only users. Of course, if you don't want to grant read access to your Public folder, you'll have to avoid placing files in the folder. You cannot deny access to the Public folder, you can only restrict that access. The Sites folder is likewise read-only to the rest of the world, as is the home of your .Mac home page. To access your Web site, enter the following URL in your favorite Web browser: **homepage.mac.com/username.**

15

Figure 15.7
Use the Internet pane of the System Preferences to configure your iDisk.

I think the iDisk is a great feature, especially if you have a broadband Internet connection. If you have a standard dial-up modem, you may find the iDisk portion of the .Mac service to be quite slow.

 TIP: For more information about iDisk and iTools, visit **www.apple.com** and click on the .Mac icon.

Accessing Files via FTP

The File Transfer Protocol (FTP) is another way to access files on remote computers, especially if they aren't Macintosh files. Mac OS X gives you the ability to access files using FTP through two very different applications, Terminal and Internet Explorer. FTP is a simple protocol that basically enables you to *get* files from and *put* files on a server using an appropriate FTP client. Internet Explorer, for example, works well when getting files, but has limited abilities when uploading, or putting, files on an FTP server. The Terminal application allows you to get and put files, but requires you to use a command-line interface, which many people find to be very awkward. However, even if you aren't comfortable with typing commands in a Terminal window, you should try it at least one to get a feel for how the pioneers of the Internet lived! Figure 15.8 shows a sample FTP session using these two FTP clients.

 TIP: FTP is not a secure protocol, but it is a common practice to download files over the Internet using FTP when connecting as an anonymous (or guest) user, in which case you are not sending sensitive user name and password data over the Internet unencrypted. To ensure the security of your computer, do not use FTP for anything other than anonymous access.

To open a connection to an FTP server using Internet Explorer, follow these steps:

1. Open Internet Explorer from the Applications folder.

2. Select File|Open Location or press Command+L.

3. Enter **ftp://** followed by the hostname or IP address of the server, as in **ftp://ftp.apple.com**.

4. Click the name of the directory you want to access; click the name of the file you want to download.

5. Close the browser window to log out of the server.

To open a connection to an FTP server using the Terminal, follow these steps:

1. Open Terminal from the Utilities folder.

2. In the Terminal window that opens, type **ftp** followed by a space and the hostname or IP address of the server, as in **ftp ftp.apple.com**.

3. Alternatively, you can type **ftp**, press the Return key, then type **open ftp.apple.com**.

4. For FTP sites that permit anonymous (i.e., guest) access, enter **anonymous** as the username, and your email address as the password.

5. To browse directories, try these commands to navigate the FTP server:

   - **pwd** (print working directory, to display your current location on the FTP server)

   - **lcd** (list current directory, to display your current location on your Mac)

   - **ls** (list the files in the current directory)

   - **ls -la** (list the files in the current directory with greater detail)

   - **cd** *apples* (move forward into a directory named apples)

   - **cd ..** (move back one directory)

   - **bin** (set the transfer type to binary to download binary file)

   - **ascii** (set the transfer type to binary to download ASCII text file)

   - **get** *filename* (download a file in the current directory named *filename*)

   - **put** *filename* (put a file from the current local directory onto the remote FTP server)

   - **help** (list of commands available for help)

   - **help** *mycommand* (more help for the command named *mycommand*)

15

6. Type **close** to end the session, and then **exit** to **quit** the FTP session.

7. Choose Quit Terminal from the application menu or press Command+Q.

Beyond Terminal and Internet Explorer, however, several full-featured FTP applications are available for a reasonable price. The FTP clients I recommend include:

■ Transmit, from Panic (**www.panic.com**)

■ Fetch, from Fetch Softworks (**http://fetchsoftworks.com**)

■ NetFinder, from Peter Li (**http://members.ozemail.com.au/~pli/**)

■ Interarchy, from Stairways Software (**www.interarchy.com**)

Each client takes a different approach to displaying files on an FTP server. I especially like the approach taken by Transmit, which is illustrated in Figure 15.9. The categories displayed (called Your Stuff and Their Stuff) are about as simple as they get.

If you need to access a Secure FTP (SFTP) server, use the **sftp** command (instead of the **ftp** command) in Terminal or download MacSFTP from MacSSH.com (**http:// pro.wanadoo.fr/chombier/MacSFTP/SFTP_info.html**).

Accessing Files via SSH

Secure shell, or SSH, is a secure alternative to the remote login (rlogin) and remote shell (rsh) protocols used by various Unix-based operating systems, including Mac OS X. SSH, rlogin, rsh, and Telnet are all forms of *remote login* to a server on which a user has an account and may execute certain types of commands, several of which are explained in Appendix C, "Learning Unix Shell Commands." **Ftp** is an example of a type of command that can be executed from a remote login session; other examples include **ls** (to list the contents of a folder) and **man** (to view the help manual for a particular application or command). SSH is widely used in Unix-based environments,

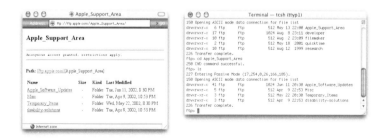

Figure 15.9
Try a graphical client, such as Transmit, for uploading and downloading files via FTP.

including scientific labs and research universities, because you can securely log in to another computer and issue commands. There are other applications for performing these kinds of tasks that use graphical interfaces, which are discussed later in this chapter.

To log in to a remote server using the Terminal application and the SSH protocol:

1. Launch the Terminal application from the Utilities folder.

2. Choose File|New Shell or press Command+N if a new terminal window doesn't automatically appear.

3. Enter **ssh** followed by the hostname or IP address of the server, as in **ssh myserver.macosbook.com** and the return key.

4. Select **Y** or **Yes** when prompted about a security warning, if you have never accessed this particular server before from the same computer.

For example, Figure 15.10 shows a remote login session to 192.168.1.12. In this example you can see the login command on the first line, as well as authentication messages between the two computers on the following lines. Eventually the remote

Figure 15.10
Use the Terminal application to open an SSH connection and control a remote computer.

computer asks for the password of the user account on the remote computer, after which the message *Welcome to Darwin!* is displayed. Next, I issued the **pwd** command to print the name of the current working directory on screen, then **exit** to close the SSH session.

Because the SSH protocol uses encryption fingerprint verification to authenticate remote hosts, it may be several seconds after you issue the **ssh** command before anything happens.

15

Sharing Resources with Timbuktu, Apple Remote Desktop, and VNC

As a system administrator, the most valuable network collaboration tool at my disposal is one that lets me see, control, and trade files with the Desktop of another computer. Timbuktu from Netopia (**www.netopia.com**) is the Ferrari of collaboration tools. It allows you to perform numerous collaboration tasks with computers running Mac OS 9.x, Mac OS X, and several versions of Microsoft Windows. Apple Remote Desktop provides more features than Timbuktu, and is an excellent tool for computer instruction, but it is only for Mac OS 8.1 through Mac OS X. Virtual Network Computing (VNC) is a freeware utility that performs most of the same screen–sharing functions as Timbuktu and Apple Remote Desktop. VNC is otherwise limited compared to the overall capabilities of the other two programs, but it's free! When you compare the features of Timbuktu and Apple Remote Desktop to the features of VNC, you'll see that both are well worth the cost of about $139 for a two-user license of Timbuktu, and $299 for a 10-user license of Apple Remote Desktop.

Timbuktu's main features include the ability to:

- Chat with a remote computer

- Control a remote computer

- Exchange files

- Exchange text messages

- Intercom with a remote computer

- Look at a remote computer without being able to control the computer

For example, I frequently exchange files between computers on which File Sharing is intentionally disabled. Because Timbuktu uses TCP/IP for all its communications, I can exchange files with any Mac or PC on the Internet that has Timbuktu installed. For example, Figure 15.11 shows a Timbuktu file exchange connection between two computers over the Internet. Note the floating palette for quick access to Timbuktu commands. The Exchange feature is very intuitive and easy to use; it allows you to move files between computers, as well as add, delete, rename, and get information about files, and create and delete folders on the remote computer.

The screen sharing feature, called Control, lets me control the mouse and keyboard of a remote computer, including the restart and shutdown commands. In short, you can perform almost any action on the remote computer that you can perform on your own Mac OS X computer, except start up the computer. To speed up the transfer of screen

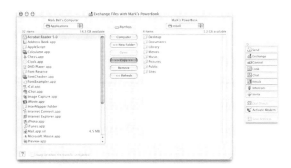

Figure 15.11
Exchanging files between two computers using Timbuktu.

information between computers, Timbuktu allows you to hide the Desktop image on the remote computer. Figure 15.12 shows an example of controlling a remote computer (Malcom) with Timbuktu.

Apple Remote Desktop also allows you to share a screen and files with another computer, but it is really targeted for the educational market where an instructor will manage many Macs. Timbuktu is a peer-to-peer sharing application whereas Apple Remote Desktop is more of a administrator-to-student application. Apple Remote Desktop allows the administrator to view multiple screens at once, which is handy for teaching computer skills in computer lab or public cluster of computers. Of course, Apple Remote Desktop can also be used on a peer-to-peer basis.

Figure 15.12
Controlling a remote computer (Malcolm) with Timbuktu.

15

Apple Remote Desktop helps administrators manage up to 5000 remote Macs by keeping track of much of the asset information of the computers, including:

- Network settings

- Memory

- Hardware profile

- Installed software

Instructors and network managers will appreciate the thoroughness of Apple Remote Desktop and the backward compatibility with Mac OS 9.x and earlier.

Unlike Timbuktu and Apple Remote Desktop, VNC requires two different pieces of software: one to enable screen sharing on your computer (referred to as a VNC server) and one to browse remote computers (referred to as a VNC client). Several Mac OS X–supported VNC servers and clients exist, and most seem to work just fine in my experience. VNC is an open source application, which means that hundreds of capable programmers are developing VNC servers and clients for a variety of platforms, including Mac OS X, Mac OS 9.x, Linux, Solaris, and Windows 95/98/2000/NT/CE, to name only a few.

Figure 15.13 shows an example of VNC on two Macs running Mac OS X Version 10.2, and the speed of screen sharing demonstrated in isn't as snappy as Timbuktu or

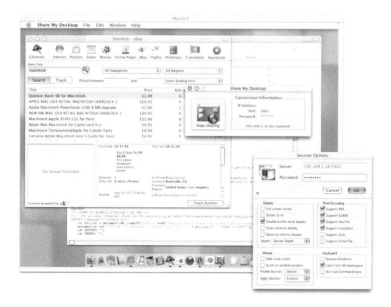

Figure 15.13
Sharing a remote computer's Desktop using VNC.

Apple Remote Desktop, but price (free) and cross-platform appeal make it worth considering if you don't want to shell out the bucks for a polished commercial application. The two VNC components I'm using in this example are:

- *VNC server*—Share My Desktop (**www.bombich.com/software**)

- *VNC client*—VNCThing (**www.webthing.net**)

The VNC server Share My Desktop, seen in the background window to the left, shows the remotely connected host; the client application is open in the foreground in the lower right, where you can see several of the connection preferences, including the IP address of the remote host and the port number used to connect to a VNC host (5901).

For more information about VNC, including a list of over 36 different operating system platforms that support VNC servers or clients, visit the Virtual Network Computing home page of AT&T Labs at **www.uk.research.att.com/vnc/**.

Storing Internet Passwords in the Keychain

The Keychain is a feature that was introduced several years ago, then withdrawn, and reintroduced in later versions of the Mac OS. The Keychain allows you to store username and password information for many types of Internet resources in a master file that is conceptually similar to the large, noisy collection of a couple of dozen keys that a building superintendent carries. In the Mac OS X Keychain, you can store login information for file sharing volumes as well as applications, including email clients (such as Eudora) and other network-related applications (such as Timbuktu). As we saw earlier, the Keychain also allows you to store passwords for encrypted disk images as well.

Using the Default Keychain

Mac OS X creates a default keychain (based on the Short Name and password) for each person who has an account on your computer. When the user logs in, the OS opens the default keychain, making the information stored in it available to servers requesting authentication or other applications. Figure 15.14 shows the default keychain for the user account markbell.

Adding Items to a Keychain

When logging into a remote computer or using any application that is Keychain-aware, look for an option called Add Password To Keychain (such as the one shown in Figure 15.3) that allows you to add an item to your default keychain. If the keychain is unlocked when you attempt to add an item to it, the Mac OS allows you

15

Figure 15.14
Mac OS X automatically creates a keychain for each user and unlocks it when that user logs in to the computer.

to proceed—no questions asked. If the keychain is locked, on the other hand, you'll be prompted to unlock the keychain to store the information. Because only the default keychain is unlocked at startup, you may encounter a message like the one shown in Figure 15.15. Expand the disclosure triangle to learn more about the keychain and what application is requesting information from the keychain.

Figure 15.15
Adding an item to a locked keychain requires that the keychain first be unlocked.

After a keychain has been selected and unlocked, information can be stored in it, as shown earlier in Figure 15.14. You can sort the items in a keychain by name, kind, date created, and date modified, as well as view the properties for a particular item by selecting it from the list of items in the upper half of the window to display various properties for the item in the Attributes tab in lower half of the window. You can also review the password for that item by selecting the Show Passphrase checkbox.

You can specify what applications have access to a keychain entry by opening the item from within the Keychain and viewing the Access Control settings, as shown in the lower half of Figure 15.16. Your access options include:

Figure 15.16
Viewing the Access Control properties of an item in a keychain.

- *Always Allow Access To This Item*—Allows servers requesting this username and password information to have it.

- *Confirm Before Allowing Access*—Causes you to be prompted for the password even though it is in a keychain.

- *Ask for Keychain Password*—Prompts you for the master password for the keychain, the same password as your Mac OS X login.

- *Allow Access By These Applications*—Allows applications listed here to always have access to the authentication information stored in the keychain item.

15

When you select the third option, a keychain not only stores username and password information for a keychain resource, it also tracks applications that have permission to access an item in a keychain. The Finder provides a good example of this feature. As you know, the Finder is the application that allows you to access file servers using the Connect To Server command, described earlier in this chapter. When accessing a file server for which an entry has been made in a particular keychain, the Keychain Access application asks you about the level of access you want to allow, including the following possible answers:

- *Deny*—Don't use the information in the keychain for this particular login attempt.

- *Allow Once*—Use the username and password for the keychain entry in this particular instance, and prompt the user again the next time this server is accessed.

- *Always Allow*—Use the username and password stored in the keychain for this particular server now and in the future.

Adding and Deleting Keychains

You can add and delete keychains in addition to the default keychain. For example, you may want to create a keychain just for file or Web servers to help you track these specific resources. To create a new keychain, follow these steps:

1. Open the Keychain Access application from within the Utilities folder.

2. Choose File|New|New Keychain and give the keychain a name and passphrase (password). Be sure to enter the same password in the Verify field. If you enter two different passwords, the Keychain will prompt you to correct the password.

3. The keychain will be created and unlocked.

Each keychain has preference settings that you can modify to suit your security concerns. To configure a keychain, follow these steps:

1. While Keychain Access is open, choose View|Show Keychains and click the appropriate keychain.

2. From the Edit menu, choose "*<keychain name>*" Settings.

3. Review the settings shown in Figure 15.17 and make the necessary changes.

The settings configuration window lets you change the master password for a keychain, as well as:

- Automatically lock the keychain after a specified period of inactivity (i.e., without touching the mouse or keyboard).

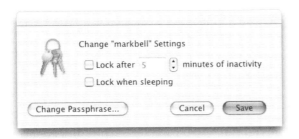

Figure 15.17
The settings for a keychain called markbell.

■ Lock the keychain if the computer goes to sleep as configured in the Energy Saver System Preferences or by choosing Sleep from the Apple menu.

■ Change the passphrase for the keychain.

Finally, you can delete a keychain just as easily as you can create a new one by following these steps:

1. While Keychain Access is open, choose View|Show Keychains and click the appropriate keychain.

2. Choose a keychain to delete by clicking it once.

3. Select the Delete button in the Keychain menu bar or choose Delete from the File menu.

TIP: Your keychain files are stored in the /Library/Keychains/ folder of your Home folder. They can be moved or copied to other computers and used if the correct password is provided.

Keychains are very handy for storing all sorts of username and password information for Keychain-aware applications such as the Finder. Whenever an application asks for a password, look for an option that will allow you to store it in a keychain for future reference.

Wrapping Up

Networks such as the Internet make it possible for computers to communicate with each other and for data to be shared among computers all over the world. The first generation of file sharing was of big servers accessed by smaller clients, but the past few years has seen a tremendous growth in peer-to-peer file sharing. Mac OS X is super-equipped to access many different types of services over the Internet, LANs, intranets, and any network that uses the TCP/IP protocol. In this chapter you've seen how to make the most of these abilities:

15

■ Using the Connect To Server command to select and mount file server volumes

■ Accessing .Mac services

■ Connecting to servers via FTP and SSH

■ Sharing files and screens with Timbuktu, Apple Remote Desktop and VNC

■ Using the Keychain to store login information for remote servers and applications

Next, in Chapter 16, I'll show you how you can use Mac OS X to share your files using many of these services to others over the Internet.

Sharing Internet Services

When it debuted in 1984, the Macintosh was ahead of its time when it came to file sharing. The first Macintosh supported the sharing of files using the AppleTalk networking protocol, allowing any number of Macintosh computers to be strung together using inexpensive telephone cable to form what is known as a *peer-to-peer network*. Later on, the Mac OS introduced a Web sharing feature, allowing Mac users to easily publish HTML documents on the World Wide Web. Web sharing was designed for individuals who wanted to share information over the Web without having to install, configure, and manage a commercial Web server. Mac OS X includes a complete version of Apache, the most popular Web server in the world; you can use it to share just about anything on your Mac, including HTML documents, images, word processing documents, spreadsheets, and much more.

Mac OS X allows you to share many types of services over the Internet, in addition to file and Web services. You can provide access to your computer via File Transfer Protocol, remotely control your Mac via Secure Shell and Apple Events, share your printer, and even share your Internet connection with other computers on your Local Area Network. Mac OS X Version 10.2 provides more robust sharing than in previous versions of the operating system. It also includes a built-in firewall to help you share these services more securely. This chapter explains everything you need to know in order to share documents safely in the multiuser environment of Mac OS X.

What Is File Sharing?

File sharing is a quick and easy way to share any file or folder with users on just about any type of network—whether it's a small peer-to-peer network of just two computers, or the mother of all networks, the Internet. But why, exactly, would you want to share files? You may be motivated to put your Macintosh on a network and share files for two main reasons:

- *Computer-to-computer communications*—Networked Macs can transfer files directly from one computer to another, eliminating the need to transfer files via *sneakernet* (using the Nike or Reebok protocol!). This form of networking is also known as *peer-to-peer* networking.

- *Centralized or distributed file servers*—Storing large amounts of data on file servers provides an easy way to share information, allows a number of people to participate in group projects, and reduces the data storage requirements of individual users. But because file sharing has its limitations, Apple also produces an industrial-strength version of file sharing in the form of Mac OS X Server, which is capable of supporting tens of thousands of users. Of course, the ultimate form of file sharing is Apple's iDisk, which supports millions of users.

In Mac OS X, file sharing is also referred to as Personal File Sharing, which allows each user to share the contents of the Public folder, located in each user's home folder. This differs from earlier versions of the Mac OS, in which you can designate up to 10 folders for sharing, regardless of their location on your computer. Because Mac OS X is a multi-user operating system, the number and location of sharable folders has been limited to prevent unauthorized access to files. However, for each shared folder within the Public folder, you can restrict access to users who have accounts on your server.

In networking parlance, when your computer is sharing files, it's acting as a server; when it's accessing files from another computer, it's acting as a client. File sharing allows every user on a Macintosh network to be a server, a client, or both. Sharing data from your Macintosh and accessing data shared by others on your network can increase your capabilities and productivity in many ways. Here are a few strategies for sharing files that you might consider:

- *Central libraries*—Reference files such as clip art, templates (or stationery), and historical records can be kept in one location and shared with the entire network.

- *Drop-box folders that send and receive files*—Each network user can define an electronic Out box and In box. By assigning access privileges, you can use an In box to let everyone add files (but not look at the folder's contents), and an Out box to let users pick up the files they need (but not add any files).

- *Temporary access*—File sharing is the perfect delivery system for members of the desktop publishing and printing industries who often transmit large files to and from customers. The alternatives are copying the files to a removable medium (such as a Zip or Jaz cartridge), or burning a CD and then mailing it; compared to file sharing, both approaches waste time and resources.

■ *Alternative to Email*—Sometimes email attachments are just too big for a mail server, which makes file sharing a great alternative for sharing multimegabyte files such as iMovies.

Mac OS X's file sharing isn't the answer to all your needs, however.

The Limits of Personal File Sharing

Although the capabilities of file sharing are impressive, it's important to understand that file sharing is only a "personal" method of sharing files over a network. Mac OS X Server, Apple's dedicated file server software, accommodates thousands of shared items and also allows Windows-based computers to connect to the Mac server. For a small number of Macs, file sharing is sufficient, whereas larger or more heavily used networks should utilize a combination of Mac OS X Server and file sharing. In most of these situations, file sharing will supplement Mac OS X Server, not replace it.

Here are a few observations about using personal file sharing that you might want to consider:

■ *Administration requirements*—As you'll see later, the administrative requirements of file sharing are not incidental. When many users need frequent access to numerous files and folders, centralized file sharing administration (provided by central file servers such as Mac OS X Server) is usually more efficient than distributed administration.

■ *Security risks*—To lighten the burden of administrative requirements, users often neglect security issues, and leave confidential or sensitive data unprotected. This is less likely to occur on centralized, professionally-managed file servers, even though Mac OS X and Mac OS X Server both have a built-in firewall. Professionally administered servers are usually staffed by people with up-to-date information about security issues who are more vigilant about protecting their servers.

■ *Performance degradation*—Even with a very fast processor and a very fast hard drive, file sharing takes a noticeable toll on computer performance. Macs or peripherals that aren't particularly speedy to begin with make the problem even worse. The benefits outweigh the inconveniences for casual or infrequent users. For frequent use, however, long delays can be annoying and counterproductive. A centralized server with resources dedicated to the burdens of serving network users is the practical alternative in these circumstances.

■ *Access limitations*—Sharing Macs must be left on all the time to ensure that files are always available to other users. Furthermore, if you need all the processing horsepower of your computer to work on a task, others might inconvenience you as they log in and copy large files to and from your computer.

A File Sharing Quick Tour

File sharing's capabilities are powerful, and therefore require more preparation and attention than most other Mac OS X features. Here is a quick tour of the steps I feel are essential to consider before enabling file sharing:

1. *Prepare your Macintosh*—This includes physically connecting to a network, placing the files to be shared in the proper locations, and activating AppleTalk (if you want older Macs to see your computer over AppleTalk networks).

2. *Start file sharing*—The Sharing System Preferences pane provides configuration information and the master switch to turn file sharing on and off.

3. *Configure users*—User accounts must be defined in the Accounts pane of the Sharing System Preferences.

4. *Specify folders to share*—To share any folder (other than the default folders identified by Mac OS X) with guests over a network, you must place the folders in a special location and review their access privileges.

5. *Confirm users can connect with file sharing*—Test your file sharing configuration by accessing your Mac from another computer before advertising it to others who may be accessing your computer. Mac OS 9.x users can use the Chooser or Network Browser.

The remainder of this chapter considers these steps in detail. See the two preceding chapters for information on connecting to the Internet and accessing Mac OS X-based file servers.

Preparing for File Sharing

File sharing success depends on physically connecting your computer to a network and properly configuring network settings. The simplest and most common Macintosh networking scheme uses standard Ethernet and a hub to connect multiple computers to each other. Sophisticated networks, which run at increased speed and use switches rather than hubs, require Fast Ethernet or Gigabit Ethernet adapters, because they can route packets of data more efficiently than hubs. All PowerMacs capable of running Mac OS X are equipped with built-in Ethernet, and additional Ethernet cards may be added via PCI slots (or in the case of PowerBooks and iBooks, a PCMCIA slot). It's also possible to implement file sharing over a wireless network using Apple's Airport networking technology.

TIP: You will need administrative privileges in order to change your network settings.

16

Once the physical elements of the network are properly configured, you need to configure your network interface using the TCP/IP and AppleTalk sections of the Network System Preferences. File sharing works without AppleTalk being active, but users on your network need to know the IP address of your computer in order to connect to it. If another user's computer is running an earlier version of the OS, your computer will not show up in their Chooser or Network Browser. If another user is working with a Windows-based computer with a utility (such as PCMACLAN) that allow them to connect to Apple-based networks, your computer won't show up in their selection tool. To configure your computer for network access, obtain the proper settings from your Internet service provider or LAN administrator. Once you have the proper network settings, launch the System Preferences, choose the Network pane, and follow these steps:

1. Choose the proper network interface, such as Built-In Ethernet, and click the TCP/IP tab.

2. In the Configure section, choose the method for obtaining your Mac's IP address, such as manually or using a Dynamic Host Configuration Protocol (DHCP) server.

3. Complete the remaining IP-related settings, such as the IP Address, Subnet Mask, Router, Domain Name Servers, and Search Domains. These options will vary depending on how your Mac obtains an IP address. For example, if you choose DHCP, you'll see a much different group of settings.

4. Click on the AppleTalk tab and choose Make AppleTalk Active if you want your computer listed in the Chooser and Network Browser of Macs running earlier versions of the Mac OS.

5. Configure any remaining AppleTalk-related options and click the Save button.

The next step in preparing your Mac for file sharing is confirming connectivity to a network. For this task, use a network monitoring tool such as the Network Utility, located in your Utilities folder. Choose the Info tab in the Network Utility window (as shown in Figure 16.1) and then select the network interface that you configured in the TCP/IP section of the Network System Preferences and confirm the following settings:

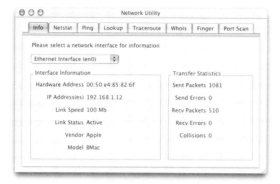

Figure 16.1
Use the Network Utility to verify your network connectivity.

- *Hardware Address*—Ensures that the computer properly recognizes the Ethernet adapter, which has a unique hardware address.

- *IP Address(es)*—Identifies the IP address or a addresses configured in the Network System Preferences.

- *Link Speed*—Determines whether your Ethernet adapter is communicating at the optimal speed with the hub or switch through which it is connected to the rest of your network.

- *Link Status*—Indicates whether you are on (Active) or off (Inactive) the network.

If you're really curious about the performance of your network connection, check out the Transfer Statistics section of the Info tab. It contains some geeky stuff, but it can also alert you to network traffic errors.

After verifying that you are properly connected to a network, the final step is to give your computer a name for use in file sharing and Rendezvous networking. The name you assign in the Sharing pane is the name that will appear in the Connect to Server dialog window when users log into your computer. This name will also appear in applications that access your computer via AppleTalk, Network Service Location (NSL), and other network-related services.

To assign a network-friendly name to your computer, follow these steps:

1. Open the Sharing section of the Network System Preferences.

2. Enter a name in the Computer Name field. For example, Figure 16.2 shows that I've entered MacDonnachaidh as the name for my computer (that's Gaelic for "son of Duncan," in case you're wondering).

16

Once you've completed all these steps, you're ready to start sharing!

Starting and Stopping File Sharing

Once your physical (or wireless) network is installed and your Network System Preferences are configured, you're ready to launch file sharing. As a security precaution, file sharing is not automatically enabled when you first install Mac OS X. By default, none of the services mentioned earlier in the chapter are enabled. To start file sharing, follow these steps:

1. Open the Sharing System Preferences (shown in Figure 16.2).

Figure 6.2
Give your computer a network-friendly name in the Sharing section of the System Preferences.

2. Select the Services tab.

3. Select the service named Personal File Sharing.

4. Select the checkbox to the left of the service, and wait a moment for the service to start up.

It will take several seconds to complete the startup task, and you can expect to hear your computer's hard drive reading and writing during the startup process. The startup process is considerably quicker in Mac OS X than in previous versions of the Mac OS; however, just *how* quick will depend on the speed of your processor and the quantity of files and folders that are being shared.

Once file sharing is running, the Start button shown in Figure 16.2 becomes the Stop button. To stop file sharing, just click the Stop button; a dialog box like the one in Figure 16.3 asks you how many minutes remain until file sharing is turned off. Enter a number between 0 (for immediate shutdown) and 999 (for delayed action). Finally, the optional warning message is sent to users as a courtesy.

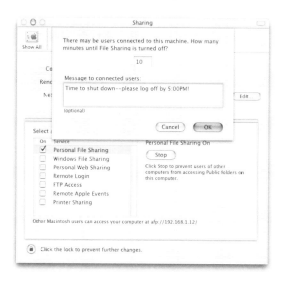

Figure 16.3
The file sharing shutdown dialog box provides the option of sending a message to connected users.

After you click OK in the shutdown dialog box, a status message informs all users who are logged into your Mac that file sharing will be turned off in the amount of time that you specified; it also conveys the message entered in the dialog box shown in Figure 16.3. If you cancel the shutdown command before the time limit expires, users will receive a second message stating that the shutdown procedure has been canceled. If you choose the 0 minutes option, cutoff will occur without warning. In earlier versions of the Mac OS, file sharing is also scriptable via AppleScript; however, this is not the case in Mac OS X Version 10.2. Perhaps a future release will include this handy feature.

If your network includes Microsoft Windows users who need to access your computer, Mac OS X Version 10.2 introduces support for the Windows file sharing protocol called Server Message Block/Common Internet File System (SMB/CIFS). Support for this protocol has been available to the Mac OS for many years via Apple's server software and through third-party applications. However, you can easily allow Windows users to access the same folders as Mac users by selecting the Windows File Sharing service, which is also visible in Figure 16.2.

Configuring User Access

Because Mac OS X is a multi-user-friendly operating system, Mac OS X's method of assigning access to users differs significantly from Mac OS 9.x. Before Mac OS X, user and group accounts were created using the File Sharing Control Panel, and access privileges were assigned on a folder-by-folder basis. In Mac OS X, file sharing is based on the user accounts on the host computer itself, and privileges are determined by the owner of each account on the computer. File sharing access is limited to three types of users in Mac OS X:

- Administrative users

- Users

- Guests

Users and administrative users have created accounts on your computer using the Accounts pane of the System Preferences. Guests can access your computer through file sharing without your creating guest accounts. Refer back to the section entitled "Working with Multiple Users" in Chapter 3 for detailed information on creating and managing user accounts. Although Mac OS X doesn't allow you to easily create and manage groups of users, users with advanced Unix administration skills can use the Terminal application to manipulate the Group ID (GID) property and configure customized groups of users. Let's take a look at the three different types of file sharing users in Mac OS X.

Administrative Users

In Mac OS X file sharing, administrative users have more read and write privileges than non-administrative users. When an administrative user logs into your Mac via file sharing, she has access to most files and folders from the root level up. File sharing allows access to files and folders that normally would be invisible to an administrative user if they were physically sitting in front of the computer. By contrast, non-administrative users are restricted to the contents of their own home folder and the Public folders of other users on the same computer, a distinction I'll illustrate a little later in the chapter.

Mac OS X file sharing doesn't distinguish between various administrators on the same computer, so it may not be in your best interest to grant administrative access to any other user on your Mac unless that person is trusted. In Mac OS X, administrative users have many of the capabilities of a Unix-style root administrator, but not all of them, and each administrator has the same level of access as the other administrators. However, even though there is a root account installed by default by Mac OS X, you cannot access a Mac via file sharing using the *root* user name and password, but you can access a remote Mac using a Secure Shell (SSH) connection using the root password. See the section entitled "Remote Access" later in this chapter for details on allowing SSH connections.

To summarize, Mac OS X file sharing is like a three-story office building: the farther you are from the ground, the more privileges you have. Administrators occupy the third floor and have the best view; the occupants of the second floor are the registered users; the ground floor is for guests. As far as file sharing is concerned, however, the building has no (root) owner—only multiple administrators. To assign administrator status to a user, read Step 3 in the following section carefully.

Users

File sharing grants access to users who've been assigned a username and password through the Accounts pane of the System Preferences. In addition to being able to access limited portions of your computer, they can also share their Public folders with other users and guests. To create a user account, follow these steps:

1. Launch the System Preferences from the Apple menu or the Dock and choose the Accounts pane.

2. Click the New User button and enter the necessary information, as shown in Figure 16.4.

3. Do not click the Allow User To Administer This Computer checkbox unless you wish to grant administrative access to the computer to the new user.

4. Click the Save button and quit the System Preferences.

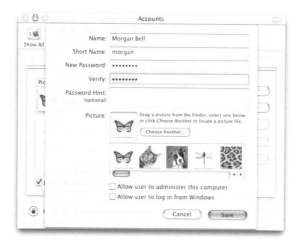

Figure 16.4
Create new user accounts for file sharing access, as well as other types of access, in the Accounts pane of the System Preferences.

16

In addition to creating the standard set of folders (such as the Desktop and Documents folders) in the new user's home folder, Mac OS X also creates a folder called Public for use in file sharing. I'll explain more about this folder in the section entitled "Sharing Folders and Volumes."

Guests

Occasionally, you may want to share files with someone who is physically connected to your network but doesn't have a user account for file sharing. This is possible thanks to file sharing's guest support. ,. By default, guests are allowed in the Public folders of each user account on your computer. In Mac OS X, guest accounts cannot be globally enabled or disabled without the assistance of a third-party utility such as SharePoints (**www.hornware.com/sharepoints**), whereas Mac OS 9.x includes this option in the Users & Groups section of the File Sharing Control Panel. Guest access is turned on by default when Mac OS X is installed; however, file sharing is not. This means that guests cannot connect to your computer by default.

If you want to enable file sharing for some user accounts but not others, it is possible to disable access to the users' Public folders, however; I'll describe this procedure later in the chapter.

Sharing Folders and Volumes

The previous section describes in detail the three different types of file sharing users; this section covers what you need to know about the various locations that can be accessed through file sharing. As you know, users of your computer can share the contents of their Public folders. However, users can also share the entire contents of their home folders. Users with administrative access can share the majority of the contents of the entire computer, in addition to their own Public folders. So, to summarize, Mac OS X file sharing allows for essentially three types of users (administrator, user, guest) and three accessible areas of the computer (the entire computer, a user's home folder, and a user's Public folder). Table 16.1 illustrates the intersection of this set of threes.

Table 16.1   Mac OS X file sharing access privileges.

Type of User	Computer	Home Folder	Public Folder
Administrator	Yes	Yes	Yes
User	No	Yes	Yes
Guest	No	No	Yes

Mac OS X preprograms, or *hard codes*, the Public folder in each user's home folder for file sharing, just as it names the home folder with each user's Short Name as configured in the Accounts System Preferences. You can't change the name or location of either of these folders. However, a user can share other folders by moving them into the Public folder and modifying access privileges. This action changes the rights that administrators, other users, and guests have to the Public and Sites folders.

Selecting a Folder to Share

Before you can share a folder with others on your network or over the Internet, you must initiate file sharing and specify access privileges in the Ownership & Permissions section of the Get Info command. If you don't, you'll be stuck with the default set of privileges. To review or change the sharing privileges of a folder located in your Public folder, select the folder and follow these steps:

1. Choose File|Get Info or press Command+I.

2. Expand the Ownership & Permissions section.

For example, Figure 16.5 shows the Ownership & Permissions section for a folder named Docs in my Public folder. This dialog box allows me to assign access privileges for this item, and transfer the same set of privileges to any folders contained in the Docs folder. Access privileges, as you learned earlier, determine who is allowed to see the folders and volumes, as well as the files inside those folders and volumes. Access

Figure 16.5
The Ownership & Permissions section of a Get Info window.

16

privileges also specify who can make changes to existing files or store new files. (I'll talk more about access privileges in the upcoming "Understanding Access Ownership & Permissions" section of this chapter.)

The Ownership & Permissions section of the Get Info window allows you to configure a number of important options, including the access privileges for the following three ownership levels:

- *Owner*—This option specifies the owner of the selected folder or volume and the owner's access privileges. Unlike previous versions of Mac OS X (in which you can reassign ownership of the folder to another user), you are the sole owner of shared folders in your Public folder and can't assign ownership to others.

- *Group*—Mac OS X automatically assigns users of your computer to a group called Staff, which you can also change. Group permissions allow permissions to be shared among users and services on your Mac.

- *Others*—This section specifies access privileges granted to guest users on your Macintosh. As mentioned before, anyone on your network can log on to your Mac as a guest—as long as you've enabled file sharing and have at least one user account with a Public folder whose privileges have not been further restricted.

When you share a folder, all enclosed folders are also automatically accessible to users with access to your computer. You can change the access privileges of an enclosed folder so that they don't match those of the enclosing folder. The Apply to Enclosed Folders button does the opposite — it resets the access privileges of the enclosed folders so they match those of the currently selected folder or volume. Think of this option as a kind of reset button.

TIP: Mac OS X creates several user accounts by default that are not visible in the Accounts pane of the System Preferences, including daemon, nobody, root, system, unknown, and others, depending on the type of installation. Additional software you install may create other user accounts as well.

Understanding Ownership & Permissions

Shared folders and volumes are available to other network users according to the access privilege settings you apply in the Ownership & Permissions section of the Get Info window. These privileges are the key to controlling file sharing. There are three access privilege options that are assigned to three different users or groups. Your choice of option settings and combinations determines how network users can access and modify your shared data and storage space.

To make a change to the permissions of a folder, follow these steps:

1. Choose File|Get Info or press Command+I.

2. Expand the Ownership & Permissions section.

3. Click the lock icon and provide the user name and password of an administrative user.

4. Change the ownership or access privileges for the owner, group, or others (guests).

Mac OS X utilizes Unix-style permissions in all areas of its tasks, including file sharing, but with its trademark user-friendliness. In reality, the levels of Unix permissions are abbreviated with a single letter and are applied individually to the owner, group, and to everyone else for each item on a volume:

■ read (r)

■ write (w)

■ execute (x)

■ no access (-)

Read means one of these three users can read a file. Write means the user can open and edit a file. Execute means the user can execute a command, or if the privilege is applied to a folder, the user can open the folder. No access means that the user, group, or others cannot read, write, or execute the item at all. To abbreviate things even further, each Unix-style permission found in Mac OS X can be reduced to a one-letter acronym using the following values:

■ read (4)

■ write (2)

■ execute (1)

■ no access (0)

Added together, a numerical value can be assigned to each file, folder, or volume in Mac OS X, one each for the owner, group, and others. The result is a three-digit number that describes the permission for an item. For example, a folder that everyone (owner, group, and others) can read, write, and execute, would have the value 777. A folder that the owner and group and can read, write, and execute, but others can only write would have the value 772. Is that geeky, or what? Table 16.2 might help you better understand the numerical values, and how the three individual values are added up to derive a permission:

Table 16.2   Unix-style numerical abbreviations for file permissions.

Value	Read	Write	Execute
7	yes	yes	yes
6	yes	yes	no
5	yes	no	yes
4	yes	no	no
3	no	yes	yes
2	no	yes	no
1	no	no	yes
0	no	no	no

For examples of how this type of information can be valuable, see Appendix C, "Learning Unix Shell Commands". I'll demonstrate how you can use the Terminal application to view and change folder permissions using Unix commands such as **ls -al** (to list the contents of a folder) and **chwon** (to change the ownership of files and folders). For now, you should know that Mac OS X translates these numeric permissions into the terms used in Mac file sharing's past —*read*, *read & write*, and *write only*. Let's look at these access privileges, the users and groups they can be assigned to, and the results of applying them in different combinations to an example folder. The following file sharing permissions are found in Mac OS X Version 10.2, with the Unix variant in parenthesis:

■ *Read & Write (read, write, and execute)*—When the Read & Write privilege is set, the user can save new files, change existing files, and create new folders. The user enjoys almost unlimited access to the folder and its contents, and can delete the contents of these folders.

■ *Read Only (read and execute)*—This option limits a user to viewing (or reading— hence the name) the contents of the folder. No changes can be made within the shared item. When the Read Only option is selected, and the status bar is displayed in Finder windows, an icon appears in the upper-left corner of the status bar to let the user know that the folder or volume is write–protected (see Figure 16.6). Users are prohibited from writing to this folder, as well as from editing or deleting files and folders.

■ *Write Only (write and execute)*—This privilege hides the contents of folders from a specified user or group—users don't even know what, if anything, is inside this type of folder (selecting Get Info will reveal "—KB" of contents). Users can place files in the shared folder, but only the owner can see and manage its contents. When a folder is shared as a Drop Box, it will appear with a small downward arrow like the folder named Drop Box in Figure 16.7 (right).

Figure 16.6
A shared folder with Read Only privileges displays a read-only icon in the upper-left portion of the status bar.

Figure 16.7
Folders with no access privileges appear with a small stop sign to indicate that you cannot read, write, or execute (open) the contents of the folder.

- *None (no privileges)*—With no privileges specified, a shared folder is inaccessible to users. If that folder is enclosed within another folder to which a user has at least read access, the folder that has no privileges will look like the Docs folder shown in Figure 16.7 (left) when a guest logs in and mounts the mbell home folder. If the Public folder is assigned this option, it will not appear in the Select The Volumes You Wish To Mount section of the Connect To Server command. In other words, when someone attempts to log into your computer and your Public folder is not shared, they will not even know you have an account on the computer. See the section below entitled "Unsharing a Folder" for a detailed example of how to disable guest access to certain users' home folders.

For example, refer to Figure 16.6 in which a folder named For Review is configured for read and write access for the owner, but read only access for other members of the Staff group and for guests. The Ownership & Permissions section of the Get Info command is as follows:

- *Owner*—Read & Write

■ *Group*—Read Only

■ *Everybody*—Read Only

In Figure 6.7, my Public folder contains a folder named Drop Box, which is created by Mac OS X to allow people to send files to your computer but not read the contents of that folder. The Ownership & Permissions section of the Get Info command is as follows:

■ *Owner*—Read & Write

■ *Group*—Write Only (Drop Box)

■ *Everybody*—Write Only (Drop Box)

Although no user will be able to see the contents of this folder, they will be able to add items to it via file sharing. The Docs folder in the same figure is open to the owner and the group called staff, but the No Access option denies access to all file sharing guests. The Docs folder has the following privileges, which you also saw in Figure 16.7:

■ *Owner*—Read & Write

■ *Group*— Read & Write

■ *Everybody*—No Access

TIP: The Mac OS uses different folder icons to indicate the level of access privileges assigned to a folder. This enables you to know at a glance whether you have read, write, or no access to a folder.

Experiment with assigning different levels of privileges to a test folder before you start sharing over the Internet. This can help prevent a file sharing mishap; you don't want a folder containing important information falling into the wrong hands. Mac OS X provides various levels of privileges to control the way files can be accessed via file sharing. Several common ways of using access privileges are as follows:

■ *Create an Inbox folder*—People can drop items into an Inbox folder, but can't see what's already there or delete items from the folder. This is accomplished by granting Write Only (Drop Box) privileges to users in all categories (except the owner).

■ *Create an Outbox folder*—An Outbox folder allows users to see files and folders, but prohibits them from adding or deleting items. An Outbox folder is an effective way to maintain an unsullied master copy of a document, because it prevents other users or guests from tinkering with the document. Granting Read Only access to everyone other than the owner, who has Read & Write privileges, designates this type of limited access.

- *Provide a workgroup area*—You can create a folder with several subfolders for access by groups who are working on related projects. For example, you can create a folder to which everyone has Read & Write access—just be sure that the users are aware of their responsibility to refrain from deleting or modifying documents that don't belong to them. Think of this strategy as a form of cooperative multitasking among file sharing users.

See the next section for information on how to stop file sharing for a particular folder.

Unsharing a Folder

Sharing folders has been the central topic thus far, but what about unsharing a folder? Mac OS X provides several strategies that you can use to stop sharing a folder, including:

- Turn file sharing off completely

- Stop sharing a selected user's Public folder

- Stop sharing a selected folder within a user's Public folder

- Remove or relocate a folder outside the Public folder

Of course, turning off your Mac or disconnecting its network cables will also do the trick!

To turn file sharing off completely, open the Sharing System Preferences and click the Stop button. When file sharing is turned off, the settings and access privileges that you set (with the Sharing command) are retained for all shared folders and volumes. These settings and privileges will be reactivated when file sharing is turned on again. This option is easiest if you're the only user of the computer. If not, you'll automatically disable file sharing for everyone else who uses your computer.

The easiest way to turn off sharing of a particular folder is to remove it from your Public folder, instead of trying to manipulate its sharing privileges. Of course, you can disable access to a folder within a user's Public folder by manipulating file-sharing permissions. Just follow these steps:

1. Select the folder and choose File|Get Info or press Command+I.

2. Expand the Ownership & Permissions section.

3. Click the lock icon, and change the Owner of the folder to yourself (if you have administrative privileges). Provide your user name and password when prompted.

16

4. Change the access privileges for the Group and Others to No Access.

5. Change the Owner of the folder back to the original owner.

6. Close the Get Info window.

To disable guest access to a specific user's Public folder without completely disabling file sharing for that user or any administrative users, follow these steps:

1. Select the folder and choose File|Get Info or press Command+I.

2. Expand the Ownership & Permissions section.

3. Click the lock icon and change the Owner of the folder to yourself (if you have administrative privileges). Provide your user name and password when prompted.

4. Change the access privileges for Others to No Access.

5. Change the Owner of the folder back to the original owner.

6. Close the Get Info window.

If you have numerous user accounts on your Mac and you want to disable guest access for all the accounts, try downloading and installing SharePoints from **www.hornware.com/ sharepoints**. SharePoints is "donationware" that allows you to easily change almost all aspects of Mac OS X file sharing, including the location and name of shared folders, guest access privileges, and creation of groups. You can also change global settings for all file sharing users such as logging, the number of concurrent users, use of file sharing using AppleTalk and the ability to disconnect idle users. For example, to disable guest access to all users with SharePoints, follow these steps:

1. Launch the SharePoints application or open the SharePoints System Preferences pane.

2. Select the Users & "Public Shares" tab, an example of which is shown in Figure 16.8.

3. Click the padlock icon in the lower-left and enter the user name and password of an administrator.

4. Select the Disable All button in the section entitled "Public" Directory Shares.

5. Select the Restart AppleFileServer button (which is required any time you make a change to any shared folder using SharePoints).

6. Quit the SharePoints application or System Preferences pane.

After one or all guest access privileges have been disabled, users will still be able to log in as a guest, but they will not see any volumes to mount. For example, Figure 16.9

shows what guests will see before (left) and after (right) guest access has been disabled in Mac OS X using SharePoints.

Figure 16.8
Try Share Points as an alternative interface for configuring file sharing.

Figure 16.9
Use SharePoints to configure file sharing users, groups, and global settings.

Web Sharing

The second way you can share files with other users over a LAN or the Internet is with Mac OS X's Web sharing feature. Although Apple has included a personal Web server with the Mac OS in the past, Web sharing in Mac OS X is different. It's more than just a lightweight Web server—it's a fully functional installation of the Apache Web server. Apache, the most popular Web server on the Internet since 1996, now accounts for 60 percent of all Web servers in use today. Because Apache is an open source Web server (much like Darwin is an open source operating system), the two are a great match. For more information about the Apache Web server and other open source projects that support or compliment Apache, consult the Apache Software

Foundation home page (**www.apache.org**). If you can point and click a mouse, then you can be a Webmaster and run an Apache Web server on your computer, thanks to Mac OS X.

"The Web" is a collection of Web servers that are accessed by Web browsers, such as Microsoft Internet Explorer, Netscape Navigator, iCab, OmniWeb, and many others. Web browsers are available for virtually every computer hardware and software platform, hand-held personal digital assistants (PDAs), such as the Palm Pilot, and mainframe computers. The Hypertext Markup Language (HTML) makes it possible for one document to be read by many different types of computers. HTML is a low-level programming language called a markup, or page description, language. It's very unsophisticated, and easily implemented into existing applications such as Microsoft Office and operating systems like Mac OS X. HTML uses simple formatting instructions like the following example to make portions of the document appear underlined, boldface, and centered, as well allowing the insertion of images and citations:

```
<HTML>
<HEAD>
<TITLE>HTML Basics</TITLE>
</HEAD>
<BODY>
<P>
<CENTER><FONT FACE="Lucida Grande">
This is an example of <U>underlined</U> and <B>bold</B>
text centered on the page.
<IMG SRC="1971.jpg" ALT="My First Bike" WIDTH="429" HEIGHT="429"><BR>
<CITE>This is a citation.</CITE>
</FONT></CENTER>
</P>
</BODY>
</HTML>
```

HTML is really just a collection of commands (written in easy-to-understand ASCII text) that tell Web browsers how to display formatted text, insert images, and link to other pages on the Web. Figure 16.10 shows what this example looks like in Internet Explorer when served using Web sharing in Mac OS X.

You'll need a good HTML editor if you plan to get serious about creating and modifying Web pages. BBEdit for Mac OS X is a great place to start if you want to learn how HTML code is actually written. To obtain a fully functional demo version of BBEdit, visit the Bare Bones home page (**www.barebones.com**). The full version costs about $120; you can upgrade to the Mac OS X version for as little as $39. It will be a worthwhile investment.

Figure 16.10
Web pages are composed of HTML code that tells Web browsers how to display text and images.

Web Server Configuration

Mac OS X implements the Apache Web server in an interesting way: it hides all the complex configuration options and expansion modules, so every user on your computer can start serving Web pages with a single mouse click. Apple doesn't disable Apache's advanced options—it just hides them by making the configuration files and folders invisible. This is not a problem for people who want to use Apache's advanced features, however. Experienced Apache users can enable many of the hidden features and issue command-line instructions using the Terminal application. This requires a working knowledge of Unix file permissions, as well as Apache administration experience. A second option is iTools from Tenon Intersystems (**www.tenon.com**), which puts an easy-to-use graphical interface on the otherwise complex configuration of Apache. A third option is an alternative Web server, such as WebSTAR from 4D (**www.4d.com**). WebSTAR is a full-featured, relatively user-friendly Web server that is best suited for robust commercial Web serving needs, and not as a personal Web server. Let's look at how to start and stop Mac OS X's built-in Web sharing feature. We'll also cover a few points about file names and folder locations.

Starting Web sharing

When Mac OS X is first installed, Web sharing isn't active by default, but starting it up is easy. Once you've configured your Mac as part of a network (outlined earlier in this chapter), you're ready to start the Web server. Just follow these steps:

16

1. Open the Sharing System Preferences (shown in Figure 16.2).

2. Select the Services tab.

3. Select the service named Personal Web Sharing.

4. Select the checkbox to the left of the service and wait a moment for the service to start up.

Because Mac OS X is a multiuser system, the amount of time it takes to complete the startup process depends on two major factors. The number of configured user accounts and the number of files and folder locations designated for serving content will affect the speed of the startup process. I'll explain this last point in just a moment. When the Web sharing startup process is completed, the Start button will transform into a Stop button.

Stopping the Web Server

Once you've started the Web server, it will continue to provide access to your computer until you stop it. If you shut down your Mac without stopping the Web server, access will no longer be available. Once you restart your Mac, however, users will again have access. To stop the server, you can either shut down your Mac, or open the Sharing System Preferences and click the Stop button in the Web sharing section.

The server will not be accessible again until you manually restart it using the steps detailed in the previous section.

Locating Web Folders

When Mac OS X is installed, the Web server and its components are installed into a variety of locations on your Mac OS X hard drive. The Web server designates two folders for files that will be served to Web browsers over the Web. The Apache Web server has a default folder in the following location: /Macintosh HD/Library/WebServer/. The Web server stores your HTML documents, images, and "other content" in this folder (which is known as the base directory, root folder, or docs folder, in Webmaster-speak). Because of an Apple-imposed limitation in the Web server, the name and location of this folder cannot be changed. It contains two folders, one called Documents (that contains documentation for the Apache Web server and also doubles as the default home page for your computer), and a folder called CGI-Executables (for storing small applications called Common Gateway Interfaces (CGIs)). CGIs provide Web site features like shopping carts and feedback forms, as well as site navigation and other interactive features. To access the content of these pages, enter a URL in a Web browser like this, substituting your Mac's domain name or IP address:

http://www.myserver.com

The second default folder is called Sites, and is located in each user's home folder.. Although each user has only one Sites folder, you can create subfolders within it, as illustrated in this example:

- /Macintosh HD/Users/username/Sites/

- /Macintosh HD/Users/username/Sites/Docs/

- /Macintosh HD/Users/username/Sites/Images/

- /Macintosh HD/Users/username/Sites/Images/gifs/

The Sites folder is owned by a specific user, and is accessible to anyone on the Web unless you manually disable access to the folder. To access the home folder of individual user accounts on a Mac running file sharing under Mac OS X, enter a URL such as these, where the user accounts are mark, virginia, and morgan:

http://www.myserver.com/~mark/

http://www.myserver.com/~virginia/

http://www.myserver.com/~morgan/

Mac OS X installs a few default documents in each user's Sites folder, and you can add and delete content to your home folder as you see fit.

As is the case with file sharing, you may encounter some users who want to share their Sites folders and others who do not. In such a situation, your only options are to completely disable Web sharing for the entire computer, or disable access to the Sites folders by following these steps:

1. Select the user's Sites folder and choose File|Get Info or press Command+I.

2. Expand the Ownership & Permissions section.

3. Click the lock icon and change the Owner of the folder to yourself (if you have administrative privileges). Provide your user name and password when prompted.

4. Change the access privileges for Groups and Others to No Access.

5. Change the Owner of the folder back to the original owner.

6. Close the Get Info window.

Anyone attempting to access a Sites folder that has been unshared in this way will be greeted with an error message that says something like this:

```
Forbidden. You don't have permission to access /~morgan/ on this server.
Apache/1.3.26 Server at macdonnachaidh.local Port 80
```

Figure 16.11
Reduce the access privileges of the Sites folder to disable Web sharing for a particular user.

Figure 16.11 shows a before (left) during (middle) and after (right) Get Info window, after revoking access to the Sites folder for the user named morgan while logged in as mbell.

You can't reduce the access privileges to the WebServer folder, however, because the operating system—rather than you or any of the other administrators of your computer—owns it. To disable access to the WebServer folder, you must completely disable Web sharing.

Selecting a Home Page

All Web servers have what is known as a *default* home page. This means that when you open a Uniform Resource Locator (URL) to that server without specifying a particular HTML document, the Web server gives you a document anyway. For example, when you go to **www.apple.com** (and you should!), the Web server gives you **www.apple.com/index.html** instead because index.html is specified as the default home page. Moreover, when you open a URL to a directory within a Web server without specifying a document, any document in that directory named index.html will be served by default. The names of the most common default pages include:

- index.html

- default.html

- home.html

Because Web servers on Windows-based PCs often use the extension .htm instead of .html, you may encounter home.htm or default.htm, for example.

Web sharing uses a file named *index.html*, which is the default file name specified in the configuration files for the Apache Web server, as the default for serving HTML documents in each directory in the Web server. You can only override this file name using a Terminal command.

Sharing via File Transfer Protocol

Before the Web was created by Tim Berners-Lee, files were transmitted among computers using a variety of lesser-known protocols such as Gopher and File Transfer Protocol (FTP). FTP is still used because it is an efficient, no-frills protocol for transferring all types of files. I like to think of FTP as the dump truck of file transfers, and HTTP as the loaded minivan. Mac OS X allows you to serve files via FTP using the Public and Sites folders for each user account, but it has an important drawback: FTP access is slightly promiscuous and will allow users who do not have administrative access to browse large portions of your Mac's hard drive(s), including the contents of system-level folders that are hidden in the Finder. For this reason, I don't like to use the built-in FTP server unless my own account is the only one on the computer. Mac OS X does not allow anonymous FTP, which is the equivalent of guest access in file sharing. As I mentioned in the previous chapter, you should consider not using FTP over public networks such as the Internet because it does not allow for the encryption of user names and passwords. For higher security, check out the SFTP server sXigen from Jomosoft (www.jomosoft.com/osXigen.html). To enable standard, non-secure FTP access on your Mac, follow these steps:

1. Open the Sharing System Preferences (shown in Figure 16.2).

2. Select the Services tab.

3. Select the service named FTP Access.

4. Select the checkbox to the left of the service and wait a moment for the service to start up.

Once FTP is enabled, users will be able to access your Mac over the Internet using virtually any FTP client, and from any type of computer capable of initiating an FTP session. What users will see, and what hidden files and folders will be revealed, depends on how a user's FTP client behaves. For example, Figure 16.12 shows how a non-administrative user can log in to a Mac via FTP and see the root folder for the Apache Web server (which normally cannot be seen when using the Finder or even file sharing).

To disable the FTP service, uncheck the FTP Access option described above.

Sharing Remote Access

In addition to file, Web, and FTP services, you can also allow users to access your Mac using a Secure Shell (SSH) connection and by sending Apple Events over the Internet. SSH, which is discussed in the previous chapter, is a secure replacement for the old Telnet service that was a staple among Unix computers for years. SSH allows

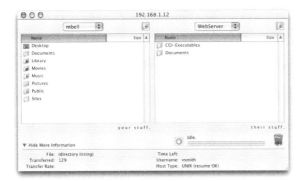

Figure 16.12
Mac OS X's FTP server allows non–administrative users to browse areas of a Mac's hard drive that would not otherwise be viewable.

users to access and command the features of Mac OS X's foundation layer over an encrypted communications link. Many Unix-style operating systems share similar commands, and most have a SSH client that can access an account on your Mac via SSH, if it is enabled.

Providing SSH can be a substantial security risk, however, because remote users can execute most of the same commands that can be executed via Terminal (as if the user was sitting down at your Mac). That means anyone with a user account on your Mac can issue commands to move, delete, and rename files, as well as execute command-line applications (such as FTP) and even SSH connections to other remote computers (not just Macs).

To enable SSH access on your Mac, follow these steps:

1. Open the Sharing System Preferences (shown in Figure 16.2).

2. Select the Services tab.

3. Select the service named Remote Login.

4. Select the checkbox to the left of the service and wait a moment for the service to start up.

Remote Apple Events is another form of remote access service that you can provide to users on your Mac. Apple Events are inter-application messages that are transmitted between the Mac OS and many applications on your Mac, and the Sharing System Preferences pane allows you to enable the exchange of Apple Events with your Mac from other Mac's running Mac OS X, as well as Mac OS 9.x. This is great for software developers, because they can write applications that utilize the resources of multiple Macs over the Internet or a Local Area Network.

The mechanics of Apple Events are quite technical, but fortunately you don't need to know much about them unless you intend to write your own Macintosh programs or AppleScripts. You'll be aware of Apple Events when your software takes advantage of its features, but the entire Apple Events operation will be translated into familiar, Macintosh- friendly commands and dialog boxes. However, if you have an interest in AppleScript (Apple's system-wide, object-oriented programming language discussed in Chapter 11), this topic will interest you because Apple Events is the fundamental messaging system upon which AppleScript is based.

You can think of Apple Events as a set of grammatical rules that make up an acceptable format for messages sent between applications. A message in this format is known as an Apple Event.

For example, an application issues an Apple Event to another application. The Apple-Event is usually a command like "Open file name and Copy Data record #, fieldname," after which the sending application pastes the data somewhere. Using this kind of mechanism, you can link a directory, a to-do list, and a calendar. In fact, some of the first and best implementations of Apple Events have been in the Personal Information manager (PIMs) category.

In addition to the Apple Events format, Apple Events provides a messenger service to transmit the properly formatted message from one application to another. Although Apple Events defines the communication format, it doesn't specify the message content. The "language" of Apple Events is defined cooperatively by Apple and by the Macintosh software developer community. This cooperation is very important—a computer language designed to communicate between a variety of software applications developed by different companies must be carefully constructed in order to accomplish its goal of facilitating precise communication.

For an application to send an Apple Event or to understand an Apple Event it receives, the application must be specifically programmed to handle it properly. This inter-operability makes it impossible for applications built to run under old versions of the Mac OS to use Apple Events. Only when the Apple Events language is clearly defined can software developers update their programs to properly engage in an Apple Events dialog.

Apple Events are described by commands and actions that act on objects. You can think of these constructs as being roughly equivalent to verbs and nouns in the AppleScript programming language.

To enable Remote Apple Events to access on your Mac, follow these steps:

1. Open the Sharing System Preferences (shown in Figure 16.2).

2. Select the Services tab.

3. Select the service named Remote Apple Events.

4. Select the checkbox to the left of the service and wait a moment for the service to start up.

5. To also allow computers running Mac OS 9.x to send Remote Apple Events to your Mac, select the checkbox entitled "Allow Events from Mac OS 9," shown in Figure 16.13, and provide a password when prompted. The computers running Mac OS 9.x will need to be able to send this password when asked by your computer.

Figure 16.13
Mac OS X provides access by Remote Apple Events to Mac OS X and Mac OS 9.x computers separately.

Like with SSH, you should probably not enable Remote Apple Events unless you are confident in the security of your network, and trust the users who will connect to your Mac.

Sharing Printers

Mac OS X Version 10.2 introduces the ability to share a local or networked printer with other Macs on your network by acting as a network print queue. Most Mac users are more familiar with peer-to-printer printing than the idea of printing to a queue. In other words, a print queue is like a middle-man in a business transaction that Mac users have traditionally cut out. Why go through a queue when you can print directly to a printer?

The answer is that in some situations the document to be printed is so large that it would slow your computer down while printing, but the more practical reason for including printer sharing is that you can share a non-networked printer that is physically connected to your Mac with other users on your network. Once again, Mac OS X reveals its practicality!

To enable printer sharing, follow these steps:

1. Open the Sharing System Preferences (shown in Figure 16.2).

2. Select the Services tab.

3. Select the service named Printer Sharing.

4. Select the checkbox to the left of the service and wait a moment for the service to start up.

To print to a printer connected to your Mac from a remote computer running Mac OS X, refer to Chapter 10, "Managing Fonts and Printers" for information on adding a printer via IP Printing. Use the IP address or domain name of your Mac in the Printer's Address field.

 TIP: You must install the BSD Subsystem as part of Mac OS X Version 10.2 in order to provide FTP, SSH, and Internet sharing.

Providing Firewall Security

Without a doubt, one of the biggest issues on the minds of computer administrators today is security. It seems like hackers are everywhere, and they're all trying to break into other people's computers. For many years Mac users have enjoyed relatively easy times when it comes to security, probably because most hackers were more oriented towards the Microsoft Windows platform. With the rise of Linux, a popular freeware version of Unix created by Linus Torvalds (see www.linux.org), hackers have focused more attention to Unix-based operating systems, including Mac OS X.

Firewalls are the best defense against intruders, but they are not fool-proof. Firewalls can be misconfigured or just ineffective against certain types of attacks, and no firewall that I know of can prevent a hacker from "dumpster diving" in your company's trash and finding sensitive user names and passwords scribbled on a piece of paper. Firewalls are just security tools, but they are your best bet for your home computer.

The first version of Mac OS X had a built-in firewall, but lacked a native interface to configure it. Mac OS X Version 10.2 includes a decent interface to the firewall, which you can turn on or off. When turned on, the firewall blocks all inbound network traffic except the services you explicitly allow. The firewall does not block outbound traffic, however.

To enable inbound firewall security, follow these steps:

1. Open the Sharing System Preferences.

2. Select the Firewall tab, shown in Figure 16.14.

3. Select the Start button.

If you have any of the predefined services (such as file sharing or FTP) enabled, the services will automatically be configured to pass through the firewall. None of the

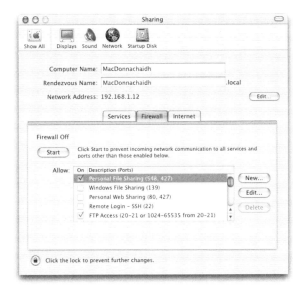

Figure 16.14
Enable Mac OS X's built-in firewall to increase your computer's security.

predefined services can be deleted from the firewall.

To enable a service that is predefined but not in use in the Services tab, such as Timbuktu, follow these steps:

1. Open the Sharing System Preferences.

2. Select the Firewall tab (Figure 16.14).

3. Select the Start button.

4. Click the New button.

5. Select an item from the Port Name menu.

6. Click the OK button, and the item will be allowed to pass through the firewall.

To add a custom port to the firewall, follow these steps:

1. Open the Sharing System Preferences.

2. Select the Firewall tab (Figure 16.14).

3. Select the Start button.

4. Click the New button.

5. Select Other from the Port Name menu.

6. Enter the port information and a description of the service you wish to allow, an example of which is shown in Figure 16.15.

7. Click the OK button, and the item will be allowed to pass through the firewall.

Figure 16.15
Use the built-in security settings with Mac OS X's firewall, or add additional ports.

If you immediately experience problems with an application, or if a user complains that something is amiss, disable the service and research the possibility that an incorrect port number has been entered.

Sharing Internet Access

Mac OS X Version 10.2 adds Dynamic Host Configuration Protocol (DHCP) capability to your Mac. DHCP capability allows other computers on your network to access the Internet through your Mac. Internet sharing on the Mac OS has been around for years through various shareware and commercial applications, but now Mac OS X lets you share access with others right out of the box. To share Internet access with other computers, refer to Chapter 14, "Connecting to the Internet," and get your Mac connected to the Internet first, then follow these steps:

1. Open the Sharing System Preferences.

2. Select the Internet tab.

3. Click the Share the Connection With Other Computer on Built-in Ethernet, as shown in Figure 16.16, and read the cautionary dialog that is presented. Click OK if you understand the consequences.

Figure 16.16
Use Mac OS X to share an Internet connection with other computers on your network.

4. Select the Start button.

5. Quit the System Preferences.

6. Refer to Chapter 14, "Connecting to the Internet," for instructions on setting the Network System Preferences on the other Macs to connect to the Internet using DHCP.

If you experience any networking difficulties, disable Internet sharing and visit the Apple support site for information on potential incompatibilities among your other computers. Not all versions of the Mac OS, Windows, or Linux will work properly with any given DHCP server, and it simply may not be possible to share the Internet connection with computers running different versions of Mac OS X. If this is the case and you want to share an Internet connection, look into a hardware-based sharing device, such as an AirPort base station or a LinkSys router.

Wrapping Up

The power and flexibility of file sharing and Web sharing can change the way you work on a local network or the Internet. File sharing and Web sharing remove almost all the barriers that prohibit the flow of data between computers. With file sharing and Web sharing, you can:

- Share the Public folder and subfolders for each user on your computer over a LAN or the Internet using TCP/IP.

- Share files with administrators, users, and guests.

- Selectively disable access to a particular user's Public folder.

- Create a Drop Box for each user that no one else can view or modify.

- Serve HTML documents for the computer and for each user with an account on your Mac.

- Create subfolders for HTML documents.

- Share the contents and resources of your computer using FTP, SSH, and Apple Events.

- Share your printers over the Internet.

- Enable and configure additional ports on your built-in firewall.

- Enable Mac OS X to share one Internet connections among other computers on your network.

Once you've connected to the Internet, accessed and shared numerous types of services, you'll want to explore the many Internet applications and utilities included with Mac OS X. I've discussed several of them along the way in the preceding chapters, and in the last chapter of this book I'll review these applications and discuss the others that have not been covered thus far.

Mastering Internet Applications and Utilities

Mac OS X lives up to the slogan "built for the Internet" by providing robust support for numerous Internet services in the operating system itself, as well as numerous Internet-enabled applications and utilities. Even more impressive is Mac OS X's extensive backward -compatibility with previous versions of the Mac OS, and its enthusiastic appropriation of cutting-edge technologies such as Gigabit Ethernet and streaming multimedia. As I've shown in the preceding chapters in this section, Mac OS X makes it easy to connect to an Internet service provider (ISP), access, and share Internet services such as file and Web sharing. These developments uphold the Mac OS's reputation for being both the easiest and the most efficient operating system to use for networking.

Along with integrating Internet connectivity into the operating system itself, Apple provides many of the major applications and utilities you'll need to master the Internet and the Web. Those that are not installed by Mac OS X can be downloaded from Apple, or located using one of several sites that track Mac OS X-specific software. In this chapter, I'll review the many components of the operating system that are Internet-related, including the applications and utilities that are essential to exploring and leveraging the vast resources of the Internet. Some of the third-party utilities are commercial products, but most are available as inexpensive shareware or even freeware.

Configuring Internet System Preferences

Numerous areas of the Mac OS X System Preferences either control Internet access or are hooked into the Internet to provide an important feature or perform a useful task. Most of these elements have been discussed earlier in the book, so I'll only review them here and refer you back to earlier chapters for more detailed information. Reviewing these features reminds us how easy it is to take for granted the many ways in which Mac OS X relies on the Internet to provide features. A review of these preferences also serves to emphasize the fact that many of Mac OS X's features, applications, and utilities may not work properly without accurate configuration of your computer's network-related settings. Apple provides numerous applications for download and during the installation of Mac OS X, including Address Book, Backup, iCal, iChat, Internet Connect, Internet Explorer, iPhoto, iSync, iTunes, Keychain Access, Mail, Network Utility, Print Center, QuickTime Player, Sherlock, and Terminal. And if that's not enough, you can download hundreds—perhaps thousands—of Internet applications and utilities for the Mac OS for free, as shareware, or as commercially–packaged software. Let's take a look at the main configuration options that allow you to take full advantage of Mac OS X's Internet-related features.

Network

The Network System Preferences pane is the primary means of configuring how your Mac connects to the Internet and for creating user-friendly network settings called locations. Mac OS X allows you to connect to the Internet using a dial-up modem, an Ethernet connection (such as a LAN, cable modem, or DSL modem), or via a wireless connection (using an Airport card). The performance of your Internet connection will depend on many factors, including hardware and software. See Chapter 14 for details on configuring your computer to access the Internet.

Date & Time (Network Time)

Keeping track of the date and the time is one of the most basic tasks of any computer operating system. Of course it's important for you to know the correct date and time, but it's essential for Mac OS X to have the correct information in order to organize its files and services properly. To accurately track the date and time, Mac OS X accesses a Network Time Protocol (NTP) server through the Date & Time System Preferences, as shown in Figure 17.1.

To configure your computer to connect to a time server, follow these steps:

1. Open the System Preferences from the Apple menu or the Dock and select the Date & Time pane.

2. Choose the Network Time tab.

3. Click the Use a Network Time Server checkbox.

4. Select a time server from the NTP Server menu or enter the domain name or IP address of a time server, such as the US Naval Observatory (USNO) atomic clock (tock.usno.navy.mil). See **http://tycho.usno.navy.mil/ntp.html** for a list of USNO clocks and information on what servers are available.

5. Click the Set Time Now button to confirm the accuracy of the selected time server and update your Mac's clock to the time server.

Figure 17.1
Synchronize to an atomic clock over the Internet to keep your computer's clock as accurate as possible.

Mac OS X will periodically check the server for the correct time and update the computer's internal clock accordingly. See Chapters 1 and 3 for more information on customizing the configuration and display of the date and time on your computer.

Internet

The Internet section of the System Preferences contains several Internet-related configuration options. Some of these options are populated after Mac OS X has been installed and the computer has been restarted for the first time. The Setup assistant asks several questions about your iDisk and email preferences and stores the answers in the Internet System Preferences. Specifically, the Internet System Preferences contains configuration information about four specific areas: .Mac, iDisk, email, and Web.

.Mac

The .Mac section of the Internet System Preferences contains information about your username (referred to as the .Mac Member Name) and password, as well as a shortcut to the .Mac Web site so you can create an account if you don't already have one. This information may be requested during the initial setup stages of Mac OS X, but don't worry if you don't have a .Mac account because it isn't required. Chapter 15 contains more information about .Mac and the many features it provides, including an email account and your iDisk (free disk space on Apple's computer system).

.iDisk

The iDisk section of the Internet System Preferences give you quick access to the usage status of your iDisk, and allows you the option of purchasing additional storage space. You can also change the permissions of your .Mac account's Public folder to make it read-only or read-write, and assign a universal password for users to access the Public folder.

Email

The Email section of the Internet System Preferences, which is shown in Figure 17.2, serves as a clearinghouse for the information your email application will likely require to connect to an email account. You can configure the following options to connect to an account that uses Post Office Protocol (POP) or Internet Mail Access Protocol

Figure 17.2
Configuring the Internet System Preferences to access an email account.

(IMAP), both of which are Internet-standard email protocols. You can't configure these settings to work with proprietary email accounts that utilize transfer protocols other than POP or IMAP. To configure your computer to access an email account using an application such as Mail, open the Internet System Preferences, switch to the Email tab, and configure the following options:

■ *Default Email Reader*—Choose Mail or the Select option from the pop-up list and locate the proper application.

■ *Use .Mac Email Account*—Click this option if you wish to bypass the settings in this section and use the settings in the .Mac tab to access your .Mac email account. Internet System Preferences will plug in the username and password provided in the .Mac tab, as well as all the remaining configuration options.

- *Email Address*—Enter the address to which people send you email.

- *Incoming Mail Server*—Enter the domain name of the server that hosts your POP or IMAP account.

- *Account Type*—Choose POP or IMAP.

- *User Account ID*—Enter the username for your email account.

- *Password*—Enter the password for your email account.

- *Outgoing Mail Server*—Enter the domain name of your Simple Mail Transfer Protocol (SMTP) server, which is used to send mail. It is sometimes different from your incoming mail server, although they can be the same.

Web

The Web section of the Internet System Preferences contains several basic pieces of information that assist in the configuration and behavior of your Web browser. Like the Email section, the information entered here is shared with whatever Web browser you set as the default application for browsing the Web. However, because some applications may not be capable of importing these settings, you may have to configure your browser manually if you choose a Web browser other than Internet Explorer. To configure your computer's Internet System Preference, complete the following fields:

- *Default Web Browser*—Choose Internet Explorer or the Select option from the pop-up list and locate the proper application.

- *Home Page*—Designate the URL to use as the default, or home, page.

- *Download Files To*—Enter the path to the location on your computer's hard drive where you want downloaded files to be placed. The default location is the Desktop folder of your home folder (/Users/<*user name*>/Desktop), although you can click the Select button to identify another folder.

The Web tab no longer allows you to set a default search page for your Web browser, as was possible in previous versions of Mac OS X.

QuickTime

Mac OS X Version 10.2 installs the standard version of QuickTime 6, including the QuickTime Player application that enables you to view and listen to streaming multimedia over the Internet. The QuickTime format specifies different file sizes for different streaming rates so computers with fast Internet connections can view more complex files than computers with slower connections. This allows QuickTime developers to create content that is viewed in a way that is more meaningful to users.

To configure QuickTime to accept data at the most appropriate rate for your computer:

1. Open the QuickTime pane of the System Preferences.

2. Click the Connection tab (shown in Figure 17.3).

Figure 17.3
Configure QuickTime to accept streaming multimedia at the appropriate speed over the Internet for optimal performance.

3. Choose a Connection Speed between 28.8Kbps and Intranet/LAN for 10Mbps and higher connections.

4. Click the Instant-On button to configure QuickTime's "instant-on" playback settings for streaming multimedia.

5. Click the Transport Setup button and either select the default protocol to receive QuickTime data or click on the Auto Configure button to let Mac OS X handle the configuration options for you.

For more information about QuickTime, refer to Chapter 9.

Sharing

Mac OS X includes a sophisticated infrastructure that enables each user with an account on your computer to share files over a LAN, the Internet, and the Web. (In the old days of the Mac OS, you could create File Sharing accounts for users and groups who didn't have Multiple Users accounts on your computer.) The Sharing pane of the System Preferences allows you to enable and disable file sharing, Web sharing, Windows sharing, remote login using SSH, FTP access, remote Apple Events sharing, and printer sharing. In the Sharing pane, you can give your computer a user-friendly name. This feature allows others to identify your computer on a network when browsing a LAN using the Connect To Server command. See Chapters 15 and Chapter 16 for information on accessing and sharing services.

Software Update

One of my favorite Internet-related features of Mac OS X is the ability to update the Mac OS over the Internet. I can still remember the old days of System 6 and 7, when updating the OS meant spending 10 or 15 minutes swapping system updates on floppy disks in and out of the computer. The Software Update section of the System Preferences allows you to check for updates to the Mac OS manually ,or on an automated basis. When an update is found, Mac OS X asks you if you want to install the update, and handles the rest of the process from there. For more information about updating Mac OS X over the Internet, see Appendix E.

Essential Applications and Utilities

Mac OS X installs a number of applications that I consider essential to working efficiently on the Internet. Depending on your needs, however, these applications may not be as essential for you. I use the following applications frequently and supplement them with several third-party applications (listed in the last section of this chapter). Every day I find new Mac OS X applications that replace the functionality of my aging Classic applications, which I retire as soon as a Mac OS X version (or replacement) becomes available. The applications in this section are installed by Mac OS X, or can be downloaded from Apple.

Acrobat Reader

Transferring files between two computers is the essence of the Internet; unfortunately, it can also be a real pain in the neck. This is especially true for documents created by word -processing and page -layout programs, because no two computers are the same. A file that looks great on one system may look like garbage—or may not even work—when transferred to another system. Even if a file is transferred between two identical computers with all the same fonts and programs, there's no guarantee that the document will look the same when it gets to its destination.

In Mac OS X, Apple has tackled this problem with native support for the Portable Document Format (PDF). Adobe Acrobat is a cross-platform (Mac, Unix, and Windows) program that creates and reads platform- and application-independent PDF files. Acrobat can also translate documents created in other programs— PageMaker, QuarkXPress, Microsoft Word—into PDF files. The new files include all the fonts, graphics, and other visual components of the original files. This feature allows users to share complex documents without worrying about losing their original look and feel.

Mac OS X uses the PDF format as the native imaging format, and most applications that allow you to print will also allow you to save a document in PDF format. You can use either Preview or Acrobat Reader to read PDF documents. But if Mac OS X includes the Preview application for reading PDF documents, what good is Acrobat Reader, you ask? For starters, Preview is only a basic PDF-reading application ,and contains only the most basic viewing features viewing. Acrobat Reader, however, allows for more advanced features. You can find text, access embedded hyperlinks, and display information as either a continuous scroll, one page at a time, or as facing pages.

TIP: Adobe has more information about Reader and the full version of Acrobat at its Web site: **www.adobe.com/products/acrobat**.

Address Book

The Address Book is the first Internet-savvy Apple application that functions as a contact manager. It's a powerful yet simple way to track information about people, including:

■ Email addresses

■ Web addresses

■ Physical addresses

■ Phone numbers

You can create custom categories, such as the Web and Mac.com fields shown in the bottom-left of Figure 17.4, as well as assign contacts to easy-to-manage categories such as Work, Family, and Friends.

Figure 17.4
Use the Address Book to manage Internet contact information, including email address and home page, for friends, family, and colleagues.

The Address Book also has the ability to search Lightweight Directory Access Protocol (LDAP) and share information among other applications that are Address Book-aware, such as Mail.

iCal

iCal is a personal calendaring application from Apple that allows you to maintain separate calendars for different categories of events, share calendars using your .Mac account, track to-do lists, access your Address Book, receive notification of calendar events, subscribe to other people's calendars, and search all your calendars. For example, Figure 17.5 shows a calendar search for the Duke University men's basketball team, and a search for events with teams whose name includes "Carolina".

Figure 17.5
iCal allows you to perform searches of your personal calendars and calendars to which you subscribe over the Internet.

See **www.apple.com/ical/** for more information on how to subscribe to calendars, and links to calendar libraries

iChat

iChat is an instant messaging application that uses your .Mac or AOL Instant Messenger (AIM) account over the Internet. At the same time, iChat uses Rendezvous to locate other users over your LAN. Instant messaging allows users to exchange files and text messages in near -real time ,and join AOL chat rooms. With over 150 million users, AIM is the industry leader in instant messaging.

Internet Connect

The Internet Connect application, discussed in Chapter 16, replaces the old Remote Access Control Panel as the means of dialing into an ISP. The specific configuration options for Internet Connect are configured through the Network System Preferences. Its only job is to connect and disconnect a dial-up connection. If you want detailed information about a PPP connection, as well as an ISPconnection, check out Net Monitor by Guy Meyer (**http://homepage.mac.com/rominar/net.html**).

Internet Explorer

Internet Explorer has become the browser of choice in recent years ,and continues to be the only browser installed as part of Mac OS X. Internet Explorer supports the main features required of most browsers, including scripting, Java, QuickTime, bookmarks, and the ability to assign helper applications to alternative protocols such as FTP, mailto, and news. The Explorer Bar is a popular feature that provides quick access to several useful resources:

- *Favorites*—A collection of bookmarks.

- *History*—A log of the Web pages you've recently visited.

- *Search*—One of several Internet search engines.

- *Scrapbook*—A scrapbook for Web pages.

- *Page Holder*—A temporary marker for a specific place in a Web page.

You can expand or collapse the Explorer Bar by clicking once on any of the five tabs, or by pressing Command+T. To further customize the appearance of browser windows, you can collapse the Explorer Bar and toolbars, thereby maximizing the space available for viewing HTML documents —all the while retaining Internet Explorer's many navigational and shortcut buttons.

See the section below entitled "Web Browsers" for several alternatives to Internet Explorer.

iPhoto

iPhoto, described in Chapter 9, is an application for managing digital images that allows users to share images over the Internet in three ways. First, you can export a collection of photos as a Web page. These photos can then be placed on a Web server manually, using AFP, FTP or whatever connection method that is required by your ISP. Second, you can publish your photo collection using the HomePage feature on your .Mac account. Finally, you can use the Mail button to attach the selected photos to an email message. iPhoto is a very well -thought -out application for sharing photos, and the Internet is the perfect vehicle for sharing images with as many people as possible. If you want to print your photos, you can also use the Order Prints feature, or have the prints bound into a book using the Order Book feature. These last two options are fee-based and the cost depends on the options you choose.

iSync

iSync is a new application from Apple designed specifically for Mac OS X . iSync enables you to synchronize Address Book contacts and iCal calendars with other computers over the Internet using a .Mac account. iSync also allows you to share this information with your iPod, certain types of cell phones, and with Palm OS devices, too. ISync works by analyzing your contacts and calendars and uploading the information to your .Mac account. You can register multiple computers, such as your work and home computers, then synchronize the information among them one at a time. For example, Figure 17.6 shows iSync with two registered computers in my .Mac account, Porthos and Archer.

Figure 17.6
Use iSync to share contact and calendar information (using Address Book and iCal) among computers.

I can make changes to my calendar and contacts on one computer, synchronize, then go to the other computer and access the same information. If I make any changes, I run iSync again, and the information will be available on the other computer.

iTunes

iTunes, Apple's MP3 player, is described in Chapter 9. iTunes is primarily used for playing MP3 audio files from your hard drive or a CD-ROM. However, I like to use iTunes to stream MP3s over the Internet from one of many Internet radio stations—with a fast Internet connection and a decent set of speakers on your computer, you'll be amazed at the sound quality . Some stations broadcast at a higher bit rate than others, as illustrated in Figure 17.7. With hundreds of free stations to choose from, why not broaden your musical tastes?

Figure 17.7
Use iTunes to listen to hundreds of free Internet radio stations.

Keychain Access

Mac OS X supports the storing of username and password information for a variety of Internet services in the Keychain, which is discussed in Chapter 15. This feature only works with Keychain-aware applications, however. The default keychain is automatically unlocked when you log in to Mac OS X; you can manually lock and copy the keychain to another computer to access Internet passwords from that computer.

.Mac

Because Apple wants to make using .Mac services as easy as possible, access to your .Mac account has been built into Mac OS X. A .Mac account isn't required in order to use Mac OS X—but it provides several valuable services, including:

- *Backup*—Backup important files from your Mac to your .Mac account, CD, or DVD.

- *iCards*—Customizable electronic greeting cards.

- *iDisk*—1000MB of storage and Web space on Apple's servers.

- *Email*—Your very own Mac.com email account with 15MB of mail storage and access over the Web or most POP or IMAP clients.

- *HomePage*—A Web site creation and publishing tool.

- *McAfee Virex* —Antivirus scanning software from McAfee.

- *Support*—Access to specialized technical support resources.

The main configuration options for .Mac are discussed earlier in this chapter, and details of .Mac services are discussed in Chapter 15. Several applications from Apple use .Mac to enable or enhance features, such as iPhoto, iSync, and Mail. Backup is a new application that allows you to select files and folder son your computer ,and back them up to your iDisk on your .Mac account. Backup has several predefined items that you might want to backup on a regular basis, such as your Address Book and your Internet Explorer settings, but you can add any item you wish by choosing File|Add and selecting the file or folder in the Finder. For example, Figure 17.8 shows four items I've backed up to my iDisk.

Figure 17.8
Use Backup and your .Mac account to back up important information.

If you have a CD-R or DVD-R on your computer, you can use Backup to store larger amounts of data than is possible with the default 100MB iDisk account that comes with your .Mac account.

Mail

Mail is a feature-rich application that supports dozens of the same features found in other popular email clients such as Netscape Messenger, Microsoft Outlook Express, and Eudora Pro. Mail hooks into the Address Book application to manage contact information and email addresses of friends and coworkers. You can send mail from within the Address Book, or you can send mail to someone in your Address Book from within Mail. You can quickly add the address of someone from whom you have received a message by opening the message and choosing Add Sender To Address Book from the Message menu (or by pressing Command+Y). The addresses of your recipients are automatically entered in the Address Book.

Like Internet Explorer, Mail has about a zillion features ,and I can only mention the highlights here. Some of the more interesting features and capabilities of Mail include:

■ Intelligent filtering of spam and junk mail.

■ Drag -and -drop attachments.

■ Keyword indexing and searching of messages.

■ A built-in spell-checker with a contextual menu for quick access to suggested spellings.

■ Formatted text, including HTML.

■ Rules for filtering messages.

■ Customizable toolbar.

And this doesn't even begin to scratch the surface. If I had to pick a favorite feature, however, it would be the rules feature, which helps filter out spam and junk mail. The junk mail filtering feature "learns as it goes" while in Training Mode by evaluating the headers and body of a selected message and color coding the messages. Once you've manually confirmed the mail is indeed junk, you can delete the messages one by one. When you select Mail|Junk Mail|Automatic, the junk mail is filtered into a special mailbox called Junk. For example, Figure 17.9 shows how Mail identifies potential junk mail while in Training Mode.

If you have a .Mac account, Mail is easily configured to access your .Mac email account. Use the Internet System Preferences pane mentioned earlier in this chapter and in Chapter 15. If you need to access your .Mac email account from the road or from any computer that has a current Web browser, go to www.apple.com and click on the .Mac link, log in, and click the WebMail button to access your messages over the Web. You can send and receive messages, manage mail folders, and use an address book to store frequently used addresses. Figure 17.10 shows an example of a WebMail inbox using Internet Explorer.

Figure 17.9
Use Mail's Junk Filter in Training to identify, or Automatic mode to identify and act upon unwanted email.

Figure 17.10
If you have a .Mac account you can send and receive email using a Web browser.

An important distinction between using Mail and WebMail is that if you delete messages from your account using Mail, these messages will not be available on the WebMail account. Also, the default mailbox storage allocation for a WebMail account is 15MB, although you can purchase additional space if necessary. Using Mail, however, you can store as much mail as you want, provided you have space on your local hard drive.

Network Utility

The Network Utility is an essential tool for network system administrators. Located in the Utilities folder, the Network Utility is used to track, trace, troubleshoot, and identify other computers on a network or over the Internet. It has several advanced features, a few of which are mentioned in Chapter 14. The main features of this utility include:

- *Info*—Provides general information on your computer's network connection.

- *Netstat*—Displays information on the routing and protocols used by your computer.

- *Ping*—Sends tiny "pings" to another computer to help verify that the computer is accessible over a network.

- *Lookup*—Performs a DNS lookup on a host to determine what DNS servers are authoritative for that computer.

- *Traceroute*—Traces the connection from your computer to another computer on a network or the Internet.

- *Whois*—Provides a type of Internet directory query for looking up people with accounts on other computers.

- *Finger*—Displays information about one or more people logged into a computer; similar to Whois.

- *Port Scan*—Scans a computer for ports in use. Don't attempt to use this command if you are connected to a cable or DSL modem because your ISP could mistake you for a hacker!

Print Center

The Print Center allows you to configure a printer in Mac OS X, including printers on the Internet or on a LAN, as long as they have an IP address. The Line Printer (LPR) protocol is used by Mac OS X as a means of connecting to networked printers using what is called 'IP Printing'. Networked printers are becoming less and less expensive, and if you have a home network (and don't want to use the Printer Sharing feature discussed in Chapter 16), consider purchasing a networkable printer. See Chapter 10 for more information on printing in Mac OS X Version 10.2.

Sherlock

Sherlock is an Internet information retrieval tool that is no longer used to search local hard drives. With Sherlock, you can search a number of information categories — called channels —that are installed by Mac OS X, and you can subscribe to additional channels, as well. The default channels include:

- *AppleCare*—Search for information and technical support on Apple hardware and software.

- *Dictionary*—Search the American Heritage Dictionary and Roget's II Thesaurus.

- *eBay*—Search and track auctions on eBay.

- *Flights*—Search for flight information from dozens of airlines.

- *Internet*—Search multiple Web-based search engines simultaneously from about.com, ask.com, bestsitefirst.com, looksmart.com, lycos.com, overture.com, and sprinks.com.

- *Movies*—Search for movies and theatres in your neighborhood.

- *Pictures*—Search for images by keyword using gettyimages.com and lycos.com.

- *Stocks*—Track stock information and recent news about companies listed on the Dow Jones Industrial Average, Nasdaq, and Standard & Poor's.

- *Translation*—Translate text between several languages.

- *Yellow Pages*—Locate business addresses and contact information using switchboard.com and infouse.com, including driving directions

When I first installed Mac OS X, a friend called and asked about a new movie that was released earlier that day. I knew about Sherlock, launched it, and within three minutes of using Sherlock for the very first time, I was able to locate the closest theatre, show times, a summary of the film, and a QuickTime preview trailer. Pretty cool! You can search for information about a specific film, as in Figure 17.11, or by theatre, in case you want to see what's playing.

Entering your home zip code in Sherlock's preferences (or providing it in the City & State or Zip field in the Movies window) will assist Sherlock in locating theatres closest to your home.

Terminal

Advanced users and Unix geeks will recognize the Terminal application as more than just a window to the local file system and a method of executing commands. Terminal is also a gateway to many of the Internet commands frequently used by system administrators, including:

- SSH

- FTP

- Ping

- Traceroute

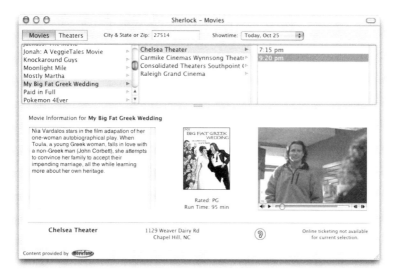

Figure 17.11
Use Sherlock to locate movies and theatres.

Although experienced users will appreciate the command-line interface to these applications, most users would rather utilize a graphical interface, such as the Network Utility application mentioned earlier in this chapter.

URL Clippings

Mac OS X is able to create Internet *URL clippings*, URLs that have been selected with the mouse and dropped onto the Desktop from applications like Internet Explorer or Eudora. It does this by parsing (translating) clippings for telltale information such as "http://" and "mailto:" before creating the Desktop clipping. When double-clicked, the appropriate application is opened, and the URL contained in the clipping will automatically be entered into the application. In Mac OS X, all URL clippings have the same Finder icon, whereas in Mac OS 9.x the icons are visually differentiated to indicate the various types of URLs, such as http, FTP, and mailto.

Essential Third-Party Applications and Utilities

In addition to the major Internet applications mentioned in the previous sections, Mac OS X hundreds and hundreds of third-party utilities have become available for Mac OS X since its initial release in March 2001. The following Mac OS X and third-party utilities are essential to ensure that your Internet toolkit is complete.

BBEdit

BBEdit from Bare Bones Software (**www.barebones.com**) is the consummate tool for HTML authoring and text editing. It has powerful search-and-replace features, tools for making HTML authoring a snap, and can be extended to include new functions through a plug-in architecture. I use BBEdit to edit all my Web pages, which is made even easier because of BBEdit's built-in FTP client, which allows documents to be opened from an FTP server directly in BBEdit. Bare Bones provides the Lite version free of charge on their Web site, but it lacks many of the important features found in the commercial version, such as a Web-safe color palette, spell-checker, and HTML tools, that make BBEdit such an indispensable tool for Web developers.

Transmit

The sole purpose of Transmit from Panic (**www.panic.com**) is to transfer files to and from FTP servers. It performs this task using an efficient, Mac OS-like interface backed by a multithreaded and Carbonized code base. According to tests performed by Panic, Transmit is the fastest FTP client available for the Mac OS. To see how Transmit works, refer to Chapter 15. Out of the many FTP clients for Mac OS X, Transmit is my favorite.

URL Manager Pro

URL Manager Pro from Alco Blom (**www.url-manager.com**) is to managing URLs as the Address Book is to managing names and addresses. It consists of a powerful URL organization menu, collections of URLs, and a small floating palette that provides shortcuts to your frequently used URLs. There are also shortcuts to your Internet applications, such as your Web browser, email client, and news client. A sample menu, which can be added to most Internet applications, is shown in Figure 17.12.

URL Manager Pro supports drag and drop, works with several Mac OS X–enabled Web browsers, is very well documented, and is fairly inexpensive ($25).

Usenet News

Usenet News is a collection of discussion lists on a wide variety of topics broken down into *groups*. Each group can contain thousands of postings that typically expire after a certain amount of time, depending on how each news server is configured. Usenet News began as a means of communicating between Duke University and the University of North Carolina at Chapel Hill, two great basketball (and academic) rivals that are about a dozen miles apart. Most ISPs have a news server that you're entitled to access for free. If not, several public news servers are available as well, but they usually don't carry all the newsgroups found on an ISP's news server because of the cost of maintaining such a system. For example, my ISP subscribes to over 49,000 groups!

Figure 17.12
Use URL Manager Pro to organize URLs and access to Internet applications.

Thoth, from Thoth Software (**www.thothsw.com**), is a great news reader. To use Thoth, launch the application and choose File|New News Server to enter the address of the news server, and then select a folder that will contain downloaded articles. Depending on how many groups are carried by your news server, it could take a minute or two to obtain the listing. Subsequent launches of Thoth are much quicker, because it only needs to update the newsgroup list. To browse groups, choose Windows|Show Full Newsgroup List and scroll through the Full Newsgroup List window, or to make it easier on yourself, type in the name or partial name of a group you are looking for. For example, in Figure 17.13 I have filtered all the groups that contain the word "Macintosh", then opened a specific newsgroup, then selected a message in the newsgroup. All three windows are shown in this example.

VNC Server/Client

As demonstrated in Chapter 15, the ability to see another user's screen is essential when it comes to supporting and troubleshooting. Freeware Virtual Network Client (VNC) clients and servers are available for numerous platforms, including Mac OS X. Timbuktu (**www.netopia.com**) is the consummate screen and file sharing application, and you can purchase Apple Remote Desktop (**www.apple.com/remotedesktop**) to work with other Macs, but my freeware picks for VNC are Share My Desktop from Mike Bombich (**www.bombich.com/software**) for the server and VNCThing from Purple Shark Software (**www.webthing.net**) for the VNC client. VNC is a no-frills Internet utility that is supported on a variety of platforms.

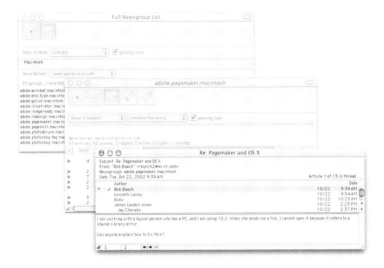

17

Figure 17.13
The Thoth newsreader is a great tool for locating information on a variety of topics.

Web Browsers

Since the initial release of Mac OS X, several Web browser have been released that offer comparable features and performance to Internet Explorer, including:

- Chimera (**http:// www.mozilla.org/projects/chimera/**)

- iCab (**www.icab.de**)

- OmniWeb (**www.omnigroup.com**)

- Netscape (**ftp.netscape.com/pub/netscape7/english/7.0/mac/macosx/sea/**)

These browsers have varying degrees of features—try them out to see if they work for you.

Wrapping Up

Apple invented the first commercial personal computer over 25 years ago, and today, Mac OS X Version 10.2 continues to improve on the basic principle of Apple's first operating system: Make it simple, make it powerful, and most importantly, make it fun! The latest version of the Mac OS implements numerous improvements and new applications to help you harness the power of the Internet and the Web, as well as the personal computer itself. I hope you find that Mac OS X meets your expectations and that you have fun!

Part

Appendixes

Getting Help

Getting help with the operating system and your favorite applications is very easy, thanks to several powerful features provided by Mac OS X. The Help Viewer application, context-sensitive help, and the **man** command are the most useful methods of getting help. Propriety help applications and the Apple support site also provide important information for Mac OS X.

Help Viewer

Getting help with a particular task can sometimes be difficult when you're not sure what terms to use in a search. (Of course, it's nothing like the frustration of thumbing through the software manual's index in the days prior to online help.) Apple's Help Viewer application gives you the very best tools to search for help with all aspects of Mac OS X. Software developers can incorporate Help Viewer–style assistance into their applications, as they did in years past, with tool tips, Balloon Help, and Apple Guide (the last two of which are not available in Mac OS X). The Help Viewer enables you to:

■ Browse help documents.

■ Search multiple help documents simultaneously.

■ View the most current help information over the Internet.

To try it out, go to the Finder and choose Help|Mac Help, which launches the Help Viewer similar to the one shown in Figure A.1, which includes Help modules for numerous third-party applications.

Let's look at each of the main functions of the Help Viewer.

Browse Help Documents

The Help Viewer allows application programmers to create help documents that can be categorized and viewed. The main view, depicted in Figure A.1, shows several

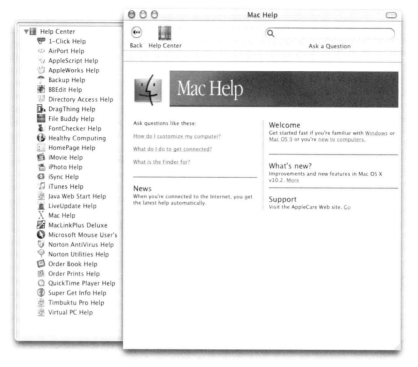

Figure A.1
The Mac OS X Help Viewer application.

subcategories of information that you can browse for detailed information. Clicking on the Help Center icon in the toolbar reveals the list to the left or right of the main window; clicking on any of the categories brings up even more information in the main window, as illustrated by the section entitled "How do I customize my computer?," shown in Figure A.2.

Typically, each of the main topics listed Help Center has multiple subcategories in which individual topics may be selected for viewing. To "drill down" into a specific help topic, such as the "Using toolbars" item in Figure A.2, you can either click on the item in the Topic section of the Help Viewer, or you can click on the topic in the detail section at the bottom of the Help Viewer. Selecting a topic using either of these methods will open the topic in the Help Viewer as shown in Figure A.3.

To pilot your way around the Help Viewer, click on the buttons in the toolbar section of the Help Viewer (at the top), or press one of the two following keyboard shortcuts which are also accessible from the Go menu:

■ Command+[(to move back one step)

■ Command+] (to move forward one step)

Figure A.2
A top-level heading of the Mac Help section of the Help Center.

Figure A.3
A detail view of a help topic.

The buttons in the toolbar are customizable by choosing View|Customize Toolbar and dragging the selected buttons to the toolbar area, just like when customizing Finder toolbars.

Search Help Documents

In addition to browsing documents, the Help Viewer also allows you to search for help topics using two search methods:

■ Keyword searches

■ Boolean searches

Depending on what components you have installed on your computer, the contents of the Help Viewer may differ. For example, applications you install separately from Mac

Figure A.4
The results of a simple, case-insensitive keyword search in the Help Viewer.

OS X may contribute additional Help documents, and when you perform a search you may end up with results relating to more than one relevant application. To perform a simple keyword search, just type a phrase such as "desktop picture" into the search field paying no attention to case, as shown in Figure A.4. Then click the Ask button.

As Figure A.4 illustrates, the Help Viewer window displays the search results in much the same way you would expect to see results of a Web search. For example, results are ranked according to how closely your term matches the contents of the Help Viewer's indices, and are displayed by group. In this example, the search returned 50 documents in 13 different Help files that you can browse.

In addition to keyword searches, you can also execute Boolean searches in the Help Viewer. Use the criteria listed in Table A.1 to further refine your Boolean searches.

TIP: It isn't necessary to insert spaces between search terms and the Boolean operators, as the Help Viewer will ignore gratuitous spaces.

Table A.1   Symbolic Boolean operators used for searches in the Help Viewer.

Character	Meaning	Example
+	and	finder + icons + size
|	or	DVD | CD-ROM
!	not	desktop ! finder
( )	group	(AppleTalk + printer) ! Chooser

For example, suppose you want to search for help on changing the size of the icons on your Desktop. Results of a search for the term "Desktop" may be so numerous that you'll be confused instead of helped. A more effective approach is to create a Boolean search using the terms and operators "finder + icons + size"; the results of this search are shown in Figure A.5.

Figure A.5
The results of a Boolean search.

Whenever you see the "Tell me more" option, you can command the Help Viewer to search further for terms related to the initial results of your search. The Help Viewer responds by summarizing the keywords of the result summaries and adding these terms to a new search. This feature is one of the first and best applications of the summarizing technology that Apple developed several years ago.

Finally, if your computer is connected to the Internet when using Help Viewer, and if the Help document in use is programmed to do so, it will search the Internet for the latest version of the file. If you aren't connected to the Internet, the Help Viewer application will just use the document at hand.

Context-Sensitive Help

Context-sensitive help is a feature of Mac OS X that senses where you're working in the Finder and offers immediate help on a selected item. For example, you can Control+click a folder, such as the Applications folder, and select Help from the resulting contextual menu. The Mac OS then launches the Help Viewer. At this printing, context-sensitive help is limited in Mac OS X, although it functions very well in the Classic environment. As updates to Mac OS X are released, context-sensitive help should improve. Ideally, you will be able to immediately access information relevant to the item you are using. For example, you could Control+click the Utilities folder and find information relevant to the Utilities included with Mac OS X.

The **man** Command

To learn more about the Unix underpinnings of Mac OS X, you'll need to get acquainted with a command-line prompt. You can access this prompt by launching the Terminal program located in the Utilities folder. A window will open showing your Mac OS X log-in at a command line. You can now see your computer in a whole new light. You can explore folders, launch programs, and manage files without ever touching your mouse. In fact, the command line holds tremendous power, so getting help—which will help you master the command line—is one of the first skills you should learn. Thankfully, Terminal features its own context-sensitive help. It's called the **man** command, derived from the word "manual." The **man** command does not execute independently, however. It is paired with the name of the command that you need help with.

For example, to see the contents of a folderin a Terminal window, type "ls" and press Return. The results would look something like this:

```
[Porthos:~] mbell% ls
Desktop   Documents Library   Movies    Music     Pictures  Public    Sites
[Porthos:~] mbell%
```

TIP: For help on using the **man** command, open a Terminal window and type **man man**.

Notice that you can only see the folder's contents listed as names. You probably can't distinguish folders from files and applications. Don't worry—the **ls** command has many options that will enhance the results. To find out more about these options, enter **man ls** in a Terminal window. You will see man pages like the one shown in Figure A.6. Press the space bar to read through each page in the man document ,or type "q" to quit. By reading all the pages on this topic, you will learn that **ls -l** will list the folder contents in long format.

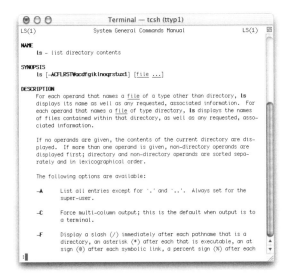

Figure A.6
Use the Terminal application to view man pages for Mac OS X's Unix commands.

Now you can brave the world of shell commands, knowing that help is only a few keystrokes away. You can learn more commands in Appendix C, "Learning Unix Shell Commands."

Proprietary Help

You can also get help from proprietary online help systems provided by applications. However, most Carbon and Cocoa applications for Mac OS X include built-in support for the Help Viewer application. Other programs may include a completely different style of help interface, or have supplemental forms of help, such as tool tips. Only the programmers' imaginations limit the inclusion of new and unique ways to provide help in their applications. For example, Microsoft Word X provides users with a well-designed help application that is independent of Mac OS X's Help viewer application. Figure A.7 shows one of the many features of the Microsoft Help Viewer feature.

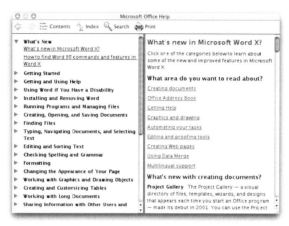

Figure A.7
Microsoft Office uses a proprietary means of provide help to users.

Apple Support

The Apple Web site has a section dedicated to providing hardware and software support (**www.info.apple.com**), including a support site just for Mac OS X (**www.info.apple.com/usen/macosx**). The Mac OS X support site provides answers to frequently asked questions (FAQs), hosts discussions on specific topics (such as customizing Mac OS X), allows downloads of software updates, provides links to additional resources, and allows access to the Knowledge Base search engine. If you sign up for a free Apple ID account (**signin.apple.com**), you can create a customized support page called My Support Page that contains the documents, downloads, and search preferences of your choosing.

Shortcuts

The Mac OS has always been easy to use—but some people (and you know who you are) just can't get enough of the many shortcuts that are available to help navigate applications and the Finder and start up and shut down the computer. Keyboard shortcuts can be more efficient than using the mouse to activate menu options and manipulate Finder objects. For example, it's much more efficient for me to use the Command+P shortcut to print a document than to take my hand from the keyboard, grasp the mouse, select a menu, choose Print, and return to the keyboard. And for those of us with repetitive-motion injuries, keyboard shortcuts are lifesavers!

If the dozens of shortcuts provided by the Mac OS aren't enough for you, at least one product that's currently in development for Mac OS X will create shortcuts for virtually anything you can imagine. QuicKeys from CE Software (**www.cesoft.com**) is a hybrid macro/scripting language that allows you to write, record, and edit strings of tasks and then execute these tasks with a click of the mouse or a tap of the keyboard. I've been using QuicKeys for several years to create simple keyboard shortcuts to my favorite applications, as well as highly complex macros to export data from one application, reformat the data, and then import the data to another application, for example. Programs like QuicKeys can make a huge difference in your computing life.

Common Shortcuts

Table B.1 lists the most common shortcuts involving starting up, shutting down, working with applications, and other miscellaneous actions. When using these or any other shortcuts, be sure to press the key combination only once and release the keys as soon as the shortcut has been activated. In the case of zapping the PRAM, release the keys as soon as the startup chime has sounded for the second time. Some CPU and monitor combinations, such as the Cube connected to the 15-inch Apple Studio Display LCD monitor (with an ADC connector), may not support all of the shortcuts. Also, some PowerBook and iBook keyboards may abbreviate the names of the keys, so choose your keystrokes carefully.

Table B.1   Common keyboard shortcuts.

Action	Keystroke(s)
Startup, shutdown, restart, or sleep	Power key
Start Classic environment without Extensions or Startup Items	Shift key (while starting up)
Zap PRAM	Command+Option+P+R (while starting up)
Close all open Finder windows	Shift (after logging in)
Boot from CD-ROM (must be bootable format)	C (while starting up)
Bypass startup disk	Option
Force quit an application	Command+Option+Escape
Force a restart (some models)	Command+Control+Power key
Stop processing (some applications)	Command+period or Command+Escape
Switching to next application	Command+Tab
Switching to previous application	Shift+Command+Tab
Take a screenshot of the entire screen (Mac OS X and Classic)	Command+Shift+3
Take a screenshot of a region of the screen (Mac OS X and Classic)	Command+Shift+4
Take a screenshot of a specific window (Classic only)	Command+Shift+Caps Lock+4
Rotate to the default keyboard layout	Command+space
Rotate to the next keyboard layout	Command+Option+space
Log out	Shift+Command+Q
Empty Trash	Shift+Command+Delete
Toggle between Show and Hide Dock	Option+Command+D
Save a file	Command+S
Save as	Shift+Command+S
Hide current application	Command+H
Hide all other applications	Option+Command+H
Hide previous application window	Option+click new application or Option+click new application Dock icon
Print	Command+P
Quit	Command+Q
Cut	Command+X
Copy	Command+C
Paste	Command+V
Undo	Command+Z
Get Info	Command+I

Finder Shortcuts

Many people use Finder shortcuts without really thinking of them as shortcuts, and you may be surprised by how many shortcuts exist for navigating around the Finder. Table B.2 lists the Finder shortcuts available in Mac OS X and the extended keyboard. PowerBook, iBook, and the standard USB keyboards lack as many as 13 of the keys that are found on the extended keyboard. However, Function key combinations that compensate for the missing keys may be available; check your computer's documentation for details.

B

Table B.2   Finder shortcuts.

Action	Keystroke(s)
Close active window	Command+W or click close box
Close all open windows	Command+Option+W or Option+click close box
Open selected item and close the parent window	Command+Option+O or Option+double-click
Expand closed subfolders one level in a list view triangle)	Click (on a closed folder's or Command+right arrow (on a closed folder)
Collapse open subfolders one level in a list view triangle)	Click (on an open folder's or Command+left arrow (on a closed folder)
Expand all closed subfolders in a list view	Command+Option+right arrow
Collapse all open subfolders in a list view	Command+Option+left arrow
Open a window to its largest possible size	Click zoom button
Minimize window to Dock	Double-click title bar or click minimize button or Command+M
Collapse all windows to Dock	Option+Double-click title bar or Option+click yellow minimize button or Command+Option+M
Move down to the next item in a list view	Down arrow
Move up to the next item in a list view	Up arrow
Select an item in a list view	Type the first letters in that item's title in quick succession
Scroll up one page in a list view	Page up
Scroll down one page in a list view	Page down
Move up one folder level	Command+up arrow
Open the selected item	Command+O
Open the selected application or document	Command+down arrow

Table B.2 Finder shortcuts (*continued*)

Action	Keystroke(s)
Locate the original of an alias	Command+R
Activate icon proxy pop-up	Command+click (on proxy icon)
Select icon proxy	Click on proxy icon from pop-up list
Scroll left, right, up, or down	Command+Option+drag mouse in window
Move an inactive window by its title bar	Command+drag title bar
Select an item in an icon view	Left, right, up or down arrow
Select next item, alphabetically	Tab
Select the previous item, alphabetically	Shift+Tab
Select multiple, noncontiguous items	Command+click
Select multiple, contiguous items in a list	Shift+click
Select multiple items	Click+drag mouse
Select everything in a window	Command+A
Copy all the file names of a window's contents to the Clipboard	Command+A, then Command+C
Create a new folder	Shift+Command+N
Create a new Finder window	Command+N
Get Info for selected item(s)	Command+I
Rename	Return, then type the name
Create an alias	Command+M or Command+Option+drag
Copy (duplicate a file)	Command+D or Option+drag
Eject removable media	Command+E
Move to Trash	Command+Delete
Toggle between Show and Hide window toolbar	Command+B
Go to Computer window	Shift+Command+C
Go to Home window	Shift+Command+H
Connect to or open iDisk	Shift+Command+I
Go to Applications window	Shift+Command+A
Go to Favorites window	Shift+Command+F
Go to Folder	Shift+Command+G, then type the path of the folder
Connect to Server	Command+K
Launch Help	Command+?

Open and Save Shortcuts

The attached sheets in Mac OS X (the Open and Save dialog boxes, also referred to simply as *sheets*) have many shortcuts that are similar to the Finder window shortcuts described in the previous section. These shortcuts may also work in the Open and Save window in Mac OS X that are not attached sheets, as well as the Classic environment if the application you are using supports Navigational Services. However, not all the listings in Table B.3 will work for all applications.

B

Table B.3   Navigational window shortcuts.

Action	Keystroke(s)
Move down one item	Down arrow
Move up one item	Up arrow
Select an item	Type the first letters in that item's title in quick succession
Scroll up one screen	Page up
Scroll down one screen	Page down
Move up one folder level	Up arrow
Open the selected folder	Right arrow
Expand closed subfolders one level	Right arrow
Collapse open subfolders one level	Left arrow
Open selected item	Return
Go to Home folder	Command+Option+H
Go to the Desktop	Command+D
Close the dialog box	Esc
Close the dialog box	Command+Period
Select all items that can be opened	Command+A

Learning Unix
Shell Commands

Early personal computers often had an operating system that allowed you to navigate the file system and execute programs using commands entered at a prompt. . Then Apple released a revolutionary operating system that used icons and mouse actions, rather than a command prompt, to control the computer. The Mac OS continued to avoid the command-line interface until the introduction of Mac OS X, which includes a utility called Terminal. Terminal gives you the option of navigating your hard drive and executing commands using keystrokes instead of mouse clicks and the Aqua user interface.

Unlike Aqua and many Carbon and Cocoa applications, however, actions performed using Terminal do not have an "undo" component, and if you type the wrong command, there is usually no going back: You can permanently remove files and folders or seriously disable your operating system, so exercise caution when using Terminal.

The Terminal Application

Although many applications developed for Mac OS X can be configured in the Finder, some of the Unix-based programs and utilities ported to Mac OS X require that you configure them manually. Terminal, an application for executing commands, provides an interface that allows you to perform these tasks.

Terminal is located in the Utilities folder, and is launched by double-clicking on the Finder icon, like any other application. . When launched, a Terminal window similar to the one shown in Figure C.1 is created, which displays the date and time of your last login, a welcome message such as "Welcome to Darwin!", and a command prompt stating your computer's name (defined in the Sharing System Preferences pane) and your user name (defined in the Accounts System Preferences pane), followed by a % symbol. Your home folder is the "current working directory" for each Terminal window.

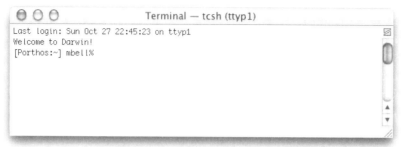

Figure C.1
A Terminal shell window, including the prompt.

 TIP: When using Terminal and working with Darwin or most other Unix operating systems, a folder is referred to as a directory.

Terminal Window Settings

Before you begin working in Terminal, you may wish to modify the preferences for the shell window. Perhaps the text is too small, or you would like more lines of text to appear in a window. To make these changes, access Terminal|Window Settings and review the various setting categories, one of which is shown in Figure C.2. As with many other programs, Terminal preferences are organized in categories. The categories are described

Figure C.2
The Terminal Window Settings.

in the following list for your information; I discourage you from changing any of these settings unless you're an experienced Unix user. The categories include:

- *Shell*—This panel displays which shell program Terminal uses. A shell is a command interpreter which passes the commands between you and the operating system. In essence, it acts as a shell around the operating system. The default shell is tcsh, a modified version of the C shell, and the path is listed in this panel. You can reveal the technical details about C shell by entering "man tcsh" at the prompt. Do not change this preference unless you're a highly experienced Unix user.

- *Processes*—Displays information about processes running within open Terminal windows, and what running applications should prompt you before closing open Terminal windows.

- *Emulation*—The Emulation settings control how your keyboard input interacts with the shell. For example, you can set the Option key to act as the meta key, which is useful for the emacs editor discussed later in this appendix.

- Buffer—When you're working in a shell window, you may need to view previous text by paging up the window. The Buffer settings allow you to set a limit (including no limit) on the amount of text stored in a window.

- *Display*— Controls the style of cursor in Terminal windows, as well as the size, style, and type of font.

- *Colors*—The shell window default is a gray world. However, if you'd like a little color, you can modify the background, the text and its different styles, and even choose different cursors. You can also make Terminal windows transparent.

- *Window*—Sets the default dimensions of Terminal windows, and controls the text displayed in the title bar of the shell window. As you modify the settings, you can see the results in the preview title bar. By default, the shell name and the device name are displayed.

Some of the changes you make in Terminal Window Settings go into effect immediately, and others will only affect windows opened after the Window Settings has been closed. Press the button entitled Use Settings as Defaults button to make the changes go into effect immediately. Experiment with the settings to customize your Terminal windows to best suit your needs.

Additional Terminal Options

Now that you've configured Terminal, you can begin using the utility. Although you can still use the point-and-click method to select options from various menus, you'll most likely begin typing commands in the shell window.

If, during your Web ramblings, you've found a complex command on a Web page and would like to run it in a Terminal window but don't want to retype the command, you can copy and paste the command into the Terminal window. You can also drag and drop a file or folder in the Finder onto a Terminal window to paste the path of that item. If you're working with long or complex paths, this can be a real time-saver and help prevent typographical errors.

Commonly Used Shell Commands

Now that you know how to configure Terminal, you can begin entering commands. Because the Darwin environment in Mac OS X is derived from BSD (refer to Chapter 1 for more details), a wide array of commands are available through Terminal. In fact, these commands often work in many Unix-derived platforms such as Linux or Solaris.

This appendix includes only a fraction of the commands and utilities available to you in Terminal. In fact, whole books have been written about these commands and all the things you can do with them. If you're serious about learning the Darwin environment and want to be productive in Terminal, you'll need additional documentation. Books for users of all levels are available. And, of course, you can find information and assistance on the Web. You will find several useful URLs listed in Appendix F.

For now, I'll review some of the most common and useful Terminal commands. The Terminal shell can be intimidating at first, so keep this information handy, especially if you are a beginner. Soon you'll be typing away. You may even discover that you're really a Unix geek at heart. The following shell commands are listed according to how often you will use them—the most frequently used commands are listed first.

ls

The **ls** (*list*) command is one of the easiest commands to remember. Typing "ls" alone simply lists the names of the files or folders in the current folder. For more information, add options to the command. Type "ls -l" to view the long listing of folder content information. This information will include whether an item is a file or folder, and tell you who created it. Type "ls -a" to see all files and folders, including hidden ones. Type "ls -la" to combine these two options into one command.

pwd

The **pwd** (*print working directory*) command shows your current path. As you begin navigating your hard drive via Terminal, you can find yourself nested deeply. The **pwd** command will show the path to your current location.

cd

The **cd** (*change directory*) command allows you to change folders. Typing "cd .." will put you into the previous directory; typing "cd /" will place you at the root. If you know the path, you can enter "cd *pathname*" to change to that location. For example, "cd /Library" will place you in the Library folder located just off the root of the Mac OS X hard drive. If you want to return to your home directory, type "cd" or "cd ~" and press Return.

cat

The **cat** (*concatenate and print*) command displays the contents of a file in the Terminal window. Type "cat *filename*" to show the file contents. If the file is large, you'll need to modify the command by adding the **more** option. For example, type "cat *filename* |more" to display the contents one screen at a time. To continue through the screens, press the space bar.

more

The **more** command displays the contents of a file, screen by screen, when you type "more *filename*" at the prompt. A status bar at the bottom of the screen indicates what percentage of the file is currently displayed in that screen. To proceed to the next screen, press the space bar. To quit without viewing the entire contents, type "q".

The **more** command can also be used as an option in conjunction with other commands, producing a screen-by-screen display of the results of the command. For example, the **ls -l |more** command results in a screen-by-screen display of results that would fly by if you entered just the **ls -l** command.

less

The less command is similar to the more command in that it is used to display information on a screen-by-screen basis, but unlike more, less allows you to move backward as well s forward. less does not read an entire file into memory, which makes it faster when viewing huge files such as multimegabyte log files.

ps

The **ps** (*process status*) command informs you about the processes running on your computer. Type "ps -aux" to see a complete listing of processes. You can also access this information in the ProcessViewer utility.

top

The top command provides statistical information on processes, including CPU and memory consumption, refreshing the screen every second or so.

history

The **history** command is pretty straightforward—it lists all the commands you've executed while working in the shell window. Use the Up and Down arrow keys to review the commands one by one.

clear

If the neat-freak in you is bothered by a cluttered shell window, type "clear" to clean up the mess. The **clear** command places the prompt at the top of a clear window.

man

The **man** (*manual*) command, which displays online help documents for commands, is one of the best tools for learning your way around Terminal. Pair **man** with the command for which you need assistance. Fox example, if you're using the **ls** command but can't remember the option to display all file information, type "man ls" to display manual pages that describe every option available with the **ls** command. Pages are displayed screen by screen; you can progress to the next screen by pressing the space bar, or access previous screens by typing "b". Type "q" to exit.

exit

The **exit** command exits the Terminal session. Depending on your Terminal settings, the window will close automatically or stay open with a message indicating that processes have been stopped.

All previous commands that I've discussed are passive—the results do not make changes to the file system and are therefore considered "safe." However, the active commands that follow do make changes to the system. A simple typographical error in the command could have devastating results. If you are new to the command line interface, practice with passive commands and *always* double-check your text before pressing Return.

cp

The **cp** (*copy*) command allows you to copy files. To copy a file to a new location, type "cp *filename directory*". For example, the command **cp apples.txt /Users/Shared** copies the apples.txt file from the current directory to the Shared folder.

To duplicate a file in the current working directory and assign a new name to the duplicate, type "cp *oldfilename newfilename*". For example, the command **cp apples.txt oranges.txt** duplicates the apples.txt file and gives it a new name.

The danger of the **cp** command lies in the possibility of accidentally overwriting a file. You will not receive a warning that you are overwriting an existing file, so use the **cp** command with caution. Also, a file's resource fork may not be copied when using the **cp** command. To ensure that both the data fork and the resource fork are copied, use the Finder to copy files.

mv

The **mv** (*move*) command is used to rename a file or move it to a new location. To rename a file, type "mv *oldfilename newfilename*". For example, **mv apples.txt oranges.txt** changes the name of the apples.txt file to oranges.txt.

To move a file to another location, type "mv *filename directory*". For example, **mv apples.txt /Users/Shared** moves the apples.txt file from my personal folder to the Shared folder.

As with the **cp** command, use the **mv** command with caution—if you're not careful you may accidentally overwrite a file. You will not receive a warning that you are about to do so.

rm

Like all active commands, the **rm** (*remove*) command can be dangerous because it is used to delete files. Type "rm *filename*" to delete a particular file. You can also delete multiple files at once by using the * wildcard character. For example, typing "rm *.txt" removes all files with the extension .txt in the current directory only; **rm *.*** removes all files, no matter what the extension, from that folder. rm -R will remove directories as well as files. Be very careful with the **rm** command (you have been warned!).

mkdir

The **mkdir** (*make directory*) command creates a new folder within the current folder. Type "mkdir *foldername*" to create the new folder. For example, to create a folder called WebDocs, I would type "mkdir WebDocs".

rmdir

Like the **rm** command, the **rmdir** (*remove directory*) command can be dangerous because it removes empty folders. For example, to remove the apples folder, I would type "rmdir myfolder" once the folder has been emptied using the **rm** command.

tar

Tar files, denoted by the file extension .gz, are recognized as compressed Unix files. Although StuffIt Expander (located in the Utilities folder) can decompress tar files, the results are not always clean. If you have tried and failed to decompress a tar file using StuffIt Expander, try decompressing these files using the **tar** (*tape archive*) command. For example, to decompress the neatapp.gz file, I would type "tar xvf neatapp.gz". In most cases, you should move the tar file to an empty directory before expanding, because the decompressed archive may contain several files that can become confused with others in the folder.

Editors

After installing some of the Unix programs that have been ported to Mac OS X, you may find that configuration files must be edited to reflect your personal settings. The fact that, in many cases, these files are hidden can be a real handicap unless you use Terminal, which gives you access to the entire file system.

Mac OS X includes several command-line text editors for use with shell environments. These editors allow you to make changes to files that you may not be able to see in Finder. In the following section, I'll briefly discuss the most commonly used editors and include only the most basic commands. For more complete directions, you can browse the man pages for each editor, or purchase a Unix manual that suits your needs.

vi

The vi editor, shown in Figure C.3, has many devotees in the Unix world. In fact, many of the instructions that are included with Unix-based software tell you to use vi to edit configuration files. But to be honest, I find vi very difficult to use.

vi operates in two modes: edit and command. If you are in command mode, you cannot edit, and vice versa. This concept is difficult for first-time users to grasp. When you open a file using vi, it is opened in command mode. You must use certain commands to place the file in edit mode before you can begin modifying the text. And while in edit mode, you must press Escape to switch to command mode, where you can then save the file or exit the editor.

To edit a file in vi, type "vi *filename*". If the file does not exist, vi will open a new document and use *filename* as the name for the new file when it's written to disk. When a new file is opened, you will see the ~ character on blank lines—note that these characters are not actually in the file. Now that you've opened the file, you can begin working with it. Table C.1 includes some useful vi commands. Keep in mind that you must be in command mode to use them. Most commands involve single keystrokes.

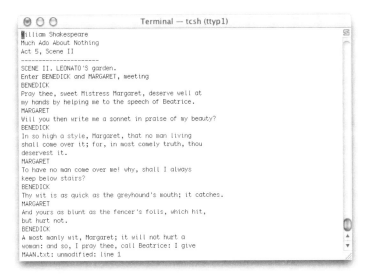

Figure C.3
The vi text editor.

Table C.1   Common vi commands.

Keystroke	Command
Escape	Switch to command mode
Control+f	Next page
Control+b	Previous page
a	Switch to edit mode and add text after the cursor
i	Switch to edit mode and insert text before the cursor
x	Delete a single character
dw	Delete the next word
dd	Delete entire line
/	When followed by a word or phrase, search the document for the word or phrase
:w	Save the file
:q	Exit vi
:q!	Exit vi without saving the file

TIP: Because vi is case sensitive, a lowercase x does not execute the same function as an uppercase X.

emacs

Although the emacs editor is not as cryptic as vi, it is not as easy to use as pico (discussed next). Unlike vi, emacs does not have different edit and command modes. You can begin typing text and you can delete text using the Delete key. Figure C.4 shows emacs in action.

In many of its commands, emacs uses the Meta key, a special key that is not available on a Macintosh keyboard—or on a PC keyboard, for that matter. If a command calls for the Meta key, press Escape followed by the other key in the command.

To edit a file using emacs, type "emacs *filename*". If the file doesn't already exist, the file name you specify will be used when you save the file. And best of all, emacs saves a copy of the file, so if you mess it up, you can always resort to the original. Table C.2 lists some useful emacs commands.

Figure C.4
The emacs text editor.

 TIP: As with vi, emacs is case sensitive. A lowercase x does not execute the same function as an uppercase X.

Table C.2   Common emacs commands.

Keystroke	Command
Control+v	Next page
Meta+v	Previous page
Control+g	Cancel the command
Control+s	Search the document for a word or phrase
Control+h	Get Help
Control+x then Control+u	Undo
Control+x then Control+s	Save
Control+x then Control+c	Exit

pico

The pico editor has one benefit that the emacs and vi editors don't —it lists some of its commands at the bottom of the screen (see Figure C.5). If you're new to shell editors, you may want to start with pico so you don't give yourself whiplash jerking your head from the screen to a manual to learn how to save your file.

To edit a file using pico, type "pico *filename*". If the file doesn't already exist, the file name you specify will be used when you save the file. Because a file opened in the pico editor is always in edit mode, you can begin typing at the cursor to insert new text or press the Delete key to remove text. Table C.3 includes some common pico commands.

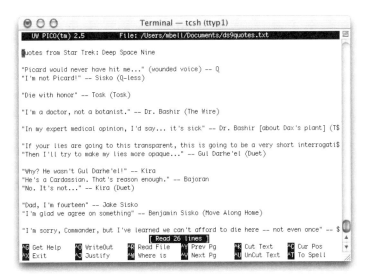

Figure C.5
The pico editor.

Table C.3   Common pico commands.

Keystroke	Command
Control+v	Next page
Control+y	Previous page
Control+c	Set cursor position
Control+w	Search the document for a word or phrase
Control+g	Get help
Control+x	Exit the file with a prompt to save the document

TIP: Pico is also case sensitive. A lowercase x does not execute the same function as an uppercase X.

If you get in a bind when editing text files using one of these three editors, you can always cheat and used BBEdit to open any visible or hidden text file. See **www.barebones.com** for the latest freeware and commercial versions of BBEdit. When working with Unix files using BBEdit, be sure to save the file using Unix line breaks instead of Macintosh, DOS, or Unicode line breaks by clicking the Options button when saving the file.

Mac OS 9.1 and Mac OS X Feature Comparison

Mac OS 9.x and Mac OS X are two different operating systems. But that doesn't mean each is alien to the other. As a user, you just have to find the similarities. Do you need to select a printer? If you're a seasoned Mac user, you may automatically reach for Chooser, only to find it gone. It may be disconcerting at first, but soon Mac OS X Printer Center will be as familiar as the venerable Chooser. If you think in terms of "tasks" rather than mouse movements or keystrokes, you will soon be able to function in the Mac OS X environment and take advantage of the improvements. Use this appendix to learn which application is appropriate for your needs in Mac OS X when compared to Mac OS 9.x.

Operating System Architectures

The Aqua interface in Mac OS X is certainly eye-catching, but the really fundamental components are "under the hood." The stability of Unix, for example, has become the foundation for Mac OS X. In the past, when an application became unstable it could render the entire system unusable. In Mac OS X, however, an application that becomes unstable doesn't bring down the whole operating system, thanks to the sophistication of Mac OS X's core foundation. Table D.1 explores some of the major differences between Mac OS 9.x and Mac OS X. Many of these differences are not seen, but are experienced instead.

Table D.1   Operating system architecture differences.

Feature	Mac OS 9.x	Mac OS X
Graphics and Windowing	QuickDraw	Quartz Extreme and/or QuickDraw
Memory	Unprotected	Protected
Multimedia	QuickTime	QuickTime
Multiprocessing	Asymmetric	Symmetric
Multitasking	Cooperative	Preemptive
Open and Save windows	Navigational Services	Attached Sheets or Navigational Services
System Extensibility	Extensions and Control Panels	Frameworks
User Interface	Platinum	Aqua

System Functions

The System Folder in Mac OS 9.x contains the components necessary to boot the system. Some files in the System Folder are just enhancements to the operating system, and some are essential (without them, the computer will be unable to boot). However, in Mac OS X most of those components are, in fact, hidden from view. Although you can access these folders using Terminal, keep in mind that Apple has hidden the system components for a reason. In the past, you could easily damage your System Folder because it was visible in the Finder, and therefore easily modified. In Mac OS X these vital folders are hidden, which reduces your chances of mangling the system. Table D.2 lists several programs or functions that are handled by the System Folder in Mac OS 9.x and shows how they are handled in Mac OS X.

Table D.2   Basic operating system tasks and functions.

Feature	Mac OS 9.x	Mac OS X
AppleTalk	AppleTalk Control Panel	System Preferences|Network
Boot disk	Startup Disk Control Panel	System Preferences|Startup Disk
Computer accounts	Multiple Users Control Panel, User & Groups section of the File Sharing	Control Panel System Preferences|Accounts
Connect to servers	Chooser or Network Browser	Go|Connect To Server command
Date & Time	Date & Time Control Panel	System Preferences|Date & Time
Desktop picture	Appearance Control Panel	System Preferences|Desktop
Dial-up settings	Remote Access Control Panel	System Preferences|Network
Energy settings	Energy Saver Control Panel	System Preferences|Energy Saver
File Sharing	File Sharing Control Panel	System Preferences|Sharing
Internet access settings	TCP/IP Control Panel	System Preferences|Network
Keyboard layout	Keyboard Control Panel	System Preferences|International
Monitor settings	Monitors Control Panel	System Preferences|Display
Multimedia settings	QuickTime Control Panel	System Preferences|QuickTime
Select printer	Chooser	Print Center
Sound settings	Sound Control Panel	System Preferences|Sound
Speakable settings	Speech Control Panel	System Preferences|Speech
System color scheme	Appearance Control Panel	System Preferences|General

Applications and Common Tasks

Mac OS 9.x and Mac OS X include a limited number of applications that may meet your needs, especially if you're interested in the Internet. In Mac OS 9.x, most applications are stored in the Applications folder. In Mac OS X, you can access the Applications folder from the toolbar. Table D.3 lists several tasks and the application you would use to perform it in each environment.

Table D.3 Applications comparison.

Feature	Mac OS 9.x	Mac OS X
Email	Outlook Express, Netscape Messenger	Mail
File Search	Sherlock 2	Find command
Image viewing	PictureViewer	Preview
Internet Search	Sherlock 2	Sherlock 3
Multimedia	QuickTime Player	QuickTime Player, iDVD, iPhoto, iMovie, iTunes
Printing	Desktop printing	Print Center
Taskbar	Application Switcher	Dock
Text editing	SimpleText	TextEdit
Web browsing	Internet Explorer, Netscape Navigator	Internet Explorer

Utilities

Both Mac OS 9.x and Mac OS X provide utilities that help you and your computer function. They can diagnose and repair your computer, as well as provide information about settings and devices. Table D.4 provides a list that compares these utilities and their functions. Note that all utilities for Mac OS X are found in the Utilities folder.

Table D.4 Utilities comparison.

Feature	Mac OS 9.x	Mac OS X
Color settings	ColorSync Control Panel	ColorSync Utility
Computer information	Apple System Profiler	Apple System Profiler
Configure computer settings	Mac OS Setup Assistant	Setup Assistant
Disk repair	Disk First Aid	Disk Utility
Font preview (some applications)	Key Caps	Key Caps, font panel
Mount and create disk images	Disk Copy	Disk Copy
Password management	Keychain Access Control Panel	Keychain Access
Screen capture	Command+Shift+3, Command+Shift+4	Grab, Command+Shift+3, Command+Shift+4

Installing and Updating Mac OS 9.x and Mac OS X

If your computer shipped with Mac OS X pre-installed, reinstalling the operating system is something that you might never need to do, or it might be something you have to do on an emergency basis. You can always let an Apple-certified professional perform the installation for you, for a fee, but Apple makes the process so user-friendly that most users can perform an installation or reinstallation in under a half hour. Reasons to install Mac OS X include:

- Upgrading from an earlier version

- Restoring the operating system after a drive failure

- Installing an optional feature not previously installed

- Reinstalling to fix a problem with the operating system or a bundled application

Mac OS X is a large and complex operating system. As such, it is constantly reviewed by Apple for issues that effect stability, performance, and enhancement. Of course, the tweaks and new features sometimes lead to more issues that must be fixed in a later release or update. Unfortunately, many users don't take the time to install these updates, and continue to use bug-ridden programs. Updates to the operating system are always in the works at Apple, and are very important for your computer for several reasons, including:

- Increased security

- Increased performance

- Fixes a known problem

Mac OS X and Mac OS 9.x have the ability to check for and install updates to the operating system, as well as most of the applications that were bundled and installed at the same time as the OS. Older computers may have come with Mac OS 9.x and Mac OS X already installed. However, if you purchased your computer in the spring of 2001 or earlier, it's likely that only Mac OS 9.x was preinstalled, and if you purchased a computer in 2002 and later, Mac OS X was probably installed as the primary OS. Starting in 2003, Apple announced that is will begin phasing out Mac OS 9.x, and I expect at some point it will not be installed in new computers. Beginning in 2003, new Macs will not boot into Mac OS 9.x, but they will run Mac OS 9.x in Classic mode.

Whatever your situation, this appendix will help you do the following:

■ Perform a new installation of Mac OS 9.x

■ Reinstall Mac OS 9.x

■ Prepare for Mac OS X

■ Perform a new installation of Mac OS X

■ Reinstall Mac OS X

■ Update the Mac OS

If you've never installed system software or components before, don't worry. After all, it's the Mac OS we're talking about, here!

I'll discuss installing Mac OS 9.x first. If you purchased Mac OS X, you probably already know that it includes Mac OS 9.x. To run versions of software that are not written for Mac OS X, you'll need the Classic, or Mac OS 9.x, environment. After Mac OS 9.x is installed or updated, you can tackle Mac OS X.

Can you install Mac OS X first and save Mac OS 9.x for later? Yes, but you must boot from a Mac OS 9.x installation CD to install the system. Think about it. The Mac OS 9.x installer is a Classic application. You can't run the installer in Mac OS X because you don't have a Classic environment installed. Save yourself some trouble. Install Mac OS 9.x before Mac OS X.

Performing a New Installation of Mac OS 9.x

With Mac OS 9.x, the mechanics of a new installation, reinstallation, custom installation, or the uninstall process are all pretty much the same. Of these processes, performing a new installation poses the most significant risk of accidentally harming your existing system software. We'll get to that in a minute; first let's look at the steps involved in installing the software.

The first step to successfully installing the Mac OS is to reboot your Mac and quit any applications that were automatically launched on startup. Like most software installation programs, the Mac OS installer requires that you quit all applications prior to beginning the installation process, to reduce the risk of new file corruption by programs already installed.

The next step is to insert the Mac OS 9.x installer CD. Of course, you can also boot from the installation CD. First, insert the CD and restart your computer. Hold down the C key until bootup begins. Once you have saved any open documents and quit your applications (or restarted the computer using the Mac OS 9.x installation CD), launch the Mac OS Install application and be prepared to perform four main tasks:

1. Select the drive on which Mac OS 9.x will be installed.

2. Read the Important Information document. This is a very important step, so don't skip it. This document details known problems and incompatible hardware.

3. Complete the software license agreement.

4. Choose the software to be installed.

After you've completed these tasks, the installation program will ensure that your hard disk is capable of containing the software, check the integrity of the hard drive on which Mac OS 9.x is being installed, and then begin the installation process. Mac OS 9.x installs everything without requiring additional intervention on your part.

 TIP: You can also uninstall portions of the Mac OS using the Mac OS installer application.

Step 1: Select a Destination Disk

Selecting a destination disk is the first step. If you have multiple disk drives, the installer automatically evaluates each one to determine whether it has enough available space for an installation of Mac OS 9.x. In Figure E.1, for example, the hard drive named Archer has been selected for installation.

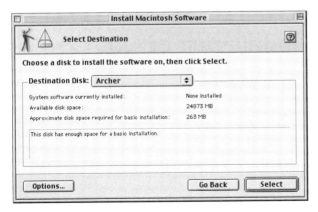

Figure E.1
Select a destination disk for Mac OS 9.x.

To perform a clean installation, which creates a new System Folder (without deleting an existing System Folder), click the Options button at the bottom of the Select Destination window. In the resulting window, check the box entitled Perform Clean Installation, as illustrated in Figure E.2. If you've run into problems on previous attempts to install Mac OS 9.x, or if you're having persistent problems with system stability, check this box.

Step 2: Read the Installation Notes

No, I'm not kidding: You really should read every word of the installation notes to ensure that your hardware fully supports Mac OS 9.x. Because your ultimate goal is to install Mac OS X, be sure to confirm that your platform will run Mac OS X, not just Mac OS 9.x. Hardware requirements for Mac OS X are listed later in this appendix. Every version of the Mac OS has known problems in relation to certain hardware, such as third-party acceleration cards; by reading the installation notes, you can find out what they are now rather than later—like when your system has deleted the report that's due at the end of the day!

Step 3: Complete the Software License Agreement

You will not be permitted to install Mac OS 9.x unless you agree to the terms of the license agreement. After all, technically you don't own the software: Apple is selling you a license (subject to terms, conditions, and caveats) to use a copy of the software on your machine.

Step 4: Choose the Software to Install

The final step is to select the software you want to install. You can choose a basic installation of Mac OS 9.x combined with certain applications and utilities, or perform a customized installation. With a customized installation, you can include all the software, or just a single program.

Figure E.2
Choose the Perform Clean Installation option to install an entirely new System Folder.

At any time between Steps 1 through 4, you can click the Help icon for context-sensitive help. A window that addresses current installation issues will be displayed. The Help window's contents should explain the function of each option, and the consequences of each possible selection.

To perform a customized installation of Mac OS 9.x (or to remove any of its components), select the Customize button and click on the checkbox beside each component that you want to install or remove. To customize the selected component even further, click on the pop-up menu for each main component, such as Apple Remote Access or Internet Access. When you select a customized installation or removal, a window like the one shown in Figure E.3 appears. In this example, the Internet Utilities portion of Internet Access is selected as part of a custom installation.

Last but not least, review the Options button at the bottom of the Mac OS Install window (see Figure E.1 for an example). It allows you to determine whether your hard disk drivers will be updated to the latest version. You can also request an installation report detailing what was added, removed, or replaced during the entire installation process.

Once you've selected the software to be installed, click the Start button to begin the process. It can take anywhere from just a few minutes to almost half an hour, depending on the software being installed and the speed of your computer and hard drive. Throughout the process, the installation program will display a progress bar.

Reinstalling Mac OS 9.x

If you need to reinstall Mac OS 9.x, go back to Steps 1 through 3. Pay careful attention to Step 1, in which you're asked whether you want to perform a clean installation. Provided that you have enough available disk space, you may want to consider performing a clean installation if your system is behaving strangely for any reason. If you're convinced you don't have enough disk space, proceed to Step 4 and install only the software that you think is needed. Note that you may not need to

Figure E.3
A customized installation for the Internet Access component of Mac OS 9.x.

reinstall the entire operating system when only one component, such as Web Sharing, needs to be installed or reinstalled.

If you select a disk that already contains a previous installation of Mac OS 9.x, the installer will recognizing that Mac OS 9.x is already installed, will ask whether you want to reinstall the OS or add or remove selected components. The remainder of the process is as described previously.

Preparing for Mac OS X

To use the Classic environment under Mac OS X, you must have Mac OS 9.x or higher installed. If you purchased Mac OS X, you also received a Mac OS 9.x installation CD. Go ahead and upgrade your operating system to Mac OS 9.x before installing Mac OS X. Although you can install or upgrade Mac OS 9.x at a later time, you won't be able to run Classic applications in Mac OS X until you do.

For those of you who have maintained the same System Folder through multiple system versions (in other words, for you long-time Mac users), be aware that your System Folder may contain software that is incompatible with Mac OS X. Although rare, this situation is certainly possible. You can detect such an incompatibility by restarting your Mac using Mac OS X; if the system can't finish booting, then you know you've got a problem. In case this happens to you, be prepared to do several things with your Mac OS 9.x installation:

- Perform a clean installation of Mac OS 9.x without adding third-party software.

- Boot successfully with Mac OS X and run the Classic environment so that Mac OS X can update it.

- Install your third-party software, but don't attempt to manually combine the contents of a previous System Folder with the new System Folder.

- Verify an application's compatibility with Mac OS X. Restart the Classic environment each time you install an application that modifies the System Folder (ie, by adding Extensions or Control Panels).

Most users can merrily install Mac OS X without a second thought; however, if you do run into problems, consider a clean installation.

Installing Mac OS X

Now you're ready to install Mac OS X. Although the installation process is quite simple—considering that you're installing a Unix-style operating system—it's also completely different from installing Mac OS 9.x.

If your hard drive has more than one partition, make sure that Mac OS X is installed on the primary partition. Refer to the Apple System Profiler to verify which partition is the primary one. You can also identify the primary partition as the first in the list of partitions in the Startup Disk Control Panel.

Mac OS 9.x can be installed on another partition or hard drive, or both Mac OS 9.x and Mac OS X can be installed on the same volume. You can also have Mac OS 9.x on more than one partition, which is useful because it allows you to have a version of Mac OS 9.x that has been modified by Mac OS X as well as one that has not. Although new software for Mac OS X is being released every day, you may find that some Mac OS 9.x applications are unstable in the Classic environment. You can select either Mac OS 9.x or Mac OS X as the operating system that boots the computer.

To install Mac OS X, insert the Mac OS X installation CD and double-click the Install Mac OS X icon. You will be prompted to restart the computer. Upon restarting, the computer will boot from the installation CD into Mac OS X. Alternatively, insert the installation CD, and restart the computer while holding down the C key to achieve the same results.

The Mac OS X installer launches automatically, and you'll need to perform four main tasks:

1. Read the Important Information document that details known problems and incompatible hardware. This is a very important step, so don't skip it.

2. Complete the software license agreement.

3. Select the drive on which Mac OS X is to be installed.

4. Choose the software to be installed.

The Mac OS X installation process is simple but lengthy. Depending on the speed of your computer, even the booting process can take so long that you may think something is wrong. Have patience—the installer will eventually launch.

To install Mac OS X, your computer must meet the following requirements:

■ A G3 or higher processor, with these exceptions: The original G3 PowerBook with the multicolored Apple logo on the cover is not supported. Although Apple maintains that processor upgrade cards are not supported, many users have reported that a wide variety of them work just fine with Mac OS X.

■ A minimum of 128MB of physical RAM.

■ 3GB of free disk space.

If your computer meets these requirements, you are ready to install Mac OS X.

Step 1: Read the Installation Notes

Once the installer has launched and you have selected a language for the installation process, read the Welcome screen. Then, click the Continue button to proceed to the Read Me window. Apple provides important information about what computers are supported by Max OS X, as well as known bugs in the operating system.

Common sense says that if you are able to boot from the Mac OS X CD, then you should be able to install Mac OS X, but this is not the case. Make sure that your computer meets all the system requirements, especially those related to memory and disk space. Once you've read the Read Me document, click Continue. Note that all the steps in the installation process are listed on the left side of the window; past steps are denoted by a gray button, an active step is denoted by a blue bullet, and future steps are faint but visible. To access previous steps, click the Go Back button.

Step 2: Complete the Software License Agreement

The Software License agreement appears next. You can read the document in English, or choose from six additional languages. After you've read the agreement, click the Continue button. If you don't scroll to the bottom of the agreement, a window will ask whether you Disagree or Agree with the license; click Agree to continue. The Mac OS X installer will then survey your computer for hard drives in preparation for the next step.

Step 3: Select a Destination Disk

You now have an opportunity to select the destination volume. If you're in doubt, choose the volume listed first in the Select Destination portion of the installation application.

Each volume icon indicates the volume name and available disk space, as in Figure E.4. Click an icon to select it; the volume's icon will then have a large, green arrow and be encircled. Once you've chosen a volume, click the Continue button and click the Install button to proceed with the Easy Install option, or click the Options button and choose from the following:

- Install Mac OS X—Installs the OS for the first time, similar to the "Clean Install" option in Mac OS 9.x.

- Archive and Install—Compresses a previous version of Mac OS X into a disk image, and performs a clean installation. This option is not available if a previous version Mac OS X has not yet been installed on the selected drive.

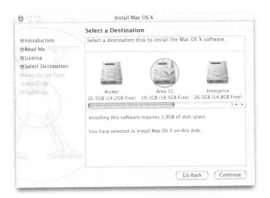

Figure E.4
Selecting a target disk to install Mac OS X.

■ Preserve User and Network Settings—If checked, this option performs a clean installation but copies the user accounts and network settings of the existing version of Mac OS X to the new installation. This option, too, is not available if a previous version of Mac OS X has not yet been installed on the selected drive.

■ Erase and Install—Erases the selected disk, and lets you choose to format the drive in either Mac OS Extended format or the more advanced Unix File System format. Unless you're an experienced Unix user, select Mac OS Extended. Erasing the drive is not mandatory—in fact, you should only do this if it is necessary. For example, if you have a previous version of Mac OS X installed but want to start with a clean slate, you could erase the disk and then proceed with a pristine installation of Mac OS X.

If you did not enable the Erase option, click Continue to proceed to the next step.

Step 4: Choose the Software to Be Installed

The next window that appears is deceptively easy. If you want to accept the default installation of Mac OS X, then you're nearly finished—click the Install button to proceed. On the other hand, if you want to customize the installation, you can click the Customize button, the result of which is shown in Figure E.5. You'll be given a listing of the packages that will be installed; if you haven't installed Mac OS X, then two of the packages, the Base System and the Essential System Software, cannot be unchecked. Several optional components can be skipped by deselecting the checkbox to the left.

The BSD Subsystem option installs additional components for the core operating system, and is required if you install tools from the Mac OS X Developer Tools CD that accompanies Mac OS X. Unless you are very short on space, you should probably leave all options enabled. The Custom Install window also reminds you of the size of the operating system about to be installed (a little more than 2GB, in this example).

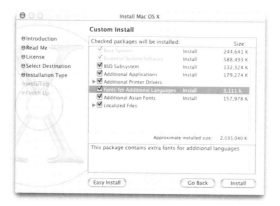

Figure E.5
A custom installation of Mac OS X,

If you decide not to customize the installation, you can click the Easy Install button, or proceed to the next window by clicking the Install button. The installer will now begin examining your disk and installing the different components. To stop the installation, click the Pause button; the installer will not actually pause until it has finished the task at hand, however. This means you may not detect a pause until the installation is complete.

As the software is installed, messages are posted under the progress bar indicating what task is active. Actual system installation, the longest part of the process, can take 30 minutes or longer, depending on the speed of your computer's hard drive and processor.

The installer requires two CDs to install everything, and after the contents of the first CD have been installed, the computer will reboot and ask for the second CD. Once the second CD has been processed, the Mac OS X registration screen appears and asks a few necessary questions. Based on your answers, a default user account is created.

Reinstalling Mac OS X

If you're reinstalling Mac OS X, follow the same steps outlined in the preceding section, with one exception. If the installer detects a previous or current version of Mac OS X, the option in Step 3 above will ask if you want to reinstall or upgrade Mac OS X. You will be asked to click the Options button and select from the appropriate choices.

Updating the Mac OS

Both Mac OS 9.x and Mac OS X have the ability to automatically update the operating system over the Internet via the Software Update feature. In Mac OS 9.x, this feature is found in the Software Update Control Panel; in Mac OS X, it's found in the Software

Update pane of the System Preferences. Because the Mac OS is modular, various components of the OS may be upgraded independently of the Mac OS as a whole. This is a real timesaver, considering how long it would take to upgrade the entire OS over the Internet! You don't have to update the Mac OS, but it's a good idea to check the Apple Web site (**www.apple.com**) often for updates that may potentially add new features, increase the speed of the OS, or fix a bug or incompatibility.

You can manually check for software updates, or schedule the Software Update feature to look automatically for new software. To check manually for new versions of Mac OS components, follow these steps, noting that you must boot the computer into Mac OS 9.x to access this feature (it cannot be used in Classic mode):

1. In Mac OS 9.x, open the Software Update Control Panel and click Update Now. In Mac OS X, open the System Preferences Software Update pane and click Check Now. Examples of both are shown in Figure E.6.

2. A status indicator will provide visual confirmation that a connection is being made to search for software updates.

3. To review what updates have been installed, click the Installed Updates tab.

4. Quit Software Update if the Software Update feature finds no updates for your particular model of Macintosh or the versions of Mac OS components that are installed.

Figure E.6
Update the Mac OS using the Software Update feature.

5. If an update is located, such as the example shown in Figure E.7, follow the onscreen instructions. You may be required to restart your computer.

6. To ignore a suggested update, select the item and choose Make Inactive in the Update menu.

You can also check for updates on a schedule that's convenient for you. This frees you from having to remember to do it manually. I prefer to check for updates on a weekly basis. To configure an automated update in Mac OS X:

1. Open the Software Update System Preferences pane.

2. Select the Automatically Check for Update When You Have a Network Connection checkbox.

3. Choose to update software on a daily, weekly, or monthly basis in the pop-up menu.

4. Quit the System Preferences.

At the appointed time, the Software Update feature will automatically launch and start searching for updated versions of the Mac OS. If no updates are found, then it will not attempt to install anything. If an update is found, you'll be presented with options similar to the ones shown in Figure E.7.

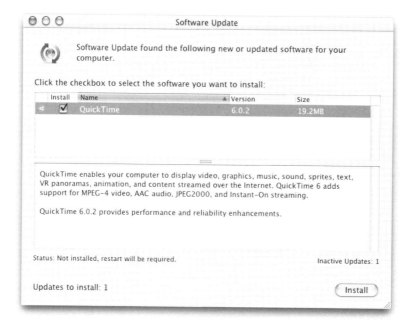

Figure E.7
An example of a software update over the Internet.

Additional Resources on the Web

Thousands of Web sites contain relevant information about the Mac OS, Apple Computer, Mac software and hardware, and news about computers in general. Too many, in fact, to be always sure where to go for the most accurate and up-to-date information. The following categories of Web sites contain the URLs of some of the best sites available at this time. Before you try any of these sites, please visit the two sites devoted to this book: my own site and the Paraglyph Press Web site. You'll find the latest information about this book, including corrections and additions, as well as information about upcoming books about the Mac OS.

The Mac OS X Book

The Author's Home Page
www.MacOSbook.com

Apple Computer

Apple Home Page
www.apple.com

Mac OS X Home Page
www.apple.com/macosx

Apple Products
guide.apple.com

Apple Support
www.info.apple.com

Apple Software Updates
www.info.apple.com/support/downloads.html

Apple News
www.apple.com/hotnews

Apple Store
www.apple.com/store

Apple Developer
www.apple.com/developer

Apple Resource Locator
www.apple.com/buy

.Mac
www.mac.com

Darwin Apple Open Source
developer.apple.com/darwin/

Mac OS X–Related Sites

Macintosh News Network: Mac OS X News
www.macnn.com

MacInTouch: Mac OS X Reader Reports
www.macintouch.com/mosxreaderreports.html

Mac OS X Hints
www.macosxhints.com

MacFixIt: Mac OS X Troubleshooting
www.macfixit.com

Macworld: Mac OS X
www.macworld.com/subject/macosx/

Stepwise.com
www.stepwise.com

Mac OS X.org
www.macosx.org

Xappeal.org
www.xappeal.org

Mac OS X Server
www.macosxserver.com

Apple and Macintosh News

Macintosh News Network
www.macnn.com

MacInTouch
www.macintouch.com

Apple Insider
www.appleinsider.com

Mac OS Rumors
www.macosrumors.com

SpyMac
www.spymac.com

MacCentral Online
http://maccentral.macworld.com/

Macintosh Security Site
www.securemac.com

Macintosh Security News Portal

www.macintoshsecurity.com

Apple and Macintosh Publications

Macworld
www.macworld.com

MacAddict
www.macaddict.com

Inside MacGames Magazine
www.imgmagazine.com

Mac Gamer's Ledge
www.macgamer.com

MacHome Interactive
www.machome.com

MacTech Magazine
www.mactech.com

Mac Design Magazine
www.macdesignonline.com

Mac Edition
www.macedition.com

Macintosh Hardware and Software

Mac OS X Apps
www.macosxapps.com

Apple Mac OS X Downloads
www.apple.com/downloads/macosx

VersionTracker: Mac OS X

www.VersionTracker.com/macosx/

ClubMac
www.clubmac.com

Deal Mac
www.dealmac.com

MacMall
www.macmall.com

MacWarehouse
www.warehouse.com/apple

MacConnection
www.macconnection.com

MacRes-Q
www.macresq.com

MacZone
www.maczone.com

Mostly Mac
www.mostlymac.com

Index